250 YEARS OF HISTORY

©ENA NIEDERGANG 2015

With best wishes
Ena Niedergang

YING HUA BOOKS
英华书

WALES-CHINA 250 YEARS OF HISTORY

I DEDICATE THIS BOOK

TO

MY LATE FATHER, CYRIL B.H. LEWIS,

WHO GAVE ME THE LOVE OF HISTORY

AND

MY HUSBAND, BARRY,

WITHOUT HIS SUPPORT, ENCOURAGEMENT

AND HELP, THIS BOOK WOULD NOT HAVE BEEN COMPILED

WALES-CHINA 250 YEARS OF HISTORY

Title: WALES-CHINA 250 YEARS OF HISTORY

Copyright © 2015 Ena Niedergang. All rights reserved.
First softcover edition printed 2015 in Wales, United Kingdom.

A catalogue record for this book is available from the British Library.

ISBN: 978-0-9934184-0-2

Printed in the United Kingdom by Cambrian Printers, Aberystwyth

No part of this book shall be reproduced or transmitted in any form or by any means, electronic or mechanical, including photocopying, recording, or by any information retrieval system without written permission of the publisher.

Published by YING HUA BOOKS
For more copies of this book please e-mail: info.yinghuabooks@gmail.com

Cover Design by Barry Niedergang

PLEASE NOTE: Although every precaution has been taken in the preparation of this book, the publisher and author assume no responsibility for errors or omissions. Neither is any liability assumed for damages resulting from the use of this information contained herein.

WALES-CHINA 250 YEARS OF HISTORY

CONTENTS

PREFACES: .... iv - vi

ACKNOWLEDGEMENTS: ……………………………………..vi - viii

INTRODUCTION: ……………………………………………… viii - ix

PART 1: WALES-CHINA A TO Z ……………………………… 1 - 264

PART 2: STORIES BEHIND MY RESEARCH …………..265 -271

GLOSSARY: PLACE NAMES…………………………………….271 - 272

ILLUSTRATIONS AND PHOTO CREDITS………………. 272 - 276

INDEX …………………………………………………………….. 277 - 285

WALES-CHINA 250 YEARS OF HISTORY

PREFACES

'Almost sixty years ago we came as a family to live in Gower in an old house that seemed full of exotic mystery. It had been extended and redecorated in the later nineteenth century by Frank Arthur Morgan, a mandarin of the Emperor of China who had been in charge of the opium traffic for many years. He and his brother, Charles Edward Morgan, appear in this book. His son, who for many years lived in one wing of the house, told me that he dared to ask his father, about 1906, why he had spent so many years at such an unworthy task as the administration of opium in China, and the old mandarin had replied that he had always had a deep love of China, that the opium trade was only a means to an end, namely that of opening up a hopelessly backward country, so that China could modernise herself and take her place among the strong nations of the world. Both father and son, in a muddled way, were aware of the paradox and ambiguity of the relationship of Victorian Wales with China, but I was left puzzled and troubled. After all, the grave of Dr Griffith John stands hard by the walls of our chapel at Carnglas, Sketty, and he spent a lifetime in China fighting the very opium trade run by our mandarin. I could only grope about in the dark for many years, looking for some light on the relationship of the Welsh with China. So after many years I was delighted to know of the work of Ena Niedergang, who has devoted a lifetime to a labour of love, compiling this book on the contacts between the two countries.

Her work takes us through the trade in tea and beautiful porcelain which attracted the Welsh to China and things Chinese during the eighteenth century, then she shows us the four trends of the nineteenth and early twentieth centuries, first the number of ships trading between Welsh ports and China, second the large number of Welsh people working in Hong Kong, such as the extraordinary governor Sir John Bowring, who was also a Welsh industrialist at Bowrington, Maesteg, third, the number of Welsh troops engaged in the three wars, the two opium wars of the mid-nineteenth century and the crushing of the Boxer Rebellion in 1900, and fourth, the immense number of religious missionaries, some of whom, such as Dr Timothy Richard, became influential figures in China. The book also takes us into the late twentieth century and even to the present day, to chronicle the many contacts between modern China and Wales, the many Chinese people living in Wales, and the movements to sustain friendship, trade and cultural or academic exchange between the two countries. Ena Niedergang has pursued her researches in many parts of China as well as in Wales itself, and has played a major part in the societies sustaining friendship between the Chinese and Welsh peoples. I have been delighted to read the book and feel that at long last I can get answers to all those questions I began to ask nearly sixty years ago about the mandarin Morgan and his world.'

Professor Prys Morgan

WALES-CHINA 250 YEARS OF HISTORY

'Thirty years are a very short period in human history, but very long in a person's life. Human beings create history and, in time, sadly, it may become lost. It is fortunate that some people will try to save it before it has been completely wiped away from human memories and objects. Ena Niedergang is one of these people.

As an educator and historian, she has been both witness and participant to a social transformation that has taken place in both countries during the past thirty years. The way of how she views the historical connections between Wales and China during the past 250 years is authentic, reliable, and passionate. The fieldwork Ena has carried out, the data she has collected, and the materials amassed during the past two decades all over Wales and many parts of China is a remarkable achievement. Even in the world of academia, it is hard to imagine how many scholars would spend twenty years to undertake a single research project. The passion and determination of writing this disappearing history is solidly built on and deeply rooted in Ena's extraordinary personal conscientiousness. It is easy to speak highly of what she has achieved and done to foster friendship and understanding between the peoples of Wales and China since the mid 1980s. Ena writes about the history of other people in this book, but simultaneously she is writing about her own history.

'Wales - China 250 Years of History' will bridge the past, the present, and the future in terms of history and time between the two countries, which has been generally neglected by scholars and historians or simply buried into the discourse of the 'UK or England'. The significant contribution made by Ena in this book is to reconstruct the historical narrative of well-known figures and relatively unknown people's lives, sketch the contours of their life tracks, and to articulate the legacies left by them in China and Wales.

Taking history as a mirror as advised by the Emperor Tang Taizong of the Tang Dynasty (618 – 907AD); it can help people to see the truth, and history as a fact and can objectively make a judgement of goodness and badness about people, events, and activities. For example, in today's China, there is a growing recognition of the contribution made by people from Wales such as the Rev. Dr. Griffith John 杨格非 (Yang Ge Fei) in Wuhan over a century ago. He is no longer seen as just a Christian missionary from Wales who established schools, hospitals and colleges in that city – but is regarded as a man who did good things for the Chinese people.

Similarly, over the years, Chinese people who have come to live and work in Wales have contributed to the evolution of a multicultural and dynamic nation within the United Kingdom. While both Wales and Chinese Governments are keen to consolidate and build upon relations between the two countries, it is also vital for both the Welsh and Chinese people to have a better understanding about this historical connection between both nations that has existed for 250 years. This kind of historical, cultural, and personal connection is what Ena offers to readers and researchers, which will be very helpful for building future dialogue and cooperation between the two governments and the peoples of each nation.

WALES-CHINA 250 YEARS OF HISTORY

Ena has highlighted the history and events that not simply retell what had happened, but also to introduce various Chinese cultures to western readers in the style of 'when Wales and China meet with each other'. She also includes examples of the contribution made by Chinese people who have come to make Wales their home.
 'Wales - China 250 Years of History' is testament to a unique relationship that has existed between two ancient nations over the centuries. '
Dr. Qian Wang

ACKNOWLEGEMENTS

This book would not have been compiled without the help, support, encouragement and generosity of so many individuals, groups, organizations and institutions. I would like to thank everyone who so graciously contributed and those who wrote articles on their specialist subjects.

In particular I wish to thank the following for their advice, assistance and contribution during the past twenty years toward the compilation of this book:
Alan Appleby, Alison Adderson, Dr. Clifford Austin, Stephen Batsford, Sandra Barnes, Prudence Bell, Sir Brooke-Boothby, Rev. Peter Brookes, Professor Huw Bowen, Gareth Bonello, E.A. Bennett, Iwan Bala, Norman Burns, Rachael Barnwell, Gregor Benton, Peter and Abby Bellan, Bill Cainan, Ying Chinnery, Very Rev. Gerwyn Huw Capon, Aliki Currimjee, Carrie Canham, Judy Chappell, Kim Collis, Katrina Coopey, Rev. Alan Chiplin, Tak Chan, Rachel Conroy, late Dr. Margaret Siriol Colley, Alex Caccia, Rhodri Clark, Jenny Childs, David Clay, Cheng Jia, Kam Yau Chen, Dr. Zhouxia Chen, Lieutenant-Colonel P.A. Crocker, Gary Davies, A.E. Dudley, Dr. Thom Davies, Tony Delamothe, Ellie Dawkins, Ding Yan, Ruby Dymond, Juliette Davies, Mark Evans, George Brynley Evans, Hywel Gwyn Evans, Major Martin Everett, John Evans, Professor David Evans, W. M. Geoffrey Evans, Oliver Fairclough, Douglas Fraser, Betty and Peter Frazer, Feng Guangsheng, Heledd Fychan, Gaynor Francis, Rev. Paul Flavell, Margaret Fernando, Simon Francis, David Gealy, David Gwyer, James Gilman, Gwylim Games, Helen Gethin, Very Rev. Geoffrey Marshall, Diane Gill, Rev. Kenneth Griffin, Rev. Canon J.W. Griffith, Mari Gordon, Keith Griffiths, late John Griffiths, Hugh Harrison-Allen, Helen Hallesy, Jean Harding Rolls, Jenny Harding Rolls, late Christopher Harding Rolls, late Edwin Harries, Dr. Peter Harries, Julie Harris, Grahan Hartill, Jo Howard, Malcolm Hasler, Andrew Hillier, H.E.T. Harris, Peter Hopkins, late Muriel Hellings, Rebekah Hunkin. Lucy Huws,, Professor John G. Hughes, Dave Howerski, A. Lloyd Hughes, Mrs. Jones (Gwynfe), Sylvia Jones, Joanna Jones, Brin Jones, Menai Jones, Pat Jones, Jack and Val Jago, Alaw Jones, Rhodri Jones, Dr. Thomas Jansen, M. Jeremiah, Mark Jones, Heather and Peter James, Steve Jones, Annwen Jones, Rt. Hon. Carwyn Jones A.M., Rev. Griffith P. Jones, Marilyn Jones, Elsie Jones, Hazel Johnson-Ollier, Frances Jones-Davies, Dr. David Jenkins, Judith Love, K. Kays, Felicity Kilpatrick, Angela Kwok, Pam Keys, Lottie Kettle, Lewis Lloyd, Chris Leggett, Len Ley, Mark Lewis, Jonathan Lee, Sir David Lewis, Robin Llewellyn,

WALES-CHINA 250 YEARS OF HISTORY

John Lyons, Dr. Li Feng, Very Rev. Bertie Lewis, Megan Lewis, Thomas Lloyd, Hon. Robert Lloyd George, Alison Lloyd, Stuart Lyden, Long Xin Min, Zhou Li, Amanda Morgan, Robert Minhinnick, Professor Prys Morgan, Dr. John Mack, Ken Morgan, Robin Maggs, Rt. Hon. Rhodri Morgan, Lady Susan McClaren, Mike McClamon, Mike Norman, Geraldine Newbury, Christine Newbury, Avril Nicholson, Jean Owen, Bryn Owen, Caroline Oakley, Pi Gong-Liang, Peter Pope, Jane Pedley, Dr. Rosie Plummer, Alison Proctor, Rev. Andrew Pierce, Kelly Powell, Jen Patrick, late Lord Gordon Parry, Pastor Peng Zhifeng, Sarah Roberts, Angela Rees, Rachel Rees, Jeremy Rye, Helen Roberts, Julian Roup, Shan Robinson, Malcolm and Ruth Ridge, Caroline Stock, Professor Qiang Shen, Elen Wyn Simpson, Stephen Selby, Audrey Speare, Julia and Kevin Saunders, Evelyn Smith, Anna and Martin Sullivan, David Saunders, Professor Michael Scott, First Secretary Su Zhimen, late Lynfa Thomas, Eiryth Thomas, Susan Thomas, David Treharne, Professor J.D.R. Thomas, K.D.G. Thomas, David Thompson, J. Hugh Thomas, Bev Thomas, John Tasker family, Rev. James Thomas, Rev. Gareth Thomas, Daphne Todd, Sîan Williams, late Bill Williams, Michael Wilcox, Dr. Frances Wood, Rt. Hon. Baron Williams of Oystermoth, David Wright, Dr. Sioned Williams, Jo Waller, Professor Wu Fu Sheng, late Professor Rev. Cyril Williams, Irene Williams, Eirian Williams, Dr Xinyu Wu, Mel Williams, late Charles Woosnam, E. Williams, Dr. Sophie Williams, late Jane Williams, T.I. Walters, Mme Wu Cuirong, Nancy Wilson, John Warmsley, David Williams, Professor Wen G. Jiang, Sheila Wheeler, Mrs. Williams (Morriston), Professor Yiling Wu, Barbara Wheadon Pauline Woodroffe, Sir George White, Dr. Xia Zhidao, Ye Ying, Dr Yan Ying, Yang Xin, Yun Li Mei, Dr Zhu Limin, Dr Zhou Xanxia, Wei Fong Lee, Hugh Lewis,

I also wish to thank the museums, art galleries, libraries, archives, churches, chapels, universities, colleges, schools, historical societies, historic houses, newspapers, journals, Confucius Institutes, hotels, photographers, local authorities, families with China connections and commercial organizations who responded with courtesy and interest in my research. I would like to acknowledge those people who discovered 'lost' plaques from chapels, locations where films on China were made; the people who contacted me over the years with information, and not least, the Welsh Government. I wish to acknowledge the support members of the Chinese communities throughout Wales for their enthusiasm and support.

In the People's Republic of China, I would like to thank the British Embassy in Beijing, the British Consulate-General in Shanghai, the Chinese People's Association for Friendship with Foreign Countries (CPAFFC) in Beijing, the Tianjin People's Association for Friendship with Foreign Countries, Tianjin Museum, and the Wuhan Museum for its research on the Rev. Dr. Griffith John, Archives of the Palace Museum in Beijing for their help on the William Hughes automata clocks. And to all my friends in China who carried out research on my behalf and supported me throughout the years.

I am indebted to each and everyone who helped to turn my research into a labour of love. Every single person and organization made the research a pleasure, and amazingly nothing was too much trouble for anyone.

WALES-CHINA 250 YEARS OF HISTORY

I am also indebted to historians, Chinese linguists and specialists for their help and advice; to everyone who opened up their collections - books, 'Chinoiserie', porcelain, Chinese garments, photographs etc. to help further my research.

I would like to thank my friends and family for their support and encouragement over the years to continue my research.

The biggest 'thank you' goes to my husband, Barry, who has supported this Project from the very beginning. Without him this book would not have been compiled as he has inputted every word and image onto the computer. He never complained and always gave the best advice.

In attempting to record Wales` historic link with China – a link that has lasted for over 250 years I am certain that the list is not finite. However, I hope that this book will act as a catalyst for future research on the subject.

(Ena Niedergang)

INTRODUCTION

My association with China and 'things Chinese' spans thirty years. In the early 1990s I worked in Wuhan, Central China. It was the city where the Swansea-born missionary, Griffith John, spent 50 years of his life and established churches, colleges and schools. I then began to wonder what other connections existed between Wales and China over the years. So my research began. Little did I realise, at the time, that it would stretch over 20 years and take me, not only to most parts of Wales, but, also to China. It was to become a labour of love.

At the beginning, I received comments such as, "Are there any links?" - "That'll take you five minutes!" - "Of course, the missionaries." For a moment I doubted myself and wondered if I was wasting my time. Thankfully, there were enlightened people who urged me to do the research and commented that it was an unknown history of Wales that had to be recorded.

It has not been an easy task as 'Wales' or the 'Welsh' rarely appeared in the indexes and was smothered under the cloak of 'England'. If there was any reference at all to 'Wales' or the 'Welsh', connections with China seemed to record the contribution of two missionaries, Griffith John and Timothy Richard. I reflected on what people had commented that they might be the only two and it would be fruitless looking for anyone or, anything else... perhaps the people who had said, "Are there any links?" were correct.

My research started unearthing remarkable people and events. There was a rich history - not only missionaries but also the military, coalminers, governors, opium traders, a clockmaker and on and on. The links with China were amazing!

It was, at this point, I thought that if people, events, plaques and gravestones were being recorded, then why not items in museums, art galleries, libraries, and stately homes etc? It also seemed obvious to record Wales-China in literature, poetry, diaries, and newspapers. What about the houses whose owners had links with China or houses with 'Chinoiserie'? The names of shops

WALES-CHINA 250 YEARS OF HISTORY

also proved intriguing as they sold Chinese items. All this knowledge should be brought together as it is an important part of our history before being lost or forgotten. There is an urgency to save our history in China - we were there and we are there now. It was important to record the people, places and events between the two countries over the centuries.

The need for a book of Wales - China connections was growing. The history of the Welsh in America and Australia has been written about, but no one, to date, has recorded and brought together the historical relationship between Wales and China.

With my husband's encouragement and help, we visited churches, chapels, graveyards, houses, shops, libraries, museums and archives throughout Wales, the rest of the UK and China (including Hong Kong and Macau) recording historical links between the two countries.

Plaques and gravestones had to be recorded for posterity before the ravages of time or encroaching ivy covered them. Revisiting some gravestones and plaques, 20 years on, emphasised the need as the wording was becoming almost illegible! The history of Welsh people in China was becoming lost and forgotten.

I spent many hours, days, weeks and months researching in archives, particularly in the days before much was accessible via the web - searching, searching and searching until, finally, a fact or a name would jump at you to send your adrenaline racing. Not only was Wales scoured for information but also return visits to China (including Hong Kong, Macau, Beijing, Tianjin and Wuhan) were necessary. Cemeteries were explored in the hope of discovering a Welsh burial. For example, a 'death' recorded in The *'Cambrian'* Newspaper in 1843 was matched with a grave in Macau. Sir Edward Youde, a former Governor of Hong Kong, has a plaque dedicated to him in St. John's Cathedral on Hong Kong Island. It was so refreshing to see that he came from 'Penarth, South Wales'. During the period of my research I have given talks to historical societies, the National Museum of Wales, been interviewed on BBC Radio Wales and written newspaper articles asking for information. People have overwhelmed me with their kindness, generosity and interest in my research. I was also interested in the Chinese people who had come to Wales, especially those who eventually were to make Wales their home and who were to contribute to Wales - China links.

In the past few years, an increasing number of Chinese people, both in the U.K. and China have shown an interest in my research.

During the period of my research I received encouragement and interest from the media, academics, official and commercial organizations throughout Wales and the rest of the UK, and from The People's Republic of China, including Hong Kong, and not least, from members of the public who were invaluable in forwarding information they had relating to personal and family links with China.

In conclusion, I hope that you will enjoy reading this book as much as I have in compiling it over the past twenty years.

Ena Niedergang

WALES-CHINA 250 YEARS OF HISTORY

PART ONE
WALES-CHINA
A to Z

A

Aberavon
MR CLAPTON'S EXHIBITION: 'This establishment, which is worthy of the attention of an intelligent and discerning public, has been open to the inhabitants of Aberavon and neighbourhood during the past week, but it has not, we are sorry to say, met with that support which its merit entitles it to. The attractions are views of the cities of Verona and Florence in Italy, Chusan in China, etc., before which people, vessels, vehicles, and animals pass and repass being ingeniously propelled by machinery, appropriate music being played.'
(The Cambrian, 25th March 1859)

Aberconwy (Henry Duncan McLaren, 2nd Lord Aberconwy 1879-1953)
Lord Aberconwy, born at Bodnant, North Wales, supported many plant collecting expeditions to China.
('Roy Lancaster Travels in China: A Plantsman's Paradise' – Antique Collector's Club 1989)

Abergavenny
'The 'Earl of Abergavenny', launched in 1789, was one of the larger ships ever built for the East India Company. John Wordsworth, Captain of the ship and cousin of the poet, William Wordsworth, made several successful voyages to India and China. In 1790, John Wordsworth, brother of William Wordsworth, joined the ship.
'The Cumberland Pacquet' reported in 1791, "Captain Wordsworth had lately the honour of receiving and entertaining on board his ship, the 'Earl of Abergavenny', at Canton, the Emperor of China, with numerous retinue." The East India Company was trying to promote trade with China and was out to impress. John Wordsworth, eventually, became Captain of the 'Earl of Abergavenny' when his cousin resigned in 1801.
The 'Earl of Abergavenny' was wrecked with loss of life, off Weymouth, in 1805 on her fifth voyage to China, Captain Wordsworth went down with his ship.'
(North-West Evening Mail April 7, 2005)

Abernant House (Builth Wells)
The Dining Room was decorated with Chinese Wallpaper in the 1930s
(See: Lord Harold Caccia)

Africa
SHIPPING INTELLIGENCE
'It is reported that the 'Africa' (American ship) sailing from Cardiff to Shanghai, went aground in the Straits of Gasper, and being surrounded by pirates was abandoned, and was on fire before the crew's last sighting of her; the latter reported as having been landed at Singapore on 9th September.'
(The Cambrian 16th November 1860)

Ah Chow
Merchant seaman from Port Tennant became the first Chinese national to be married in Swansea. The ceremony took place at Swansea Registry Office on 31st January 1910.
(West Glamorgan Archives Service)

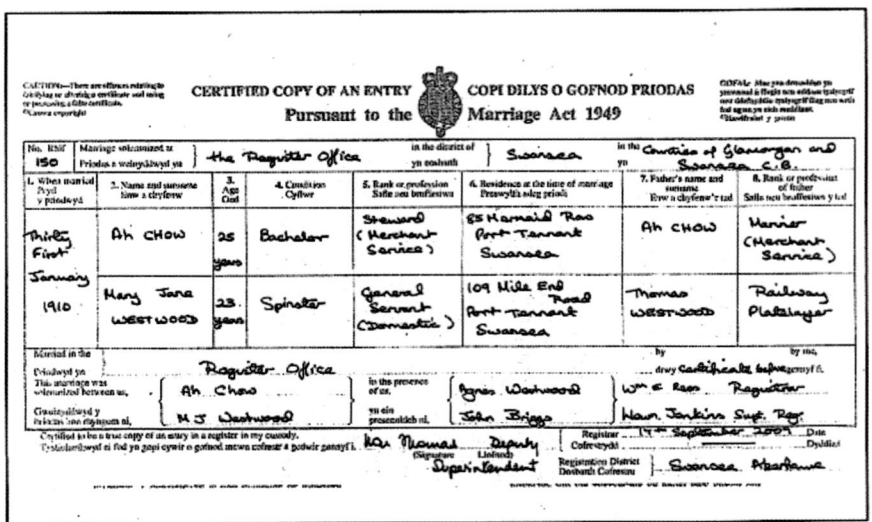

Marriage Certificate of Ah Chow and Mary Jane Westwood

Alderman Davies' Church in Wales Primary School, Neath
A group of pupils and staff from the School took part in the 'China 89' Project – Wales' first ever schoolchildren's performance, cultural and educational tour to China in March 1989. They were joined by a group of pupils and staff from Cwrt Sart Comprehensive School, Briton Ferry.
(See: 'China 89'; Cwrt Sart)

Allen (C.F. Romilly J.P)
'Born 1844: son of L. Bough Allen, Cilrhiw, Pembrokeshire; Former H.M Consul, Fuzhou. (Address: Southfield, Woodchester, Stroud, Gloucestershire).'
('Who's Who in Wales' 1921)
('China Consuls' by P.D. Coates (Appendix) 1990 p.4, pub: Asian Affairs)

Allen (E.E.)
MARRIAGE
'On the 28th February, at St John's Cathedral, Hong Kong, by the Rev E.E Allen, MA, rector of Porthkerry, Glamorganshire, and Honorary Canon of Llandaff, to Florence Hope, daughter of Francis Julian Marshall, Surveyor of Her Britannic Majesty's Office of Works for China and Japan.'
(The Cambrian 12th April 1889)

Allen (E.L.B)
The son of a Glamorganshire clergyman; a former British Consul in China. Died aged sixty-six.
('The China Consuls' by P.D. Coates 1990, p.139, 169 (Appendix II), pub. Asian Affairs)

Allen (Herbert James)
'Born in India, where his father was in the Civil Service. He came to China as a student interpreter in 1861. He retired from the consular service in 1888 and died in Wales in 1911. He wrote various papers, translations, etc; his best-known work being 'Early Chinese History or are the Chinese Classics forged?' (1906).
('Encyclopaedia Sinica' by Samuel Couling M.A. (1917) – Page11)
('The China Consuls' by P.D. Coates 1990, p.93 (Appendix II), pub. Asian Affairs)

Amelia
SHIPPING INTELLIGENCE
'Liverpool, July 31st ……………. The 'Amelia', from Swansea bound for China, put into Rio de Janeiro, leaking.
(The 'Cambrian', August 5th, 1859)

'Amethyst'
HMS Amethyst was one of the Royal Navy ships involved in the 'Yangtze Incident' in 1949 when it was on its way to Nanjing to relieve HMS Consort from its duty of protecting the British Embassy. The 'incident' started on April 20th 1949 and ended with the Amethyst's escape to freedom on July 30th. It was Britain's last naval involvement in China. There were Welsh crewmembers serving on the ship.
A plaque commemorating the sailors who died on the 'Amethyst', 'Consort' and the 'Blackbird' (another one of the ships involved) was dedicated and placed in the Memorial Garden at the British Embassy in Beijing on 16th June 1994.
(Barry Niedergang)
(See: Owen Baker, Geoffrey Locke, Len Ley and Sir Edward Youde)

Andromeda
'HMS Andromeda, a first class protected cruiser launched at Pembroke Dockyard on April 30, 1897. She saw service in the Mediterranean, Indian Ocean and on the China station. She later served as a training ship and was broken up in Belgium in 1956/57.' ('A Short History of Pembroke Dock in Words and Pictures' by F.D. Days 1985)

HMS Andromeda built at Pembroke Dockyard and launched 30th April 1897

Ann Lucy

**FOR HONG KONG DIRECT
FROM APPLEDORE NORTH DEVON CALLING AT
SWANSEA
THE BRITISH BUILT CLIPPER
BARQUE**

'500 tons berthed A1 at Lloyds, John Butcher, Commander has room for a limited number of cabin and steerage passengers and will sail on or about 18th February next, having all her crew engaged. Apply to owner, Mr William Lucy, at Yeo's Richmond Dock, Appledore; Mr James Strick, Ship and Insurance Broker, Swansea Messer's R.G. Jones, Price and Co., Clements Lane, London; W. Wickham Esq: Bideford, Devon'
(The Cambrian 6th February 1863)

Anna Maria
SHIPPING INTELLIGENCE
'The 'Anna Maria' left Cardiff for Shanghai on 8th October, 1860.'
(The 'Cambrian')

Arber-Cooke (Alfred Theodore)
Alfred Arber-Cooke was Town Clerk for Llandovery. He came from Wimbledon, London and lived at Tŷ Cerrig, Stone Street, Llandovery. Arber-Cooke accumulated a vast collection of Chinese robes and other Chinese antiques. He also had a vast collection of Chinese coins. He wrote: 'Pages from the History of Llandovery' Volumes 1 and 2 (1994) Llandovery Civic Trust.]
(Source: David Gealy, Llandovery.)

Arthur (William Hawken)
'The Arthur family, who lived at Highway, Pennard, during the latter years of the 18th century, were noted for their smuggling and other related activities. One son, whose baptism was registered in 1774, became a country Parson in Devonshire and was the father of the Naval Officer, who, in 1860, surveyed the area of the Liaodong Peninsula in northern China. Port Arthur, on that Peninsula, was named after him.'
By H.R. J Davies and L. A. Toft
(The Magazine (3rd Edition) - The Parish and Church of St Mary, Pennard, Gower)

Arthur (William C.)
'Lieutenant Royal Navy: During the Second Opium War, 1860, Lt. Arthur's frigate was towed into the harbour at Lushun for repairs. Lushun, at this time, was a simple fishing village which, after this event, became known as Port Arthur. It has reverted to its Chinese name of Lushun Port and is situated near the City of Dalian.' (B. Niedergang)

Atlantic College
The United World College was founded in Wales with the opening of Atlantic College, St. Donat's in the Vale of Glamorgan. The College forms part of the historic St Donat's Castle, the former home of the American Newspaper Tycoon, William Randolph Hearst. The college accepted its first intake of Chinese students in 1973.
In 2012, twenty students from the College visited China as part of their 'China Project'. The students taught in ten schools in Gansu Province.
In 2013, John Walmsley, the College Principal, invited Mayor Wang Yang from the City of Changshu, near Shanghai to visit St Donat's and to see for himself what the College had to offer as it had inspired the prospect of establishing a new international college in Changshu.
Over the years, many Alumni from the College have become members of the Chinese Government. (Atlantic College)

Photographs from the 'China Project ' (Atlantic College)

Austin (Dr. Clifford)
Dr Austin, of Swansea, worked in Guangdong, Southern China in the 1950s. In November 1989, he attended the Annual Conference of Friends of the Church in China in London. It was at the Conference that he met two nurses from Kunming, who had crossed the Chinese border on the same train as him in 1951.'
('Ni Hao' Newsletter WCFS July 1990)
The late Dr Austin was a great supporter of friendship and understanding between the people of Wales and China.

Austin (Griffith Rosser 1848-1889)
DEATHS
'On August 25, at sea while on a voyage to Shanghai, for the benefit of his health, Griffith Austin, pilot, son of John Austin, one Geoffrey's place Swansea, aged 42 years.'
(The Cambrian January 2, 1891). He is remembered on the family grave at Saint Mary's Church, Swansea.

Austin family gravestone at Saint Mary's Parish Church Swansea

Automaton

> EXTRAORDINARY NOVELTY
> Arrival of the Chinese Automaton Juggler
> FREE ADMISSION
> THE LOUNGE AND PROMENADE
> 3 TEMPLE STREET SWANSEA
> Opposite the Branch Bank of England
> *MESSRS MIER and CO. have the honour to inform their friends of the above arrival, from which there will be no charge in exhibiting*

(The Cambrian 7th August 1841)

Aylward (Gladys 1902 – 1970)
Born on the 24th February 1902 in Edmonton, north London, Gladys Aylward lived in Page Street, Swansea for two years and worked with her good friends John and Evie Jago at the Mission in the Hafod area and also worked at the Walter Road Home for Girls who had gone astray in order to earn money for her journey to China.
1932 - Left London for China, travelling across Siberia before, eventually, arriving at Yungchen, Shanxi Province. Worked with Mrs Lawson. Took in orphans and adopted some.
1936 - Became a Chinese citizen.
1938 - China was invaded by Japanese forces. Gladys led about 100 orphans over the mountains.
1948 - Returned to Britain. Tried to return to China but Communist Government prevented her entry.
1958 - Taiwan-founded the Gladys Aylward Orphanage.
1963 - 'This is Your Life' TV programme with Eamonn Andrews.
1970 - Died in Taiwan, 3rd January, aged 67 years.
1991 - South Wales Evening Post article on Evie Jago and Gladys Aylward.
Evie and Jack Jago recorded memories of Gladys Aylward on Swansea Sound. After her death, the Weir Secondary School in Edmonton changed its name to the Gladys Aylward School.
2010 - The school became an Academy and renamed itself Aylward Academy.

The 1958 film, 'The Inn of the Sixth Happiness' featured Gladys's struggle to cross the mountains with, approximately, 100 orphans. The film starred Ingrid Bergman and was filmed on location at Nantmor in North Wales. Nantmor, near Beddgelert became the fictional city of Wang Cheng. In China, Gladys Aylward was given the Chinese name of 'Aì Wěi Dé'- 'The Virtuous One'.
(See: Nantmor; Beddgelert; 'Inn of the Sixth Happiness')

Gladys Aylward at Mount Pleasant Baptist Church Swansea (1963)

Gladys Aylward's dress and jacket left with the Jago family in 1963

Note: In 2014 the Author became the 'guardian' of Gladys Aylward's Chinese jacket and dress.

B

Baker (Owen)

Aged 22 years, a medical orderly from Port Talbot, was killed on board HMS Amethyst in 1949 as it was taking supplies to the British Embassy in Nanjing, China. The attack on the Amethyst became known as the 'Yangtze Incident' when the Chinese killed 40 British personnel.

A memorial plaque to Owen Baker was displayed at the Royal Naval Hospital in Hong Kong. Following the closure of the hospital, it was transferred to the British Military Barracks. In 1997, when Hong Kong was returned to China, Mr Baker's brother, John, worked with various authorities to rescue the plaque. The plaque to Owen Baker is on display at Neath-Port Talbot Council Office in Port Talbot.

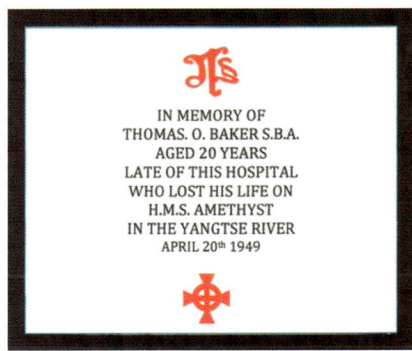 

Photo of Owen Baker and brass plaque at the Civic Centre Port Talbot

Bala (Iwan)

Artist, writer and Senior Lecturer in Fine Art at the University of Wales Trinity Saint David, Carmarthen. In 2009, he was one of the leading artists from Wales who took part in 'Celebrating the Red Dragon' exhibition, supported by Wales Arts International and the British Council. The exhibition toured Chongqing, Guangzhou, Shanghai and Beijing.

Bangor University

Bangor University is the first university in Wales to establish a campus in China. 'Bangor College' accepted its first intake of students in September 2014 and offers undergraduate teaching programmes in banking, accountancy and electronic engineering. The University is collaborating with the China Central South University of Forestry and Technology in Changsha, Hunan Province. Those present at the official signing ceremony included Professor John Hughes, Vice-Chancellor of Bangor University, Secretary-of-State for Wales David Jones MP, Lord Dafydd Wigley and Li Guoqiang First Secretary (Education), from the Chinese Embassy in London. The University formally launched a Confucius Institute in September 2012.

Vice-Chancellor Professor John G Hughes and Professor Xianyan Zhou sign the agreements with Dr Xinyu Wu, Director of International Development, Bangor & Professor Zhuqing Yang, Dean of Bangor College, China.

In May 2014 the Symposium 'Reading China – Translating Wales' took place at the University organized by Dr Yan Ying and Dr Sioned Puw Rowlands of the 'Wales Literature Exchange'. The Symposium was officially opened by Professor John Hughes, Vice-Chancellor of Bangor University and, Mr Wu Hong Vice Editor-in-Chief of the Shanghai Translation Publishing House. Featured speakers included Jon Gower, Nia Davies, Jerry Hunter, Hu Dong, Heather Inwood, Li Yuyan, Patrick McGuiness, Francesca Rhydderch and Angharad Price.

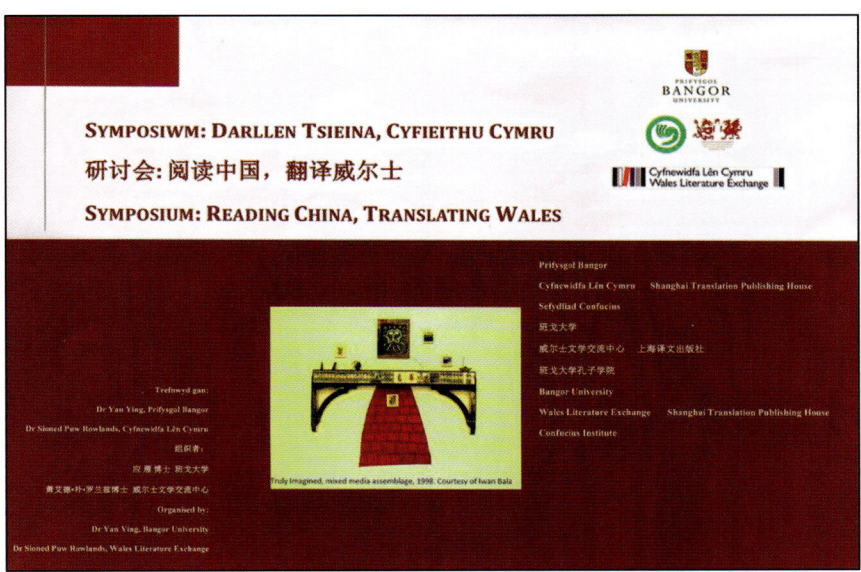

Examples of Chinese porcelain from the Dr Owen Pritchard Collection at Bangor University

Barnard (Sir Charles Louden K.C.B)
'Born 1823. Retired 1888; son of Admiral E.Barnard; Married Julia, daughter of Captain Edwards R.N, 1858. Served in China 1859 -1860.' Address: Castle House, Usk, Monmouth.' ('Who's Who' 1897 Edited by Douglas Sladen/Page 180)

BBC (Cardiff Singer of the World Competition)
Singers from around the world come to Cardiff to compete for the title of 'Singer of the World'.
Chinese Winners
1997 – Guang Yang
2007 - Shen Yang

BBC National Orchestra of Wales
2012 First China Tour. The Orchestra undertook a twelve-day tour of China and performed at Tianjin, Beijing, Shanghai, Shenzhen, and Guangzhou. The tour was part of the 'UK Now' Festival.

Beddgelert

The 'Inn of the Sixth Happiness' (1958) was filmed in and around Beddgelert and Nantmor. During the filming, many of the cast and film crew were based in Beddgelert. A member of the original cast, Burt Kwouk, unveiled a commemorative plaque on 28th May 2004. See (Nantmor; 'Inn of the Sixth Happiness')

Commemorative plaque at Beddgelert unveiled by Burt Kwouk May 2004

Bei Dao

The Chinese poet, Bei Dao, read from his selection of poems entitled 'The August Sleepwalker' at the Welsh Arts Council's Gallery, Oriel Cardiff (1990). Bei Dao found inspiration from Dylan Thomas. He is widely acknowledged as one of China's most gifted and controversial writers.

Beijing

Beijing Haidian Foreign Language Middle School took part in the Llangollen International Music Eisteddfod in 2013.

Beijing Acrobatic Troupe

Production of 'Shang Hi' from the international hit 'Dralion' at the Grand Theatre Swansea, April 2012

Bell (Prudence)

'Lives from a Black Tin Box' by Prudence Bell and Ronald Clements (Published by Authentica Media 2014). The story of Herbert and Elizabeth Dixon, missionaries to China, killed by the Boxers in 1900. They were Prudence Bell's great grandparents.
(See: Elizabeth and Herbert Dixon, Peter B.S. Davies)

Bella Donna

'From Swansea to Hong Kong, floundered in a gale in the China Sea; Captain, Mate and part of crew landed at Singapore previous to 4th ult.'
(The Cambrian' 17th January 1868)

Benton (Gregor)
Gregor Benton, formerly Professor of Chinese Studies at the University of Leeds and Associate Professor of Anthropology at the University of Amsterdam, is Professor Emeritus of Chinese History at Cardiff University. He has published more than a score of books on China, Chinese History and the Chinese Diaspora. His research portfolio includes Chinese Communism, Chinese in Britain, Chinatowns worldwide and the Chinese in the Cuban Revolution.

Betts (George Edgar)
Born, 1876 at 94, High Street, Merthyr Tydfil - Left for China to become a missionary in 1882 aged 25 years.
(Overseas Missionary Fellowship 1991)

Beynon (Owen Gwynne Richard)
1894 - Born Llanelli
1921 - Appointed pharmacist and radiographer to the Lester Hospital Shanghai.
Interned 1945 - Returned to Wales.
(Overseas Missionary Fellowship 1991)

Beynon (Rev. William Thomas 1860-1900)
Born Haverfordwest, Pembrokeshire. His formative years were spent at Nantyffyllon. He later trained as a missionary at Allencliffe College, London.
1884 - Attended University College Aberystwyth where he met his future wife, Emily Turner, from Leeds.
1887 - 19th April, Rev Beynon was presented with the Bible by Siloh Sunday School Nantyffyllon on his departure to China. This Bible was the only possession of the Rev Beynon returned to Wales. It was presented by his sister, Mrs J Evans, to Siloh in March, 1927. The Bible is now displayed at the Historical and Cultural Centre in Pontypridd along with a portrait of the Rev Beynon.
1885-1895 - The China Inland Mission appointed Rev. Beynon to work with the Mongol people of North China.
1887 - Married Miss Emily Turner in China.
1889 - Daisy Beynon born
1892 - Kenneth Beynon born
1893 - Norman Beynon born
1896 - Appointed sub-agent in Shanghai by the Bible Society.
1900 - Beynon family massacred in Taiyuan by the Boxers on 9th July.
1927 - Memorial tablet the Rev. Beynon unveiled at Siloh Chapel on 28th March.

This Bible was presented to the Reverend William Thomas Beynon by the Sunday School of Siloh, Nantyffyllon on his departure as a missionary for China On 19th April 1887.

In 1900 William T. Beynon, his wife and three children were martyred in the Boxer Risings.

This Bible was the only possession of the missionary that came back to Wales.

It was presented back to Siloh by Mr. Beynon's sister, Mrs J.R. Evans, Nantymoel, in March 1927

Photographs of William Thomas Beynon and memorabilia at Pontypridd Museum

'In memory of Martha, beloved wife of John Beynon, of this place who departed this life 24th June, 1880 aged 45 years. Also Thomas, their son, who died 1869, aged 4 years. Also in memory of W.T.Beynon aged 40 years, Missionary, son of the above named with his wife Emily, aged 30 years, and their children Daisy, aged 11 years, Kenneth, aged eight years and Norman aged seven years massacred at Taiyuan, China, 9th July 1900.'

Beynon Grave at St. John's Church

Memorial plaque to the Rev .W.T Beynon at Siloh Chapel, Nantyffyllon

A memorial to the murdered missionaries and their families was placed outside the South Gate of Taiyuan that no longer exists.

Reference:
– WT Beynon, pages 31 and 32, 'Hanes Eglwys Nantyffyllon 1841-1941
– William Thomas Beynon (1860 – 1900), pages 280 and 281, 'History of the Llynfi Valley' by Brinley Richards
– Rev WT Beynon (1860 – 1900), pages 67 and 68, William Hopkins Memorial Book 1937, 'The Advertiser', July 3rd, 1929, Siloh Church and W.T.Beynon

Bishop W.
Served with the Royal Welsh Fusiliers and was awarded the China Medal (1857-1860) with bars (Pekin 1860 and Dagu Forts 1860).

Bitten (Nelson)
Author: 'The Story of Griffith John, the Apostle of Central China.' (Published by The Sunday School Union)

Bonello (Gareth)
Welsh folk artist The Gentle Good, aka Gareth Bonello, swapped his hometown of Cardiff for the unknown terrain of Chengdu in China's Sichuan Province to complete a career-changing six-week musical residency. He worked with the Chengdu Associated Theatre for Performing Arts and wrote the album based on the poetry of Li Bai (701-762AD) the Tang Dynasty Poet. The trip encouraged the singer songwriter to meld traditional Welsh folk melodies with Chinese instrumentation and scales, in an ambitious project sponsored by PRS for Music Foundation and the British Council (October 2011).

Bowen (William)
'On the 1st ult. on a voyage from China, the death of Mr William Bowen, aged 48 years, youngest son of the late Mr David Bowen, of Goat Street, Swansea.'
(The Cambrian 4th November 1864)

Bowlby (Thomas William)
'Thomas Bowlby, the correspondent for The Times was captured in Pekin in 1860 along with Private John Phipps of the King's Dragoon Guard (See Private John Phipps). The bodies of Bowlby and Phipps, and those of the remaining Sikhs, were brought in on the 16th. Quicklime had destroyed their features, but we recognised them by their clothes, and Bowlby, poor fellow, we also knew from the peculiar formation of his head and brow, and by a peculiarity in one of his feet. Strangely enough, about six weeks earlier he had related to us his having gone to Wales to the spot where the ROYAL CHARTER had been wrecked, the search amongst the bodies of those washed onshore for that of a brother who had been lost, and after several days he had recognised one............ the features of which were defaced from the length of time the body had been in the sea............ to be that of his brother by a peculiar formation of his foot caused, I think he said, by a broken bone. It was a singular coincidence that almost the only way by which his own body was identified with in so short a time of his telling the story, was by a similar peculiarity in one of his feet.'
(Extract from: 'A Number of Events in China' by Henry Brougham Loch (1900 pub. John Murray) Chapter 14 page 160)
(See: John Phipps)

Bowring (Charles Algernon)
Deaths
'We have to announce the death, at Rome, of the younger son of Sir John Bowring, Governor of Hong Kong. The deceased gentleman, who was in his 30th year, was a Jesuit priest.'
(The Cambrian 18 December 1857)
Deaths
On the 18th ult., at Rome, aged 30 years, Charles Algernon Bowring Esq, Youngest son of John Bowring, Governor of Hong Kong.'
(The Cambrian 18th December 1857) (See: Sir John Bowring)

Bowring (Sir John)
1792 - Born Exeter, 17th October
1806 - At 14 years of age, worked for his father, Charles Bowring, at the family owned woollen mill for four years. As a wool merchant, his father exported to China. During this time John Bowring visited Spain, Russia, Sweden, Finland and Germany.
1816 - Married Maria Lewin. They had five sons and four daughters.
1824 - Joint Editor of the 'Westminster Review'.
1828 - Commissioned by Chancellor of the Exchequer on various projects.
1829 - Made honorary Doctor of Law.
1832 - Secretary of the Commission for the Reform of Public Accounts.
1834 - Elected MP for Kilmarnock.
1841 - 1849 - Member of Parliament for Bolton.
1845 - Invested in Llynfi Ironworks.
1846 - Presented with silver salver by the workmen at the Llynfi Ironworks.
1847 - Robbery at Llynfi Ironworks.
1848 - Court case.
1849 - At 49 years, Consul of Canton (Guangzhou) for four years.
1854 - Advocate for Decimal Currency and wrote 'The Decimal System in Numbers, Coins and Accounts'. The Florin was introduced into the currency mainly due to his efforts.
1854 - 1859 – Knighted and became the 4th Governor of Hong Kong.
1857 - Son, Charles died in Rome, aged 30 years.
1858 - Wife, Maria died.
1859 - Gave lecture at Swansea on China at the Society of Arts.
1860 - Married, Deborah Castle.
1861 - Commissioner to Italy.
1872 - Died 23rd November, aged 80 years at Claremont.

SIR JOHN BOWRING ON CHINA

'At a crowded meeting of the Society of Arts last week Sir John Bowring delivered a long and highly interesting discourse on China and its relation to British commerce. Numerous persons could not obtain admission, and the confusion round the entrance, owing to the crush of visitors struggling for entrance, rendered the commencement of Sir John Bowring`s observations indistinctly audible. He began by describing the vastness and importance of China, its immense population of 400, 000, 000 the general character of the country and the extent of its imports and exports. The average exports of China to this country during the last five years was stated to exceed 9, 000, 000 sterling, and its imports of British manufacture amounted to only 2, 000, 000, and but for the opium imported from India the balance would be required to be paid in bullion. Sir John Bowring dwelt with much force, and at some length on the misconception that prevailed in this country with respect to the trade in opium, for the purpose of disabusing the public mind respecting the alleged immorality of the trade in opium, and the injurious effect the drug is reputed to produce on the people. To prove that the Chinese law does not forbid the use of opium, it was sufficient he said, to state that opium was cultivated in China to a great extent and that the quantity it imported from India does not amount to so much as the produce of China itself. His experience of the effect of opium on the people led Sir John Bowring to conclude, that it is far less pernicious than spirits; and he mentioned that in Hong Kong during the period he was governor of the island there were two-thirds more deaths caused by DELIRIUM TREMENS than by taking opium.

He adduced instances in which the introduction of opium eating had tended to improve the morals of the people by putting a stop to the excessive use of spirituous liquors, and the effects of the two kinds of excess, were greatly in favour of opium. The effect of it is altogether different from that of spirits. It may deaden the faculties and produce stupor, but it does not incite to the commission of crime, and among a people who take opium there is a much less amount of robberies, assaults, and of vice than among those who indulge too freely in spirits. It had been stated he said, as one of the evil consequences of the encouragement of opium-eating that it prevented the diffusion of Christianity; but this was so far from being the case that in one district into which opium had been introduced as a substitute for intoxicating drinks, the people had been found particularly willing to receive Christian missionaries and had become ready converts. In his intercourse with the mandarins and other Chinese officials he said he had never heard any of them speak against the importation of opium, and he felt persuaded that the prejudice which had been excited in this country against the opium trade was without foundation, and that the recognition of the trade and the import of opium into China at a low duty was one of the most beneficial measures that could be adopted for the promotion of commerce. The average annual imports of the drug into China had amounted to about seven millions sterling; and but for the teas and silks exported there would have been a most exhausting drain of the precious metals from this country. After entering into several statistical details of the exports and imports from China and Hong Kong which have already been published, Sir John Bowring proceeded to notice the ports which had been opened to trade by the treaty which, Lord Elgin, some of which, particularly, Ning-po, he considered had been ill-chosen, for it was not the place of residence of any principal officer of the Chinese Government. The port of Tchao-Tchou, however, which was the residence of Mandarins of the first rank had not proved favourable for commercial transactions with the Chinese, though possessing those advantages. Shanghai has become the principal shipping port for Chinese produce; and as it is in the neighbourhood of the tea districts, it is favourable for the export of that commodity, more than half the tea exported from China being shipped from that port. Sir John Bowring remarked that all the seaboard of China was remarkable for the absence of any large towns; the provincial ports being situated on the estuaries of rivers, as remote as possible from the sea, for the sake of protection against the numerous pirates who infest those waters. Having noticed at length the statistics of imports and exports, Sir John Bowring proceeded to consider the habits and qualifications of the Chinese, and the prospects of an increasing trade with the vast country, which extends 5,000 miles in length, and upwards of 3,500 miles in breadth. That vast territory is scarcely sufficient to accommodate its 400,000,000 of inhabitants, and the rivers swarm with boats in which hundreds of thousands of the people live and spend their lives. Some of the institutions are of the more republican character than could have been supposed possible in so despotic an empire. Competitive examinations for public office have been established in China, and some of the principal officers of State had risen to those positions from low conditions of life. Amongst these was the celebrated Commisioner Lin, who, in early life, kept a small stationer`s shop. In many of the manufacturing arts the Chinese, it is well known, were far more advanced of Europeans. It appears from the records that silk dresses were worn 4,000 years ago, though woven silks were not known in Europe until 200 or 300 years after the Christian era, and were not much worn, even in Italy, 600 years later. The mariner`s compass was also known to the Chinese long before it was applied in Europe, and in the ceramic arts the Chinese were celebrated for the perfection they attained.

The great obstacle to the progress of improvement in China is the constant recurrence to the past instead of looking in advance, and many of the Chinese manufacturers are not now as good as they were hundreds of years ago.

This state of circumstances presented great advantages to a manufacturing country that was enabled to supply goods by the aid of machinery at a much cheaper rate than can be made by the old loom.

At present, however, the Chinese principally weave for themselves, as there is a loom in every house, but if their attention were directed more to the cultivation of the raw produce of cotton and of silk to supply the manufacturing machines of this country, we might be enabled to supply them with cotton and silk manufactures at a cheaper rate than they can make them. The cultivation of cotton in China is a subject Sir John Bowring observed that deserves earnest consideration. There is at present a large amount of cotton grown to supply the native loom; and by the introduction of better seeds and an improved mode of cultivation the Chinese might be in a condition to supply us with the raw produce, which we might then return to them in muslins, The great advantages of machinery had enabled the British manufacturers to surpass the celebrated Dacca muslins both in cheapness and quality, and we have now possession of the Dacca markets; and Sir John hoped that in the course of a few years the same result would occur in China. One of the advantages attending the commerce with the Chinese was that they were always ready to purchase the best article at the cheapest price, without regard to the country whence the goods might come; and if the British manufacturer could produce his cotton goods in the Chinese markets of a better quality and cheaper than they could be made there, they would be bought without any prejudice. Sir John Bowring said that the result of his experiences taught him that the Chinese are a people who may be easily deceived and he expressed the opinion that the Emperor of China had been kept in ignorance of the full effects of the treaties that had been entered into with the English, and that if direct communication were to take commercial relations with them, they would have the eject of allaying the present angry feelings, and be the means of bringing hostilities …. hostilities there must be…… shortly to a close. At the end of Sir John Bowring`s discourse, the Chairman Mr. Bodrin complimented him on his able address, and a vote of thanks was passed to him with loud applause, Sir John Bowring again rose to return thanks, and in doing so he alluded in a very energetic manner to the circumstances of his refusing the demand by the Chinese Commisioner to give up the Chinese sailors, who had taken refuge under the English flag. The demand he said, was made by a man who had immolated more victims than any human being who had ever existed; and he (Sir John Bowling) had delivered over those men, who were under protection of the British flag to be victimized, he should never afterwards have enjoyed repose. He felt assured that there was no Englishman, who, under the same circumstances, would not have done the same. He sat down, amid tumultuous applause.'

(The Cambrian 2nd December 1859)

In Maesteg many places and streets were named after Sir John Bowring. In the mid-nineteenth century a district of the Llynfi Valley in Glamorgan was known as Bowrington as it was built-up when John Bowring was chairman of the local iron company. Bowrington's ironworks community later became part of the Maesteg Urban District. The name was revived in the 1980s when a shopping development in Maesteg was called the Bowrington Arcade.

Bowrington Arcade, Maesteg

References:
- 'Illustrated London News'
- 'History of the Llynfi Valley' by Brinley Richards (1982)
- The Cambrian newspaper
- 'The Dragon Wakes – China and the West 1793-1911' by Christopher Hibbert (1970)
- Western Mail (11th March 2013: 'A supreme charlatan and worse: a cheat, liar and …….a swindler' by Martin Shipton)

Brecon (Theatr Brycheiniog)

An exhibition of contemporary Chinese art from Xi'an was held at Theatr Brycheiniog, Brecon in 2012. The Exhibition entitled 'Harmony' included works by artists Li Fenglan, whose paintings have been used on postage stamps in China, Li Qiong and Zhu Bin.

Bridge (Albert Henry)

Albert Henry Bridge, b. Ferndale 1868 - Missionary in Weicheng, China.
(Overseas Missionary Fellowship 1991)

British v Chinese

'London Liner`s Story At Swansea. Crew Who Mutinied: Officer`s Views. The vexed question "British v. Chinese" seamen was localised somewhat on Monday when a Daily Post reporter boarded the London steamer 'Foxley' (Capt. C. Mathieson) as she lay in the Prince of Wales Dry Dock, undergoing treatment for sundry "nips" in the ice which she sustained near Vladivostok. The Foxley carries nearly 7,500 tons and loads 1,700 tons of tinplates for New York (all sizes). She usually goes in ballast, by the way. This steamer is the one which has been brought into much prominence by the circumstances of a mutiny occurring on board among the Chinese crew, and which has been eagerly seized upon by the Seamen`s Union as an argument against the employment of Asiatic labour on board British steamers. On March 20th, when in the Red Sea, on the way home from Hong Kong, the chief officer, it appears, ordered the look-out-man, a Chinaman, named Chang-Tee, to remain in the "crow`s nest". This the man declined to do, and came down on deck, going on the bridge and threatening the officer, who promptly ordered him off. He refused to go, and then the man at the wheel, Chang Kiven, rushed at him with a knife and then eight others …… deck-hands and firemen, took a hand in the "fun", and matters looked extremely ugly until the men were got under control.
One of the Foxley`s officers, on Monday, told the Post man that the result of the trial of the men at Hull last week was a grievous disappointment. "The men were discharged," he said bitterly, "and they are now free to go and do the same kind of thing again. It`s too bad, it is." "The occurence is being used as an argument against the employment of Asiatic seamen." remarked the pressman "Is it? Don`t see why it should. There are good and bad in all classes of seamen, and we have to get what we can, you know". "They say that you pay the Chinamen less than the British seamen", he asks. "Not this crew, anyhow," was the reply; "and there are 32 of them, which we had brought down from Cardiff. As a matter of fact, we really had no option at this time, as we have stores for a Chinese crew on board, and had we shipped Britishers all these would have to be thrown away". "Are these Chinamen really dependable?" was the next question. "As I said, there are good and bad in both British and Chinese, but the Chinese, I may say, are slow."

'They are assimilating European ideas," the officer added slyly, "As to this particular voyage on which the trouble occurred, the alleged grievance appears to have been that the Chinese complained of the food." "Pooh," was the rejoinder, "they are fed too well, really. And on the voyage in question, we had European stores!" It is a bit of coincidence that a sister-boat of the Foxley`s ..,. the S.S. Headingly, on her last voyage had a "double event" of a disturbing nature, a perilous fire on board and the murder by an insane Chinaman of a shipmate, the murderer, afterwards leaping overboard. This is the Foxley`s first visit to Swansea.'
(The Cambrian 5th May 1911)

Britten. F. J.
Author: 'Old Clocks and Watches and their Makers'
Mentions a Henry Levy as being in possession of a William Hughes Automata watch taken from the Summer Palace in 1860.
(See: William Hughes)

'Brodland'
In January 1913 the steamship 'Brodland' ran aground on Aberafan Beach. On board were 33 Chinese who were rescued and taken to the Asiatic Sailors Home in London. An account of this event can be read in the following: South Wales Daily Post (20th January 1913), and Western Mail (23rd January 1913).

Bronzes (Ancient Chinese)
In the early 1980s the Palace Museum, Beijing, produced a limited edition of copies of ancient Chinese bronzes. The copies were identical to the originals as possible. A foundry was constructed within the walls of the Palace Museum for the production of the copies. A representative selection of 32 bronzes was chosen from the Museum's reserve collection.
Copies were reproduced from:
Shang (16th-11th Century B.C.)
Western Zhou (1050 – 770 B.C.)
Warring States (475 – 221 B.C.)
Han Dynasty (206 B.C. – A.D.220)
Tang Dynasty (A.D.618 – 906)
They represented 2,500 years of the best periods of Chinese bronze making.
The National Museum of Wales: Exhibition of Ancient Chinese Bronzes (1985)

Exhibition poster and catalogue

'Brownell' (Barque)
'The Barque 'Charles Brownell', built in Pwllheli at the Yard of William Jones and Sons, was intended for the China trade' (November 1846)
('PWLLHELI- The Port and Mart of Llŷn' by Lewis Lloyd (1991))

Bryant (Evan 1832-1918)
Born Hirwaun, Glamorgan. Arrived in Shanghai,
1865 - Spent many years working with Rev. Dr. Griffith John in Hankou and Wuchang. Together with Griffith John made many journeys along the Yangtze River.
1873 - Worked in Beijing and Tianjin.
1880 - Left the Hankou mission as his wife's health was suffering.
1884 - 1892 Agent of British and Foreign Bible Society in North China.
1906 – 'Griffith John- The Story of Fifty Years in China' by R.Wardlaw Thompson (Chap vii, p198): '………. Rev. Evan Bryant, whose appointment gave Mr. John special satisfaction, because he also was a Welshman, a native of Glamorganshire and a student at Brecon College.'

Bryant (Evan Evans)
Born 1878 in Wuhan, Central China. Married Myfanwy Rowlands. Worked in Beijing and died in Tianjin.
Note: There is an E.E.B. in the 1901 Census – China Hankou, British Citizen.

Bryant (Myfanwy)
Born 1880 in Madagascar; daughter of Welsh missionary parents. Married Evan Bryant. Served in Hong Kong and Zezhou in North China. Wrote 'On the Banks of the Grand Canal' (1930). Died (1935) on a voyage home.

Bryson (Mary)
Wife of Rev. Thomas Bryson - a prolific writer on Chinese themes. Usually wrote under the name of 'Mrs Bryson of Tientsin'. Written works include:
'Croes a Choron' (London Missionary Society) (1906)
'Cross and Crown' (London Missionary Society) (1905)
'The Land of the Pigtail.' (National Sunday School Union)
'James Gilmore and the Mongol Mission'. (National Sunday School Union)
'John Kenneth Mackenzie; Medical Missionary to China' (Hodder & Stoughton) (1891)
'Fred C. Roberts, of Tientsin or for Christ to China' (H.R. Allenson) (1895)

Bryson (Rev. Thomas)
Arr. Hankow, January 11th, 1867. Worked with the Rev. Dr. Griffith John in Wuchang from 1867 to 1884 when he was transferred to Tientsin (Tianjin).
(Chronicle of the London Missionary Society, November 1882. Swansea Library)
Birth On August 17th 1882 at Hankow north China to the wife of the Rev. T. Bryson, a son.
(Chronicle of the London Missionary Society, November 1882. Swansea Library)

Buddha

The Buddha, used in the film 'Inn of the Sixth Happiness' (The story of the missionary Gladys Aylward filmed in North Wales), found a home in Portmeirion. (See Gladys Aylward)

Bute Park (Cardiff)
'There is an avenue of Gingko trees at Bute Park in Cardiff. Gingko is one of the oldest types of tree in existence. Fossils of it dating back about 200 million years have been discovered in its native China. Chinese monks cultivated it for centuries before people started planting it in European gardens during the 18th Century.
The avenue of trees in Bute Park was planted in 1880. Originally, there were two rows of trees each side, later reduced to one. When the trees needed replacing in the 1950s, Bill Nelmes, Cardiff Council's Chief Parks Officer, chose Gingko. He took a keen interest in Botany and even planted Gingko trees along some of Cardiff's suburban streets.'
(History Points)

Avenue of Ginko trees, view looking south at Bute Park, Cardiff.

C

Caccia (Harold Anthony, GCMG GCVO GCStJ 1905-1990)
Harold Anthony Caccia (Baron Caccia of Abernant) was born on Dec. 21, 1905 in British-ruled India where his father was a senior official in the Indian Forestry Services. After Eton and Trinity College, Oxford, he entered the Foreign Service in 1929. **His first posting was to Beijing, in 1932, where he and his wife Nancy stayed for three years.** Returning to London in 1935, he spent some time as Assistant Private Secretary to Foreign Secretary Anthony Eden and Lord Halifax. Died, October 31st 1990 at Abernant House, Builth Wells.

Cadwaladyr (Betsy 1789-1860)
Elizabeth 'Betsy' Cadwaladyr was born in 1789 at Llanycil, near Bala, north Wales, one of 16 children to Methodist preacher Dafydd Cadwaladyr. Betsy called herself 'Elizabeth Davis'. At the age of 14 years, she left home and went to Liverpool. She spent many years touring the world. In one chapter of her autobiography ('Betsy Cadwaladyr; A Balaclava Nurse' – First published 1857, subsequently 1987-, 2007, 2015 - Honno) she describes a visit to Canton, China (pages 83 to 87) without mentioning the year.

In the book 'A Foreigner in China' by O. M Green (1942- Hutchinson and Company), Chapter 3, 'Factory Days in Canton', Green wrote: "Not until 1830 did any white woman dare to visit the factories."

Betsy wrote about a remarkable visit to Canton when she had an audience with the Emperor of China. She, in later life, went on to become a nurse at Balaclava where she made a name for herself and is respected in the 21st Century for her contribution towards nursing. She was buried in a pauper's grave in Abney Park Cemetery, Stoke Newington, North London. A memorial stone and bench, in her honour, at the cemetery is the result of the hard work by Professor Deidre Mead, OBE.

The following is an extract from 'An Autobiography of Elizabeth Davis – Betsy Cadwaladyr: A Balaclava Nurse' edited by Jane Williams (Ysgafell) Chapter 9 pages 84 – 87:

'There we loaded a general cargo, with fine woods and ivory for Canton. On reaching that city, we anchored in Cock Lane to discharge the cargo, and then went up to the East India Company's factory, and loaded the ship with tea. The foreman there was an old Chinaman, who had been thirty years in the factory. He used often to come on board the 'DENMARK HILL' for a meal of beef, and biscuits, and grog; and I made a joke of asking him to take me to see the city. One day I told him that I would give him no more beef and grog until he did take me. I thought the thing impossible, and only said it to tease him. The old man looked very hard at me, as much as to say, "Are you in earnest?" He went on shore, and I thought no more about it. He spoke English very well. The next morning about nine o'clock, I was very much surprised to see a grand native boat come alongside our ship. This great boat was of all the colours of the rainbow, with the Union Jack and the Company's flag, flying together at the stern. The rowers were ten Chinamen, dressed all in white, with green sashes. The boatswain wore a pink robe, with a red sash, and had a white and green cap on his head with a very large green and red feather. They all wore satin slippers, with wooden soles to them, and very narrow, turned up toes. At the same time the old foreman, Fa Pooh, came on board the 'DENMARK HILL' from the factory, bringing a passport in his hand for my mistress and me to see the city. She was afraid, and would not go; but I would not lose such a chance, so I dressed myself up in a pink gingham dress, and went alone in the barge in the care of the little boatswain.

Neither he, nor any of the crew were able to speak English, when I talked English to them, they stared foolishly at me; but when I spoke Welsh to them, they pointed out the different places that came in sight as we went along the river, and I never will believe but they knew what I said.

They took me as near as the barge could go to the gates of Canton, and I landed and had to take care afterwards of myself. Fa Pooh had taught me what I was to do. I gave in my passport, expecting that it would be looked at, and returned to me, but instead of that, I was kept waiting so long that I grew very uneasy, for the Tartar sentinels were staring fiercely at me all the time. The gatekeeper at last, gave me a new passport, which he had been writing out while I stood there. The same thing was done at all the other gates which I passed through that day.

I think that I had twelve in going through the city. Being let in, I wandered about and saw a great many craftsmen at all sorts of works. Some were weaving; and others making cabinets; others turning with a lathe. Everyone was busy that I saw, and they were all gentle and civil in their manner towards me; but they eyed me, I thought, as if they mis-doubted me, there was not a woman among them. I felt uneasy, and was sorry that I had come. None of them uttered a word to me, nor did I speak to them. Not knowing where I went, I got at length into the Royal Square, where I found a great number of women all very industrious and working in sets at all kinds of things: some were at embroidery; some were weaving silk or camels' hair textures; some were turning Ivory; and others making fans, and pretty toys. I was very much pleased to see them. I should think there were five hundred there. They all seemed by their manners to be ladies. They were beautiful creatures, very fair and had a delicate pink colour on their cheeks. I do not know whether it was paint or not. Their eyes were some dark and some light in colour; but too small to have life enough in them. They were very silent, but looked pleased at me.

I was told afterwards that this was the Emperor's harem. I began to talk Welsh to them, and the leader of them, who seemed to act as foreman in their works, took me round, upstairs and downstairs, and showed me everything. I think she understood what I said. I am sure there is some connection between the Welsh and Chinese languages.

This old princess looked at my dress, and smiled, and patted my face, and stroked me down, and we were very good friends. I stayed some hours with these kind ladies; and, when I was coming away, the old princess fetched a small parcel, folded up in a China silk-gauze handkerchief. I did not examine what was in it, but I felt very thankful for her kindness, and I offered to shake hands with her, saying "Diolch yn fawr i chwi", and making a curtsey. She kissed my hand, and I went away.

I did not know where I was going; and got into a gallery, and passed along it for some distance. It skirted the Royal Square, but all ways seeming the same to me. I stopped short at a door, which I saw in it, and passed into the longest room I have ever beheld in my life. The walls were bare, and there was no furniture, excepting two images, with a great deal of Chinese writing about them. In the further end of the room several men were sitting together in a group upon the ground.

I had scarcely time to notice these particulars, when a gentleman came rushing after me, saying – "For God's sake, don't go there! It's as much as your life is worth.' I was frightened, and asked – "What have I done?" He answered -

"Do you know where you are? Down on your knees! and stop so until I tell you." I sat down on the floor; and he fell on his knees, and raised his joined hands, as if he had been praying.

One of the men from the other end of the room now got up. He wore a long robe, glittering with precious stones, and had in his hand a sceptre, about three yards long, with a sort of crown on top of it. With that he came towards us, and measured from the spot where Mr Cruickshanks knelt, thrice its length along the ground.

Mr Cruikshanks then walked the distance on his knees, with his hands lifted up as they were. The man measured a second distance, and Mr Cruikshanks passed it in the same way. When he reached the party, they made him sit down cross-legged, and gave him a pipe to smoke, and talked with him.

By and by, he was brought back again with the same ceremonies to the spot where I was sitting on my heels. He told me to do everything as he had done; and that he had explained about me. The way was then measured for me, as it had been for him, but I found great difficulty in getting along, for my petticoats hindered me, and I was obliged to tuck the princess's parcel across the back of my legs, to have both my hands free for holding up. When I got to the group of gentlemen, I sat down cross-legged, as Mr Cruickshanks had done. They all looked at me and laughed; the youngest and most plainly dressed of them handed me a pipe. I never thought that they could intend me to smoke it, but supposed they wished me to see how pretty it was, so I took it all to pieces, and looked at it bit by bit, and gave the biggest branch back again to the young emperor who had passed it to me. At this they were more amused than ever, and laughed very heartily.

Thinking it was time to go, I arose and stood upon my feet, but in an instant the chamberlain who had measured the ground, and was sitting cross-legged with the rest, planted his fingers so firmly in the palm of my hand that he pulled me down again. My hand was black and blue for days after that pinching gripe. He measured the ground again, and I tried to imitate the way in which Mr Cruikshanks had walked backwards on his knees with his hands lifted up together. I scrambled and crawled some how or other along the first distance, but when the chamberlain measured the next I lost all patience, for the party all shrieked out, and the old man shook me with angry looks for not going in the right posture, so I suddenly started to my feet and ran out of the room face foremost, and down a flight of many hundred marble steps, and into a fine chapel, and through it to the river's bank. I could go no further in that direction, so I recrossed the chapel - it was inlaid with dazzling stones, and there were no idols in it. In going up the marble steps, I met Mr Cruikshanks coming towards me. He said it was a mercy he had seen me, or I never should have come out of the room alive. The young emperor had only arrived at Canton the day before, and was sitting in council when I went in upon him.

Mr Cruikshanks was a Scotch merchant, who had lived twenty-eight years in Canton. He took me to his house in the square, and there I saw his wife, who was a Scotch woman, and their children. They were very much surprised to see me there. I took tea with them, and that being over, Mr Cruickshanks walked with me through the city to the last gate, where the boat was waiting for me.

About eight o'clock in the evening I got safe back to the ship. My friends there feared I was lost forever, and Fa Pooh had been several times on board showing a great anxiety from my safety. The next morning I opened the princess's parcel, and found in it a fine camel's-hair dress, of a yellow and white striped pattern - the white being like open needlework. It had hanging sleeves, and strings with tassels to draw it into shape. I thought it was too short to me, so I gave it to Mrs Foreman, who asked me for it. I heard afterwards that she was offered eighty pounds for it.

Many years afterwards I met and talked with Mr Cruickshanks in London.'

(Honno, Cardiff 1987) 'An Autobiography of Elizabeth Davis – Betsy Cadwaladyr; A Balaclava Nurse' Edited by Jane Williams (Ysgafell)

Cambria Magazine
Article by the Author entitled, 'Griffith John, Wuhan and Me' describes her return visit to Wuhan, Hubei Province after 20 years and the search for the legacy left by Griffith John, the Swansea – born Missionary, who lived there from 1861 to 1911.
(Cambria Magazine Vol 13, Number 4, P26)

Campbell
SHIPPING INTELLIGANCE
'Lisbon Jan. 31st: The 'Sir Colin Campbell, Ralph', from Cardiff for Hong Kong (coals), foundered at sea; crew saved and arrived here.'
(The Cambrian, 10th February 1860)

Campion (Mary Anne J)
Marriage
'On June 30th, Chicago, USA, James Draper Bishop, Late Imperial Chinese Service to Mary Anne J Campion of Brecon and France.'
(The Cambrian 20th July 1888)

Cardiff (Anti-Chinese Sentiment)
During the Cardiff riots of 1911, every one of the City's Chinese laundries was attacked.
(BBC Radio 4 – 'Chinese in Britain'

Cardiff and Xiamen
In 1983 the City of Cardiff signed a twinning agreement with Xiamen City, Fujian Province, South China. Cardiff was the first UK city to establish such a link with China.
(See: Xiamen)

Cardiff Christian Chinese Church
The Church is located in the Canton area of the City. Its aim is to be a spiritual home for Chinese Christians and to reach the Chinese in Cardiff and surrounding areas. Services are held in three languages: Cantonese, English and Mandarin.

Cardiff University (China Studies Centre)
The Centre was established in 1985 and officially opened by H.E. Mr. Chen Zhaoyuan, the Chinese Ambassador, in March 1986.

Carey
The 'William Carey' was built by William Jones and Son in Pwllheli and was intended for the India and China trade. It sailed under the command of Captain W. Webb. As principal owner, William Jones, offered free passage to Baptist missionaries and their families who were travelling to India. It is not known whether his offer extended to China.
('PWLLHELI – The Port and Mart of Llŷn by Lewis Lloyd 1991)

'Carmarthenshire' (S.S.)

The S.S. 'Carmarthenshire' was built in Pembroke Dock in 1865. She belonged to the Shire Line and was eventually wrecked off Terschelling, 10th January 1865. The second 'Carmarthenshire' was built in 1887 and owned by the Shire Line by Captain J Jenkins, whose father was a Master Mariner from Haverfordwest.

The Company was one of the pioneers of steam ship services to Hong Kong and Japan. In 1886 another of the Shire Line vessels - the steamer, 'Breconshire', was lost off the Chinese coast.

The 'Carmarthenshire' entering Hong Kong Harbour, April 23rd, 1897' by an unknown artist (Amgueddfa Cymru – National Museum of Wales)

Cenhadwr Americanaidd

'CENHADWR AMERICANAIDD (News From Overseas – CHINA 1840 p. 317) 'What follows is an appraisal in a few words of the current situation in China with particular reference to the war between that country and Great Britain, as clear as light and as, no doubt our readers will be happy to read although some of the facts referred to have been published before.

Britain is at war and not any old war but war with a third of the world. As for wanting to colonise mighty China, the rest of the world marvels at our boldness and, as it is said to be an unavoidable war, let us hope that it will all be worth it in the end.

A few days ago, a couple of coded letters were received from the Far East, one from China, and one from India. The word from the former, as recently as 13th March and latter from 30th April, is that it would appear that the Chinese are tightening their resolve in the face of attack from the English, who are determined to show their strength and power to the ultimate degree. On the 16th April two ships, called the John Adams and the 'Rustomjee Cowasjee', carrying battalions, sailed out of Madras bound for this far flung conflict, On the other side, the Chinese are reported to have bought two American merchant ships and have illegally seized three Danish vessels for the purpose of converting them all into warships. And in order to understand the British viewpoint a bit better, it is said that the Emperor has not only commanded that all trade with the English as well as with the rest of the world be stopped immediately and forever, so that from that moment no China Tea would be available outside China. To make this sanction more effective, the Chinese Commander Lin has been given authority to instigate any measures that he considers necessary without having to wait for the necessary authority from the Government in Pekin. At around 10 pm on the night of 8th February, the Chinese attempted to set the British vessels in Canton ablaze. Into this mayhem, at the same time, two blazing Chinese junks boats, accompanied by a number of barges loaded full with combustible materials, sailed out towards the ships, but a full wind carried them out between and past the ships to where there were a number of small Chinese craft some of which caught fire.

However, the only damage suffered by the British vessels was to the bowsprit of one of them but the blaze was soon put out. Therefore, the fire boats, i. e. those which sailed past the target having been propelled by the wind to the shore, where they burnt boats from their own side without causing an eruption, although they are reported to have been loaded full of fine powdery material glass chippings etc. A second attempt was made the following evening which ended unsuccessfully as the previous one. It so happened that the wind had dropped and the evening was still, and besides, the English would be more on their guard.
Meanwhile, many Chinese families were fleeing to Macao, with anti-war feelings starting to spread amongst the population even in the capital city Pekin and also in the second city, Monkden. They chose this action rather than take part in arresting the rioters.
The battalions of soldiers previously referred to, who had sailed out of Madras on 16th April had in their midst a large number of important officials, from the medical corps, artillery men and so on. On the same day, as well a considerable number of men started out from Calcutta and Sir Z. G. Bremmer and his cohorts followed them out about a week to ten days later, which completed the expedition to take on the might of China. The adventure is a hazardous one for those taking part. Officers were to receive four months' pay in advance and non-commissioned ranks two. A deliberate decision was made not to make liqueur available to the European soldiers but instead they were given the equivalent of the liqueur ration in money. However, some was available on board the ships although the orders were that no man was to receive more than two drams a day.
Moreover, given the preparations that the Chinese are making, a letter dated 25th April from St. Helena, gives the following information. The ship 'Iris' came here today from China and we heard that a large army of Chinese soldiers are heading to Macao with the intention of capturing Captain Elliot and other English craft. On the departure of the 'Iris' the 'Volage' and the 'Hyacinth' were the only two warships in China. Other ships arrived recently in England direct from China, having left there in February showing that the Chinese Government understood clearly that a mighty force was amassing against them seeking revenge because the Queen of England had been insulted. Why, therefore, had they gone to such lengths to withstand the attack by buying several foreign boats to convert into warships to defend the ports?
Battalions were despatched as well, to reinforce the garrison in Canton against which the English were expected to make their main thrust. Meanwhile, the Chinese were making every effort to force Captain Elliot and the British traders to leave Macao by sending a huge army there which led to the Captain having to seek help from the Portuguese Governor of Macao to help defend the lives and possessions of the English. Although the Governor was prepared to do this, he was wary about giving the Chinese cause for vengeance. By the end of 21st February, the Chinese had not advanced on Macao, but a few days before that, the ship 'Morr' from England had arrived there after a sea journey of 113 days bringing information to Captain Elliot from the British Government. This therefore, is the latest news from those parts and it would appear that the next news will be of the fighting between the two sides and the result will be awaited with great interest.'

CENHADWR AMERICANAIDD (CHINA FEBRUARY 1842)
'P.57…. The sailing ship 'Albion' reached the port of New York on the 17th January direct from China, having left Canton on the 15th September. It brought important information from China this time again.
The Chinese people in an effort to defend themselves had tipped ship loads of large stones into the depths of the river to prevent the large English ships gaining access to the city of Canton.
The English looked upon this delaying tactic as a crime against the covenant of war, and when the 'Albion' started her journey for New York, the villages along the shores of the River Canton had been burnt down by British soldiers.

As she sailed, the smoke was still rising, surrounding Canton, and they were to expect that the City itself would be put on fire. On the other side about two thousand Chinese soldiers had gathered to repair and strengthen the defences of the Bogue. Another piece of important information received was the city of Amoy to the North had been taken by the British. Few facts were known about this, the whole through secret letters, and not through official announcements, but it was no doubt true. It was said that the British had first taken possession of a small island opposite Amoy and from there were able to bombard fireballs over the City walls, which had caused much slaughter. The Chief Military Mandarin and his deputy were both killed. (Both were wearing red buttons) and that the British soldiers had gone in and taken the town by the edge of the sword. It was also said that a retinue of a thousand armed men and three of the military ships are to be left there while the Navy goes forward towards the outskirts of Pekin.

Amoy is 1200 miles from Pekin, the strongest fortress in the Empire after the fall of Bogue. If it has been taken according to the above report, this will most likely affect the mind of the Emperor and will be ready to accept measures to conclude the quarrel.'

CENHADWR AMERICANAIDD (NEWS FROM CHINA APRIL 1842 P.12l)
'It would appear from the latest news from China (up to 22 Nov) that the British Army have won some more victories, besides those named in our previous numbers. Soon after taking Amoy, a number of soldiers were left to occupy the garrison, and the Navy sailed to Chusan, and on the first day of October, they retook the city after more vigorous opposition and bloodshed than anything previously experienced on the part of the Chinese to defend their country. British soldiers took the fort and thirty-six new cannon together with a quantity of government supplies of rice from the town. From here the Navy went forwards toward the city of Chinhae.

This city is portrayed as having walls 37 feet thick and 22 feet in height, encircling for two miles. This city is to the north, at the mouth of the River Tahee or Ningpo. In this town there are exceptionally strong defences, about 250 feet above sea levels and is encircled by strong walls as well as the inner city walls with heavy iron gates and archways to the East and West of it.

There were also Chinese forces in the defences which were built recently at the riverside making the most vigorous efforts to obstruct the coming of the Navy and British soldiers to enter but, however strong their defences the British ships came closer and on the 10th October they penetrated the strong walled defences and landed 15,000 soldiers, who took the city.

About fifteen miles up-river is the city of Ningpo, which was captured on October 13th without opposition. The Chinese soldiers fled as the British army neared the town, as winter approached there was little likelihood that they would do anything more before the spring, when Pottinger intends to receive additional numbers of soldiers and sailors so as to attack the main city of Pekin. The British army, well known for the successes, have also met with much hardship and losses since they arrived at the outskirts of China early in the year 1840. Many among the soldiers and sailors were cut down through disease. The ship 'Nerbudda' was wrecked on the outskirts of Formosa, and about half of their number slaughtered, and the rest were sent to China and most likely met with a similar end. The steamship 'Madagasgar' was also wrecked, the officers and all hands have fallen into the hands of the Chinese, and no more has been heard of them. It is assumed that there will have to be a substantial addition to the army before they will be able to proceed to the Capital city.'

CENHADWR AMERICANAIDD (NEWS FROM CHINA MAY 1842 p.154)
'China has broken the truce which was agreed between England and China outside Canton. The result is that Pottinger has had to return back to attack his enemies there, before starting his intended assault on Pekin.'

CENHADWR AMERICANAIDD (NEWS FROM CHINA UP UNTIL MAY 27th P.318)
'Many new British warships had reached the outskirts of, and anchored in the port of Hong Kong. More were expected within the next few days.

With their arrival it was expected that Pottinger and his fleet would sail to the north and attack forthwith like he threatened a few times last year on the city of Pekin. The English township of Hong Kong was expanding fast.
The Canton Press dated May 21st had a strange statement saying that it had been reported from a good source that the Emperor was afraid of an English raid on Pekin, so he and his family had fled to Tartary, but before leaving he had sent out orders to his people urging them to resist the Barbarians for as long as they could. Tartary is the native ancestral place of the present Emperor, so perhaps the story is true that he has fled there. Wouldn't it be strange if the vast China would be governed by one of its sons who would have to pay homage to Victoria.'

CENHADWR AMERICANAIDD (NEWS FROM CHINA AUGUST 1842 P.255)
'The latest news from China was March 18th and Bombay 23rd. It revealed that the Chinese believed that by making a concerted attack in different places at the same time will wholly destroy the British army. Forces of between ten to twelve thousand armed men were sent to Ningpo, a City in the hands of the British Militia, and at the same time, fire-ships were sent out towards the Naval Vessels.'

CENHADWR AMERICANAIDD (SEPTEMBER 1842 P.288)
'News received from China was up to the 12th April and from Singapore up to-the 5th May. The report stated that a fierce battle had again taken place between the British and the Chinese in which six thousand Chinese were defeated by eleven hundred British. Some five to seven hundred Chinese were killed, but only four of our own men and about twenty wounded. It was said that at that time, Yang, who was the Emperor's messenger was on his way to the British camp to offer 40 million dollars in compensation for the opium and towards the expenses of the war. Also that Hong Kong would be given over to England as a peace offering.'
(CENHADWR AMERICANAIDD NEWS FROM CHINA Translated by Huw Davies, London)

Chang Jung
Author of: 'Empress Dowager Cixi–The Concubine Who Launched Modern China' 2013. Pages 118, 239 and 240 about Timothy Richard. (Published by Jonathan Cape – London)

Charlotte (HMS)
(See: Admiral Oliver Jones)

Chen Kam Yau
Hong Kong–born Mr Chen ran a number of businesses in Abergavenny; a widely respected member of the Chinese community in Wales. Over the years he has played an important part in promoting links between the Welsh and Chinese communities. He has been a keen supporter and long-time member of the Wales - China Friendship Society. Several years ago he and his wife returned to live in Hong Kong.

Cheng Jia
Cheng Jia translated R.S.Thomas' 'Selected Poems 1946-1968' 'Collected Poems 1945-1990' and 'Collected Later Poems 1998-2000' into Chinese. She teaches at the College of Foreign Studies, Jinan University, Guangdong Province, China and spent one year as a visiting scholar at the R.S. Thomas Study Centre, Bangor University in 2009, supervised by Professor Tony Brown.

Chin Fong Sui
Chin Fong Sui and her husband Chi Mau Chin, were among the first Chinese to make Swansea their home. In the 1950s, they opened the KKK Laundry in Bryn-Y-Mor Road and later opened the Ming Yuan Restaurant.
(From: 'All our Stories' Project by the Swansea Chinese Community Co-op Centre 2013)

China 89

'CHINA 89' Logo

'China 89' was a project organized by the Wales China Friendship Society. It involved two schools – Alderman Davies' Church in Wales Primary School, Neath and Cwrt Sart Comprehensive School, Briton Ferry. The Project took 18 months in preparation and involved over 100 fundraising activities.

The 'China 89' Project took young students from Wales to perform – Welsh culture, song and dance to the people and students of China. The visit took place during March 1989. It was the first of its kind from Wales. The 25 young students were aged between 9 and 15 years.

'China 89' Party with the Mayor and Mayoress of Neath (1989)

Before leaving for China, the students appeared on the BBC TV programme 'Blue Peter', on St David's Day, 1st March 1989.

The 'China 89' party performed in Beijing, Shanghai, Nantong (Swansea's twin city) and Nanjing. The concerts took place mainly in Children's Palaces (China's equivalent to the Urdd movement), schools, theatres and, on one occasion, at an arena in Nantong. The visit was covered throughout by CCTV news and radio.

Chinese TV made a documentary about the visit. When the 'China 89' party was in Shanghai a special two-way phone link was set up between Swansea Sound and the hotel in Shanghai where the students were based – the first of its kind from Swansea Sound.

To commemorate this historic visit a brochure and video were produced and copies sent to the British Library and the National Libraries of Wales, Scotland and Northern Ireland. A copy of the commemorative video was presented to the Wales Film Archives.

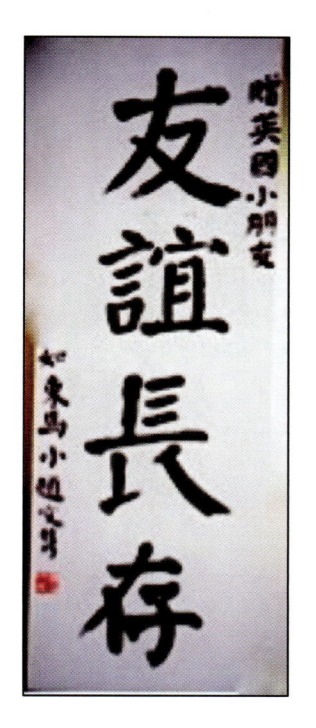

FRIENDSHIP

I met a friend,
You came from another land,
I couldn't speak her language,
But I took her by the hand.

We sang together,
And had a lot of fun!
Singing is a language,
We can speak with anyone.

By SHEN YI

Poem written by a Chinese student about the 'China 89' visit to Nantong

'Friendship Lasts Forever' Calligraphy presented to 'China 89' by students from Rudong County School, Nantong

A song called 'NI HAO' (Hello) was composed for the China 89 choir to sing on tour. The music was composed by John Mills and lyrics by Ena Niedergang.

'NIHAO'
1st Verse
We're taking to China our love, our joy.
To the children of China, to each girl and boy.
The peace and the friendship we bring in our hearts.
To our brothers and sisters in those distant parts.

CHORUS
We want to say "ni hao" from Wales to Zhongguo .
We want to say "xie-xie" and much more.
From the Welsh dragon our song we sing.
To the Chinese dragon our love we bring.

2nd Verse
We're going to China to climb the Great Wall.
Forbidden City we'll give you a call.
Then on to Shanghai; bye bye Beijing
Women qu Zhongguo , xiao pengyou , huanying.
(We are going to China, little friends, welcome)

CHORUS
We want to say "ni hao" from Wales to Zhongguo .
We want to say "xie-xie" and much more.
From the Welsh dragon our song we sing.
To the Chinese dragon our love we bring.

3rd Verse
We'll sail up the Yangtze, the Yangtze so wide.
We're going to Nantong with friends by our side.
With greetings from Swansea, from Swansea so fair.
We're going to Nantong to see our friends there.

CHORUS
We want to say "ni hao" from Wales to Zhongguo .
We want to say "xie-xie" and much more.
From the Welsh dragon our song we sing.
To the Chinese dragon our love we bring.

4th Verse (Repeat of lst Verse)
We're taking to China our love, our joy.
To the children of China, to each girl and boy.
The peace and friendship we bring in our hearts.
To our brothers and sisters in those distant parts.

CHORUS
We want to say "ni hao" from Wales to Zhongguo .
We want to say "xie-xie" and much more.
From the Welsh dragon our song we sing.
To the Chinese dragon our love we bring.

Note: ni hao (Hello), Zhongguo (China), xie xie (Thank You), Huanying (Welcome)

China Challenge Cup
'Competed for annually at the Wimbledon Meeting by Ten Volunteers from each County. A subscription is being raised among the Ladies of Glamorganshire to pay the expenses of a team to represent the County in this Competition in 1876. Lady Aberdare, Aberdare; Mrs Booker, Velindre, Cardiff; Miss Talbot, Margam; and Miss Dillwyn, Swansea, will be happy to receive the names of ladies who wish to subscribe.
No subscription to exceed £1.'
(The Cambrian 31 December 1875) (See: China Cup)

China Contract

CONTRACT FOR CHINA
'Department of the Storekeeper General of the Navy, Somerset Place 1st June 1860.
'The Commissioners for Executing the Office of the Lord High Admiral of the United Kingdom of Great Britain and Ireland, do hereby give notice, that on TUESDAY, the 12th instant, at two o`clock, they will be ready to treat with such persons as may be willing to Contract for Supplying and Delivering into Store, or on Board Her Majesty`s Ships and Vessels at Hong Kong, 20,000 Tons of South Wales COALS, fit for her Majesty`s Steam Vessels. Conditions of the Contract and the Form of the Tender may be seen at the said Office. No Tender will be received after two o`clock on that day of the treaty, nor will any be noticed unless the Party attends, or an Agent for him duly authorised in writing.

Every Tender must be addressed to the Secretary of the Admiralty, and bear in the left-hand corner the words Tender for Hong Kong, and must be delivered at Somerset Place, accompanied by a letter, signed by two responsible persons, engaging to become bound with the person tendering, in the sum of 15,000, for the due performance of the Contract.'
(The Cambrian 8th June 1860)

China Cup
The China Cup was first presented for annual competition by English volunteers in China. To celebrate the winning of the Cup, by the Glamorgan Rifle Association in 1894, a banquet was held at St. Fagan's Castle outside Cardiff.
(See: China Challenge Cup)

China Ginger

ORIGINAL JAR CHINA GINGER

We have just received some original jars of China Ginger,
containing about 6 pounds each. Price 5s. 6d. per Jar

TAYLOR & COMPANY

Agents for W & A GILBEY   6 Castle Square

Swansea

(The Cambrian 27th September 1872)

China Run
'A biography of a Great Grandmother 1829-1893' by Neil Paterson (1948).
Neil Paterson's great grandmother, Christian West, was born in Banff, Scotland. She married Captain Dai Evans of the 'Dee' in Aberdeen in 1845. In Cardiff, Captain Evans renamed his ship the 'Christian Dee' and set sail for Garwyth on Cardigan Bay............ his home port. The new Mrs Evans spent her life here when her husband was away at sea.
At this time the 'Christian Dee', which was running the China seas and returning with rice and tea, had been designed for the opium trade. On one of these voyages, Captain Evans took Christian with him, but she had no intention of being just a passenger. She learned how to sail the ship and earned the respect of the sailors.
When her husband died she became the ship's captain and made a name for herself in the days when women were not expected to tackle a man's job – let alone with spectacular success.
('A biography of a Great Grandmother 1829-1893' by Neil Paterson 1948)

'Chinaman, John'
IN SEARCH OF 'JOHN CHINAMAN'
PRESS REPRESENTATIONS OF THE CHINESE IN CARDIFF
1906-1911
By John Cayford
('LLAFUR' – Journal of Welsh Labour History Llafur Vol.5 No.1 (1988). p16.)

Chinese Armorial Porcelain

"In the 18th century, it was very fashionable for rich families in Britain and mainland Europe (especially if a family member was involved in eastern trade or serving with the East India Company) to order fine porcelain dinner or tea services from China embellished with their coat of arms. About a hundred are known with Welsh coats of arms. Most of these services were made for descendants of old Welsh families who had left their ancestral homes in Wales and gone on to find fame and fortune elsewhere, in London or, for example, the Navy....... i.e. typically the second son of the family. So not many of the services would have been brought back to Wales, even though they bear old Welsh family heraldry, and few of the services can definitely be associated with one individual (the person who ordered it). James Seys, of Penrhos, and Sir Thomas Stepney at Llanelly House are two, but services like that for the Jones of "Monmouthshire" have no certain owner: all we know is that the coat of arms shown was born by people called Jones who once traced back to that country."

Thomas Lloyd

The following form part of a private collection of 18th Century armorial china dinner services with the coats of arms of Welsh families. It is estimated that during this period (18th Century) less than 50 of the wealthiest Welsh families ordered dinner services from China.

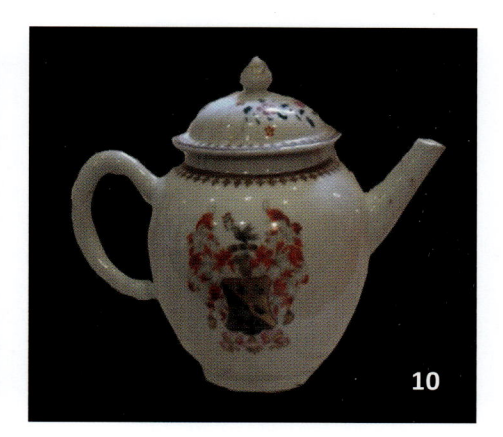

1. Pryce- ex Breconshire, of Rose Hall, Jamaica, c. 1760
2. Roberts – Glamorganshire, c. 1785. The family were traders and lived in the West Indies.
3. Jones – ex Monmouthshire, c. 1730
4. Edwardes – Pembrokeshire, c.1760
5. Langford – Denbighshire, c. 1750
6. Howell – ex Carmarthenshire, c.1760
7. Jones – Garthgynan, Denbighshire, c. 1775
8. Crowther impaling Meredith – Knighton, Radnorshire, c. 1760
9. Seys – Glamorgan/Monmouthshire, c. 1745. The service was made for James Seys of Penrhos, Monmouthshire (Arms are quatered with Seys of Boverton, Glamorgan.
10. Probably Allen, of Dale Castle, Pembrokeshire, c. 1760

Chinese and the Language Test

'Chinese seamen (except natives of Hong Kong or other British territory) are subject to the provisions of the new Merchant Shipping Act which requires every foreigner on British vessels, to have a working knowledge of the English language. Upon the language test coming into operation, the Chinese in many cases claimed they were British subjects, but these claims were rigidly examined, with the result that many were rejected, and a considerable number left Cardiff in consequence. For vessels trading in the Far East the rule, it is stated, has been somewhat relaxed, and, as in the case of Indian lascars crews, the principal firemen and deckhands only have been required to pass the full test. This matter has been made the subject of a question in Parliament. It being claimed by the Seamen`s Union that there has been an evasion both of the letter and the spirit of the new Merchant Shipping Act.'
(Western Mail 14th May 1908)

The Chinese Attack

'The subjoined is a copy of a letter which has been received from an assistant surgeon on board 'Magicienne', written soon after that unfortunate affair at the mouth of the Peiho River, in China:
'HMS Magicienne', Gulf of Pechili, July 1, 1859.
My Dear Father, A few days ago we had one of the most bloody actions that we have had for years but thank God I somehow escaped scatheless. We left Shanghai on June 15th, and arrived here on the 20th, and anchored about 7 miles off the Peiho forts.

The remainder of the fleet had been here for some days previous, when they found the entrance of the river had been completely blocked with stakes and successions of booms and chains across the whole being commanded by extensive forts and batteries. Several communications had been held with the Chinese, when they were requested to allow us to proceed up the river, which they endeavoured to put off by various excuses. However, on the 23rd ult. the Admiral ordered all the gun-boats and boats of the fleet to start on the morning of the 24th for the mouth of the river which we did about 7 a.m., and anchored about 2 miles from the forts, where we remained all day and night but during the night a party with a few boats were sent off to blow up the booms, which they partially succeeded in doing but had two guns fired upon them from the forts, which did no mischief to our boats. On the following morning (25th) about 8 a. m., we started and went further in, some of the gun-boats getting close to the first row of stakes, when several grounded and the whole forenoon was occupied in getting them off again. At 1 p.m., a signal was made to prepare for action, when all took their respective positions. At 2 p. m., the Admiral started in the gunboat 'Plover' towards the booms with a few gunboats following him, but directly he touched the booms all the forts opened fire upon us, which of course we immediately returned. All the gun-boats were in a position as to be under cross-fire, the shot dropping around us and into us as thick as hail in a hailstorm ……..it was something terrific.

The Chinese had 8 forts besides a great number of embrasures, loop-holes for wall pieces; and on the summit a covering of gingalls and rifles. Two of the forts we blew up by 5 p. m., and the guns on the south side were apparently silenced when the gun-boat I was in (Forester) was ordered down to the junks that we had and boats about a mile off to bring the landing party which consisted of marines and blue jackets (being the reserve).

We then returned to our former position by about 6.30pm and shortly afterwards, by doing so, those guns which we thought had been silenced opened a frightful fire on our landing party, besides gingalls, rifles muskets arrows and fire balls, all of which made frightful havoc among our men, especially as they had to wade some distance and through some feet of mud. Those few who managed to get up found that there were three ditches flooded with water and the third filled with stakes. Some of the men succeeded in getting across the two first ditches under a raging fire, when finding the attack useless, the retreat was sounded and they returned to the boats and came off to the gunboats, our firing ceased about 10 p.m.

I was ordered from the Forester to the 'Coromandel' (the Admiral `s yacht where the wounded were ordered to be taken) as the two surgeons and three assistant surgeons were unable to attend to all, I found the deck completely covered with wounded all imploring to be looked at and dressed, but they were so numerous that we had to take the worst cases first and the others in their turn, which occupied us until 5 am, without any intermission; the whole time the shot was falling around us in every direction. I am very sorry to say that we had a very large number killed and wounded numbering about 460, the missing included the entire force we had in action amounted to about 1300 men; I am sorry to add that Captain Vansittart was very severely wounded. I enclose a list of officers killed and wounded which I have collected to this time. Of officers and men on board we have had 26 killed and wounded. Five gun-boats and one despatch boat were sunk; three of which we have since been able to recover by plugging up and baling out at low water, though they are daily endeavouring to get them up. Out of 266 marines who landed 172 were killed and wounded. The Chinese have kept their fire day after day since the action, but without much success. They are endeavouring to prevent our getting up the gunboats. I do not know what the people of England will say to all this, especially to our being defeated by the long-tailed gentry. I believe nothing more will be done until orders are received from England. A French and American gunboat were also in the thick of the fight the whole time, they have lost several men killed and wounded and the French Admiral had a very narrow escape. JULY 5th, 1859 .... All the wounded were sent, yesterday, on board the 'Assistance', which has been converted into a hospital ship. Captain Vansittart remains on board he is getting on pretty fairly. I cannot yet give any information with regard to our further movements, but I believe we shall remain up here a short time for the benefit of the wounded on way from Gulf of Pecheli to Shanghai.'

JULY 7th 1859.

'On the 5th we were ordered down to Saddle Islands, which are outside Shanghai, where we are to remain for some little time for the benefit of our Captain`s health; Mr. Bruce and the legation leave us there for Shanghai. The authorities were very anxious to take Capt. Vansittart out of the ship, but were overruled by the medical department.

We take the mail from England down with us to Shanghai. One more gunboat has been raised, two others and the despatch boat have been abandoned. We have on board 100 additional marines and their officers, taken out of the Assistance, to make room for the wounded. The Chinese are inclined to make up with the Americans, and allow them to go up to Pekin, provided they eat "humble pie." Our operations, I believe, are terminated for this year: and our forcing our way up to Pekin will I expect depend entirely on the state of Europe and our ability to send out more ships and troops here, and also a few mortar vessels, which would very soon silence the Peiho Forts. I am glad to say that in the late attack all our men behaved most nobly, especially as they were under a most destructive fire the whole time, which swept them down by dozens.

The Commander-in-Chief (Hope) has issued an order thanking the whole that were under fire for their gallant conduct. By the time you receive this, you, I expect, will have seen a full account in the papers, which will be by far better than what I can give, as ever, since the action, I have been so much engaged with the wounded etc., that I have had hardly time to write. One surgeon on board the 'Coromandel' performed 30 amputations in two and half' hours, i.e. before 8 p. m. SUNDAY JULY 10, 12 a.m. .... The Saddle Islands are in sight, off which we have to remain, and as the mail bag closes this afternoon, I have no time to add more.
I am William H Clarke

To: Rev. T. Clarke,
Pontardulais,
Llanelly
'PS …. I am sorry to say that our Captain is not doing so well to-day,
but still I hope he will get over it.'
(The Cambrian 30th September 1859)

Chinese Cemeteries
Special areas have been set-aside in a number of cemeteries throughout Wales for the burial and commemoration of members of the various Chinese communities. In the Cathays Cemetery in Cardiff there is a memorial to all the Chinese who have died in Britain. The inscription reads:

'THIS MEMORIAL WAS ERECTED IN
1961
IN MEMORY OF ALL CHINESE
WHO DIED IN GREAT BRITAIN

Chinese memorial at Cathays Cemetery,
Cardiff

Chinese Crew Mutiny

CREW OF CHINAMEN MUTINY
ON CARDIFF SHIP AT NEW YORK
CURIOUS STORY ABOUT THE REVIVAL

'About the British steamer Dordogne a Chinese crew, shipped at Cardiff three months ago, mutinied in New York on Tuesday (says the "Daily Telegraph'). They attacked and wounded the second engineer, Millar, with knives, because, as alleged, he struck one of their number. The first officer heard Miller`s cry for assistance and ordered the men below deck. They refused. Then the captain and officers, armed with revolvers, drove the mutineers to quarters, where they were kept until a police boat from New York arrived. The boatswain and all deck hands were locked up on a charge of assault and mutiny. Miller says that ever since the crew learnt that they were debarred from landing in America because they were Chinese they became very morose and threatening, evidently associating Americans and English together as "oppressors of the Chinese". This feeling, he says, doubtless led to the outbreak. The chief officer of the Dordogne stated to the magistrate that it was impossible to engage a crew of Britishers at Cardiff owing to a religious festival conducted by Evan Roberts. The men there did not seem to think that service aboard a tramp steamer was exactly a Christian occupation.

Statement Confirmed
The owners of the vessel, the Cardiff Steamship Company Limited, have received a telegram from Captain Gray, the master of the ship, confirming the statement that the Chinese crew had mutinied, but no further particulars are given of the affair. The name of the wounded man is W. Mueller, and not Miller, and he lives at 202 Clarence Road, Grangetown. Captain Gray is also a local resident, living at Kyveilog Street and the other Britishers on board are C. Evans, third engineer, of Pengam, W. McGrather, Chief Mate, of Belfast, and R. Eglinton, chief engineer, of Glasgow. The deck hands and firemen were Chinese, shipped from the Chinese boarding house at 28, Patrick Street, Cardiff. The Dordogne left Cardiff for Baracoa, Cuba, on February 6 last, and was engaged in the banana trade between the West Indies and New York.

Christians on 'Tramps'
Some of the leading ship-owners of Cardiff were seen by a representative of the Western Mail, with reference to the statement made by the chief officer, that it was impossible to engage a crew of Britishers at Cardiff owing to the religious revival conducted by Evan Roberts. The suggestion was ridiculed and laughed at. Some said "Bosh. What utter rot." And others "Just as though Evan Roberts and the revival would affect the engagement of crews. It was generally agreed, however, that it was difficult to get a crew composed of all Britishers. If this were possible it would be more satisfactory to all concerned, but as there are very few British sailors about very few British crews could be got together. On the other hand, there were plenty of good mixed crews to be got, Britishers, Scandinavians and Southern Mediterranean people. And - if properly treated - good work may be expected from them. '
(Western Mail, Friday 11th August 1905)

Chinese Crews for British Ships

EXCITEMENT IN LONDON AND CARDIFF
UNEMPLOYED WHITES UP IN ARMS

'The Chinese seamen question has made its appearance under various guises in the past few months, as we have detailed on a number of occasions. The proportion of Chinamen employed on British ships is not great as yet, but the increase in their numbers has been so rapid of late that British seamen fear that they are in danger of being seriously prejudiced by the yellow race. For some reason, presumably because ship owners find that the Chinese crews are more economical, they have become more widely employed, and they find their way into other trades than those in which they until recently were almost exclusively engaged.

While this development has been in progress the shipping industry has fallen upon evil days, and thousands of British sailors and firemen are out of work. In the Bristol Channel ports alone some 40 or more vessels are "laid up", throwing out of work fully 1,000 ships` officers and men. At Cardiff alone the number of sailors and firemen of various nationalities out of employment is computed to be from 500 upwards. The fact that many of these men have practically exhausted their resources is calculated not to improve the position, as starving men are not given to think calmly when they see their means of livelihood being steadily reduced.

The latest trouble has arisen over the selection of the crew for the steamer 'Strathness', now loading at Cardiff for eastern waters. This vessel has usually carried an Eastern crew, and, finding that the number of Chinese available at Cardiff, although there is a considerable colony in the port, was insufficient, the captain proceeded to London to "sign on" his hands.

Up to the present the protests against the Chinamen at Cardiff have been confined to words. In London, however, matters have become different, angry scenes were enacted on Saturday, and again on Monday and Tuesday. When the master of the Strathness appeared at Poplar Board of Trade Office with a Chinese crew for the purpose of signing them on and taking them to Cardiff; about 300 white seamen were waiting, and great excitement prevailed. The Chinese assembled two or three times for the purpose of going to the office, but when they saw the threatening demeanour of the white seamen they beat a hasty retreat. Eventually the Chinese were brought to the office under the protection of Inspector Walmsley and a posse of fifty police. They were allowed to enter the office, but were unable to pass the language test, and were not signed on. When they left they were followed back to their boarding houses by a crowd of upwards of a thousand indignant whites. A rush was made upon them by some of the whites who evaded the vigilance of the police; and many Chinamen received blows about the head and face.

As the result of the difficulty, other arrangements to secure a crew are being made by the owners of the vessel, and these men will, if necessary, be conveyed on board under police protection. It was stated that a crew had already been despatched from London for Cardiff; but the local agents on Wednesday stated they had not been advised of the fact. Mr Havelock Wilson MP., President of the National Sailors And Firemen's Union, addressing a protest meeting of seamen, said he could see no difference between employing Chinese in South Africa and on British ships. During 1907, he said, some 6,000 Chinese were allowed by the Board of Trade to serve on British vessels. Outside the Cardiff Shipping Office on Wednesday morning, a meeting of seamen was held to protest against the employment of Chinese, and the following resolution was submitted and unanimously adopted: "We, seamen sailing out of the port of Cardiff strongly protest against the increase in the employment of Chinese seamen on British ships, and urge upon the Government to take steps to deal with the question." Mr. Henson (Barry) referred to the recent incidents at the London Docks and advised local seamen to "watch the 'Zambezi' when she came into Cardiff" As Britishers they made no objection to Chinese competing with them on equal terms in regard to wages and general conditions of employment. As a dumping ground for foreigners, Cardiff was known as the scrapheap of Europe. (Shouts of: "Quite right.") Instead of the Union Jack the Shipping Federation ought to fly the Chinese flag. The Chinese were less able to endure the heat of the engine-room than Britishers, and every year one out of every 400 Chinese employed committed suicide, the corresponding figures for Britishers being one for every 800 employed. Mr. Henson added that hardly any ship sailed out of the Port of Cardiff that was not under-manned. This matter was under the consideration of the Board of Trade.'

(WESTERN MAIL, Thursday 14th May 1908)

Chinese Junk

**CHINESE JUNK
NEW TEA ESTABLISHMENT
CASTLE STREET, SWANSEA
Opposite the 'Wheatsheaf'
WILL OPEN ON SATURDAY NEXT
HUMPHREY AND CO., PROPRIETORS**

'Humphrey and Co., from UNDERWOOD BROTHERS, respectively announce to TEA CONSUMERS of ALL CLASSES, that they have opened the above PREMISES, for the SUPPLYING of TEAS and COFFEE at such equitable and economic terms by placing the greatest advantage in the hands of their supporters, command one of the most extensive TEA TRADES in this locality. With much pleasure they also announce that TEA was not only CHEAPER THAN EVER, but the quality of their present imports is undeniably superior so that this establishment, the most careful buyer as well as the most fastidious connoisseur, maybe satisfactorily suited.

The system adopted will have for its object the establishment of a Ready Money Family Tea Trade, and the only solid and lasting basis, namely, THE MUTUAL BENEFIT of both BUYER and SELLER; and to the effect this object, the best teas will be sold, and the most limited profit adhered to. As, however, professions without practice are nothing worth, families are requested to test the truth of these observations by a trial, the Proprietors well knowing they cannot expect a continuance of favour if not found to deserve them.'

	s.	d.
Very strong congou	3.	4.
Fine Suchong kind	3.	8.
An excellent Tea, and deservedly in repute; strongly recommended **Splendid Rich Old Suchong**	4.	3.
We might refrain from quoting a higher price, this being so superior an article.		
THE VERY BEST BLACK TEA	4.	0.
At THE FINEST MIXTURE, combining all the choicest qualities.	5.	0.
Good Young Hyson	3.	6.
Fine GUNPOWDER, full of strength	4.	0.
Fine Silvery Leaf GUNPOWDER	5.	0.
This is a delightful Tea, possessing great strength and full rich flavour.		
FINEST PEARL LEAF DITTO	6.	0.

(The Cambrian 31st August 1849)

> **To GROCERS and FAMILIES.**
>
> MR. T. GLOVER begs to announce that he has been instructed to SELL by AUCTON, on the Premises, THE CHINESE JUNK, CASTLE BAILEY-STREET, SWANSEA, on TUESDAY, the 15th day of JANUARY, 1850.—
>
> All the well-selected STOCK, which comprises TEAS of the first quality, FRUIT, SUGARS, SPICES, RICE, MUSTARD, &c.
>
> The SHOP FIXTURES, &c., consist of a modern Plate-glass Front, Counters, Drawers and Shelves, Japan Canisters, Scales and Weights, superior Gas Fittings, with "The Chinese Junk."
>
> The FURNITURE is modern and useful.
>
> The Sale will commence at eleven o'clock in the forenoon, and the Grocery will be put up in lots adapted for family purchases.
>
> The Shop Front and Fixtures may be taken at a Valuation, with the House.

(The Cambrian 11th January 1850)

Note: 'CHINESE JUNK' only opened on 31st August 1849

CPAFFC
CHINESE PEOPLE'S ASSOCIATION FOR FRIENDSHIP WITH FOREIGN COUNTRIES (CPAFFC)

The Chinese People's Association for Friendship with Foreign Countries (CPAFFC) is one of the three major foreign affairs organizations of the People's Republic of China. It aims to promote friendship and mutual understanding between the Chinese people and foreign nations.

The organization was founded in May 1954. Its current President Madame Li Xiaolin. The Wales-China Friendship Society has had a long and close association with the CPAFFC since 1975 including a number of delegation visits to Wales and China by each organization. In 1989 the CPAFFC arranged the China part of the 'China 89' Project (See 'China 89').

Delegation from Chinese People's Association for Friendship with Foreign Countries hosted by the Wales-China Friendship Society, pictured with the Lord Mayor of Swansea Councillor Howard Morgan JP at the Guildhall (1989).

Chinese Poems
'Y Cocatw Coch' by Cedric Maby 1987
A selection of Chinese poems translated into Welsh.
(See: Cedric Maby)

Chinese State Circus
Performed in Wales in 2013 at Rhyl Pavilion (April 2013) and Swansea Grand Theatre (May 2013). Performance theme: 'Yin and Yang'.

Chinese Staircases
Chinese style staircases featured in a number of houses and buildings in Wales. They appear to have been mostly concentrated in North-West Wales and Pembrokeshire including the following locations:
- Bishopsgate House, Beaumaris, Anglesey
- Tan yr Allt, Bangor
- Trefeillir, Anglesey
- East Hook Farm, Haverfordwest
- Old King's Arms Hotel, Pembroke
- Royal George Hotel, Pembroke
- Treleddyn Uchaf, St.Davids
- Cresselly House, Pembrokeshire
- Freestone Hall, Cresselly, Pembrokeshire

Reference: 'Ascending in the Chinese manner' – The Pin Mill at Bodnant (Garden Pavillion) by Emile de Bruijn in 'Treasure Hunt' – the National Trust Collection.
Old King's Arms Hotel, Pembroke (History Point)

East Hook Farm, Haverfordwest, Pembrokeshire

Royal George Hotel, Pembroke

Freestone Hall, Pembrokeshire

Treleddyn Uchaf, Pembrokeshire

Old King's Arms Hotel, Pembroke

Cresselly House, Pembrokeshire

A 'Chinese' Chippendale staircase at Bishopsgate House, Beuamaris, Anglesey

EXTRACTS FROM AN ORIGINAL ARTICLE BY RACHAEL BARNWEL
Chinese' Staircases in North - West Wales
'Between 1755 and c. 1760, when the vogue for interior design "partly after the Chinese manner" was at its peak, a series of unique staircases emerged in the wealthy households of north-west Wales. The Royal Commission on the Ancient and Historical Monuments of Wales, which compiled detailed inventories of the archaeology and built heritage of Anglesey and Caernarvonshire between the 1930s and 1960s records 'Chinese Chippendale staircases at Tan-yr-Allt in Bangor, Caernarvonshire; Bishopsgate House in Beaumaris, Anglesey; and Trefeilir in Trefdraeth, Anglesey. Tan-yr-Allt and Trefeilir were both originally country houses built or occupied during the eighteenth century, while Bishopsgate House is a townhouse owned and used by the Bulkeley family based at Baron Hill, also in Anglesey. The houses are all within a seventeen-mile radius of one another, and have 'Chinese' staircases that survive to the present day, though in variable conditions.

Tan-yr-Allt, Bangor
Tan-yr-Allt was visited by Royal Commission investigators in the early 1950s while preparing the Caernarvonshire Inventories, which were published in three volumes between 1956 and 1964. A plan of the property was made, and photographs were taken of key features of the house and its interior, which was by that time in use as Bangor University Student's Union.

Records at the Commission indicate that at the time of its initial survey the interior features of the building had survived well. They date the main staircase, windows, fireplaces, cornicing and ground floor panelling to the building's original construction in 1755. Particular attention is given to the main staircase, which the final inventory notes is 'a good example of the local Chinese Chippendale style'.

It ascends from the main entrance of the property to the first floor in a single flight, with a railing on the landing and fluted reveals to the window at the head of the stairs.

It features a latticework design, with two contrasting patterns repeating in sequence to form the balustrade. The stair rail on the landing uses two different but equally contrasting patterns across the span of the landing.

In addition, the tread end of each step is carved with a stylised wave design.

Although the staircase is now painted white, the photographs from the initial 1950s investigation show the original staircase as being dark wood, though it is not possible to ascertain from the images whether its appearance is inherent in its materiality (i.e. whether it is made from mahogany or similar), or whether it is a result of wood staining.

Bishopsgate House, Beaumaris
Bishopsgate House in Beaumaris, Anglesey was built in the early eighteenth century by the Bulkeley family, who used the property as a dower house. The family's main residence on Anglesey was at Baron Hill, about a mile from Beaumaris. The house is substantially eighteenth-century in its fabric but with later alterations to the front room and façade of the property, probably dating to the nineteenth century. There is a 'Chinese' staircase at the house, which is not contemporary with the original construction of the building. Following a visit to the property in the 1930s, investigators suggested that the staircase was installed in the house in c. 1760. It was noted that the panelling in the ground floor rooms and the back stairs of the property are likely contemporary with the installation of the staircase and suggest a broader programme of interior change at the house in the 1760s. This home improvement work occurred following the death of its owner James, 6th Viscount Bulkeley (1717 – 1752) in 1752, and possibly in the same year that the Dowager Lady Bulkeley, née Emma Rowlands (d. 1770) married her second husband, Lt. Col. Hugh Williams (d. 1794) of Nant, Caernarvon and Caerau, Anglesey.

The 6th Viscount Bulkeley was succeeded by his posthumous son Thomas James Bulkeley (1752 – 1822) who was born eight months after his father's death, and who therefore had little influence on the interior design of the properties in his ownership at that time. The staircase is the main stairway in the building, and ascends from the ground floor to the first floor in two flights.

The staircase rail features a repeating pattern of alternating and contrasting latticework designs In addition, the tread ends are decorated with a carved, stylised wave design.

Trefeilir, Anglesey
Trefeilir is an eighteenth-century house near Trefdraeth, Anglesey. The majority of the extant structure of the building was constructed in 1735, incorporating the remains of a sixteenth-century house, representing all that remains of an earlier building, into one wing of the property. Inside, key architectural features include two sixteenth century fireplaces and the main staircase. The 'Chinese' staircase was probably added to the house in c. 1760. It is possible that the new staircase was added to the house in preparation for the marriage of owner Charles Evans (1726 – 1802) to Elizabeth Lewis (1740 – 1805) in 1761. The staircase appears to be made from dark wood, and has a reasonably plain handrail, newel and newel cap. The tread ends are carved with a stylised wave design.
The staircase ascends from the central hall to the first floor in two flights, with different sequences of patterns used for each flight and the landing.

A 'Local' Style
The Royal Commission's inventories indicate that all three of these staircases were installed in the five years between 1755 and c.1760. In each example, the staircase is either part of the original interior design of the building or appears to coincide with a change in the marital status of its owner. From the Commission's photographs, the staircases appear to be constructed from similar materials (though further investigation is required to ascertain the particulars of their fabrication) and feature designs that are extremely similar to one another, as at Tan-yr-Allt and Bishopsgate House, or that share basic, characteristic motifs and patterns that have been arranged differently, as at Trefeilir.
All properties share the stylised wave motif carved into their tread ends, though at Trefeilir this is more ornate than at the other properties.
It should also be noted that the quality of the craftsmanship exhibited in the construction of each staircase is high. When examined in close detail, the photographs reveal a fine finish to the woodwork, with close, precise joints between component parts. However, at the time of writing it has not been possible at this time to uncover the identity of the craftsmen that physically installed these staircases.
The geographical and chronological proximity of these staircases relative to one another, as well as their similarities of design and construction suggests that their appearance in these houses in north-west Wales in the mid-1750s to c. 1760 may also be related. Furthermore, the Royal Commission's Caernarvonshire Inventory notes that the staircase at Tan-yr-Allt 'is a good example of the local Chinese Chippendale style' (emphasis added).[i] There are also several "missing" 'Chinese' staircases in the region that were mentioned in the record, but that could not be located. In visiting local archives, museums and history groups in Anglesey and Caernarvon a number of 'Chinese' staircases were reported to have been in place in private households and even in shops up until the 1970s. However, with no evidence to support this they remain unconfirmed occurrences.
Despite this, their frequent appearance in local history discourse hints that 'Chinese' staircases may have been more prevalent in the region than records suggest. How, then, might a 'Chinese' style become 'local' to north-west Wales in the eighteenth century?
Firstly, all three properties are connected by one shared characteristic: each was owned or occupied by wealthy and socio-politically influential families.
John Ellis, as Archdeacon of Merionedd, was in a position of power both locally and nationally through the Church of England.

The Bulkeleys of Baron Hill owned a significant amount of land in north-west Wales and had lived at Baron Hill since its construction in the early seventeenth century as a residence for Prince Henry, son of King James I and Anne of Denmark, for use on his journey to Ireland (a purpose that was ultimately unfulfilled, as Henry died of typhoid fever in 1612 before he reached Anglesey).

Charles Evans (1726 – 1802) of Trefeilir was High Sheriff of Anglesey in 1751, then of Caernarvon in 1752. All three families were invested in local politics; the Bulkeley family were even involved in a prolonged political rivalry with the influential Bayly family of Plas Newydd, in which both parties competed to represent Anglesey in Parliament. All three families were well - connected in society, both within and beyond Wales, holding numerous political positions and posts. They were well - travelled, and held property in London; they were well embedded in fashionable, metropolitan culture. It is likely therefore that the decision to install 'Chinese' staircases at the three houses considered in this study was mostly affected by much broader consumer trends for interior design and furnishings across Britain in the mid-eighteenth century.'

(Adapted by the author from a case study first published on blogs.ucl.ac.uk/eicah in January 2014.)

Chinese Temple Tea Warehouse - Swansea

Pearse's Commercial Directory to Swansea and the Neighbourhood for 1854

Chongqing (Municipality)
Wales has a close relationship with the City and Municipality of Chongqing in South West China. The partnership between Chongqing and Wales was recommended by former Premier Wen Jiabao during a visit to Wales (as Vice Premier with responsibility for the Western Provinces) in 2000.

A Memorandum of Understanding (MOU) between the Chongqing Municipal Government and the Welsh Assembly Government, agreeing to collaboration and co-operation in a number of areas, was signed during the visit to Chongqing by First Minister for Wales Rhodri Morgan in March 2006.

In September 2006, a Welsh Affairs Officer was appointed to the British Consulate General in Chongqing to take forward the Chongqing-Wales relationship. A second post was added in September 2007. In January 2011 the two posts were relocated to a separate Wales Government office in Chongqing.

A formal Co-operation Agreement between Wales and Chongqing was signed during First Minister Rhodri Morgan's visit to Chongqing in March 2008. The Mayor of Chongqing, Wang Honju, visited Wales in August 2008. In 2013 Chongqing staged the 'Wales, Land of the Red Dragon Exhibition'.

(See: Welsh Assembly Government, National Museum of Wales)

Celebrating Wales Week in Chongqing in 2009

Christ College (Brecon)
Christ College received its first student from Hong Kong in 1966, followed by others in 1977. In 1999, the first student from China arrived and the intake has grown year by year. Every two years, 20 students, accompanied by teachers from the College, visit China for two weeks. In 2013, the College visited Xi'an High School, which is affiliated to Xi'an Jiaotong University and Fengxian Senior High School in Shanghai.

Clydach
In the 1920s the district of Clydach in the Swansea Valley was locally known as 'Shanghai'.

Coal In China
'There seems to be no doubt that the coalfields of China are practically inexhaustible. There are said to be 400,000 square miles of coalfields. Can we hope ever to supplement our own supply in these islands by importing Chinese coal? Sir Rutherford Alcock, late British Minister in China, who ought to be one of the best authorities on such a subject, answers this question in the negative.
"Of course, by and by, coal might be brought to this country from China; and at what price? It is declared that the very existence of England as a great nation depends upon the continuance of a supply of good quality coal at prices not much higher than it has now reached.
But, even supposing Chinese coal could be bought at the pit's mouth at five shillings per ton, we must add to this sum the costs of its transport to the coast, and £3 per ton for freight to England, as well as seven shillings or 10 shillings per ton for inland carriage on arriving here.
Thus, Chinese coal would cost us at least £4 per ton before it could be used in English factories or houses. It would be far cheaper to import American coal, having regard to the distance and cost of freight. Further, the Chinese have hitherto resisted all attempts at opening mines within the Empire.
European capital and mining skill has no attraction for them, when coupled with the necessity of encouraging European trade and complications with the Western Powers.

The Chinese Government says Sir Rutherford Alcock, is not ignorant that by means of European science and capital a great source of wealth might be developed, and a large increase of revenue secured, through the opening up of coalmines.

The customs revenue of China, obtained by intercourse with foreigners, is now £4 million per annum, and this might be easily doubled or trebled if the Chinese government were willing to allow free intercourse with the Western nations. But the Mandarin is deliberately inclined to accept these advantages, knowing that they would be accompanied with trouble, with riots and with possible aggression. The utmost, however, we could expect from an abundant supply of coal in the treaty-ports in China is that we should not be required to export from this country, and that steamers might call in China instead of consuming English coal out and home. Sir Rutherford Alcock rebukes the English merchants for their impatience to obtain everything they desire from the Chinese, and all at once. He reminds us that the Chinese are not of our opinion as to the advantages of Foreign Trade. Their rulers think there is something of higher importance than flourishing revenue. They are not willing to send us their tea; but they do not want our opium; and in fact would rather remain isolated without doing any trade with us. They may be very much to blame in this view. At all events they are consistent and disinterested in rejecting the temptation of hard cash. Japan presents a curious contrast with China in this respect. The Japanese are going ahead, we fear, even too quickly. The Chinese, in spite of such invitations as cannonballs and rifle bullets, continue to wish for no further acquaintance with us. They have tried the acquaintance and do not like us: they neither wish for European gold nor for European civilisation. On the contrary, the Japanese, having once taken the plunge, are adapting themselves with wonderful rapidity to European habits, and that taking acute advantage of every useful European invention.

They are introducing railways and telegraphs into Japan; they have introduced the study of English into the schools, apparently with a view to its ultimate adoption in preference to their own tongues; and they have come to England for a loan, which is even popular upon our Stock Exchange.

That the Japanese Government has been able to launch a loan successfully here is a signal proof of their sagacity. Never was a revolution in national ideas, language and customs more rapid. We only hope that, unlike most revolutions, it may be safe as well as rapid.'

(The Cambrian 14th February 1873)

Concert (Celebrated Chinese Steel Band)

'*The Nobility, Gentry, Patrons of Music and the Public from Swansea are respectfully informed, that M. Richardson and his MONSTER BACK BAND and the CELEBRATED CHINESE STEEL BAND will have the honour of giving TWO GRAND CONCERTS OF SACRED AND CLASSICAL MUSIC consisting of morning and evening, for the first time in Swansea in the Assembly Rooms, on Saturday, 10 April 1847 on their brilliant and silvery toned Chinese Steel Band. Morning Concert is to commence at 11 o'clock and, Evening Concert at eight. Notwithstanding the addition of the far famed Chinese Steel Band, the prices will still remain as usual.*

Tickets for the morning concert, two shillings and sixpence, or family ticket to admit five, ten shillings; children and schools, one shilling each. Programme, with full particulars is, to be had from Bookseller, 17 Wind Street, Swansea.

A Morning and Evening CONCERT to be given by the above celebrated Bands in the Assembly Rooms, Merthyr on THURSDAY, April 8th, and in the Assembly Rooms, Neath, on Friday 9th.

Programmes may be had off Mr White, bookseller, Merthyr and of Mr Whittington, Post Office, Neath.'

(The Cambrian: April 2nd, 1847)

Confucius Statue

A statue of the Chinese philosopher, Confucius, was presented to Swansea University by the European Federation of Chinese Organizations. The statue was unveiled at the University on 15th September 2009.

Confucius Conference

In 1994 a Conference to celebrate the 2545 years since the birth of Confucius took place in Beijing. The Conference was significant in that China celebrated the return of Confucianism to Chinese life after it had been banned during the Cultural Revolution. Ena Niedergang, President of the Wales China Friendship Society, represented Wales at the Conference where she was presented with a commemorative watch to mark the occasion.

The Conference played host to delegates from all over the world, including Lee Kuan Yew, former Prime Minister of Singapore and former US Secretary of Defence, Robert McNamara. Ena Niedergang was invited to meet the President of China, Jiang Zemin, in the Great Hall of the People in Tiananmen Square. The President, through the Conference, wanted to show the world that China had changed.

President Jiang Zemin (centre) with a number of delegates at the 1994 International Conference to celebrate the 2545th anniversary of the birth of Confucius at the Great Hall of the People, Beijing.

Presentation case and watch to commemorate the 1994 Beijing Conference

Confucius Classroom (CC)
Wales' first Confucius Classroom at Llandovery College was opened by H.R.H. Prince Charles the Prince of Wales and the Chinese Ambassador to the United Kingdom H.E. Liu Xiaoming on St. David's Day 2011.
Confucius Classrooms are also located at:
Ysgol Aberconwy, Conwy
Argoed High School, Mynydd Isa, Flintshire
Ysgol Gyfun Gymraeg Bryn Tawe, Swansea
Cathays High School, Cardiff
Ysgol Dyffryn Taf, Whitland
Ysgol Eirias, Colwyn Bay
Ysgol Gyfun Emlyn, Newcastle Emlyn
Lansdowne Primary School, Cardiff
Ysgol Penglais, Aberystwyth
St Cenydd Community School, Caerphilly

Confucius Institute
The Confucius Institute (CI), which has its headquarters in Beijing, was inaugurated in 2004 to deliver Chinese language and culture programmes. It is overseen by the 'Office of Chinese Language Council International' (Hanban), a non-profit organization affiliated with the Ministry of Education of the People's Republic of China and the United Front Work Department. The Institutes operate in co-operation with local affiliate colleges, universities and schools around the world, and financing is shared between Hanban and the host institutions.
2007 – First Confucius Institute established at University of Wales Trinity St. David's, Lampeter
2008 – Cardiff University
2012 – Bangor University
2013 – Swansea Metropolitan University (now University of Wales Trinity St.David's)

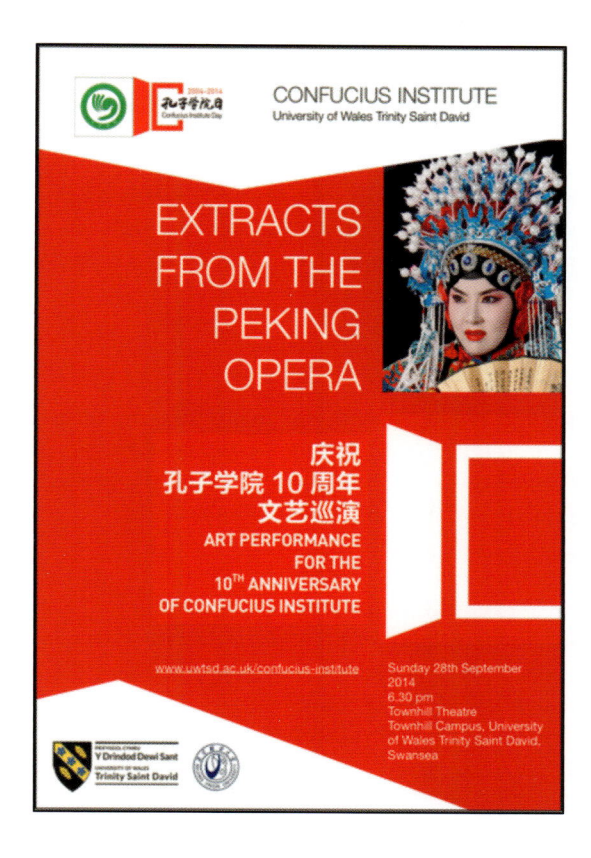

Peking Opera performance held at the University of Wales Trinity Saint David, Swansea to celebrate the 10th Anniversary of the establishment of Confucius Institutes worldwide.

Conway H.M.S
In 1840, the Conway made the first examination of the Yangtze River as far as Fushan. Became involved in the capture of Chusan (Zhoushan) and Canton (Guangzhou) – hoisting the Union Flag on the British Factory there.
A $6 million ransom imposed on the Chinese authorities was transported to Britain in HMS Conway. The ship was awarded Battle Honours in China (1842).

China – 'Treasure From China, July 1842'
'There came into London from China, $6 million in compensation to the British Government. It arrived in wooden chests that filled 10 wagons and carts conveyed over London Bridge to the Bank. This money weighed over 65 tons and was brought from China in HMS Conway.'
('Cenhadwr Americanaidd' Translated by Huw Davies)

Cordell (Alexander 1914-1997)
Alexander Cordell was the pen name of George Alexander Graber. He was born in Sri Lanka. He married twice - his first wife was Rosina Wells and they had a daughter, Georgina.
His second marriage was to Elsie May Donovan. Although he adopted Wales as his home, he was educated in China the setting of many of his novels. These included 'Traitor Within', 'In the Sinews of Love', 'The Bright Cantonese', 'The Dream and the Destiny', and 'Dreams of Fair Women'.

Cors-y-Gedol
(See: Richard Vaughan)

Cory (Reginald 1871 – 1934)
Reginald Radcliffe Cory, third son of John Cory of Dyffryn Gardens, Vale of Glamorgan, pursued his passion for collecting plants. Plant collectors, such as 'Chinese Wilson' and Richard Gilbertson, brought back plants for Cory. He also collected garden ornaments.
(See: Dyffryn Gardens)

Craft Council for Wales
The Craft Council for Wales contributed many 'dragon themed' items for a Welsh Dragon Exhibition held at the British Consulate-General, Shanghai (1988). The Exhibition was opened on St David's Day to welcome the year of the Chinese Dragon in 1988. The Exhibition promoted Welsh industries in China.

Cwmdulais Uchaf ('Links with China')
A joint-article by George Brinley Evans and the Author about the Rev. Dr Griffith John who, at the age of fourteen, worked at the Onllwyn Colliery and Ironworks Shop and in later life become a missionary in China.
(Cwmdulais Uchaf Magazine, Spring 2010, Issue 18, P.8/9)

Cwrt Sart Comprehensive School
A number of students and staff from Cwrt Sart School, Briton Ferry formed part of the 'China 89' Project along with Alderman Davies' Church in Wales Primary School, Neath. Both schools were among the first in Wales to host teachers from China during the 1980s.

Mr. Zhongbao Liu from Nantong Number 1 Middle School with students and staff of Cwrt Sart Comprehensive School, Briton Ferry who were part of the 'China '89' touring group to China in 1989.

WALES-CHINA 250 YEARS OF HISTORY | 53

Cyfarthfa Castle Museum and Art Gallery
The former home of the Crawshay family, historical ironmasters of the Cyfarthfa Ironworks in Merthyr Tydfil. The Museum collection includes a number of Chinese artifacts (pictured).

Decorative Chinese porcelain bowl

Chinese Celadon glaze ceramic dish

Glazed figures (ridge decoration) – Summer Palace, Beijing

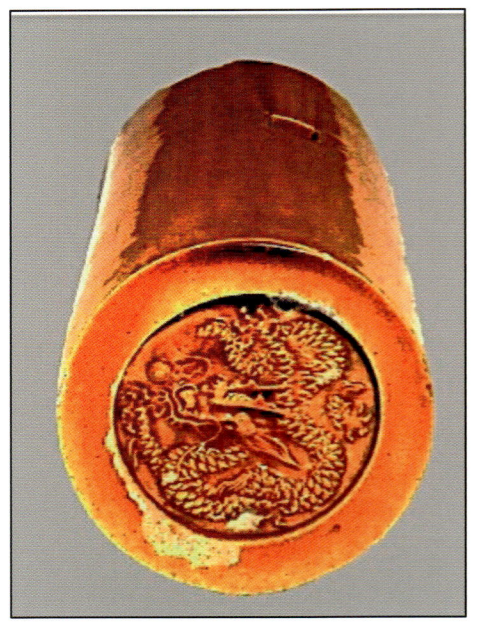

Five - Clawed Chinese Dragon glazed earthenware roof decoration

D

Dagu (Taku) Forts
The Royal Welch Fusiliers would have known them as the 'Taku Forts'. The Forts were attacked by Britain and her allies in the wars of 1860 and 1900. The following is an excerpt concerning the attacks from the Chinese viewpoint.

Chinese fortress at Dagu (Taku)

'Each fort accommodated three cannons and over 400 soldiers. In 1870, Li Hongzhang, a Qing Dynasty Officer, built up three more forts while reinforcing the then old ones. The Dagu Forts played an outstanding part in the Chinese people's struggle against imperialist aggression. When the invading warships attempted to land at Dagu and attack Beijing during the Second Opium War (1856-1860), the patriotic soldiers led by Shi Rongchun, a Qing officer, fought 24 hours at Dagu Forts on June 25, 1859. They damaged and sank eight invading warships, captured two warships, wounded and killed nearly 500 enemies and severely wounded the British fleet commander James Hope (1808-1881). Again when Dagu was invaded by the Eight Power Allied Forces sent by Britain, the United States, Germany, France, Tsarist Russia, Japan, Italy and Austria in 1900 to suppress the anti-imperialist Boxers Movement of the Chinese people, the Qing court officer Luo Rongguang led his army to fight shoulder to shoulder with the Boxer Movement soldiers and Dagu residents and added an illustrious chapter to the annals of the Chinese people's struggle against foreign invaders. In 1901, the Qing court was forced by the Eight Power allied Army to sign the unequal Treaty of 1901 protocol, according to which the Dagu Forts were demolished by force. What were left are only fort vestiges, mounds and a broken cannon. However, streams of tourists come to cherish the memory of the ancient battleground and the heroic and moving feats of the national heroes.'
(Tianjin Museum)

Dahl (Roald 1916-1990)
Born in Wales, to Norwegian parents, rose to prominence in the 1940s, with works for both children and adults, and became one of the world's best-selling authors. His book 'Charlie and the Chocolate Factory' has been translated into Chinese.

Dale (Arthur Leonard)
'Arthur Leaonard Dale, 6th November, 1914, South Wales Borderers, 10724, Private, Sai Wan (China) memorial, Newport Cenotaph – First World War'
(History Points)

Davey (William James)
Born 1865, at 22 Warwick Street, Grangetown Cardiff. In 1882, he arrived in China to begin his missionary work, aged 26 years. Married M. Lawson in March 1896.
(Overseas Missionary Fellowship 1991)

Davidson (Henry, Captain, Hon. East India Company Navy)
Captain Davidson lived at Grove House, Llanstephan, Carmarthenshire and distinguished himself when he preserved the lives of the crew of the Frigate 'Alceste' during a dangerous voyage to the Embassy in China'
February 18th 1817 The 'Alceste' was wrecked in the Gasper Straits (107° E, 3° S)
August 17th – Embassy landed at Spithead.
Earl Amherst .... Jeffrey William Pitt – Ambassador Extraordinary to China
References:
'The Morris Family of Carmarthenshire' by D.L. Baker-Jones
The Carmarthenshire Antiquary', Volume VII, Page 98 (1971)
'The Chronicles of the East India Company Trading to China-1635 to 1834' by Hosea Ballou Morse LL.D

Marriage
'On Wednesday, the 11th inst., at Llanbadarn Fawr Church, Cardiganshire, Capt. H.D. Davidson, of the Hon. East India Company's services, to Jane, daughter of the late William Morris Esq, of Carmarthen.'
(The Cambrian 21st September 1822).

Death
'On the 31st ult., after a short illness, Captain Henry Davidson, regretted by all who knew his worth.'
(The Cambrian 12th November 1842)

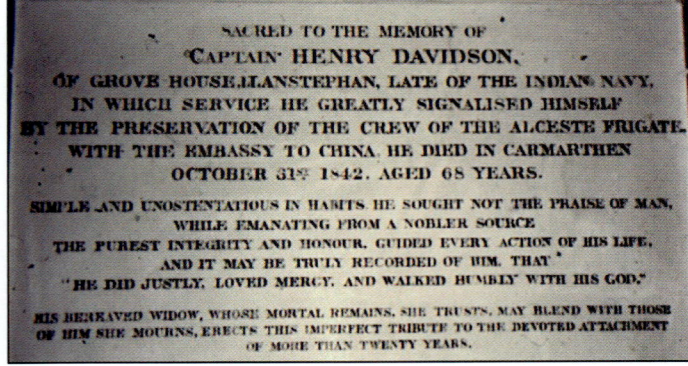

Memorial to Captain Davidson at Llansteffan Church, Carmarthenshire.

Davidson (Robert)
Robert Davidson founded the Friends Mission in Sichuan Province, China where he was followed by three of his brothers.
'Friends to China', written by Charles Tyzack, a former lecturer at University College Cardiff, gives an account of the Quaker missionary work in China from 1860 onwards.

Davies (Arnold)
Born 1879 at Menai Bridge. Appointed as a missionary and medical service to Zezhou in 1907. He returned to Wales in 1909.
(Overseas Missionary Fellowship 1991)

Davies (D)
'Driver: Number 3 Battery, 13th Brigade Royal Artillery. Awarded the China War Medal (1860) – Pekin Bar and Daku Forts Bar.'
(Carmarthenshire County Museum)

Davies (David and Jean)
'David and Jean Davies were missionaries in China at the same time as Gladys Aylward. David was captured and tortured by the Japanese who tried to make him confess to being a spy but without avail. He was born in Cardiff and is buried with Jean in the Western Cemetery in Cardiff. His son Murray lived in Swansea.'(B.B.C. Press release for the programme 'Blinded by Her Faith- The story of Gladys Aylward' (2004)
'David Davies – Born to Burn' by Fredrick A. Tatford (1972) 'Nightmare in the East', Western Mail, June 6th, 1998

Davies (Evan)
Evan Davies was born at Hengwm, Lledrod Carmarthenshire. He was apprenticed to a local draper before going to join his father in London. He returned to Wales and started preaching at Mynyddbach, near Swansea. Eventually, he joined the London Missionary Society (LMS) and was sent to work in Penang in 1835. By 1840, he returned due to ill - health and took up several posts in England before retiring to Crug - y - Bar in Carmarthenshire. He was buried at Abney Park Cemetery, London. Evan Davies published several books, amongst them: 'China and Her Spiritual Claims' and 'Memoirs of Samuel Dyer'*
* Samuel Dyer (1804-1843) was a British missionary in Penang (1827). He devised a steel typeface for printing Chinese characters to replace the traditional wooden blocks.
('Welsh Biography on Line' by the Rev Dr Evan Lewis, D. Th)

Davies (Florence M.E. 1897-1984)
'The diary of Florence Mary Davies was found on the stairs of a second-hand bookshop in Llandudno in the late 1990s. It was handwritten, not in a very good condition, but its contents were interesting. She studied Medicine at Liverpool and practised as a doctor in China from 1928 to 1939. She died in 1984, aged 87 years and was buried at Nercwys in Flintshire, where her father had been vicar.
Her diaries describe a range of things such as treating wounded soldiers, the flora and terrain of China, which she likened to parts of north Wales. She also wrote about the people. The diary is now at Hawarden Record Office.'
(Alison Proctor and Sylvia Jones Women's Archive Wales)

Davies (Hannah)

'Among Hills and Valleys in Western China' by Hannah Davies (1901). The following account appeared in the Cambrian, September 1902

PONTARDAWE LADY MISSIONARY IN CHINA
'One of the most recent books on missionary enterprise should appeal forcibly to Welsh readers, as apart from the interest of the matter it contains, it is the work of a Welsh lady, Miss Hannah Davies, who is a native of Pontardawe, and the daughter of the Rev. W. Davies, Llangwstenin Rectory, Conway. The experiences of Miss Davies were rather exciting, as a period was put to her labour in Si-Ch`uan (the largest of the Chinese provinces) by the Boxer rising, when she was ordered to the coast. Miss Davies left for China in 1893, and for the first six months was engaged in the acquiring of a smattering of the Chinese language. Of the language Miss Davies tells us some amusing things (says the Vicar of Aberpergwm, in review). Speaking of the Chinese characters which, as is well known, were in their original form of little pictures representing, like the Egyptian hieroglyphics, ordinary objects in life she says the Chinese idea of home is represented by a pig under a tree. The character for peace shows a woman extinguished. In her journey inland, Miss Davies was much impressed by the Yang-tse gorges. One spot reminded her at first of Wales, and one of her companions thought it looked like Scotland, but they soon decided that it far exceeded them both in grandeur and beauty. At one rapid, especially difficult to negotiate, more than a hundred men were employed in tugging up the boat. The missionary party had no sooner got through the gorges safely than they had to return again to Hankow, owing to the spread of riots in Si Ch`uan. At Ch`en-tu, the capital, the various mission houses were burnt, and the missionaries had to flee for refuge into the Yamen. The period of waiting was spent by Miss Davies in evangelistic work at Ta-Ku t`ang, where the people were friendly, though not many eager listeners. In her class for women, was one member, bright and ever cheerful, who confessed to her with great indifference, that she had six little girls, all of whom she had got rid of in their babyhood. As Miss Davies looked at her horrified, she said she did not want them; they were only girls, and did not her neighbours do the same?'
(The Cambrian 12th September 1902)

Davies (H. Tudor 1816-1863)
Barrister and Chief Magistrate in Hong Kong, 1856-1859. He left Hong Kong and became Commissioner of the Chinese Imperial Maritime Service. He died in Shanghai in 1863.
(St. David's Society Hong Kong)

Davies (Murray)
The son of missionary parents, David and Jean Davies, born in 1932. In his article, 'Nightmare in the East' published in the Western Mail 6th June 1998, he relates about his early life in China.

Davies (Peter B.S.)
St. David's based local historian and author. 'The Footsteps of Our Fathers' (Chapter XVII p.91 – 'Martyrs of the Faith' (Published by Merrivale (1994) with reference to Herbert and Elizabeth Dixon
(See: (i) Herbert and Elizabeth Dixon missionaries in China (ii) Sue Bell)

Davies (Tanya)
'Tania Davies, from Ystradgynlais, Swansea Valley, worked as an English, music and drama teacher in Beijing for four years. She was appointed as co-director to the official children's choir of the Beijing Olympics.'
(South Wales Evening Post, Friday, March 19th, 2010)

Davies (William)
Unpublished thesis: 'Relations with China – 1854 – 69
(National Library of Wales)

Day (Lieut. Col H.J)
Born 1804, commanded 99th Regiment, awarded China Medal and Pekin Clasp.Died, 1874.

Day (Lieut. Col H.J)
Born 1835, commanded 99th Regiment, awarded Second China War Medal: 1857-1860 with Pekin Clasp, died, 1892.
Tenby Museum and Art Gallery display five generations of the
family of Lieutenant Colonel Francis Day.
Ref: 'China, 1860' by Michael Man (p.25)

Day Family Honours on display at Tenby Museum

Dazu (Chongqing Municipality, China)

Major exhibition at National Museum of Wales – 'From Steep Hillsides: Ancient Rock Carvings from Dazu, China' (2011). It was the first time that ancient rock carvings from Dazu left China to make their debut in the West at the National Museum of Wales, Cardiff.
(See : Western Mail Article, Friday, 21st January 2011.)

The Dazu Rock Carvings were declared an UNESCO World Heritage Site in 1999. For many years they were closed to the public that helped to preserve them. The Chinese were allowed to visit Dazu in 1961 and foreigners had to wait almost twenty years later before they were allowed entry. The carvings are famous for their grand scale and are amongst the best preserved of this form of Chinese cave temple art. They are in the form of religious sculptures and carvings dating as far back as the 7th Century AD. The carvings depict and are influenced by Buddhist, Daoist and Confucian beliefs.

Deer (Père David)

'The French naturalist, Father Armand David, (Père David) brought these unusual Deer to the attention of the West. He had found them in the garden of the Summer Palace, on the outskirts of Beijing, in 1865.

Père David Deer were introduced into Margam Country Park, in the 1990s by Nigel Davies then Head Ranger. They were on loan as part of a breeding programme from Whipsnade Safari Park as they were becoming a rare breed. The group thrives at Margam Country Park and the numbers have grown to around 40 (2014). The environment of the Park, with extensive rhododendron cover, is very similar to the natural habitat that they would be used to in China.'

(Alison Lloyd) (Margam Country Park, NPT County Borough Council)

Dey (Emily Maud)
'Born 1903 in Cardiff. Worked at the Lester Hospital, Shanghai in 1930. With the Red Cross Unit in China: 1942-45. Died 1952.'
(Overseas Missionary Fellowship 1991)

Diamond Sutra
The Diamond Sutra, from Dunhuang, was printed in AD 868. It is the earliest dated, printed book in the World. It is now kept at the British Library but, previously at the British Museum. During World War II the Diamond Sutra and other Chinese antiquities were deposited, for safe keeping, at the National Library of Wales, Aberystwyth.
'The Diamond Sutra is a copy of the Buddha's sutra and sermons. The scroll is just under five metres long. A final part of the text proved to be the most important as it gives the date when it was printed. A printed colophon reads -' Reverently (caused to be) made for universal free distribution by Wang Jie on behalf of (his) two parents on the fifteenth day of the fourth month of the Xiantong reign'........a date equivalent to A.D. 868.It was brought to London by Sir Aurel Stein (1852-1943) who acquired it in 1907. It was found hidden in the Caves of the Thousand Buddhas, Dunhuang, at the edge of the Gobi Desert, Gansu, western China. The Diamond Sutra was well over 500 years older than the first European printing. Over the years conservators have tried to preserve the fragile paper that usually had the opposite effect. In the 1990s, a decision was taken to restore the Diamond Sutra. Conservation started in 2003 and was completed by 2010. Mark Barnard, Conservator at the British Library, has, through his skilled efforts, brought it close to the state in which it was first printed over 1100 years ago. '
From: 'Diamond Sutra' by Frances Wood and Mark Barnard. Frances Wood the former Head of the Chinese Department at the British Library

Dinosaurs from China Exhibition
The 'Dinosaurs from China' Exhibition from December 1986 to April 1988, at the National Museum of Wales, was the largest exhibition of dinosaurs ever held in the UK. The Exhibition included unique specimens that had not been seen before outside of China.

Exhibition poster

Dixon (Elizabeth, née Williams)

Elizabeth Dickson was born at St David's and attended Tabernacle Chapel. She married Herbert Dixon and they went as missionaries to China in 1885. Taken prisoners by the Boxers and executed outside the walls of Xin Zhou on August 9th, 1900. Fortunately, their four children were in Britain at this dreadful time. A plaque to their memory is at Tabernacle Chapel.

Their great granddaughter Prudence and her husband, the Rev Canon Stuart Bell, visited the places in China associated with her great grandparents and discovered a wonderful story.

(See: Prudence Bell and Peter B.S. Davies)

Herbert Dixon and Family

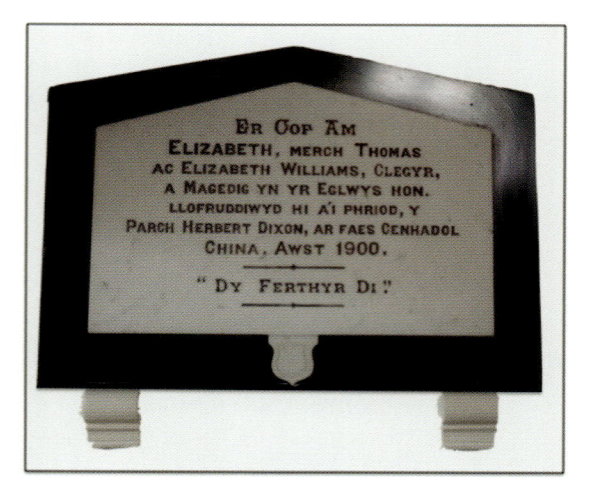

Memorial plaque to Herbert and Elizabeth Dixon at Tabernacle Chapel St. David's

Memorial to Elizabeth and Herbert Dixon on Thomas William's grave at St. David's Cemetery, Pembrokeshire

ELIZABETH
AND HER HUSBAND
HERBERT DIXON
BAPTIST MISSIONARIES BOTH MARTYRS
OF THE FAITH IN CHINA AUGUST 1900
THEY LOVED NOT THEIR LIFE EVEN TO DEATH

Memorial inscription to Elizabeth and Herbert Dixon on the grave at St. David's Cemetery, Pembrokeshire

ST DAVIDS MISSIONARY MURDERED IN CHINA

A diary kept by Revd. Herbert Dixon, Baptist Missionary during the late Boxer Rising, has recently been recovered by Western troops pursuing the rebels. It recounts the harrowing experiences of a group of Europeans, including his wife Elizabeth Dixon formerly of Clegyr. For nearly a month they travelled in secret to escape the Boxers who were intent on the capture and execution of all Christians.
(Cambrian News and County Echo)

Centenary of murder of St David's Missionary
'Wednesday next week 9th August 2000, will be the centenary of the murder of St Davids missionary Elizabeth Dixon who was killed in China during the Boxer Rebellion.
A total of 8 missionaries were killed at Xinzhou (Shanxi Province) during the Rebellion. Among the 4 men and 4 women cruelly put to death were the Rev Herbert Dixon and his wife Elizabeth.
Elizabeth Dixon had been born in St David's on 14th July 1855, the daughter of Thomas and Elizabeth Williams of Clegyr Isaf. After a childhood spent in St David's and Cardiff, the young Elizabeth left home for London where she trained to become a nurse. In London she met Rev. Herbert Dixon, a Baptist minister and missionary. They married and had 4 children who were born between 1886 and 1891. In 1899 Rev and Mrs. Dixon returned to China leaving the children at home.
By April 1900 they were settled comfortably in Xinzhou, a walled city some 250 miles southwest of Pekin. Here Mrs. Dixon had opened a school for the daughters of Chinese Christians. The missionaries were still unaware of the anti-European feelings among native Chinese.
These resulted in the formation of the secret society 'The Righteous Harmonious Fists' or 'Boxers' dedicated to driving out or killing all foreigners as well as Christian Chinese. 29th June, Rev Dixon heard of the attack on the mission at the state capital of Taiyuan.

Warned of the danger, the 8 missionaries left Xinzhou in secret as Herbert Dixon recorded in his diary. With friendly Chinese acting as guides they were led by night to the relative safety of a Christian village. It was a nightmare journey, particularly for the ladies, in darkness in complete silence through ravines and along treacherous mountain paths. For several days they sheltered in the village. By then the Boxers were on the trail and they were forced to leave. Another hazardous night march ended at a tiny damp cave, deep in the mountains. By this time Mrs. Dixon was seriously ill. For nearly a fortnight they had been lying on cold, damp bedding, able to emerge only at night; sometimes to move between caves.

Food and water were becoming increasingly scarce as the Chinese Christians fled. There had been no response to messages asking for help from European troops stationed near the coast. In spite of all their close relations they retained their Christian Faith, but as they realised, the end could not be long delayed.

On Saturday 21st July the cave was discovered by the pursuing Boxers. The missionaries were armed and the first attack was driven off. At that point the diary ends.

The precise sequence of events which followed is uncertain. The missionaries were in the end captured and taken back to Xinzhou. There, nearly three weeks later on 9th August 1900, they were all executed.

Elizabeth Dixon and her husband still lie in distant China. In St David's they are remembered by an inscription on a family tomb in the cemetery and by a plaque in Tabernacle Chapel where the young Elizabeth Williams once worshipped.'

(Cambrian News and County Echo 4th August 2000)

Memorial Service for Murdered Missionaries

'*Last Sunday morning, 13th August, a memorial service was held in Tabernacle Presbyterian Church, St David's, to observe the centenary of the tragic death of the missionaries, Mrs Elizabeth Dixon (a former member of Tabernacle from Clegyr and her husband the Rev Herbert Dixon a Baptist minister.)*

As recorded in an earlier report in the County Echo the Reverend and Mrs Dixon were killed in Hsin Chou China during the Boxer Rebellion. The Rev Richard Williams MA of Woodstock conducted the service and gave an account of the experience of the Dixons in China until their murders on 9th August 1900.

The Rev Williams expressed appreciation to Mr. Peter S. Davies, a local author and historian, for his research and information about the Dixon family.

Mrs Edna Morgans, the oldest member of the tabernacle, presented an arrangement of flowers on behalf of Church members, at the plaque in Tabernacle which commemorates the Dixon's sacrifice.'

(Cambrian News and County Echo August 2000)

Doré (William)
LECTURE
'*The lecture was delivered in the Wesleyan Schoolroom by Mr William Doré last night, descriptive of life in China, and of a visit to Japan, and illustrated by specimens of native workmanship.'*
(The Cambrian 29th March 1872)

Dragon Boat Race

Dragon Boat racing commemorates the Chinese poet Qu Yuan (340-378 BC), who was a wise and learned man. He fought against the corruption at the court of the King of Chu but ministers plotted against him and the King sent him into exile. Qu travelled widely, and, during his travels, wrote many poems and important works. He loved Chu so much that on hearing that his beloved State had been conquered by the State of Qin, he threw himself into the River Miluo, in Hunan Province. Fishermen rushed out in their boats to try and rescue him. They splashed the water with their oars and beat drums to keep away the fish from Qu Yuan but were unable to rescue him. Dragon Boat Racing is held in many places throughout Wales. On 25th May 2014, the first Welsh Dragon Boat Championship, organized by Narberth and Whitland Rotary Club, took place

Dragon Music

Peter Rees, Brian Roberts and Ian Thomas, Swansea musicians, composed two pieces of music entitled 'The Dragon Sleeps' and 'The Dragon Wakes' for the Welsh Dragon Exhibition held at the British Consulate General in Shanghai to welcome the Chinese Year of the Dragon in 1988. Their compositions were played on Shanghai Radio.

Dragons
How two cultures use their dragons

Chinese Dragon, Shanghai (1986)

Welsh Dragon near Swansea Leisure Centre (1987)

Dragons (Welsh Dragons for China Exhibition)
The Wales-China Friendship Society worked with the British Consul- General, Mr Iain Orr, in Shanghai on the first non-Chinese Dragon exhibition to be held in China which was opened on St David's Day 1988.
People from all walks of life contributed from throughout Wales.
 Artist, Sharon Patterson, designed a special Welsh   Dragon stained-glass window. Musicians, Peter Rees, Brian Roberts and Ian Thomas composed two pieces of music- 'The Dragon Sleeps' and 'The Dragon Wakes' which were played on Shanghai Radio.
Pat Price, of the Love-spoon Gallery, Mumbles, Swansea, commissioned a lovespoon featuring the Chinese and Welsh Dragons.
The Craft Council for Wales contributed many items and informed the Princess of Wales about this unique exhibition held at the consulate to promote business between China, Wales and the UK.

Pupils at Alderman Davies' Primary School Neath showing their dragon T-Shirts

The Consul - General in Shanghai involved Chinese children in painting Chinese dragons which were sent to Alderman Davies' Church in Wales School, Neath. The Neath schoolchildren returned the compliment by drawing Welsh Dragons for the Chinese children. The Consul- General sent Dragon T-shirts to the children at Alderman Davies' School.

Dyffryn Gardens
Designed by eminent landscape architect Thomas Mawson. The gardens in the Vale of Glamorgan are the early 20th-century vision of industrialist John Cory and his son Reginald. The mansion and gardens are in the ownership of the National Trust. The gardens include a number of oriental bronzes.

The Chinese philosopher Laozi

Chinese Dragon Bowl

Dymond (Emslie Chambers 1902-1980)
Dr Emslie Chalmers Dymond (Jimmy) was born in Yunnan Province, China where his parents were missionaries. He qualified as a doctor at St Mary's, London and returned to China in 1930 where he was in charge of the British Hospital on Nantai Island and Port Health doctor where he attended British Consulate staff.

Dymond (Ruby)
'*Ruby, the wife of Dr Dymond, was born in Liverpool in 1904. They worked together at the Treaty - Port of Fuzhou, Fujian Province. Ruby wrote about this period of her life in a book 'Threads of Circumstance'. She recalls their nine years in the British Treaty Port and the world of diplomats and protocol. In 1933, after a short stay in South Africa, they returned to Fuzhou. In 1938 they left China because of the Sino-Japanese War and retired to North Wales.*'
(British Medical Journal Volume 282, 10th January 1981)

St David's Day

The Wales China Friendship Society and the Confucius Institute at University of Wales Trinity Saint David Lampeter jointly celebrated St David's Day 1st March 2008. It was the first time that the two organizations had come together to celebrate Wales' national day.

St. David's Society (Beijing)
The Society, established in 2008, brings together the ex-pat Welsh community in Beijing and throughout China.

St. David's Society (Hong Kong)
The first recorded meeting of the St David Society was on St David's Day, March 1st, 1911.

E

East India Company
Extract of a letter from London, dated Wednesday evening last.
'For several days past, reports had been circulated respecting the capture of Saint Helena by Admiral Linois, the fact is not credited, and the report loses ground daily. At a quarter of directors held at the East India House this day, the following captains were sworn in to the command of their respective ships, namely, Captain Dixon Meadows, of the 'Baring'; Captain Jasper Sweate, of the 'Lord Eldon'; Captain Thomas Jones, of the 'Tottenham'; Captain John MackIntosh, of the 'Airy Castle'; Captain John Santer, of the 'United Kingdom', all for Madras and Bengal.
The following commanders took leave previous to the departure for China: Captain William Donaldson, of the 'Neptune', and Captain Richard Franklin of the 'Royal Charlotte'.
It is expected the fleet for Madras and Bengal, will be dispatched in the course of next week.
The Victor sloop of war arrived at Trincomalee early in June, after experiencing a very tempestuous passage from the Malabar Coast. On 28 May, she was struck by a most violent shock of lightning, which did much damage to the vessel, but fortunately no lives were lost.
Petitions represented to the House of Commons, last week, praying for leave to bring in a bill for the improvement of Swansea Harbour, and for making a canal from Swansea to Oystermouth.
The importation of grain, flour, butter and other articles of provision, into the town, has been much greater this week than for some time past.
John Symmons, Esq., High Sherriff of the County of Carmarthen, with his usual benevolence, has instructed his deputy, Thomas Lewis, Esq, of Llandeilo, to divide ten pounds indiscriminately.'
(The Cambrian: 3rd March 1804)

Ebbw Vale
(See: Miners)

Edwardes (Thomas)

'Sacred to the memory of Thomas Edwardes, second son of Admiral David Edwardes, of Rhydgorse, in the County of Carmarthen, by Ann his wife, who died on board the 'Goddard Indiaman' in China, on the 13th day of October, in the Year of Our Lord 1786, aged 23.'

Memorial to Thomas Edwardes at St. Mary's Church Llanllwch, Carmarthenshire

Edwards (Jack OBE 1918-2006)
Born in Cardiff and served in World War II. He was taken prisoner of war. He was a member of the British Legion Hong - Kong and China Branch. He fought for the rights of Hong Kong war veterans and was also dedicated to tracing Japanese war criminals.
(St. David's Society Hong Kong)

Eisteddfod (National Eisteddfod of Wales)
'The Chair for the 1933 Wrexham National Eisteddfod was the gift of the Shanghai Welsh Society at the instigation of Mr. John R. Jones, of Hong Kong, a native of Llanuwchllyn, Meirionnydd. It took four Hong Kong craftsmen, working eight hours per day, sixteen months to make the Chair. The intricate carvings depict various Chinese folk tales. The Chair was won by the late Edgar Phillips ('Trefin'). It was donated to the National Museum of Welsh Life, St. Fagan's in 1981.'
(National Museum of Wales)

Wrexham Eisteddfod Chair at the Museum of Welsh Life St Fagan's

The 1933 Wrexham National Eisteddfod Chair and Chinese craftsmen

The 1933 Wrexham National Eisteddfod Chair was the gift of the Welsh Society, Shanghai. Pictured are the Chinese craftsmen who made the chair.

Elba Tinplate Company (Swansea)
'Workers of the Elba Tinplate Company at Salisbury House, Wind Street, Swansea, sent a further donation of £23.15s.10d to British United aid to China, bringing their total contributions to £43.1s.2d.'
(From the Section 'THIRTY YEARS AGO' South Wales Evening Post, Monday, May 10th, 1976 (www.southwales-evening post.co.uk)

SS 'Emperor of China'
FOR CALCUTTA DIRECT
'The splendid new ship 'Emperor of China', 12 years A1 at Lloyd's, 700 Tons Robert Brown Commande, will sail from Liverpool on or about the first of June. This splendid ship was built expressly for the East India Trade, and has superior accommodation for passengers. For further particulars apply to Mr. W Jenkins, the owner, St. Mary Street Swansea.'
('History of the Port of Swansea by W.H. Jones – Facsimile Edition, West Glamorgan County Archives Service 1995)

Arrival at Swansea Docks
'We can imagine the suppressed excitement under which Captain Robert Brown brought in the 'Emperor of China' on a brilliant day in May, 1848, returning with cargo and passengers from Adelaide, Southern Australia.
This magnificent ship, belonging to our townsman, Mr W Jenkins, entered this harbour on Sunday afternoon, preceded by the 'Catherine Jenkins', a fine barque, the property of the same owner. The appearance of the two noble vessels, as they furrowed the deep, afforded a very pleasing spectacle, which was witnessed by at least 5000 persons. The Western pier and the promenade were crowded, and presented a very animated scene.'
(The Cambrian: 11th May 1848)

The 'Emperor of China' was painted by James Harris, the marine artist. William Henry Jones, in his book 'History of the Port of Swansea' (1922), gave an account of the last days of the 'Emperor of China'.
'She lay dismantled after a Typhoon in the China Seas, and so badly battered that a bill of £6000 was incurred for repairs in China, she was sold with her liabilities in that country.'
('History of the Port of Swansea' 1922)

Evans (Professor David)
David G. Evans studied chemistry at Jesus College, Oxford as both undergraduate and research student. Several visits to Chinese university chemistry departments in the early 1990s convinced him of China's potential for development in this area and he moved to Beijing University of Chemical Technology in 1996, where he is currently a member of the State Key Laboratory of Chemical Resource Engineering. He was awarded a 'Friendship Prize' by the State Council of the PRC in 2001 and an 'International Scientific and Technological Cooperation Award of the PRC' in 2005. He is a Fellow of the Royal Society of Chemistry. Professor Evans, through his 'Fun with Science Programme' has brought the study of Science to the children of migrant workers in Beijing as part of the non-for profit 'Migrant Children Foundation' which works with migrant communities in Beijing. Although not having lived in Wales, his grandfather came from Cwmaman, near Aberdare. The Royal Society of Chemistry and the Beijing University of Chemical Technology hosted the' Ludwig Mond Award' Symposium, March 2011 The welcome address was given by Professor Evans, Chairman of the Royal Society of Chemistry Beijing.
(See: Alfred Mond)

Evans (Elizabeth Gwendoline)
Elizabeth Evans, from Llangain, Carmarthenshire, married Dr. Alec Anthony Lee. They worked in Xi' An, China in 1919.
(Overseas Missionary Fellowship 1991)

Evans (F.W. Price)
Writes about Timothy Richard in 'A Narrative of Christian Enterprise and Statesmanship In China.'

Evans (Hywel Gwyn)
'CYFARCHION O KAIPING A BROOKLYN' (1993)
'SONS OF THE ROCK' (1996) by Hywel Gwyn Evans of Cwmllynfell -The story of Lewis Williams who left The Rock Inn, Penrhiwfawr in 1889 to work at Tong Colliery, Kaiping, Tangshan, China.

Evans (Janet née Rees)
'Janet Elizabeth Evans was the daughter of W Hopkyn Rees. She was born in Beijing in 1884, brought up in Tianjin. In 1906 appointed as a missionary to Xiaochang. In 1909 she married Robert Kenneth Evans who came from Liverpool but was brought up in Caerleon. Both of them served in Wuchang. In 1926-27 she returned to China to work after the death of her husband.'
(Overseas Missionary Fellowship 1991) (See Kenneth Evans)

From 1902 to 1905 she was Governess to the children of Yuan Shih K'ai who would become the first President of China. She also taught the children of Tong Shuo Ti who was to become the first Prime Minister of the Republic. In 1909 she married Robert Kenneth Evans-missionary and professor at Pekin University.

Janet Rees (Evans) pictured with children at a school in China

Evans (Rev. Alfred and Bessie)
Missionaries in Yunnan province in China from 1906 to 1951; they adopted a little Chinese boy, about 1922, and they called him John. In 1945-6, John went to the USA.
(Evans Family History 2001)

Evans (Rev. Robert Kenneth)
Professor at Pekin University Originally from Liverpool but was brought up in Caerleon. He left for China in 1911. Married Janet E. Rees, daughter of W. Hopkyn Rees. Both served at Wuchang, Central China (1923). Returned to Wales 1925: Robert died at Barmouth. Janet returned to China and worked in Tianjin (1926-27).
Robert Evans drowned in Barmouth on Sept. 15th 1925. He is buried at St. Mary's Church, Llanaber, near Barmouth. The inscription on his grave includes three Chinese characters 'Yī Wén Sī – the nearest sounds in Chinese to EVANS.

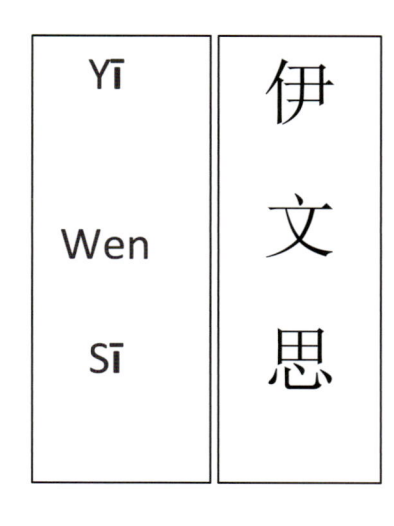

Yī Wen Sī 伊文思

The three Chinese Characters were the nearest in sound to 'Evans'

The Evans Grave at Llanaber Cemetery near Barmouth

Evans (Thomas)
Thomas Evans of Oxwich, Gower died in Tianjin China on the 6th November 1869, aged 30 years. Buried at St. Illtyd's Church Oxwich.

Headstone and inscription at St. Illtyd's Church Oxwich,

Exhibition (China)

THE MOST SPENDID EXHIBITION EVER IN WALES
THEATRE SWANSEA.
FOR SIX NIGHTS ONLY
Viz., MONDAY, TUESDAY, WEDNESDAY, THURSDAY, FRIDAY an
SATURDAY DEC. 2, 3, 4, 5, 6, and 7 1846.

'M.GOMPERTZ respectfully announces Six Performances of his
Celebrated PANORAMA THE WAR WITH CHINA!
SECTION 1: PANORAMA, painted on 4500 square feet of canvas, the largest ever exhibited out of London, illustrating, in Thirteen Views, the principal events connected with THE WAR WITH CHINA!
There is no series of panoramic Views that have ever been produced which have been witnessed with more intense interest, combined with greater satisfaction and delight than the Panoramic Views illustrating the recent War in China, which has attracted numerous and fashionable audiences in every Town it has been exhibited. In order to give additional effect, a splendid Band is engaged, and will perform between each part selections of Music from the most popular Authors.
View 1: The City of Canton View 2: Fleet of War Junks View 3: Explosion of a War Junk View 4: The Island of Hong Kong by moonlight View 5: Terrific Descent of the Burning rafts at Moonlight View 6: The Bombardment of Amoy View 7: Long Battery, Amoy View 8: Island of Ting Hae, Chusan View 9: Rice Sellers View 10: City of Ningbo and Cage with Mrs; Noble View 11: The Repulse of Ningbo View 12: The City of Nankin View 13: Porcelain Tower of Nankin.'
(The Cambrian 27th November 1846)

F

Film Festival
Wales celebrated 60 years of Chinese cinema in 2009. Organized by the Confucius Institute, University of Wales Lampeter, 1st to 31st October, 2009

Fitzwilliams (Edward Crawford Lloyd)
'Lieutenant-Colonel Fitzwilliams,CMG Royal Army Service Corps, late 71st Foot, now Welch Regiment, was born in 1872, the eldest son of Charles Home Lloyd Fitzwilliams, Cardiganshire. Col Fitzwilliams of 'Cilgwyn', Newcastle Emlyn, served in China in 1900. He died aged 64 in London.'
(Bryn Teifi, Llandyssul, Cardiganshire.) (Ceredigion County Council Biographies)
(Who's Who in Wales: 1920)

Fong Lai
'Fong Lai, born in China, was a marine artist who worked in Calcutta (Kolkata) from about 1887 to 1910. He painted the 'Riversdale', a merchantman or windjammer, 2,200 tons gross, Calcutta in 1898 was, probably, commissioned by her Captain, John Griffiths. The 'Riversdale' was built in Glasgow in 1894, for the Leyland Line by William Hamilton & Co. It is said that Captain John Griffiths, of 'Riversdale', Lampeter Road, Aberaeron, supervised her building and then took command of her for several years. She was one of the largest fully rigged ships sailing out of the Mersey. The painting was given to Aberystwyth Town Library as part of the collection of Captain T.O. Griffiths (Son of Captain John Griffiths) of 'Sunnycroft', Aberaeron in 1954. The painting of the 'Riversdale' by Lai Fong is on view at the Ceredigion Museum, Aberystwyth.'
(Carrie Canham)

'Riversdale' by Lai Fong

Fonmon Castle

Fonmon Castle is a fortified medieval castle near the village of Fonmon in the Vale of Glamorgan. Since the castle was built by the St. John family in around 1200, it has only changed hands once. Oliver St John of Fonmon was one of the Twelve Knights of Glamorgan who took part in the Norman conquest of Glamorgan. Fonmon is still a private residence and the present owner, Sir Blake Boothby, is a descendant of Colonel Philip Jones, who bought the house in 1656.

The Castle houses a collection of Chinese imperial robes and Chinese antiques collected by Admiral Oliver jones RN. (See: Admiral Oliver Jones RN)

Robes and Chinese Porcelain at Fonmon Castle

Chinese Imperial Robe with the five-clawed dragon

Chinese High Official's Ceremonial Robe with the four-clawed dragon

Chinese ornamental vase and plate

Armorial Plate with Jones Family Coat of Arms

Fordyce (Emilie)
'The death on Sunday, 6 August, 1893, at Penmaenmawr, after a few days illness, Emilie Fordyce, wife of Wyndham R. Dunstan, of 3 Percy Villas, Campden Hill, London W, and second daughter of the late George Francis MacLean, of Chefoo, China.'
(The Cambrian 11th August 1893)

Forerunner
'The 'Forerunner', from Swansea for Hong Kong, drove on-shore on reef off the Island of Sairgao* during a storm 3rd January, and broke up: Master and thirteen men lost.'
*Philippine Sea
(The Cambrian 12th April 1867)

Fort Regent
SHIPPING INTELLIGENCE
'The ship 'Fort Regent' from Swansea for Shanghai, Nov.1, 6N, 24W.'
(The Cambrian 14th December 1866)

Fossils
(See: Dr. Xiaoqiao Wan)

Francis (Simon)

Born and brought up at Onllwyn in the Dulais Valley a Chemist by profession. He has worked in the Pharmaceutical Industry (Operations) for 18 years in the areas of Quality, Supply Chain and Manufacturing and since 2002 has worked for the German Pharmaceutical Company Boehringer Ingelheim. In April 2009 he and his young family moved to China to take up the position of Vice-President of Pharmaceutical Production with Boehringer, based in Shanghai. After five years in China he returned to Germany where he is currently Head of Production at the Company's Headquarters in Ingelheim. Mr Francis has a vast knowledge of living and working in China and has a great empathy with the Chinese people.

Fraser (Douglas)

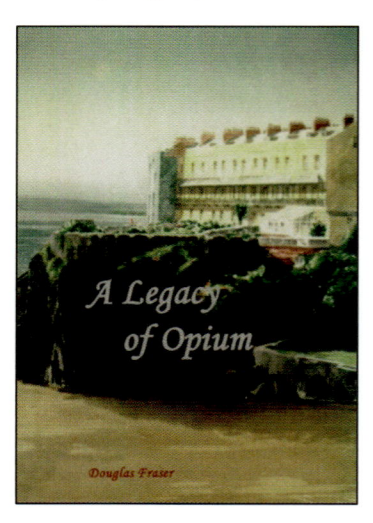

Douglas Fraser and his wife, Elizabeth, moved to Tenby and bought a house in Lexden Terrace which is in a beautiful position overlooking the bay. He began researching the history of his house only to discover it had a past history of piracy, smuggling and the opium trade in the South China Sea.
His book, 'A Legacy of Opium', published by Tenby Heritage Publications, in 2010, tells the story of how three brothers, George, Thomas and John Rees, from Tenby became opium traders in China, and their legacy.
'All the Tea in China'- an article by Douglas Fraser, in two parts, was published in Pembrokeshire Life in 2009.

(See: George, Thomas and John Rees)

Fund (China Relief)
'CHINA FAMINE RELIEF FUND
TO THE EDITOR OF 'THE CAMBRIAN'
'Sir, --- Three weeks ago you were good enough to insert an appeal in the Cambrian for this fund. Will you permit me now to acknowledge, through you, the result.I have received the sum of ONE POUND, THREE SHILLINGS -------- five shillings only of which came from Swansea proper. I trust others have sent their contributions direct. In addition to this, the Rev Mr Milland, Port Eynon, kindly made a collection of four guineas, which I have forwarded to the Rev Arnold Foster, as a separate collection.
Yours truly,
Samuel B. Power
Lismore House, Swansea May 30, 1878'   (The Cambrian 31st May 1878)

Funeral
CHINESE FUNERAL AT CARDIFF
Remarkable Scene at the Graveside
Quaint Ceremonies and Customs.
'There could hardly be a stranger funeral than one at the Cardiff Cemetery on Tuesday. It was half Christian and half Chinese, and showed again how different is east from west. The funeral was that of Ah Pow, a Chinese seaman, who was taken to the workhouse on Thursday from a lodging-house in Patrick Street. He was then in a dying state from pneumonia and expired not long after his admission. The funeral procession left the workhouse soon after twelve. The coffin was conveyed in an ordinary hearse, and was followed in mourning coaches by about a dozen Chinamen, the lodging-house keeper and other compatriots.
Chinamen frequently conduct their funerals without the assistance of priests or ministers, and these had made no arrangements for a clergyman. When they got to the cemetery, however, they suddenly decided they must have one, and although the dead man was said to be Roman Catholic they sent for the Rev, Caradoc Griffiths, a Baptist Minister, he being the nearest. He came in a few minutes in a cab. Meanwhile the Chinese and the undertaker`s men waited in the driving wind and rain by the open grave. In the soft mound by the side a black piece of wood, with Chinese characters in red, had been planted. Mr. Griffiths went through the Burial Service briefly, and then the Chinamen took charge of affairs.
They had their own ideas of how the ceremony should finish, and, with these in view, dragged a big hamper to the graveside. One Chinaman, a short little man, with a fat, chubby face, solemnly opened it. First, he produced three small bowls of rice, which he put carefully on the ground. Then, strangest of all, appeared a bottle of Buchanan`s Scotch whisky! After the spirit came a plate of oranges, a plate of apples, a plate of chocolates, and other sweets and, finally, an emaciated boiled fowl, and a lump of boiled bacon. It next seemed necessary to light a fire. For this numerous sheets of coloured tissue paper were produced, and beneath the shelter of two umbrellas the Chinamen tried to set it alight. They had a struggle, and one who caught a spark on his cheek said something much like an expletive, though, of course, it may have been a Chinese prayer. When the paper was fairly blazing and being blown about the cemetery, the ceremony ended. One Chinaman threw the rice on the coffin and around the edges of the grave. The oranges, sweets and apples, and, at last, the boiled fowl and bacon, quickly disappeared into the grave, and while the Chinamen walked to the coaches, the gravediggers began to cover up everything with clean fresh earth,'
(Western Mail Wednesday 2nd January 1907)

G

Garden Festival
The National Garden Festival (Wales) held in 1992 at Ebbw Vale, hosted guests of the Wales China Friendship Society, from the Chinese Embassy, London and The Chinese People's Association for Friendship with Foreign Countries (CPAFFC), Beijing.

Garnier (Albert J.)
'A Maker of Modern China' (Pub: London, Carey Press, 1945); The story of Timothy Richard a missionary to China.

Genghis Khan
(See: Marco Polo)

Gibbard (Noel)
Author: 'Griffith John – Apostle to Central China' (Bryntirion Press 1998)

Gladstone (William)
Prime Minister William Gladstone invited Chinese statesman Li Hongzhang to Hawarden Castle, Flintshire in August 1896.
(See: Li Hongzhang)

Glamorgan University
The South Wales and Monmouthshire School of Mines at Treforest opened in October 1913 with 17 diploma students, three from China. The University merged with the University of Wales, Newport in April 2013 to form the University of South Wales.

Glamorganshire Rifle Association
'The 15th annual general meeting of the Association was held at the Town Hall, Neath on Friday last………
The Committee desired to call attention to the very handsome manner in which the Ladies of the County have come forward with a subscription to defray the expenses of a team to compete at the next meeting of the National Rifle Association for the China Cup.'
(The Cambrian 12th May 1876)

Glory Church
The Church, originally named the Griffith John Church, was built to commemorate the centenary of the birth of the Rev. Dr. Griffith John in 1831. It was damaged during the Japanese invasion. After the Second World War, it was repaired with donations from church members. In 1951, it was renamed the Glory Church. It had to close during the Cultural Revolution, but, in 1980, it opened its doors again to the people of Wuhan.

The Glory Church was the first reopened Protestant church in the province of Hubei and is now recognised as having 'Outstanding Historic Architecture'. Currently, over 1500 people attend the church for worship on Sunday.
(See: Wuhan; Griffith John)

Interior of the Glory Church, Wuhan

Gogerddan
(See: Lewis Pryce)

Gordon (General Charles George CB)

Charles George Gordon, CB (28 January 1833 – 26 January 1885), also known as 'Chinese Gordon', Gordon Pasha, and Gordon of Khartoum, was a British army officer and administrator. He saw action in the Crimean War as an officer in the British Army, but he made his military reputation in China, where he was placed in command of the "Ever Victorious Army," a force of Chinese soldiers led by European officers. In the early 1860s, Gordon and his men were instrumental in putting down the Taiping Rebellion, regularly defeating much larger forces. For these accomplishments, he was given the nickname "Chinese" Gordon and honours from both the Emperor of China and the British. Gordon of Khartoum served as a young lieutenant in the Royal Engineers with the East Surrey's at Pembroke Dock. Later in his career was looked after by Frank Morgan of Bishopston. The Photograph shows Gordon dressed in Chinese robes.

At Pembroke Dock – 'As an officer he was privileged to live 'out' while at Pembroke Dock and he lodged in a house at the top of Lewis Street.

He was a man who kept to himself and was not altogether popular with his fellow officers. Many, who will have watched the Regiment depart Pembroke Dock that cold, grey morning, had frequently seen him walking to and fro at the foot of the Barracks Hill studying a book.' ('A Short History of Pembroke Dock in Words and Pictures.' 1987) ('Gordon's Farewell to the Garrison Town' by Vernon Scott p.38)

Reference: 'The Story of Chinese Gordon' by A. Egmont Hake 1884 (Pub: London, Remington and Company, 1885 (See also: Frank Morgan)

Gorseinon College
'Gorseinon Tertiary College, Swansea held the first of its kind course on China. The course was designed and organized by the Wales-China Friendship Society Secretary Ena Niedergang.
The First Secretary of the Chinese Embassy, Cultural Department, Mr Su Zhimen awarded certificates to the students at the end of the Course.'
(South Wales Evening Post, September 16th, 1987 www.southwales-eveningpost.co.uk)

Certificate of Participation at Gorseinon College (1987)

A student visits the China Exhibition at Gorseinon College (1987)

Study of China - First in Wales
'THE CHINESE WON'T seem so inscrutable to those who take part in a 10 week course at Gorseinon Tertiary College.
'China-A Study', is the first ever of its kind in Wales and is designed to give students at the evening classes a glimpse of the history culture and pastimes of a fascinating people. The course has been designed by Mrs Ena Niedergang, of Pontardawe the Secretary of the Wales China Friendship Society.
Each week a different aspect of Chinese life or culture will be examined by visiting lecturers, including calligraphy and Tai Chi. Sitting in on the classes will be members of the Yellow River Society. They are Chinese students living in Swansea, who are looking forward to 'opening up' windows on their native country. Certificates will be presented at the end of the course and Mrs Niedergang hopes they will be handed over by representatives of the Chinese Embassy and the Hong Kong Government.
In October the Shanghai Theatre visits Swansea's Grand Theatre giving Jacks and Jills another opportunity to view Chinese art.
The course begins on September 30 and enrolment takes place on September 23 when a small exhibition on China will be set up in the main College entrance. Fees for the 10 week course £12 but those in receipt of benefits join free of charge.'
(South Wales Evening Post, Wednesday, September 16, 1987 www.southwales-eveningpost.co.uk)

Gower (Sir Erasmus William - Admiral RN, 1742-1814)

'Born at 'Glandovan' in Cilgerran. A Naval officer and Colonial Governor, he was knighted in 1792. Gower was named Commander of the British Expedition to the Chinese Imperial Court and sailed in the 64-gun HMS Lion to convey HM Ambassador, Lord George Macartney to China. He was made Admiral in 1809. The Gower family eventually moved from 'Glandovan' to Clunderwen, Pembrokeshire. He died at Hambledon, Portsmouth, 21st June 1814, 'in his seventy-second year. '(The Dictionary of Welsh Biography Down to 1940 p.285, 1959)

References
Burke's Landed Gentry (1952 – Extracts)
P.1034 'Erasmus William Gower, of 'Glandovan', Cilgerran. Father, Abel Gower, had 9 sons and 8 daughters. Promoted to Vice-Admiral of the White in 1804. After his death, succeeded by his brother Abel Anthony. There is a memorial to Sir Erasmus Gower at St Llawddog's Church in Cilgerran.'
(1792-1801, journal, letter book and notebook at National Maritime Museum)
(1792-1794, journal of voyage to China at British Library, Manuscripts and Collections.)

SACRED TO THE MEMORY

OF

SIR ERASMUS GOWER

ADMIRAL OF THE WHITE

INTERRED IN THE CHURCH OF

HAMBLEDON IN HAMPSHIRE

HE WAS CONSISTENT AND

AFFECTIONATE IN COMMAND

PROMPT INDEFATIGABLE AND BRAVE

AND PATRON OF MERIT UNBIASED

BY FAVOUR OR CONNECTION IN SOCIETY,

FRIENDLY PLACID CONCILIATING AND FIRM

UNDER LONG AND SEVERE AFFLICTION

HE DIED RESPECTED BY HIS FRIENDS

AND LAMENTED BY THE POOR

IN THE 72ND YEAR OF HIS AGE

AND THE 58TH OF HIS PUBLIC SERVICE

JUNE 26TH 1814

Preparations for the Embassy
'Every branch of the sea service Captain, now Sir Erasmus Gower, was known to be fully equal………….. he had, twice, at an early age, been round the world.
At Lord Macartney's desire, he was appointed to the command of the 'LION' man-of-war, and gratified with the choice of his own officers, whom he selected from a personal knowledge of their merit.'
'The Authentic Account of an Embassy from the King of Great Britain to the Emperor of China.' P. 34. By Sir George Staunton, Baronet (1797). Printed by W. Bulmer and Company, for Nicol, Bookseller to His Majesty, Pall Mall.
(Thomas Phillips Collection - The Roderic Bowen Library and Archives, University of Wales Trinity Saint David's Lampeter.)

Memorial to Admiral Sir Erasmus Gower at St. Llawddog's Church, Cilgerran.

Graham (Angus Charles 1919 – 1991)
'Professor of Classical Chinese at the School of Oriental and African Studies (SOAS), University of London, was a noted sinologist. He was born in Penarth, to Charles Harold and Mabelle Graham, the elder of two children. His father was originally a coal merchant who moved to Malaya to start a rubber plantation, and died in 1928 of malaria. Graham attended Ellesmere College, Shropshire, 1932–1937, and went on to read Theology at Corpus Christi College, Oxford (graduating in 1940), and Chinese at the School of Oriental and African Studies, University of London (graduating in 1949). In 1950 he was appointed Lecturer in Classical Chinese at SOAS, promoted to Professor in 1971, and to Professor Emeritus after his retirement in 1984.

He also held visiting positions at Hong Kong University, Yale, the University of Michigan, the Society of Humanities at Cornell, the Institute of East Asian Philosophies in Singapore, Tsing Hua University in Taiwan, Brown University, and the University of Hawaii. He was elected a Fellow of the British Academy in 1981.'
(Timothy Richard Centre for Cultural Communication)

Grand Theatre (Swansea)
CULTURE AND THE ARTS AND SCIENCE, BUILDINGS, THEATRES
'George Dance's Company present the musical comedy, 'A Chinese Honeymoon' at the Grand Theatre, Swansea.'
(The Cambrian 22nd September 1903)

Chinese performances and events that have taken place at the Grand include the 'Shanghai Kunju Theatre (17th October 1987), Photographic Exhibitions from China and Welsh schoolchildren's Chinese artwork. Cirque du Ciel 'Shang Hi' (2012)
(See: Shanghai Kunju Theatre)

Griffiths (Griffith)
'Born Gwynfe, Carmarthenshire, 1854. Appointed to Shanghai in 1881 where he served until 1882, prior to working as a Missionary with the American Missionary Society.' (Overseas Missionary Fellowship 1991) 'No one really knew his story. It was discovered in the archives of the London Missionary Society at the University of London and the kindness of the Minister, 'Deri Bach',Capel Maen, and Tabernacle.
Griffith Griffiths was born at Deri Bach of humble parents when this church was but two years old. His family worshipped here from about 1867 to 68 under William Thomas. He accepted Jesus Christ as his Saviour and Lord. He gave his vows of faithfulness to go where the Lord would send him and do what the Lord told him to do. After 2 to 3 years of education, the norm in those days, at least for humble people, he was appointed to a cord -winder in Llandeilo. But he didn't leave his God although he left Capel Maen. He worshipped at Tabernacle and so faithful and serious was he that his minister asked him to go and preach in chapels. He felt the call from on high to go in the name of the Lord God. He went back to school at the age of 20 when most going to school were far younger than him. At the age of 22, he wrote to the London Missionary Society and said "I think God wants me to go further afield to carry the Word to those places where the fields are white under the harvest and the harvesters are few." He said, "I do not have much education, five or six years, and I have studied algebra, Euclid's geometry, physics, chemistry, natural philosophy, literature, history and now I have learnt English, German, Latin, Greek and Hebrew." They said to go to the Brecon Congregational College and when you have finished there go to Plymouth to the Congregational College. And so he did. Then returned, was ordained and both commissioned and set sail for Shanghai, China.

He was in love with a young lady from Plymouth, but Miss Harding was not yet sent to China with him. Their marriage, apparently, was postponed. She waited and waited and waited for her orders to go, but her orders did not come. The young unselfish young man, from Deri Bach, wrote to the Board. I saw this letter in his own hand to the University of London, said, "Please send Miss Harding quickly. The boat on which you sent me was slow the seas were perilous and we nearly lost our lives in the Indian Ocean.

We were delayed a month in Burma. Please send her by the fast P.O. package boat and I will pay the difference in cost myself."

He was in China learning the customs of the Chinese people. He started learning the language so he could speak in Chinese to Chinese amongst whom he would minister in that church, in that school and in the medical work which was carried out in the name of Jesus Christ.

He was summoned, one day, before the elder missionaries and they said, "We notice that you have been seeing a good deal of a Chinese lady, Miss Ling, who works at our Mission. What is your relationship with Miss Ling?" It was more than a question it was an accusation. Griffith said "I am friendly with Miss Ling." Then came the next question, which you, who are young and even, we, who once were young, can understand............. "How friendly is friendly?" Clearly whatever his relationship with Miss Ling, he had lost the confidence of those amongst whom he worked. He was asked to resign after less than a year in China. He submitted his resignation.......... pathetic letter, yet a letter which preceded something which was in the inner core of one who was later to do such great things.

He said "I resign all hope and all intention of ever again taking any public part in Christian work. But God helping me, I am more determined than ever to do all in my power in a quiet way for the advancement of the work for which God has so early directed my thoughts. He gave up all hope of remaining a missionary or a practicing minister, but, in his own way he committed still to be an ambassador for Jesus Christ. He came back to the United Kingdom.

The year of his life that follows is yet a closed book which someday may be opened for us. The next we know comes from the records of the churches of California where he sailed into San Francisco harbour in December 1883. He was met by one Dr Warren, who would be like the General Secretary of the churches of California and said "I am an ordained independent minister. Can you use me?" Dr Warren said. "There are seven people 400 miles away from here in a county town with no church. Last summer they wanted to become a Church and a minister went and met with them. In prayer they formed themselves into the first Congregational Church of Alturas, California. They met in a home. Six weeks later their minister died. They have been five months without a minister, no church building and no leadership. I can find no one who will go that far away to serve them." Griffith Griffiths said, "Though I am one of unclean lips, I will go."

He and Miss Harding were married on Christmas Eve and spent Christmas Day in San Francisco. On Boxing Day they boarded the stagecoach for a 400-mile journey to a remote small place on the frontier of California where the deserts of Nevada and the plateau County of Origon come together with California to form that little outpost of civilisation. There he was greeted by the people and remained as their minister for six long years. A tenure which was unequalled until I went to serve that same church 70 years later.

In that place, where there was no church, the Permission Board had promised to loan some money so that the building could be built. So he signed a contract with the builders and built a church, but the money did not come. The builders would not let them use the church. They continued to worship at the manse. In America, you pay rates on the manse and the church didn't have enough money to pay rates on the manse. So out of the tiny stipend that Rev Griffiths received, he paid the rates on the church manse where they were worshipping. The church was finally opened and they worshipped there.'

All about them were American Indian people. They were treated very badly in those days, and are still treated very badly in much of that county.

Most of them could not speak the English language nor could they understand the Gospel of Jesus Christ for there was no one to speak of Christ in their language. So the man who had learnt so many languages, including Chinese, now learned American-Indian. He preached to those people in their own tongue and started a school where the Indian lads could learn English as well. They could have the kind of education which would allow them to become full citizens in that country. He was concerned about alcoholism and drinking. So founded the Temperance Society.

When not as many came to the church to hear the Word as ought to, he began being a writer for the newspaper that his influence might find a wider audience in the community. Also, knowing that many of the major decisions in life are made through government, he became active in politics.

After some years he was called across the state of California to where the great redwood forests meet the ocean. There was a church which had been a fine church, but there had been a controversy. The church had been split apart and half formed another church. Debts were huge and spirits were low. For 13 years he served as a minister at that church in Eureka. When he left, this man, who had been described by the Editor of the Alturas paper as 'the hardest working and poorest paid man in town' left with the accolade of the Eureka people that he had paid off the debt and healed the wounds of the church and left behind him a solid legacy.

Then, would you believe it, he went to San Francisco, where he began, to serve among the Chinese people. He thought he was going to serve in China but he went back around the world the other way. In San Francisco he met Chinese who sailed east. There, in the Chinese Congregational Church of that great city, he served those people in the name of Jesus Christ.

One of those sons born in Alturas, growing up in Eureka returned to the United Kingdom as a Rhodes Scholar, studying at Oxford University and becoming a solicitor. The grandson of that man has just retired as a Professor of History at the University of Washington, Seattle. What a legacy growing out of a person worshipped here in these pews and took his oath here.'

(From a sermon by the Rev. Carl Olsen on his visit to Gwynfe. Taken from the recording on a cassette of the sermon.)

Griffith Griffith's house, Capel Gwynfe

Mrs M.H. Jones, Ty Gwyn, Capel Gwynfe, Nr Llandeilo. Saturday, 11th November 1995.
From the book: 'HANES Y TABERNACLE, LLANDEILO' gan W.T. Gruffydd (1951)
P32. Y GENHADAETH DRAMOR
Ymysg y teuliau am y flwyddyn honno gwelwn I Griffith Griffiths gael anrheg o £8.7.61/2. Tailwyd hefyd dreuliau ei urddiad, £15.10.6d. Aeth I China, ac yn ddiwddarach I America .... presentation of £8.7.61/2 and for his ordination £15. 10.6d

Griffiths (Captain John)
(See: Lai Fong)

Griffiths (Keith, RIBA, FHKIA b. 1954)

Architect who founded Aedas (www.aedas.com) one of the largest global architecture and design practices. Keith Griffiths was born in Merthyr Tydfil, but brought up in St. Davids where he attended Ysgol Dewi Sant. He read architecture at St John's College, University of Cambridge where he received a Masters in Architecture in 1976 and a Diploma in Architecture in 1979. Since 1985 and for most of his career he has resided in Hong Kong. He was a member of the design team for the new Hong Kong and Shanghai Bank headquarters (HSBC) in Hong Kong. In conjunction with Anthony Hackett he set up Hackett and Griffiths in Hong Kong. Their first commission was the new Royal Hong Kong Yacht Club sailing Centre at Middle Island. Among the more recent buildings designed by Aedas in China include: *'Hengqin International Financial Centre'*, *'Zuhai Fortune Plaza Phase 1, Beijing'*, and *'The Heart of Yiwu - An Urban Living Plaza, Yiwu'*.

He was Chairman of the Asian Youth Orchestra from 2010–2013 and is a Director of the City Chamber Orchestra of Hong Kong.

His personal commitment to the City of St. Davids and the County of Pembrokeshire continues through his work with the 'Griffiths Roch Foundation' and 'Retreats Group Ltd' through which he has purchased and restored three significant historical buildings in the St. Davids peninsula as 5 star hotels. (rochcastle.com, penrhiwhotel.com, twryfelinhotel.com)

In 2012, he was awarded an Honorary Fellowship of the University of Wales, Trinity Saint David in recognition of his contribution in restoring important historic buildings in Wales as exclusive five star hotels and retreats. In 2014, he was made an Honorary Fellow of Cardiff University.

Griffiths (Captain William)
'Captain William, Milford Haven, died 1944'
(Dyfed FHS Journals 4.6, 223)

The following letter to the Author from Mr David Saunders of Milford Haven regarding Captain Griffith's house name – 'Woosung' at Milford Haven

'Dear Mrs Niedergang
Thank you for your letter about the name of the house.
When we moved here some seven years ago it was called the 'White House,' and previously 'Ivy Nook'. The ivy on the garden walls may be appropriate, the nook certainly not, for it stands in a very prominent position on the waterfront here.
A dear friend of ours in the local maritime history society, who as a boy can vaguely remember the first owner, a Captain William Griffiths who died in 1944, said that the house then had a Chinese name. At first we didn't believe him as he was always a great storyteller. However my wife made some enquiries in the Haverfordwest Record Office and found a small file of papers relating to Captain Griffiths, and, yes, the house, from 1910 when it was built, was called Woosung.
I have subsequently carried out a great deal of research into the career of Captain Griffiths. In brief he first went to sea in 1877 sailing from Cardiff in the 'Malabar' for Rio de Janeiro and then to the Guano Islands off Chile. He rose steadily, taking his first command, as Captain of the 'Cumbrian' in 1895. He only served in sailing ships and his longest command was as Captain of the 'Galgate' of Liverpool, in which he sailed from 1898 to 1916 when she was sunk as a result of submarine attack. He then served as Captain of the 'Neath' but she was sunk by a German submarine the following year and on that occasion Captain Griffiths was taken prisoner. After the war he lived in retirement at Woosung, with Mrs Griffiths.

His first two voyages on the 'Galgate' were to Shanghai; these were the only occasions that he visited China. There seemed to be two local stories as to the house name.

One says that after encountering a tremendous storm in the China Sea, on reaching Woosung Mrs Griffith said that when they retired from the sea they would call their house Woosung, because it means peaceful haven or something similar. Mrs Griffith sailed as a stewardess on a number of voyages.

The other is that Captain Griffiths made his fortune as a result of his two voyages to China. Certainly he seems to have been a wealthy person owning at one time some property in British Columbia as well as here in Milford Haven. However I prefer the first story. I hope that all this is of interest, pray let me know whether you need more information. Perhaps you can tell me more about Woosung and its meaning?

Good wishes with your research

Yours sincerely

David Saunders' (16th December 1993)'

Grove (William)

'A SWANSEA YOUTH DROWNED' - We have received an extract from a private letter from Captain Cathiss, of the ship Empress of China, Aangoon, India November 23, 1872, in which he conveys the melancholy intelligence of the death of one of his apprentices, named William Grove, son of Captain Grove, of Russell Street, in the town, a gentleman well known and highly respected. When Captain Grove last arrived home he received the sad tidings of the death of his wife, now he has to learn the distressing fact that his son has been suddenly taken away. We are sure that he will receive the sympathy of his numerous friends under these distressing bereavements. The following is the extract:-

"I am very sorry to have to inform you of the death of William Grove, apprentice, by drowning at 5 o'clock last night.

He and one of the able seamen were tarring the bends, when Grove slipped off the stage into the water. The mate and one man got into the boat in less than a minute; they picked his hat up close to the ship, but the poor boy never rose.

Will you kindly inform his friends of the sad news, as I am not aware of their address. Captain Wright is well acquainted with his father Captain Grove of Swansea. I will bring his effects home with me. I am truly sorry for his death, as he was a promising boy. Owing to the heavy under current in the river bodies never rise to the surface.'

(The Cambrian January 10th, 1873)

Guangzhou (COSCO)

The arrival of the 'Ping Chuan' (owned by the China Ocean Shipping Company COSCO) to Swansea in 1987 was the first Chinese ship to have berthed at the Port for 40 years. Members of the Wales-China Friendship Society visited the ship to make a presentation to the Captain and crew.

Presentation to the Captain (centre right) of the 'Ping Chuan'

Guo Brothers

Guo Yue and Guo Yi with the help of their sister Yan formed one of China's famous folk musical ensembles in the 1980s and went on to record their music and work on film soundtracks. Since then, they have performed at various venues and festivals throughout Wales, including the Sherman Theatre Cardiff and the Pontardawe International Folk Festival.

Gwynne (Major J.H.)
'Major Gwynne of Llanddetty, Brecon commanded the 2nd Battalion, Royal Welch Fusiliers and took part in the Relief of Pekin. He was promoted to Brevet Major.'
(The London Gazette 25th July 1901)
'Regarding the capture of the native quarter of Tianjin, 13th-14th July, 1900' Brigadier-General (JG Dorward) in his dispatch stated that the Royal Welch Fusiliers were well handled throughout the day by Captain Gwynne, and "that they wasted less ammunition than any other body of troops on the ground." Page 254 'A history of the Royal Welch Fusiliers' by Howell Thomas (1916). 'Major Gwynne and a Pekinese dog' Chapter 5-'Points and Pearls' (p. 143) 'A Glanbrane Boxer was given to Major J.H. Gwynne of the 23rd Welsh Fusiliers by Prince Ch'ing in return for special services during the chaos of the Boxer Rebellion in Peking. Prince Ch'ing was a high official of the Imperial Court, so these two – there was a bitch as well – were indesputedly palace dogs.'
('The Butterfly Lions......... The Pekingnese History, Legend and Art.' By Rummer Godden.

There is a brass plaque (pictured) and memorial inside the St Tetti's Church at Llanddetty in memory of Major Gwynn and family.

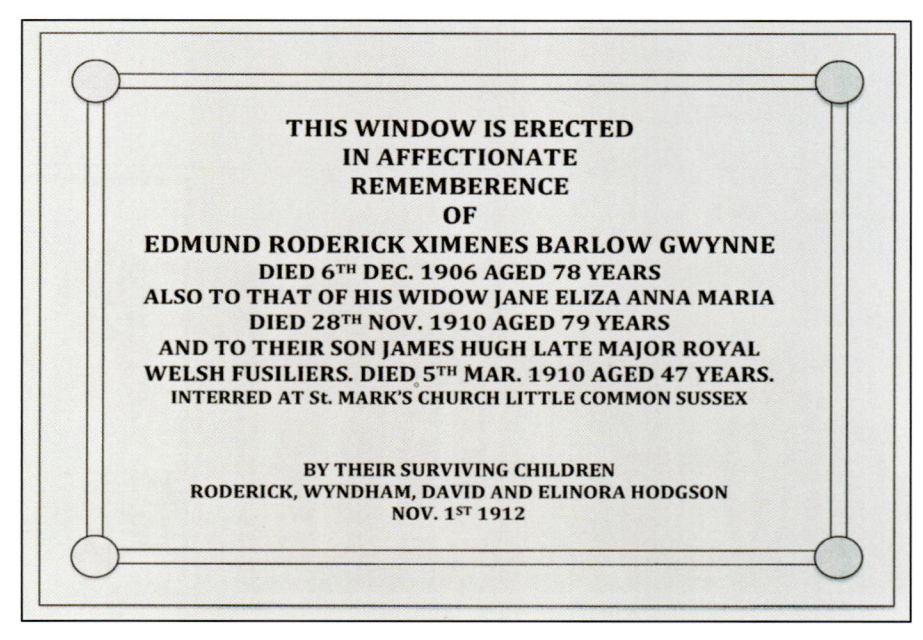

**THIS WINDOW IS ERECTED
IN AFFECTIONATE
REMEMBERENCE
OF
EDMUND RODERICK XIMENES BARLOW GWYNNE
DIED 6TH DEC. 1906 AGED 78 YEARS
ALSO TO THAT OF HIS WIDOW JANE ELIZA ANNA MARIA
DIED 28TH NOV. 1910 AGED 79 YEARS
AND TO THEIR SON JAMES HUGH LATE MAJOR ROYAL
WELSH FUSILIERS. DIED 5TH MAR. 1910 AGED 47 YEARS.
INTERRED AT St. MARK'S CHURCH LITTLE COMMON SUSSEX**

**BY THEIR SURVIVING CHILDREN
RODERICK, WYNDHAM, DAVID AND ELINORA HODGSON
NOV. 1ST 1912**

Memorial Plaque at St.Tetti's Church Llanthetty to Major Gwynne and Family

H

Harding (John Reginald 1858-1921)

The son of John Taylor and Patricia (née Rolls) Harding of 'The Hendre', near Monmouth.

'Engineer spent nearly 30 years in China and established a reputation as a designer and builder of lighthouses on the Chinese and Taiwanese coasts. He designed the Royal Palace in Seoul for the Emperor of Korea, who, as did also, the Emperor of China, conferred decorations upon him. He assisted in Shanghai during the Boxer Revolution.'
(Who's Who in Wales – 1920)

John Harding married Elizabeth Margaret Saunders (daughter of Captain John Saunders of Fuzhou, China) and had five children.

One of J.R. Harding's lighthouses situated around the coast of China.

Decorations and Orders conferred on J.R. Harding by Korea and China.

The Royal Palace Seoul designed by J.R. Harding

Book Plate

Harries (Thomas)
Born 18th September 1883, he was the nephew of Noah Williams* who encouraged him to study and to go to university. His mother, Ann (1859-1931), was Noah's elder sister. Tom left school at the age of fourteen and worked at his father's small mine, 'The Gover', in Cwmllynfell. He graduated from the University of South Wales and Monmouthshire, Cardiff in Mechanical Engineering (Applied Science) and, in 1910, in Mining and Mine Surveying. He obtained a position with the 'Peking Mining Syndicate' in Henan Province, Northern China.
(Dr. Peter Harries)
(* See Noah Williams)

Tom Harries in Henan, circa unknown

Harries' garden in Henan, circa unknown

Harris (David)

REVIVAL OF RELIGION IN CHINA
TO THE EDITOR OF THE CAMBRIAN

Sir,
The friends of missions will be pleased to see the following letter from the Rev. G. John, of Hankow, which was printed in one of the Chinese papers and received by his relatives and myself in Swansea.
Some of your readers will remember Mr. John at Swansea (His native town) some three or four years ago, and call to remembrance his able address at the Music Hall on behalf of the Missions to China during the session of the Congregational Union in the Autumn of 1873.
Yours respectfully,
DAVID HARRIS
Swansea, Dec 8th, 1875
The following is an extract:
'We are having wonderful meetings these days. Talk about the apathy of the Chinese. Why here are Chinese sobbing all at once in the Chapel while confessing their sins and praying for the outpouring of God's spirit upon themselves individually, and upon the Churches, upon their friends, their families, etc. Mrs …… says she never expected to see such a sight among the Chinese; and Mr….., of the Inland Mission, says that he never saw a sight in his life. I never did in China. And it was on Saturday last I was enabled to believe, for the first time in my life, that such a baptism was possible.'
(The Cambrian 10th December 1875)

Harris (James)

James Harris, marine artist, was commissioned by many ship-owners to paint their vessels. William Jenkins, of Swansea, was one such owner. James Harris painted, among others, the 'Rajah of Sarwarak' and 'Emperor of China'; both were involved in the China trade. His grave is at Reynoldston Church, Gower

'At this time the harbour had become adapted for vessels of more ample proportions, and amongst the ship sailing from the Port was the 'Chelydra' of 500 tons burthen, owned by Mr James Meager, built in 1838 at Newport for smuggling opium in China, and fitted for passengers. James Harris, senior, a Swansea artist, went on a voyage around the Horn in this ship, with a commission from Mr C.R.M. Talbot, to paint marine pictures whilst at sea, and he often told of his adventures and experiences.'
'History of the Port of Swansea' By W. H. Jones (Facsimile Edition) 1995
('Shipping and Shipbuilding of the Port' p.281) (Exhibition at Glynn Vivian Art Gallery, Swansea - 'Under Sail') (Photo: James Harris' grave at Reynoldston Church, Gower.)

Harris (John)
Lovespoon artist, created a Chinese and Welsh Dragon Lovespoon commissioned for the first non-Chinese Dragon Exhibition held at the British Consulate General in Shanghai (1988).
(See: Lovespoon)

Hay-Williams
Lady Sarah Hay-Williams (née Pitt Amherst) 1801-1876 married Sir John Hay-Williams in 1842 and lived at Plas Rhianfa (now re-named Chateau Plas Rhianfa), Beaumaris Anglesey. She was the daughter of William Pitt Amherst, 1st Lord Amherst, who was appointed Ambassador Extraordinary to China and led the second embassy in 1816 to establish commercial relations between the two countries.

On the return voyage, Lord Amherst's ship, the 'Alceste' was wrecked in the Gaspar Strait. The Ambassador and his embassy were rescued.
(See: Captain Henry Davidson)

'Hendrina'
'HONG KONG`.... NOV.14: The Dutch barque Hendrina arrived in Harbour, Oct 29, from Swansea, after a tedious passage of 148 days. Reports experiencing a typhoon on the 18th and a hard gale the two following days. It commenced from the N.W., and finally finished at S.E., but since had light southerly airs till within a short distance of Lema, from which having to beat up has detained her nearly a week. During the gale, and when, hove to, the greater part of her bulwarks and moveable commodities on deck were washed away; stanchions, cathead etc. were more or less materially injured; but although the ship laboured heavily, she made little or no water. One main topsail was blown into ribbons. Barometer at lowest 29.9, showing that by her heaving to on the first approach she had escaped the severest part the hurricane. When about half-way between Christmas Island and Java, an able seaman fell overboard from the forehelms, and the poor fellow instantly sank.'
(The Cambrian 6th January 1860

Hensol
Hensol House, Glamorgan (later Castle) home of Charles Talbot (1685-1737),
1st Baron Talbot of Hensol .
(See: Talbot)

Hickey (Frederick Captain RN)
'The following Memoir of the late Captain Hickey, we copy from the GENTLEMAN'S MAGAZINE for the present month; and which, from the gallant and much-lamented Officer`s long residence in our neighbourhood and the esteem in which he was generally held cannot fail to prove interesting to any of our readers:
'May 18. At Bath, aged 64, Frederick Hickey, Esq., Post-Captain, R.N
'He was born on the 23rd August 1775, and entered the Navy in 1787 as Midshipman, on board the 'PORCUPINE', in which he served under Captains L. Brabazon and G.Martin, on the Irish and Scottish stations, until 1792, when he was removed to the 'LION', commanded by Sir Erasmus Gower, and then setting out to take Lord Macartney to China. On his return from the memorable voyage he was promoted to the rank of Lieutenant.'
(Extract from Cambrian, 29th August 1840)
(Mathews `s Swansea Directory 1830: Captain F.R.N Hickey, Park Wern)
(See: Erasmus Gower)

Hill (David)
A SWANSEA MAN
'Number 8684 Private David Hill of the Plymouth Battalion of the Royal Marine Light Infantry served as a legation guard at Pekin and survived the siege.
On August 17, 1900 he wrote to his parents that: "it was a matter of impossibility for me to write on paper what we have really been through.
When the Chinese try to rush the Legations we have to go outside and drive them away. It has been what I may say a proper hand-to-hand fight right the way through, and when even we had to go outside the legation they used to ask for volunteers.'
(Source: John Griffiths)
('The siege of Peking' by Peter Fleming 1939)

Hillier (Raymond)
Gunner Raymond Hillier of Emrock Street, Goitre Port Talbot was aboard 'HMS Black Swan' when she attempted to rescue 'HMS Amethyst' on the Yangtze River, April 1949, in what was to become known as the Yangtze Incident.
('Gripped by dash to Freedom by Jill Forward in 'The Way We Were' Series)
(The South Wales Evening Post April 23rd, 1996 www.southwales-eveningpost.co.uk)

Hinton (Wilfred John M.A. (Wales)
'Wilfred Hinton (7th November 1887 – 20th June 1949) was educated at Howard Gardens School in Cardiff, the University of Wales and Jesus College, Oxford. In 1912, he was appointed the registrar of the University of Hong Kong, remaining there until 1929 and becoming Professor of Political Economy, Dean and a member of the Court and Council; published numerous articles. In 1929, Hinton was appointed Director of Studies for the Institute of Bankers, having developed a reputation as an economist and expert in international affairs of the Far East. Hong Kong Defence Corps from Nov, 1914.'
(Who's Who in Wales)

Holtam (Sidney Harry)
'Sidney Harry Holtam, died 8th July, 1943. Aged 43 years. Son of Sydney Harry Holtam of Tonyrefail. Husband of Galina Holtam of 65 Great West Road, Shanghai. Died at Shanghai Isolation Hospital. His police force protected Shanghai's International Settlement, which remained neutral until 1941 and was officially handed over by Britain and the USA to China in early 1943, although the City remained under Japanese control. Tonyrefail War Memorial, Trane Cemetery. His demise is officially classed as a war death.'
(History Points)

Hornby (Sir Edmund)
MARRIAGES
'On the 26th ult, at Llandygwydd, Cardiganshire, by the Rev D Lewis, Vicar, the Rev WB Money, Curate in Derbyshire, son of the Rev J.D. Money, to Edith Belinda Hornby, only daughter of Sir Edmund Hornby, Judge, Supreme Court of China and Japan.'
(The Cambrian 6th October 1871)

Huang Xiuqi

A former student at Cardiff University in the early 1990s produced a book of poems entitled 'HILARIOUS FESTIVAL'. The following poem 'REFLECTIONS' is taken from his book.

'REFLECTIONS'

Face smiling	Eastern music
Hand shaking	Rings in a new topic
Xiamen, Cardiff	Echoes the Hall
Ten Years Twinning	In promising call
Gongs beaten	Ribon swayed
'Lions' woken	Paves the way
Get to dance	To span a bridge
With jubilance	Requires courage

Hughes (Hugh Brythan 1848-1913)
School teacher and author. Born 8th April 1848 at Tregarth, near Bangor. Author of several Welsh schoolbooks and readers including 'Rhament Plat y Pren Helyg' ('Romance of the Willow Pattern Plate') published 1916.
Article: 'Tra Môr Tra Brythan (1843-1913)' p.7 by Eryl Wyn Rowlands

(Y Casglwr Rhif 110 Rhifyn y Gwanwyn 2014 (Spring 2014 Issue No. 110)

Hughes (Hugh Michael)
'Independent minister born 13 Aug. 1858 at Llanllechid, Caerns; son of Michael and Elizabeth Hughes. He was educated at the Memorial College, Brecon and at Aberystwyth and Cardiff university colleges. His publications included 'Griffith John, Arwr China' (1914)'
(Dictionary of Welsh Biography to 1940, National Library of Wales

Hughes (William d. 1794?)

The image is a glass negative presumed to be that of William Hughes by M.A. Shee at National Museum of Wales

William Hughes, of Llanfflewin, Angelsey must have left for London before 1755. He was in business until 1794 at the 'Dial', near King Street, High Holborn.

1755: Vice-President of the Honourable Society of Cymmrodorion.
1781: Made Honorary Freeman of the Clockmakers Company
1860: William Hughes made a musical Automata Watch and other clocks for the Emperor Qianlong of China who collected Western technology. During the Second China War (1860), the Automata Watch was stolen from the Summer Palace near Beijing.
1917: It appears in 'The Horological Collection' of Henry Levy, Esq, deceased, late of 11 Hyde Park Place, West London to be auctioned at Messrs Christie, Manson and Woods at their Great Rooms, 8 King Street, St. James' Square, London, on Tuesday, November 27th, 1917, as Lot No. 36.
1953: 'Antiquarian Horologist', March, 1953 – 'Captain Cook's Cabin Clock and its Maker William Hughes' by R.K. Foulkes p.29
1954: The Automata Watch was auctioned in the' Percy Webster Collection' at Sotheby's with the added information that it was made 'circa 1780' and that it was taken in 1860 by Lt. Smith from the Emperor's bedroom at the Summer Palace, Peking. The Catalogue stated that William Hughes specialised in the Far East trade. It was bought by Spink & Company for £650.
1955: 'Five Centuries of British Timekeeping Exhibition', Goldsmiths Hall, London. William Hughes's Automata watch was the centre page of an article by Cecil Clutton (see illustration).
1959: The Automata Watch was again auctioned at Sotheby's as the Property of a Lady, Lot No. 107, for £580. Again, bought by Spink's.
1994: At the request of the Director of the Palace Museum, Beijing, the Author presented her research of the William Hughes Automata Watch to the Palace Museum Archives, as previously the Archives had no knowledge of the Automata Watch.

'A Catalogue of various clocks, watches, Automata, and other miscellaneous objects of European Workmanship Dating from 18th and early 19th Centuries, in the Palace Museum and the Wu Ying Tien, Peiping.' By Simon Harcourt-Smith (1933). 'Qian Long, while affecting to despise the West......... during his reign clocks and mechanical toys of beauty and ingenuity never before seen flowed into China from the West at the rate of some thousands a year.'
(William Hughes, p.21 No. 725 (Plate 24 A and B.)

'Freemen of the Worshipful Company of Clockmakers' by George Daniels. Privately published – Isle of Wight 1984) ('Clocks and Watches of the Qing Dynasty' (From the Collection in the Forbidden City - 2002)

'Clock and Watch Makers in Wales' by Iorwerth C. Peate : Published by National Museum of Wales, Cardiff (1945)

William Hughes' Automata Watch

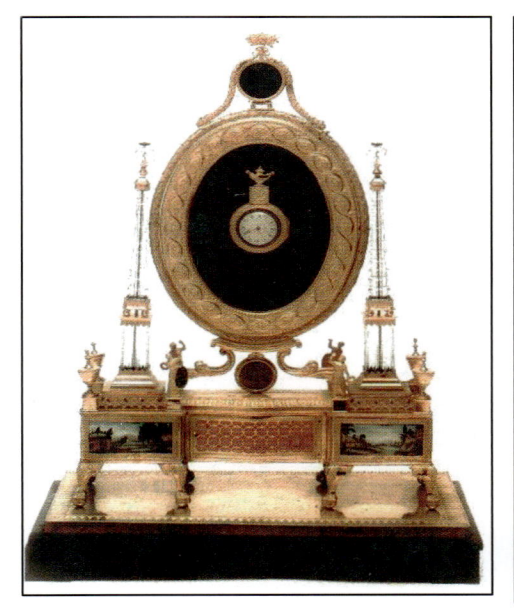

A William Hughes clock and matching mirror at the Hall of Clocks and Watches, Palace Museum, Beijing

Huws (Lucy)
Aberystwyth born, studied Chinese at Edinburgh University under the eminent Sinologist the late Professor John Chinnery. In 1980 she was part of only a second group of students to spend a year in China after the Cultural Revolution. A fluent speaker of Mandarin, she returned to China to work as a language teacher at Shandong University and on E.U. funded development projects in Hainan and Jiangxi provinces. She later worked at E.U. Headquarters in Brussels on training and developing translators, before returning to Asia to work for a trading company in Hong Kong where she married and had two daughters. She returned to Wales in 2003. In 2009 she was appointed to the MFL Department at Ysgol Penglais, Aberystwyth where she teaches Mandarin and Chinese Studies.

I

India and China Tea Company
The shop, in Brynamman, was in existence from 1895 to 1930 (approx).

India and China Tea Company at Brynamman

Inglis (Iain)
Cardiff-born university lecturer in China found fame by singing Chinese revolutionary songs, which featured on the TV competition 'China's got Talent' in 2009. Mr Inglis, a Russian and German language graduate, lives on the tropical Chinese island of Hanya with his wife, Yu Yanling.

'Inn of the Sixth Happiness'
Ingrid Bergman starred in the 1958 film, based upon the life of Gladys Aylward, and was filmed on location in Snowdonia. Nantmor, near Beddgelert, Gwynedd was chosen as the fictitious city of 'Wang Cheng'.
(See: Gladys Aylward Beddgelert; Nantmor)

Ingrid Bergman arriving for filming

The 'Walled City of Wang Cheng' at Nantmor

Action shot during filming at Nantmor

'Inspired by Wales'
Published in Chinese to promote Wales in China (2008). The Welsh Assembly Government worked with the Chinese authors, Feng Jianxin and Liu Jianchun, to produce 'Inspired By Wales'. It was published by the South West University in Chongqing and is, probably, the first book about Wales to be published in Mandarin. The two authors looked at Wales through Chinese eyes. Former First Minister Rhodri Morgan wrote the Foreword to the book.

'Isabel'
SHIPPING INTELLIGENCE
'Sailed from Cardiff to Shanghai September 22^{nd,} 1867. The voyage took 29 days.'
(The Cambrian 1st November 1867)

J

Jacob (Henry Thomas 1864 - 1957)
Congregational Minister, lecturer, writer and poet. Born in Treorchy, Rhondda. It was his interest in church missionary work, and his service to it, that prompted him to write a biography of Hopkyn Rees
('Hopkyn Rees China', published 1925 by Cymdaithas Grenhadol Llundain.)

Jago (Jack and Val)
Evie and John Jago were friends of the Missionary Gladys Aylward, who worked in Swansea before leaving for China. On her last visit to Swansea in 1963, Gladys left her Chinese jacket and dress with Evie. When Evie died, her son, Jack, and daughter-in-law, Val, became the 'guardians' of the garments. In May 2014, Jack and Val passed on the guardianship of Gladys' garments to the Author as they are historical memories of the Missionary.
(See: Gladys Aylward)

James (Heather)
Concert Pianist, and Teacher of Music. Graduated from Cardiff University and Birmingham Conservatoire. Examiner in Hong Kong for the Associated Board of the Royal Schools of Music – 2003 to 2010. Taught ABSM Teaching Course for piano teachers in Hong Kong. Visiting speaker at seminars in Singapore and Malaysia on Practical Musicianship skills.

Heather James (centre) with piano teachers in Hong Kong

James (Ivor)
SWANSEA MAN'S POST IN CHINA
To take charge of Native Police in Shanghai
'News has been received in Swansea for the appointment to the Shanghai Constabulary of Mr Ivor James, 8 Myers Street, St Thomas. Mr James will leave on October 16 to take up his post as officer in charge of native constables.'
(The Cambrian 11th October 1929)

James (William)
'On 9th December last, on-board the 'Camilla,' from Shanghai to London, Mr.William James, son of the late Mr Eli James of Swansea'.
(The Cambrian 1866)

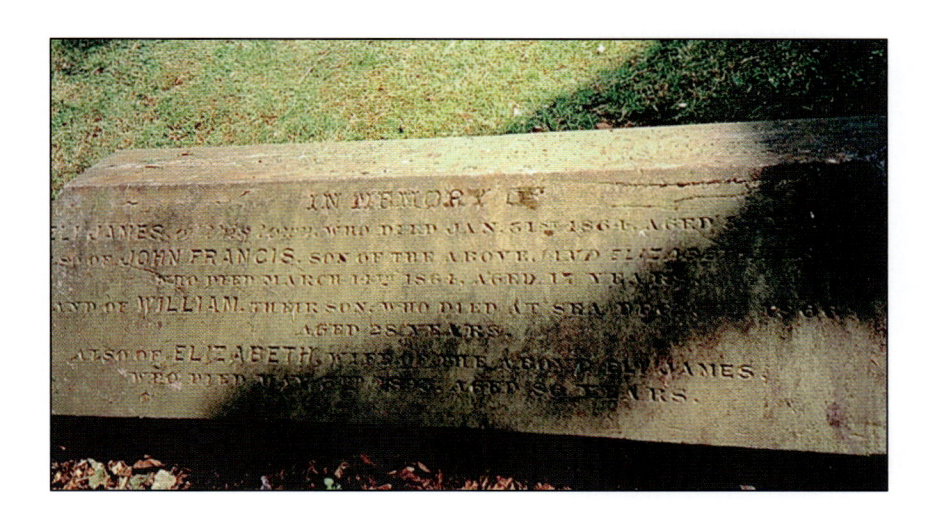

Eli James' Grave with a memorial to his son, William at St. Mary's Church Swansea

Jasper (Vincent John and Ceridwen neé Lloyd)
'Originally from Blaina, Jasper worked in the colliery at 14 years of age. The National Coal Board (N.C.B.) funded him to study for a degree at Cardiff University. In 1936, he went to China as a missionary and Ceridwen followed later. They were married in Beijing. Both of them taught in China and Hong Kong. Bandits attacked them during the troubles in China. Two from their group were killed and Ceridwen was injured in the attack. They also worked at Zhoucun and Taiyuan. Jasper spoke nine languages and, for a time, worked for the BBC as an interpreter and translator. They returned to the UK in 1965 and settled at Seven Oaks where Jasper taught at the local comprehensive school. They then relocated to Porthcawl and, in 1980, moved to Abergavenny. (Pam Key - niece)

Jeffreys (George B.)
UNIFORMED FORCES, NAVAL
'George B. Jeffreys of Swansea on HMS Pylades – Attacks Chinese Pirates.'
(The Cambrian 13th February 1841)

Jenkins (Frank)
'DEATHS – On the 3rd March, at 39 Queen's Road, Hong Kong, China, Frank, the beloved second son of Alderman Samuel Jenkins, of Pembroke Dock, South Wales, aged 27 years.'
(The Cambrian 11th April 1890)

Jenkins (Karl C.B.E b.1944)
Karl Jenkins was born and raised in the Gower village of Penclawdd, in the County of Swansea. His father, who was a local schoolteacher, chapel organist and choirmaster, gave him his initial musical instruction. He began his musical career as an oboist in the National Youth Orchestra of Wales. He went on to study music at Cardiff University, and then commenced postgraduate studies in London at the Royal Academy of Music. He is highly regarded as a composer and musician of international standing and was awarded the OBE in 2005 and the CBE in 2010. He was guest of honour at the world premiere of his work 'ZHI JIANGNAN' ('On visiting Jiangnan') performed by the chorus and orchestra of the Shanghai Opera in 2010. In 2015 he was knighted.

Jenkins (Richard Ceredig)
1866 - Born near Aberystwyth
1893 - Appointed to Chizhou, China
Became member at Union church, Tianjin
1896 - Returned home
(Overseas Missionary Fellowship, 1991)

Jenkins (Robert 1824-1894)
'Robert Jenkins, Naval Officer of Welsh descent from the Shrewsbury area, and saw service in many parts of the world. He entered the Royal Navy in 1838. In 1842 he took a stirring part in the China War, his service especially mentioned in the 'Gazette', and was awarded the China Medal.
In 1855 to 1856 he engaged on the 'Comus' in the suppression of piracy and took an active part in the subsequent China War, receiving the China clasp. On retirement, he took up residence in Shrewsbury. He was buried in Wroxeter.'
(Eminent Welshmen: a Short Biographical Dictionary of Welshmen who Have Attained Distinction from the Earliest Times to the Present, by T.R. Roberts Volume 1, 1908)

Jenkins (William)
William Jenkins was a butcher as well as the owner of a fleet of vessels. He commissioned the artist James Harris to paint many of his ships that he had built for the Cuba and China trade. He lived at Sketty Hall. Jenkins died on 7th February 1850, aged 70. He is buried at St. Mary's Church in Swansea.

Ji Chaozhu

'H.E. Ambassador Ji Chaozhu opened the business seminar – 'China and Business Affairs' at the China Study Centre, Cardiff University. The day before the seminar Ambassador Ji presented a collection of books to the China Study Centre. Cardiff was among only a few universities in the United Kingdom that were selected to receive the gift of books from China.' (1988)

John (Rev Dr. Griffith 1831-1912 - Chinese Name: Yang Ge Fei)

Griffith John was a Welsh Christian missionary and translator in China. A member of the Congregational church, he was a pioneer evangelist with the London Missionary Society (LMS), a writer and a translator of the Holy Bible into the Chinese language.

1831
Born Dyfatty, Swansea.

1845
Worked at Mr and Mrs John Williams' shop at Onllwyn. Gave his first sermon at Onllwyn, aged 14 years and started to preach regularly from the age of 16 years.

1855
Ordained at Ebenezer Chapel, Swansea. Married Margaret Griffiths. They sailed for China and worked for the London Missionary Society. He worked in Wuhan (Hubei Province, Central China) where he established schools, colleges and hospitals – which have continued under different names into the 21st Century. A fluent speaker and writer of Chinese, he translated the Bible into Chinese.

1911
Returned to London.

1912
Died London and buried at Carnglas Cemetery, Sketty, Swansea.

1963
Original commemorative plaque and garden at Brynmelin flats Dyfatty. The flats and street were named after the missionary.

2006
Bust of Griffith John at Wuhan Union Hospital

2012
Wuhan Union Hospital presented a bust of Griffith John to the College of Medicine, Swansea University to celebrate the linking of the two medical schools. The bust is on display at Swansea Museum. An 'Onllwyn Plate' which features an image of Griffith John was presented by Mr and Mrs Niedergang to Union Hospital.

2012
A new memorial garden and commemorative plaque were placed outside the Griffith John Flats at Brynmelin, Dyfatty. The Flats and Griffith John Street are named in his memory.

2013
A Blue Plaque to Griffith John erected at Ebenezer Chapel, Swansea.

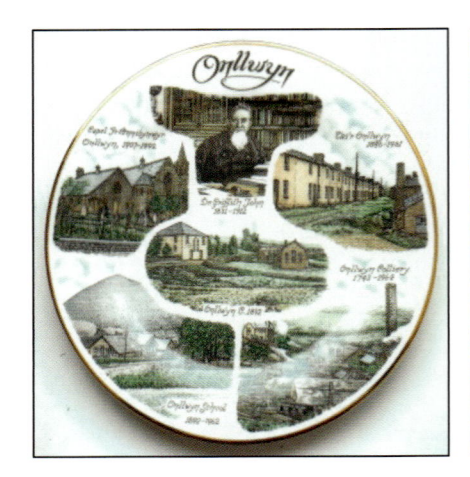

'Onllwyn Plate'

Griffith John Memorial Garden, Brynmelin, Swansea

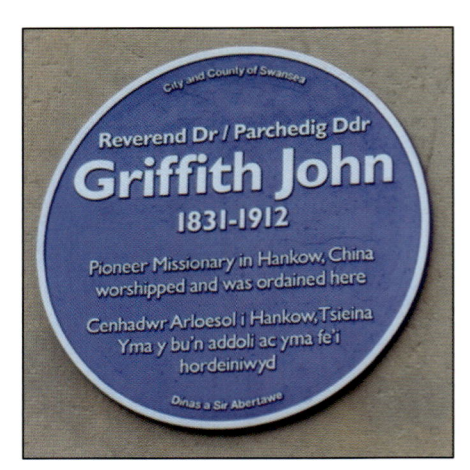

Plaque at Ebenezer Chapel, Swansea

Bust of Rev. Dr. Griffith John at Swansea Museum

PLAQUE WILL COMMEMORATE MISSIONARY
'Alderman Percy Morris drew the attention of the Swansea Council to the fact that the famous Welsh teacher, preacher and missionary in China, Dr Griffith John, had been born at a spot near where the new flats are being built in Llangyfelach Street, Brynmelin.
Two or three years ago, said Alderman Morris, he heard Lady Stansgate, mother of Mr. Wedgwood Benn, speak of the work Dr. John did in China in the interest of the Christian religion.

The London Missionary Society felt it would be very appropriate if a plaque was affixed to one of the buildings indicating that he was born in that part of Swansea.
It might perhaps influence other people to undertake work of such importance. The plaque would be provided by the Missionary Society and by local churches. He moved that the plaque should be affixed to the building.
The ex-Mayor, Cllr Sydney Jenkins seconded and the Council agreed.'
(South Wales evening Post 21 July 1961 www.southwales- eveningpost.co.uk

> ON THIS SPOT
> STOOD THE HOUSE IN WHICH
> DR GRIFFITH JOHN
> WAS BORN ON DECEMBER 14TH 1831
> HE SERVED AS A CHRISTIAN MISSIONARY IN CHINA
> WITH GREAT DISTINCTION
> 1855 — 1911
> "GOD'S GRACE HE GAVE TO THE PEOPLE."
> "GRAS DUW A RODDODD I'R BOBL."
> 百年紀念

Original Griffith John Memorial Plaque at Brynmelin, Swansea (1963)

The Chinese characters on the plaque translate as:
'REMEMBER ME FOR 100 YEARS in other words 'DON'T FORGET ME!'

Newspaper articles about Griffith John
Missionary among the Mandarins (South Wales Evening Post (SWEP) 27th August, 1959)
Article by Kate Bosse Griffiths (South Wales Evening Post 14th May, 1964)
'From Swansea went China's First Inland Missionary' (LF Davies, South Wales Evening Post 19 August, 1965)
Chinese scroll tribute to a saintly son of Swansea (South Wales Evening Post)
City's unsung Hero of China (South Wales Evening Post Saturday, February 25,1989)
'Griffith John, Wuhan and Me' by Ena Niedergang, (Cambria Magazine, 2013)
'The Welsh Academy - Encyclopaedia of Wales' pub. University of Wales Press (2008), Page 416-Griffith John
Diaries and personal belongings etc are held at the National Library of Wales, Aberystwyth.

DEPARTURE of the Rev Griffith John for China
'The Rev gentleman will leave Swansea next week for Liverpool, en route for China.ON MONDAY EVENING, February 3rd, a FAREWELL MEETING will be held at Ebenezer Chapel, to commence at 7 PM. EM Richards, Esq., MP, will preside. Prayers will be offered, and suitable addresses delivered, by the following Ministers- Rev Dr. Rees, W Jones, and T Jones, Swansea; T Davies, Llandeilo; E Jacobs, Ebley; T Davies, Llanelli; D Jones BA, Merthyr, and several others. ' (Cambrian 7th February 1873)

FAREWELL TO THE REV. GRIFFITH JOHN.
MISSIONARY TO CHINA

A public meeting held at Ebenezer Chapel, on Monday evening, for the purpose of publicly bidding farewell and wishing God speed to the Rev Griffith John, a native of Swansea, well known throughout the country as an able and zealous missionary among the Chinese, and will, after two years leave of absence, is now about to return to the scene of his labours in the celestial Empire.

In the absence of Mr EM Richards, MP, who was announced to preside, but was unavoidably prevented, the chair was taken by the Mayor of Swansea……….. The Rev Mr Davies, of Llanelli; the Rev W Jones (Castle Street); Mr Alderman Phillips; the Rev E Jacob of Ebly; the Rev T Jones (Walter Street)………… In the course of the evening a large portrait of Mr John, painted in oil colours by Mr Jones of Merthyr, was exhibited.

It was announced that it would be on view for a month or so at the shop of Mr Griffiths, bookseller, High Street; it will then be placed permanently in the library of Brecon College where Mr John received his education.

(The Cambrian 7th February 1873)

TREASURE CHEST OF CHINA MISSIONARY'S BELONGINGS

The contents of a steel trunk and other containers, which have reached Swansea, will provide an interesting exhibition at Ebenezer Congregational Church schoolroom in connection with the opening of the Dr Griffith John commemorative garden and the dedication of a plaque in Brynmelin, Swansea on November 23.

The variety of articles, books, schools, photographs and an elaborate gown of many colours decorated with bells and Chinese characters the possessions of Dr John, Llangyfelach Street. A Swansea boy who gained nationwide fame for his work as a missionary in China for more than 50 years. The treasure chest was sent to Swansea by Mr Brynmor Sparham, whose brother, the Rev Griffith John Sparham will unveil the plaque. Both are grandsons of Dr Griffith John.

The Rev Glynn Richards, who will be the chairman at the Garden ceremony, is arranging the exhibition at Ebenezer where the famous missionary was a member during his boyhood and where he was ordained in April, 1855.

It is likely that some of Dr John's writings, with the parchment of his honorary Dr of Divinity degree of Edinburgh University and the invitation sent to him to accept a degree of the University of Wales, will be sent to the National Library of Wales.

There are other items which will probably be offered to the Royal Institution of South Wales.

Illuminated addresses presented to Dr John by Swansea and Wrexham when he attained his Jubilee are in striking contrast to greetings presented to him by groups of Chinese converts in the form of scrolls.

Three of these are many feet in length, evidently designed for ceiling to floor wall decorations. They are in scarlet silk with golden Chinese characters and with embroidered letters. Another scroll has huge characters. Others have black characters on a pale golden background.

There is a copy of the New Testament in the Wen-li dialect which Dr John translated from the English in 1885, one of the many translations he made, as well as finding time to write a book.

One interesting exhibit will be an album containing some old photographs of Swansea, probably greatly prized by the doctor in view of the fact that there was one period of 30 years between his return to England from Hankou.

By GEORGE LONG
(South Wales Evening Post 14th November 1963
(www.southwales-eveningpost.co.uk)

Griffith John 'Fundraising Tour Caravan' (The wording on the front of the caravan says 'Griffith John'. The side has 'Madagasgar' written on it.)   Location unknown.

A Griffith John event – Location unknown

In 1931 the centenary of the birth of Griffith John was celebrated at Onllwyn. The gentleman pictured far left is Mr Dan Lewis, Headteacher of Maesmarchog School.

Grave of Griffith John at Carnglas Cemetery Sketty in Swansea.

John (Margaret Jane)

Born in Madagascar to missionary parents who came from Machynlleth.
1855
Married Griffith John in Swansea before they sailed for China.
1873
Died while entering Singapore Harbour on returning to China after a visit home.
1891
The Margaret Memorial Women's Hospital was opened in Hankou. It was built mainly at Griffith John's expense as a memorial to his wife and companion of the early pioneering days in China. (See: Margaret Memorial Hospital)

Johnson (Dudley Graham V.C., D.S.O and Bar, M.C.)
'Major (Temp. Lieut. Col) Dudley Graham Johnson, South Wales Borderers, Born February 13th, 1884, entered the Army in 1903……… served with South Wales Borderers at Qingdao (Dispatches, D.S.O.)
(Who's Who in Wales – 1920, p. 224)

Jones (Benjamin)
Death: 'On the 17th inst. aged 47 Mr. Benjamin Jones, Chinaman, of Swansea; and on 10th inst. Aged 27, Mr. Thomas Heywood, brother in law to Mr. Jones.'
(The Cambrian 25th August 1832)

Jones (Edward)
Private, 2nd Battalion Royal Welch Fusiliers from Neath. Died at Pekin, China on September 12th, 1901, aged 23 years. (John Griffiths)

Jones (Eleanor)
'Born Llanberis; left for China in 1912 aged 30 years to become a missionary.'
(Overseas Missionary Fellowship 1991)

Jones (F. Elwyn)
Author of 'Justice in Modern China' (1956). It was written after a visit he made as a Member of Parliament to China in 1956. He later became Right Honourable the Lord Elwyn Jones of Llanelli.

Jones (Gareth Richard Vaughan 1905 - 1935)
'Linguist, journalist and son of Edgar and Gwen Jones of Barry, South Wales. Father was head of Barry County School; Foreign Affairs Secretary to David Lloyd George. Joined the staff of the Western Mail in1935 and began a world tour.
After a hazardous journey through mid-China, he was murdered by bandits in Inner Mongolia, 12th August 1935. The University of Wales Memorial travelling scholarship was established by public subscription. His 'In Search of News' was published posthumously.'
(Dictionary of Welsh Biography to 1940) (1959)
'Last letter by Gareth Jones, Western Mail and South Wales News, Tuesday, October 29th, 1935. 'Gareth Jones-Hero or Villain?' by Toby Thacker, Western Mail, Saturday, 9th April 2011. ' Was Welsh journalist killed for defying Stalin's orders?' - John Sweeney talks to Aled Blake. Western Mail, Thursday, 12th January, 2012.'
'Gareth Jones – A Manchukuo Incident' by Margaret Siriol Colley published by Nigel Linsan Colley 2001

Jones (Hannah)
'Born 13th November,1858. Left home to become a missionary in 1881, aged 22 years. Married W.E. Burnett.'
(Overseas Missionary Fellowship 1991)
'History of the Vale of Neath by D. Rhys Phillips (1925): p.773
'In 'Additional Notes': Letter from China, the author printed, in full, a letter from Hannah Burnett, dated, November 10th, 1924. Hannah relates that she was born in the chapel house of Capel Llwyn Adda, Llechryd. At about the age of three and a half she moved to Resolven. At the age of thirteen, whilst at her Grandfather's house, she heard 'Dr Griffith John of China'. At about ten years of age she moved to Pant-y-Geifr, near Resolven.
At the end of the letter, Hannah comments that: 'The railways are not in good working order, as they are in the hands of the soldiers.' She would send the letter to Mr Phillips via Siberia.'

Jones (Captain John 1751-1828)
'John Jones was born in Swansea on 20th August 1751. He was apprenticed in the West Indian trade, served as a seaman in the East India Company (1770/1771) and then had a continuous ten-year period of serving in the Royal Navy. After this varied (and global) early career at sea, he re-entered the East India Company in 1785. Over the next 15 years he held senior positions in various East Indiamen, initially First Mate on the 'Carnatic' (1785/86), the 'Deptford' (1787/88) and then as the Captain of the

'Boddam' which he commanded on three voyages to Madras and China (1790/91, 1793/94, and 1800/01).

Command of an East Indiaman was a plum position for an 18th Century mariner, and the commanders formed a small maritime elite. Like all officers and commanders in the East India Company's service, Jones took advantage of the private trading opportunities that were open to him in Asia, and through a variety of commercial transactions he was able to generate a substantial personal fortune which set him up for a comfortable retirement. There were very few Welsh commanders of East Indiamen. The English and the Scots dominated the Company's maritime service. Thus, Jones is of considerable interest to historians because his career demonstrates how some men from 'a periphery' of imperial Britain were perfectly capable of making their way in the trading world of Asia. Jones is also of great interest because, unlike many of his colleagues, he chose to retire to his place of birth, and he invested his fortune in Swansea, notably in his development of St Helen's House.

St. Helen's House, Swansea

It has been possible to build up a good picture of Jones's career in the maritime service of the East India Company because some of his private logs and journals have been discovered in the West Glamorgan Archives (SL 19/1-3). These volumes relate to voyages in the 'Carnatic'(1785/6) and the 'Boddam' (1790/1). Taken together with the official logs and journals returned to the East India Company at the end of a voyage, these richly detailed sources allow Jones's East India career trading activity to be reconstructed in some detail. They provide a fascinating insight into the maritime world of the East India Company, and will form part of a study of how Wales and a Welshman played a key, yet often ignored role in the extension of British influence in the Indian Ocean world.'
(Professor Huw Bowen)

(Extracted from: 'Cymru A'R MÔR - Maritime Wales (2010); The Swansea History Journal-Minerva Number18 2010/11, published by Royal Institution of South Wales (RISW)
Note:
i) The portrait of Captain John Jones was painted by Spoilum a Chinese artist in Canton Ref: Carl L. Crossman, 'The Decorative Arts of China Trade (A.C.C. 1991) pp.35-53. It may be the only such portrait of a Welshman. (National Museum of Wales)

ii) St. Helen's House; Artist, British School 19th Century circa.1820. A painting of the villa owned by Captain John Jones at St. Helen's Swansea before 1792 (demolished 1910) with his horses, cattle and sheep in the foreground, representing the fruits of his professional success. The background is a panorama of Swansea Bay with the Mumbles lighthouse and Oystermouth Castle and Church, together with a horse-drawn omnibus. (National Museum Wales)

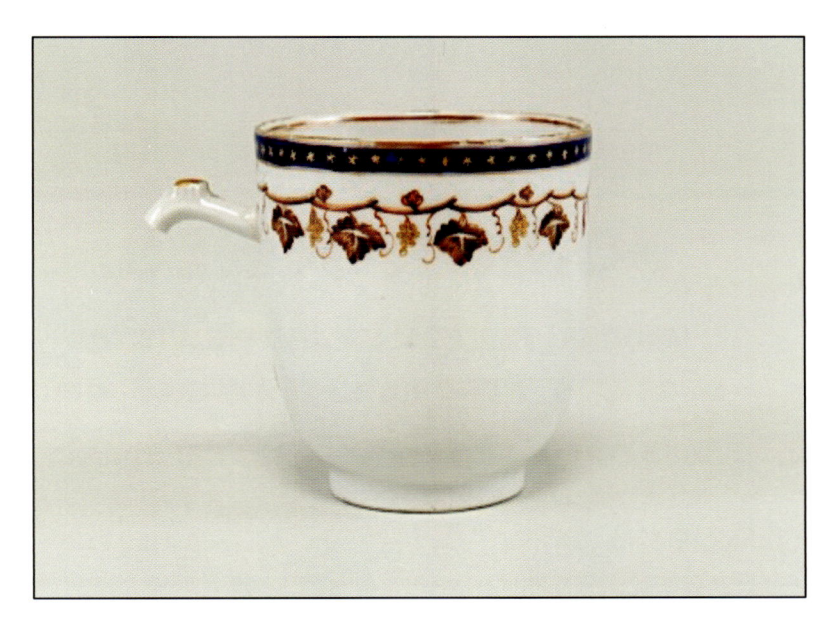

China porcelain cup bearing the monogram of Ann, wife of Captain John Jones of the East India Company at the National Museum of Wales.

Jones (J. Frank)
'Appointed a member of the Electricity Department in Shanghai, China. Secretary St David's Society, Shanghai.'
(Who's Who in Wales-1920)

Jones (John)
'1700s - "A Welsh tea salesmen in very ordinary circumstances". His son Samuel bequeathed £5000 to Manchester University College.'
(Eminent Welshmen by TR Roberts-Volume 1)

Jones (Dr. John Robert CBE, MC, K St.J, LL.D, JP 1887-1976)
'John Robert Jones of Llanuwchllyn had a very distinguished life before entering the China scene. His record shows that he continued his career in and around China in no less a manner. He practised in the Supreme Court for China. Later, he was to become Secretary General of the Council for the International settlement of Shanghai, President of the Shanghai Committee of the International Red Cross, Chairman of the British Residents Association, a member of the War Office Intelligence Staff, adviser on international affairs to the Hong Kong and Shanghai Banking Corporation, and chairman of the Public Services Committee of the Government of Hong Kong.

He was also a member of the St David's Society in Shanghai and Hong Kong. At his instigation, the St David's Society in Shanghai donated the Eisteddfod Chair for the National Eisteddfod of Wales which was held in Wrexham in 1933.'
(Sir Emrys Evans M.A., B.Litt., LL.D.)

Jones (John. T.)
'Grocer, Tea Dealer and Provision Merchant ('HONG KONG TEA WAREHOUSE') at Clydach and a branch at Graig Cefn Parc.'

JOHN T. JONES,

GROCER, TEA DEALER AND PROVISION MERCHANT, HONG KONG TEA WAREHOUSE

CLYDACH and Branch at CRAIG CEFNPARC.

Telephone No. 10y.   Posting Travellers.

(Purrier's Directory – Swansea District Section 1913-14)

Jones (Lewis)
'Born in 1865, Lewis Jones left for China on 28th October, 1892, aged 26. Arrived in China in December 1892. Occupation: Draper's Clerk.
Address: Bryn-y-Mor House, Towyn. Married Miss G. Ardern in March 1897. He retired from the China Inland Mission in 1942. Died, August, 1950.'
(Overseas Missionary Fellowship, 1991

Jones (Mark)
In 2001, Mark Jones gave up his job and joined the Voluntary Service Overseas (VSO). After obtaining a TEFL qualification was sent to Shaoyang, Hunan Province, China to teach English at a teacher training university. Initially, he expected to stay for only 2 years but stayed on for another year having met his future wife and then for a further year in Hangzhou, Zhejiang after working for a short period for a Fujian-based company that was seeking to establish a UK presence. In 2006 he returned to his native North Wales to become an International Officer at Bangor University with responsibility for student recruitment and marketing for China and Hong Kong. In 2008, he joined the China Britain Business Council (CBBC) to manage its office in Cardiff, working closely with International Business Wales the trade and investment arm of the Welsh Government at the time. His current role is the China-Wales Consortium Manager, based at the University of South Wales - working with all eight Welsh universities to deliver bespoke training programmes to Chinese organizations on behalf of its members. In addition, identifying collaborative opportunities with universities across China.
(2014)

Jones (Admiral Oliver John R.N.)

Oliver Jones was born on 15th March 1813. He was the second son of Major General Oliver Thomas Jones and grandson of Robert Jones of Fonmon Castle in the County of Glamorgan, after a life spent in the service of his country, died at Westfield House in Braunston, Northamptonshire, on the 11th January 1878, aged 64 years. His grave is in the grounds of All Saints Church, Braunston. Admiral Jones saw service on the receiving ship HMS Princess Charlotte in Hong Kong among other locations. Captain of HMS 'Furious' (East Indies and China).

Extracts from the Admiralty Boxes of Admiral Oliver Jones R.N., stationed on HMS Charlotte at Hong Kong

ADMIRAL LETTERBOX: 1866-70………………….No. 31
Respecting the cost of passage from Hong Kong to England of Mr T Huard, Engineer, as an invalid.
 H.M.S. Princess Charlotte,
Hong Kong 22nd November 1869
Sir,
 In reply to your letter MM of first of October 1869 I have the honour to state that, as Mr Thomas Huard, engineer, was sent home in the sailing ship Carmarthenshire, a ship taken up for the conveyance home of invalids and time expired, it was my impression that he and all invalids, whether Officers or not……………… sent by her would have a free passage…………. except the usual charge for messing………… and it was with this view knowing that Mr Huard could not afford to pay a third of the passage money to the Peninsula and Orient Company's route that I sent him by the Carmarthenshire, that I respectfully submit such being the case their Lordships would be pleased to remit the payment by him of the sum in question.
I enclose documents showing that there was no more accommodation in her Majesty's Ship 'Tamen', and that the Commander-in-Chief approved of time expired (on station) Officers being sent home by private vessel; a conclusion was therefore drawn that no invalid officer would be called on to refund any part of the cost of his passage any more than the time expired Officers.

HMS Princess Charlotte,
Hong Kong 5th Aug 66
To the Secretary
of the Admiralty
 Whitehall
London
Sir,
I have the honour to inform you that the person has this day given himself up as a deserter from the Navy. He states that he was a First Class Boy, paid off in Her Majesty `s Ship 'Eldgar' in December 1865, and was granted twenty-one days leave; instead of returning to the Fisgard at the expiration of his leave he joined an American Merchant Ship at Cardiff, South Wales, in which ship he arrived at Hong Kong and was, with the rest of the crew, discharged.
Signed
Oliver Jones
Commodore

Price paid for steam coal at Hong Kong
HMS Princess Charlotte
12th May 1869
Sir,
With reference to the price paid (£2.19.6) for the Coal sent from England for Hong Kong for the use of the Squadron……………… I have the honour (in compliance with the circular letter of the seventh of January last) to inform you that screened coal, half Cardiff and half Newcastle, is now being placed on board His Italian Majesty's ship 'Principessa' by Messes Blackhead and Company of this place at the rate of $11 (equal to £2.6. 9) per ton, including the labour of storing the coal in the bunkers.
Signed
Oliver Jones
Commodore

To the Secretary
of the Admiralty
Whitehall
……… Commodore Jones wrote
Respecting bills left unpaid at Hong Kong by acting naval and Sub Lieutenant Sullivan on his leaving the China Station.
I have the honour to enclose a number of bills unpaid by Mr N. I. Sullivan, which have all been incurred during the three months he was aboard this ship awaiting passage. In addition he had run up the mess and wine bills of £17. 1. 11 which is charged upon his pay documents.
This officer appears very deficient in honest principle; he has even stooped so low as to leave his bill with a little Chinese boy in the gun room mess……… for lemonade etc.… unpaid.
(Glamorgan Record Office – See also: Fonmon Castle)

Jones (Owen 1809-1870)
'Architect and ornamental designer; born 15 February, 1809 in Thomas Street, London, the only son of Owen Jones; buried at Kensal Green Cemetery.'
(Dictionary of Welsh Biography to 1940, p.500)
'Examples of Chinese Ornament' was first published in 1867. Owen Jones looked at the intricate patterns of Chinese ornaments that were coming into the West as trade with China expanded. It was originally published in a limited edition of 300 copies and, because of this, has become a very rare book. The reprint received the title of 'Examples of Chinese Ornament' (1987) and was produced from one of the 300 copies.' (Owen Jones from 'The Grammar of Chinese Ornament' pub. Studio Editions London)

Jones (Rachel)
1892 - Born Cardiganshire
1919 - Appointed to Wuchang, Central China
1940 - Died in China'
(Overseas Missionary Fellowship, 1991)

Jones (Rhodri)
Rhodri Jones was born in Gwynedd, Wales, and is presently based in Italy. He first went to China in 1995. He has been a professional photographer since 1989 and worked on two main themes in China: "Internal Migration in the People's Republic of China" and "Minorities in the People's Republic of China".

'The Migrant Worker' from 'INTERNAL MIGRATION IN THE PR CHINA (Images from 2005-2007 by Rhodri Jones)

Jones (Steve)

Born Llandrindod Wells; MD at Venture Xtreme Ltd. He has over 30 years of experience in the world of adventure sport and in senior roles from instructing, to manufacturing and project management.

As an experienced caver he has been involved in a number of world firsts, including, discovery of the world's largest underground river in Irian Jaya, the first ever descent through Lowes Gulley in Borneo and the deepest ever cave dive in China. Since 1987 he has visited various regions of China on several occasions for caving expeditions that included the Provinces of Guizhou and Guangxi as part of the China Caves Project. He also assisted in the setting up of a manufacturing company there.

(Photograph – China Cave Diving Expedition to Duan County Guangxi, China)
 South Wales Evening Post Article
'Steve Jones, of Llandrindod Wells, and studying at Trinity College Carmarthen, is one of four British divers helping Chinese scientists to explore the Ti'su River which is thought to be the longest underground river in the world. Steve will join an 18 strong party of cave diving experts to explore the uncharted cave system in Guanxi Province.
(South Wales Evening Post 24th December, 1987 www.southwales-eveningpost.co.uk)

Jones (Tom)

> **TOM JONES**
> Family Grocer and Provision Merchant
> 'HONG KONG'
> The Square, CLYDACH-ON-TAWE
> 'Try our delicious Tea – A real luxury-You will enjoy it'

Jones (Sir William 1746 - 1794)
Anglo - Welsh by birth, was known as 'Orientalist Jones'. By the end of his life he had learned 28 languages, including Chinese-many of the languages were self-taught. He had learned enough of the Chinese language to enable him to translate an ode of Confucius. T.C.Fan wrote of him in 'The Review of English Studies':-
Sir William Jones
'It was not until the late 18th century, when Sir William Jones taught himself to decipher Chinese characters, that there were signs of direct cultural contact.
…………. With the endeavors of Sir William Jones as an Orientalist, haphazard, unsuccessful as they were, Sinology as such in English may be said to have begun.'
('The Review of English Studies-Volume 22, Number 88, October, 1946'

Jones (William 1826-1899)
'Secretary of the Peace Society - The son of John Jones, a Ruthin Quaker and great-grandson of Jonathan Hughes, the bard mentioned by Borrow in 'Wild Wales'. Educated at Ackworth Quaker School. He was later appointed head of the commission for the relief of distress during the Franco-German war 1870-1. He had discussions with President Cleveland, Li Hong Zhang and other statesmen on the principle of arbitration as an instrument of world peace. He was buried in Sunderland.'
(Dictionary of Welsh Biography to 1940 (1959), page 526)

Jones (William and Son)
'William Jones and son of Pwllheli built barques and fully rigged ships for the India and China trade in the 1840s.'
(Lewis Lloyd - 'Pwllheli Port and Mart of Lleyn' 1994)

St John's Cathedral Hong Kong
A memorial tablet to Sir Edward Youde, of Penarth, a former Governor of Hong Kong.
(See: Sir Edward Youde)

K

Kenrick (John P. and Hubert Wynn)
The Kenrick Brothers of Wynn Hall, nr Ruabon, Wrexham.
Captain William Wynn built Wynn Hall in 1649. It passed to the Kenricks when William Wynn's granddaughter, Sarah Taylor, married the Rev. John Kenrick in 1723.
John P. Kenrick worked for the Pekin Syndicate Ltd, in China.
(Papers, photographs and photo albums (2) of John P. Kenrick at the Bangor University Archives)
Hubert Wynn Kenrick married Alice Beale. They had a son also called Hubert Wynn. Hubert Wynn (father) was a captain with the P&O Line. Letters sent home to his wife, at Wynn Hall, were found in woods near the Hall (about 1990). Hubert wrote about the various ports of call that the ship visited, including some that were sent from Shanghai. In one he mentions leaving Shanghai on the P&O 'SS Chusan'.
(The letters are held at the A.N.Palmer Centre for Local Studies and Archives Wrexham)

Pekin Race Course 1920s

Pekin Syndicate Ltd

Kymer (Thomas 1722-1784)

Thomas Kymer was associated with the Kidwelly and Llanelly Canal and Transport Company. He died in 1784 and was buried in the Chancel of the parish church of St. Mary, Kidwelly. In his will, Kymer requested that he should be buried 10 feet deep in the Chancel and commemorated with an inscription on a square of Welsh marble recording the dates of his birth and death. He bequeathed to George Talbot Rice an oil painting of himself in a Chinese robe and red Chinese hat which was painted by George Hamilton of St James Street London in 1754. The painting now hangs in the National Trust property Newton House, Parc Dynefwr, Llandeilo, formerly, the property of Lord Dynevor.

('The Canals of the Gwendraeth Valley Part 1 by WH Morris MA)
(The Carmarthenshire Antiquary 1970 Volume 6)
(The Curator, Newton House, Llandeilo)

Kingfisher
SHIPPING INTELLIGENCE
Ships and Shipping Port Departures Swansea
'The ship 'Kingfisher' sailed from Swansea to Hong Kong on January 10th, 1860.'
(The Cambrian January 13th 1860)

Kitto (Mark)
Mark Kitto was formerly a Captain in the Welsh Guards. He became a metal trader in London and China. He published a magazine in China called 'Thats' and opened a coffee shop, with his wife and two children, in Maganshan Village in the mountains outside Shanghai. Author of 'China Cuckoo'. (Constable & Robinson 2009)

Kublai Khan
See: Marco Polo

Kuo (Jimmy)
Prominent businessman and member of the Chinese community in Wales during the 1980s and 90s. He and his wife Esther, were active in promoting community relations in Swansea and South Wales. Jimmy described how he and his brother, as young teenagers, escaped to the West from Shanghai during the Cultural Revolution by making their way across China to India. In their later years Jimmy and Esther left Swansea to be with their family in Essex.

Kwok (Angela)
Originally from Hong Kong, has made Cardiff her home since 1972. In 2013, was honoured by the Asian Women's Achievement Awards with a 'Lifelong Service Award' for her work in the Chinese community. She established the Cardiff Chinese Community Services Association (CCCSA) to provide help for women who had difficulty speaking and understanding English in the local community.

L

Laughing Water
ANNOUNCEMENT OF DEATH
'On the 9th September, being unfortunately washed overboard from the ship 'Laughing Water' on her voyage from Swansea to Hong Kong Mr Nicolas Williams, of Swansea………… leaving a wife and a large family to deplore his loss.'
(The Cambrian 9th January 1857)

Laundry (Chinese)
'In 1911, due to the resentment against the Chinese, all Chinese laundries were attacked during the Cardiff riots. However, in the 1960s, with the growing popularity of washing machines Chinese laundries closed. Their owners reinvented themselves and opened restaurants and takeaways.'
(The Chinese in Britain - History Line by Zak Keith 2009)

Leeder (John M.)
Auctioneer Oxford Street, Swansea

> Mr. JOHN M. LEEDER
> Has been instructed by Mr. J. M. Curnow,
> TO SELL BY PUBLIC AUCTION,
> On the above premises,
> On MONDAY, the 24th day of MARCH, 1873,
> (In consequence of his removing to No.   )
> A PORTION of the STOCK-IN-TRADE, Chinese Curiosities, Vases, &c..
> Sale to commence at Eleven o'clock.
> Oxford Chambers, Swansea.

(The Cambrian 21st March 1873)

Lewis (Benjamin Thomas)
'Born in Llanfyrnach, Dyfed 1886. He worked in Hong Kong (1922) and returned home in 1925.'
(Overseas Missionary Fellowship 1991)

Lewis (Sir David)
Born in Hong Kong in November, 1947 but brought up in Malaya and Singapore. In 1978, he moved with his family to Hong Kong where he became Managing Partner in the international law firm Norton Rose, whose headquarters are in the City of London and has a joint venture with the Hong Kong law firm Johnson Stokes and Masters. In London, 1982, he served as a senior partner and chairman of Norton Rose from 1997-2003. He served as Sheriff of London from 2006-7 and became 680th Lord Mayor of London 2007-8, being only the eighth Welshman to become Lord Mayor since 1197. He and his wife live at Cwrt Cadno, near Pumpsaint, Carmarthenshire, where his family have farmed for several generations (2014).

Lewis (David William)

'David Lewis, from Dyffryn Cellwen in the Dulais Valley, served with South Wales Borderers at Qingdao in 1914 and was known as 'Dai Shanghai' on his return home.'
(Source: Barbara Wheadon (granddaughter) and George Brinley Evans)

Lewis (Dr John 1881 to 1960)

'Born Cardiff 1881. Heard Timothy Richard speak and thought he could offer something to China. He joined the Student Voluntary Mission. He was sent to Taiyuan. He died of typhus in 1916. His wife, Nelly, remained in China and worked as a teacher in Suzhou.'
(Overseas Missionary Fellowship 1991)

Lewis (Megan)

Educated at St Paul's Girls' School, Hull University and the School of Oriental and African Studies, she is a former Head of Geography at a London girls' school. Formulated and organized 'The Long Horse Ride' (thelonghorseride.com) which involved riding on horseback starting from Shanghaiguan on the Great Wall of China and ending at Worm's Head on the Gower Peninsular - to bring a message of goodwill from the Beijing Olympics (2008) to the London Olympics (2012) and to raise funds for the charity 'CHALLENGE AID' (challengeaid.org), to support 'Schools of Hope' in some of Africa's most impoverished areas. Now lives on a farm in West Wales where she breeds welsh ponies and large welsh Part-breds under the 'Cwrtycadno' prefix. She is a Fellow of the Royal Asiatic Society and the Royal Geographical Society.

Lewis (Private Z.)

'Private Lewis, of the 2nd Battalion Royal Welch Fusiliers, is with the British Land Force in North China, writing from Tientsin to his parents, who live at Green Oak Cottage, Pontymister, and states that they had a terrible battle on July 13. Before they could enter the city they had to get through three great walls. It was a terrible day, and he should never forget it. There were thousands of Chinese killed and 26 wounded. He continues………. There was a shell fired into us, there were 50 Americans and the same number of ourselves holding a railway station. When the shell came in upon us it was a horrible sight, three Americans being killed on the spot, while five were wounded. We had six wounded. Some had their arms blown off, while others were wounded in three or four places. The day we took the city some of us were lying in the trenches, when one of the Chinese big guns fired three shells at us. I have not had such a narrow escape since I've been out here……….. and I have seen some rough times. One shell came right in front of us, and it did not explode, while another came right over us. We were firing all the time. Then another shell came and brought right over us. I can tell you I thought my time had come, but, thank goodness, it did not hurt one of us. We are having a rest now before we march on to Peking. We have lost nine killed and 41 wounded, so our regimental numbers are diminishing.'
(The South Wales Weekly Argus, Newport Saturday, 8th September 1900)
(Photo: China War Medal 1900 with Pekin Bar awarded to Private Z. Lewis, 2nd Battalion Royal Welch Fusiliers)

Ley (Lennard)
Mr Lennard Ley, of Ystradgynlais, at the age of nineteen was a seaman aboard HMS Alacrity at the time of the 'Yangtze Incident' involving HMS Amethyst in 1949. (See also: Owen Baker; Geoffrey Locke; Sir Edward Youde)

Lee Wai Fong MBE

Mrs Wai Fong Lee arrived in Swansea from her native Hong Kong with her family in 1975. It was a lonely place to be. The language barrier accentuated the sense of isolation, but years later, after settling into a new way of life, she set about trying to ensure that other incoming members of the Chinese community would not have to share the same feeling. She founded the Swansea Chinese Community Co-op Centre in 1997 and today it has 500 members, stretching from Haverfordwest in the west to Newport in the east. Such has been her contribution to Chinese/Welsh relations that an MBE followed in 2006.
(South Wales Evening Post 21st January 2013)
(www.southwales.eveningpost.co.uk)

Liddell (Sir Charles Oswald 1854-1941)
Charles Oswald Liddell was born in 1855 at Edinar, Midlothian, Scotland, the son of William Hodgson Liddell and Catherine Oswald . He married Elizabeth Kate Birt at the Anglican Cathedral in Shanghai (c1880) and died in 1941 at Shirenewton Hall, near Chepstow, Monmouthshire. He held the office of High Sheriff of Monmouthshire in 1918.
He ran the family's firm in Shanghai from 1877 to 1913 at which time he developed a keen interest and knowledge of Chinese art. During this time he collected Chinese antiques which he eventually brought back to Wales, including a Moon Flask (photograph) or 'baoyueping' in Chinese and is also traditionally known as a 'pilgrim's flask' in the West. It is said to be only one of five such vessels produced for the Qianlong Emperor (1736 - 1795). The Flask was sold at Bonhams in November 2013 for nearly £1.5 million to a Hong Kong buyer.

IMPERIAL CHINESE DRAGON MOONFLASK HIDDEN FOR A CENTURY FOR SALE AT BONHAMS

'A stunningly beautiful flask made for the Qianlong Emperor and hidden for a century will be sold at Bonhams on 7th November 2013.

The turquoise vase with its rampant red Imperial dragon is estimated to command a price of £500,000 to £800,000 because of its rarity, beauty, and its Imperial provenance, says Colin Sheaf, Bonhams Asia Chairman. This flask is one of less than five such vessels known made for the Qianlong Emperor, who reigned from 1736 to 1795. A distinguished connoisseur of ceramics in his own right, the Qianlong Emperor presided over one of the greatest flowerings of Chinese art production, and pieces from this period are amongst the most highly sought-after today.

This flat-sided full-bodied flask – round like the moon, hence its name 'moonflask' in English and 'baoyueping' or 'bianhu' in Chinese– is also traditionally known as a 'pilgrim's flask' in the West, since it takes its form from a Middle Eastern prototype for water flasks, which were often carried by travellers.

The auspicious five-clawed Imperial dragon flying amongst clouds follows a traditional design dating back to the 14th century. Collected in China by Captain Charles Oswald Liddell (1854-1941), the vase was brought back to England by him to his country house Shirenewton Hall, a Grade II listed house near Chepstow in Monmouthshire. The Liddell home provided a suitably impressive setting for this Chinese treasure, surrounded by parkland with views over the 'Golden Valley', the Bristol Channel and beyond to the Mendip and Quantock Hills.

Colin Sheaf who has headed Bonhams Chinese Art Department for more than a decade says: "The reappearance of this flask, unknown to collectors for nearly a century, is a very exciting event in the world of Chinese art."

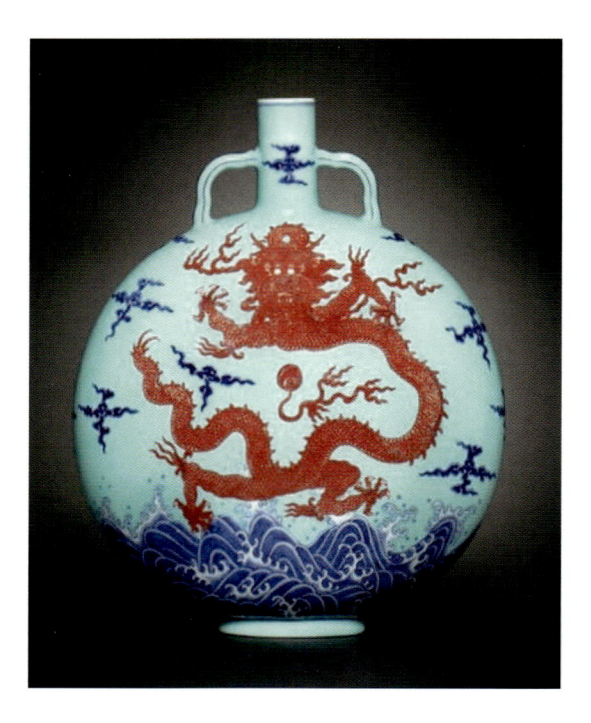

RARE IMPERIAL BLUE AND COPPER-RED TURQUOISE-GLAZED 'DRAGON' MOONFLASK, BIANHU Qianlong seal mark and of the period made for the Qianlong Emperor (1736-1795)

Captain Liddell was based in China from 1877 to 1913, running his family's firm for more than three decades whilst also developing his eye for and knowledge of Chinese art. He was fortunate to be present at a crossroads in Chinese history, just as 2,000 years of Imperial power was ending and Imperial pieces were becoming available to Western collectors astonished by their beauty. On his return from China, Captain Liddell created a Japanese Garden and erected an immense 1.5 tonne temple bell under a pagoda roof on the east lawn, reflecting his appreciation of Asian cultures.

'Flasks of this type are much sought after by the world's leading museums for the extremely rare decorative style combining underglaze painting in cobalt-blue and copper-red minerals further enhanced by a fine translucent turquoise glaze. An artistic and technological triumph, it is expected to be fought over by the new generation of collectors emerging from China, eager to acquire a piece of Imperial history and willing to pay exceptional prices for such exceptionally rare treasures.' (The flask was sold for £1,482,500 inc. premium)
(Bonhams Auctioneers London November 2013)

Li Feng

DR. 'Li Feng, of the Beijing Art Museum, gave a presentation and slideshow on the 'Wuhan Chime Bells'- the ancient orchestra discovered in Wuhan central China. The orchestra had been buried with its owner, Marquis Yi in 433 BC. Dr. Li was the guest of the Wales China Friendship Society.' Dr Li was a member of the team that worked on the excavation of Marquis Yi's Tomb in 1978. The tomb was discovered near Wuhan, Central China. It was later to become known as the 'Tomb of the Underground Orchestra' or 'Marquis Yi's Tomb from 433 BC.'
(Wales-China Friendship Society)
(See: Welsh Dragon)

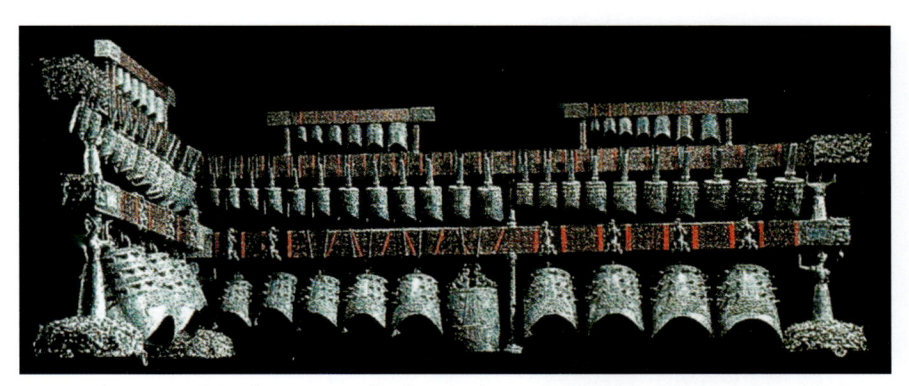

Underground Orchestra on display at the Hubei Provincial Museum, Wuhan

Li Hong Zhang (1823 – 1901)

Li Hong Zhang was a politician, general and diplomat at the Qing Court. He was the guest of Prime Miniter William Gladstone and his wife at Hawarden Castle whilst on his visit to Britain in 1896.

Lin Jixi

Professor Lin Jixi (Jeffrey) from Xiamen spent several years at the China Studies Centre, Cardiff University where he held business seminars. He also involved himself in the work of the local Chinese community, Chinese student associations and a valued supporter and friend of the Wales-China Friendship Society during his time in Wales in the 1990s.

Llangollen International Musical Eisteddfod

'His Excellency the Chinese Ambassador Ma Zhenyang (pictured left) fulfilled his promise of attending the Eisteddfod in 2002. He commented that it was a great honour to be invited to the Eisteddfod and an even greater one to be the Day President. It was the first time that competitors from China had taken part in the Eisteddfod.'
(Shropshire Star)

Llanelly House

The family home of the Stepneys. The Stepney Chinese porcelain armorial service has been described by the late David Sanctuary Howard, the outstanding expert in this field, as 'arguably one of the finest services of this mid century date'. It is now on display at the house. The service was commissioned around 1760 by Sir Thomas Stepney (1725-1772). The service is also unusual in that it includes two different shapes, octagonal and circular, which are used for the plates, soup plates, serving dishes and matching tureens.

Stepney Armorial Dinner Plates

Llewellyn (W.D.)
TRAVELS OF MR.W.D.LLEWELYN, PENLLERGARE.
MR.W.D. LLEWELLYN AND HIS TRAVELS.
SECOND LECTURE AT PENLLERGARE.
'On Monday, the 27th February, at the Penllergare Sunday Schoolroom, Mr. William Dillwyn Llewellyn, of Penllergare, delivered a second lecture (illustrated by lantern views) on his travels last year. The room was again crowded, as at his former lecture, and Mr. Webber, jeweller, Oxford Street, Swansea, successfully manipulated the lantern. The views were excellent, and came out clearly and distinctly, and graphic explanations were given of them by the lecturer. The chair was taken at 8 p.m. by Sir John T. Dillwyn-Llewellyn Bart, Penllergare. Before the lecturer commenced his work, the audience was invited up to the platform to inspect the skin of a crocodile shot by the lecturer whilst on his travels. The cruel-looking teeth and ponderous and powerful jaws were enough to make one shudder. The great difficulty with these great saurians is, that when shot they rush off at once into deep water if they can manage to do so, and are thus lost to the hunter; but Mr. Llewellyn managed to secure his crocodile, and its skin was displayed in triumph to the audience. The lecturer started at Bombay, then going to Ceylon, an island at the southern extremity of India; thence through the Straits of Malacca to Penang and Singapore, and thence to Hong Kong in China, a foul-smelling place ceded to the English by the treaty of 1842. The Empire of China is one of the oldest, if not the very oldest in existence. It was at the zenith of its prosperity 4,000 years ago, when the great Assyrian and Babylonian Empires were in their most flourishing condition; but in consequence of the persistent refusal of the Chinese Emperor to have anything to do with other potentates no treaties could be made, which might have secured intercourse with other parts of the world, and give to China, a fair amount of commercial prosperity. The reasons why the Chinese Emperors thus keep away from all other governments is because they are considered to be direct descendants of their god, and far too august to fraternize with other monarchs. The English Ambassador compelled the Chinese Emperor to meet him in 1842, and forced him to cede Hong Kong to the English; but the reason the Emperor gave for ceding it was that being an unhealthy place, he was in hopes the English would die out! The English, however, are still there, and by planting trees and shrubs, they have managed to do away with much of the malarial fog which formerly made the place so unhealthy, and they further preserve their health by retiring from the city in the evening to the adjacent high table land, where the air is much purer, just as many a Londoner retires to his house in the suburbs beyond the smoke of London, after the day's work is over.

The Chinese Empire has a population of about 370,000,000, or about one-5th of the population of the Earth. Its climate varies from Arctic cold to tropical heat. Every kind of tree, shrub and vegetable will grow there, and as a matter of fact is grown within the limits of the Empire, and every kind of mineral is to be found there, but in consequence of this exclusiveness of the Emperor, it is a totally undeveloped country. There is but one railway in the whole Empire. This was first laid down years ago, but the people, fearing they were becoming too like the outer barbarians, would not have the work completed, and destroyed what had been done.

The lecturer, however, informed his hearers that this railway was reconstructed and re-opened last year. If China were once opened up on fair terms to English commerce, there would be no reason to complain of bad times. One fact may illustrate this. It would give full employment to all the Tin-plate works in the United Kingdom for a whole year to make one tin cup for every inhabitant of the great Chinese Empire. From Hong Kong the lecturer proceeded to Canton, a town of 1,000,000 inhabitants, half of whom live in houses, and the other half in boats on the river. The Chinese forms of punishment are most cruel.

There were some vivid views of some of these. One punishment is to hang a heavy piece of board, about two inches thick, round the neck of the offender, which prevents him from resting comfortably in any position, and this is sometimes left on for a long time, whilst several criminals thus ornamented are huddled together in a Chinese "Black Hole of Calcutta". This punishment is inflicted on minor criminals, such as thieves. Another cruel punishment is the bastinado, too well known to need description, and when a great state official is murdered, as sometimes happens, his murderer is tied up and slowly cut to pieces. The lecturer informed his audience that the great point of male beauty in China is stoutness; nobody but a fat man having much chance of gaining favour in the eyes of the Chinese ladies; so that China may be called the paradise of the fat gentleman!'
(The Cambrian 3rd March 1893)

Lloyd (Ceridwen)
(See: Vincent John Jasper)

Lloyd (Elizabeth)
'Born 1876 in Clwyd. North Wales. Appointed nurse in Beijing in 1909. She resigned from service in 1912 to marry Dr Moses Chiu.'
(Overseas Missionary Fellowship 1991)

Lloyd (Professor Sir Geoffrey)
Born 1933 in London of Swansea parents. Visiting professor at Beijing University in 1987. Warden of Darwin College, Cambridge (1989-2000). Research interest include Ancient Science and Comparative Studies in Chinese and Greek philosophy and science. He was awarded the Kenyon Medal for Classical Studies and Archeology (2007)

Lloyd (Miss)
'Born in 1875 she left for China in September 1907. Occupation: housemaid at 'Boothdale', Llandudno.'
(Overseas Missionary Fellowship 1991)

Lloyd George (Hon. Robert John Daniel b. 1952)
Robert Lloyd George is the great grandson of former British Prime Minister David Lloyd George and son of the late Owen Lloyd George, 3rd Earl Lloyd George of Dwyfor, Ffynone Mansion, Pembrokeshire.
He was educated at Eton where he was a King's Scholar, and Oxford University. Following a banking career in London and New York he moved to Hong Kong in 1980 and from 1984 to 1991 was Managing Director at Indosuez Asset Management. In 1991 he established Lloyd George Management, which he sold in 2011 to the Bank of Montreal.
The author of several books including: *'Guide to Asian Stock Markets'* (1990), *'The East West Pendulum – A risk reward analysis of Asia to the year 2000'* (1992), *'David and Winston – How the Friendship Between Lloyd George and Churchill Changed the Course of History'* (2008).
Presently, he concentrates on his writing and philanthropy through an educational foundation which supports poor children around Asia as well as a number of schools and colleges in the US and Britain.
During the past thirty years he has become a keen student of Chinese history, culture and a collector of Chinese artifacts.

Local Intelligence
'It is stated that the gentleman has just started from Swansea for China to engage a number of the natives for some metal works in South Wales.'
(The Cambrian 23rd May 1873)

Locke (Geoffrey)
'Geoffrey Locke, of Felindre, Port Talbot, was on board HMS London when a rescue mission was attempted to free HMS Amethyst in what became known as the 'Yangtze Incident' in April 1949.'
(Article:'Gripped by dash to Freedom' by Jill Forward in: 'The way we Were Series'
South Wales Evening Post Tuesday, April 23, 1996
(www.southwales-eveningpost.co.uk)
(See: Owen Baker, Len Ley and Sir Edward Youde

Loveridge (Miss)
'Originally from Llandaff, she married Dr Herbert Stanley Jenkins. He worked at Xi'An and died of typhus in 1913.'
(Overseas Missionary Fellowship 1991)

Lovespoon

A 'Two-Dragon Lovespoon' was commissioned by Pat Price of the Lovespoon Gallery in Mumbles, to mark the occasion of the first non-Chinese Dragon exhibition held at the British Consulate - General at Shanghai in March 1988 to celebrate the year of the Chinese Dragon.

Ena Niedergang, on behalf of the Wales China Friendship Society, worked with Iain Orr, the British Consul-General in Shanghai, on the development of the Welsh Dragon Exhibition that was to promote trade and cultural exchanges between Wales and China. The Wales China Friendship Society coordinated the Exhibition in Wales.

M

Maby (Cedric)
Cedric Maby worked in Beijing before the Second World War as a probationer Vice- Consul. During the War the Japanese interned him. He translated 100 short Chinese poems into Welsh in his book entitled 'Y Cocatw Coch' (Gwasg Prifysgol Cymru 1987). He also wrote 'Dail Melyn o Tseina' Dinbych, Gwasg Gee (1983); retired to Penrhyndeudraeth.'

Madden (Richard)
'Richard Madden, of Margaret Street, Velindre, Port Talbot was reported safe on board HMS Consort when 9 of the crew were killed and 13 wounded. HMS Consort had sailed down the river from Nanjing in an attempt to help HMS Amethyst in what was to be known as the Yangtze Incident.'(1949)
('Gripped by dash to freedom' by Jill Forward from 'The way we were' Series: South Wales Evening Post, Tuesday, 23rd April, 199
www.southwaleseveningpost.co.uk)
(See also: 'HMS Amethyst'; Len Ley; Sir Edward Youde; Owen Baker)

Magic Lantern (Views on China and the Chinese)

> **GREENHILL WESLEYAN SCHOOLROOM** - *On Wednesday evening last, an exhibition of Magic Lantern Views, entitled 'China and the Chinese', took place in the above schoolroom, in connection with the Band of Hope which has recently been re-established there. The views were shown by Mr John Griffiths, accompanied by a descriptive lecture by Mr Skeet. Mr William Mill (Superintendent of the Sunday School), occupied the chair, and Mister W.P. Wearne presided at the harmonium.*

(The Cambrian 20th October 1876)

Magna Bona
SHIPPING INTELLIGENCE
'The ship Magna Bona from Swansea for Shanghai put in to Rio de Janeiro with loss of the mainmast.'
(The Cambrian 6th April 1860)

Margaret Memorial Hospital
The Margaret Memorial Women's Hospital was opened in 1891. It was built mainly at the expense of her husband, the Rev Dr Griffith John, as a memorial to his wife and companion of the early pioneering days they had spent in China. The Margaret hospital brought down barriers for the employment of women missionaries in Wuhan. It made it possible for women doctors to examine and treat Chinese women. Only one year after its opening the first lady medical missionary in central China, connected with the London Missionary Society, was appointed.
('Griffith John-The Story of Fifty Years In China' By R. Wardlow Thompson pub. The Religious Tract Society London 1908)) (See: Margaret John)

Margaret Memorial Hospital for Women

Marier (Frances Edith)
HOME LETTER FROM THE BRIDE
'Our marriage column of this week contains the announcement of the marriage, at the Cathedral of the Holy Trinity, Shanghai, of Frances Edith, eldest daughter of Mr James Marier, Wind Street, Swansea, to John, son of Mr Robert Talbot of Wellington, Somerset. The pluck and devotion of these young people in leaving the land of their birth and friends, to devote their lives to the religious distractions and improvement of the so-called heathen Chinese, lends an interest to their personalities and some account of the wedding will be pursued with pleasure. The young couple were married on Saturday. A pouring rain came down at the time of the ceremony, but the sky cleared off beautifully in the afternoon, so that the couple had, as was said to them, the double blessing………….. of shower and sunshine. The whole of the arrangements passed off admirably, the ceremony itself, the wedding breakfast, the taking of photographs, etc. The bride and bridegroom left the same evening for Chin-kiang, where they were to remain until the sisters came down from Yang-chan to join them on their way to Honan. With them were to depart reinforcements from that place for the different missionary stations. The Bride was given away by Mr Slimmoer the Deputy Director of the Mission, and Miss Kaye, the lady superintendent, took the place of the Bride's mother, and presented her with a bride cake and a set of silver buttons. There was also a goodly list of presents. The bride herself wore a silvery grey silk dress, trimmed with blue, and white and other blossoms in her hair. The Bridegroom wore a grey silk gown.

The bridesmaid was Miss Maud Fairbank. Archdeacon Moule, who performed the ceremony, and Mr Stevenson made congratulatory speeches at the dinner table, which was excellently laid, and the bridegroom responded for his wife. The wedding party went to and fro in one carriage and several rickshaws, which are small hand carriages, like the Japanese 'jinrickshas'. The remainder of the letter is filled with loving salutations to relatives and friends at home.'
(The Cambrian 2nd June 1893)

Marriage (St John's Cathedral Hong Kong)
'On 28 February, at St John's Cathedral, Hong Kong. By the Rev E.E. Allen MA, Rector of Porthkerry, Glamorganshire, and Honorary Canon of Llandaff, to Florence Hope, daughter of Marshall, Francis Julian, Surveyor of Her Britannic Majesty's Office of Works for China and Japan.'
(The Cambrian 12th April 1889)

Matthews and Company
MESSRS MATTHEWS' NEW ESTABLISHMENT (Number 6, Castle Square, Swansea)
'In being a little more than 12 months in the building of it, the Messrs. Matthews have opened their new splendid tea and grocery establishment in Castle Square, and a more handsome and tastefully arranged shop we have never seen in the provinces. Every department is most complete, whilst underneath the shop is a very spacious cellar, with the requisite machinery for removing heavy goods, etc. When lit up, the premises have certainly a most imposing view and on Friday and Saturday evenings last attracted the curiosity of hundreds of spectators.'
(The Cambrian 16th January 1857)

McFarlane (Rev. A.J.)
Headmaster of the Griffith John College, Hankow, China. He wrote about the College in 'China's revolution 1911-1912 a historical and political record of the Civil War', page 78 (Unwin London 1912)

Medhurst (C.S.)
'Missionary, born Cardiff and left for China in 1885.'
(Overseas Missionary Fellowship 1991)

Merthyr Tydfil
'Merthyr Tydfil in the 1830s had a district known as 'China'. It was an area where God-Fearing people rarely ventured. One of the inhabitants, Shoni Sgubor Fawr, gave himself the title 'Emperor of China' and terrorised the area.'
(Glamorgan Historian Vol.3 p41 – 'Law and Order 1830s)
(See: Shoni Sguborfawr)

Milledge (James Sibree)
'James Milledge was born in China to the Welsh Missionaries Miriam and Geoffrey Milledge. In 1943-45, as a young boy, he was imprisoned with his parents, in a camp. As times were becoming very difficult, his parents left China with him and the three of them settled in India. James Milledge became a doctor and married Dr Betty Averil Astle. They both stayed and worked in India. In 1970, he climbed part of the Himalayas with Sir Edmund Hillary.'
('Vehicles of Grace and Hope'-Welsh missionaries in India 1800-1970)

Milledge (Miriam, née Thomas)
'Miriam Milledge was born in Arthog, Merionethshire. In 1929, she married Dr Geoffrey Milledge and they set sail for China. In 1929 to 1931 and 1933 to 1939 they worked at Changzhou Hospital.
The years 1932 to 1933 was spent at Xiaochang. The years 1943 to 1945 were spent in a prison camp with their son, James. By 1950, China was becoming a difficult place to be so they left for India. In 1970, Miriam retired to Hertfordshire and died in 1980.'
('Vehicles of Grace and Hope'-Welsh missionaries in India1800-1970)

'Mimosa'
The ship 'Mimosa' started out as a tea clipper on the China run before being converted to take settlers to found a Welsh colony in Patagonia in 1865. The 'Mimosa' Cafe in Ystradgynlais was named after her.

Min (Anchee)
Author of 'The Last Empress' (Pub. Bloomsbury 2007) mentions the Welsh Baptist and political activist Timothy Richard.
(See: Timothy Richard)

Minhinnick (Robert)
Robert Minhinnick (born Neath 1952) is a Welsh poet, essayist, novelist and translator. He was invited to the First Chinese-English Poetry Festival at Huangshan, Anhui Province, China. He used the visit in stories published in a subsequent collection – 'The Keys of Babylon' (2011)

Miners
THE MINER'S STRIKE IN SOUTH WALES
'In reference to the strike at the Ebbw Vale Companies Works, Mr Phillips, the Deputy Chairman of the Company, writes to say that he hopes soon to resume the operations of that immense company 'on a new system', as an eminent contractor has offered to import any number of Chinese labourers (many of them skilled miners) and place them at the works in Wales at so much per head, and the offer was to be brought before the Board of Directors yesterday (Thursday). Mr Phillips adds: 'The Trades Unionists will probably Broadhead me, but I shall do my duty by my shareholders, some of whom are widows and orphans, whose property I will not stand by and see ruined by a pack of idle men who neither work themselves nor let others do so.' It is stated that while colliers are earning an average of £3 to £4 a week, the shares in the Ebbw Vale Company have only yielded dividends for the last six years averaging £3 8s. 4d. Should this threat of Chinese labour be carried out it is not difficult to foresee the consequences. A new element of competition in the labour market (which may soon extend to other occupations than coalmining); the introduction of a most undesirable variation in the population; constant hatred and disturbances between the two nationalities; the necessity for a strong armed force throughout the coal districts to protect the newcomers; and a heavy blow inflicted on the native workers at one of our chief national industries.'
(The Cambrian 31st January 1873)

Missionaries Remembered
EYES TURNED AGAIN TO CHINA
'On the handover of Hong Kong to China two famous missionaries were remembered; Griffith John and Gladys Aylward.'
('Down the Years' by Jill Forward, South Wales Evening Post Thursday, June 12th, 1997
(South Wales Evening Post www.southwales-eveningpost.co.uk)

Missionary Dolls

They were made in the early 20th Century for European children who lived in China. They became known as 'missionary dolls'. This little missionary doll was found in Wales. This particular doll is from the Author's private collection.

Mitchell (The Hamilia)
SHIPPING INTELLIGANCE
'The Hamilia Mitchell, from Cardiff, which arrived at Shanghai, January 3rd, encountered a succession of gales from October 2 to the 12th, during which she lost a complete set of canvas, a quarter boat, and the lifeboat, and had all the other boats stove on their skids.'
(The Cambrian 22nd March 1867)

Moldairen
SHIPPING INTELLIGANCE
'Spoken: The Moldairen (barque) from Swansea to Shanghai, January 12th off the Pellew Islands.'
(The Cambrian 23rd March 1866)

Mond (Dr Ludwig 1839-1909)

The Royal Society of Chemistry and the Beijing University of Chemical Technology hosted the 'Ludwig Mond Award' Symposium, March, 2011. The welcome address was given by Prof David G Evans, FRSC, Chairman of the Royal Society of Chemistry Beijing.
The 'Ludwig Mond Award' is given for outstanding research in any aspect of inorganic chemistry.
The Mond Nickel Works, Clydach, Swansea, was established in 1902 by the Mond Nickel Co to refine nickel matte from Canada by means of the nickel carbonyl process devised by Ludwig Mond. A statue to Ludwig Mond is situated opposite the entrance to the refinery at Clydach.
(See: Professor David Evans)

Moore (Sir John)
SHIPPING INTELLIGENCE
'Sir John Moore's, ship, 'Robertson', from Cardiff to Hong Kong, was passed in a sinking state on the 10th instant by the 'Amelie Chusco', which took off crew and landed them at St. Nazaire 17th.'
(The Cambrian, 29th March 1867)

Morgan (Charles Edward 1836-1911)
Brother of Frank Arthur Morgan
'Landowner in Gower and Berkshire who inherited his father's house Cae Forgan, Llanrhidian. Entered the Army just before the Crimean War (1854). Joined the 67th Regiment, eventually becoming Colonel. Went with the Army to China at the start of the 2nd Opium War; marched to Peking (Beijing) and took part in the sacking of the Summer Palace (1860). After returning home, he persuaded his younger brother Frank Arthur Morgan to join the Chinese Imperial Customs (c 1864).
He married and had one daughter who inherited and eventually sold Cae Forgan in the 1920's' (Prys Morgan 2014)

THE WAR IN CHINA
The following is a letter sent home by a young officer well known at Swansea (the son of the late Mr Morgan of Cae Forgan). The incident that he witnessed is described with much spirit, and doubtless, will be read with great interest:
China Transport Tasmania, Pehtang Forts, August 5, 1860.
'My dear mother,………….. Curious world we live in and no mistake……….. Don't you think so? Who would ever have thought of my being in this extra ordinary part of the world! It will please you, I daresay, (though it is not particularly pleasing to me) to know that I am not landed yet, although we were ordered to land twice, but are now ordered to remain till Tuesday. We were told on Friday evening to land on Saturday morning; so after I had been up nearly all Friday night getting provisions for three days for all the men, and making arrangements, Saturday arrived and with it a 'mem' to remain till Tuesday. Pleasant, eh? After having packed up everything even to one's toothbrush, and this with a thermometer at 94 in the shade, making all exertion doubly irksome. Such is life! And probably before you receive this we shall (or at least those who think of us), be either on the way to India or wintering at Tientsin……….. The former I hope. On Friday several bodies of our troops and some French effected a landing, took possession of the small forts at Pehtang, and were attacked by Tatar cavalry. Several wounded on our side…………. MH Greathead amongst others. The enemy retired in excellent order. That's all I know, as we are about 5 miles from land and can only hear the firing and see the forts. The transports can get no nearer inconsequence of the mud, and our men are landed in small boats…………. very few are landed yet; however, nothing will be done until we are landed as the Chinese are in great force. It is rumoured that they are all at Tientsin, about 30 miles up, and intend to make a grand stand there. I had drawn out a map for you, but in the hurry of packing have lost it, and fear shall not have time to make another.
We are fine fleet here, about 150 sail, and of course it is a fine sight and all that sort of thing, but we might as well be at the world's end; for the sea is too rough for much communication with each other.'

August 9
My dear mother……………. I'm safe within the Pehtang Forts, of which we have possession. I'm sitting up to my knees in water, in consequence of a thunder shower. I'm very hard worked but jolly under the circumstances.
Your affectionate son, C Morgan

Tientsin, August 25, 1860

My dear mother……………….. All right in every respect, or at least as far as I am personally concerned. Well, you see, I don't give you any circumstantial information; but, however, we landed at Pehtang Forts on 1 August, 1860, remained there till the fifth I think on which day we marched out early, i.e. about 3 am, and after marching about 11 miles through mud up to our knees, arriving in front of some forts near Sinho, where we were surrounded by some Tartar Cavalry, 'we 'means the 3rd Buffs, 44th, 67th, Royal Marines, 4th Dragoon Guards, Fane's horse, Probyn's Horse, Madras Sappers, Armstrong Guns etc and the French in another direction. I'm too tired to describe it all, just come off march now…………. suffice it to say that I was with our left-wing (about 300 men), which was a rear guard. We were surrounded by about treble our number of Tartar Cavalry, and I began to think it was all up with us, but our rifles soon made them 'hook it'. I rode out to the front and caught a pony whose rider was down, thinking I had a prize, and when I brought it up to the square they found it was shot through the throat and it died in a few minutes.

Well, our guns have knocked down the Forts and our Cavalry licked the Tatars, so we camped on the ground without tents or any harm. This fight was fought by us on a plain where we could see neither tree nor anything rising up to the horizon………. It is a splendid prairie.

Well, that night and the next we were harassed by the Tatar Cavalry; no sooner did we lie down and bang bang, and in rushed the piquet with a "Here they come! Here they come!". And this about every hour………. very trying. Here we remained two or three days and captured several Tartars and lots of the ponies of the poor devils we shot. They could not make out our rifles picking them off at all; they fought well and I fancy I saw about 100 dead cavalry in all exclusive of the heaps that must have been killed in the Fort. It was rather a sickening thing at first to see both men and horses perhaps mortally wounded and still struggling for life horse rolling on the rider and so forth; but I am accustomed to worse now. Well, then, we marched on to Tougho, above four miles from Sinho, and took it, though I must say it looked a very ticklish affair for we could see nothing but a line of forts for miles; however, in about three miles the Armstrong had blown down the gate and made a breach ………….. in we all rush, but not under much firing as the Chinese were retreating. This Fort was too big for their force to hold they fled leaving heaps of dead and dying; also all their towns full of women, children, and old men. We treated them all as well as we could. ………… gave them bread, etc; but they were afraid of our treating them as they would treat us i.e., torture us to death. Here I saw most ghastly wounds from Armstrong; shells ……. fearful horrible! And, here I saw what was worse, the poor women strangling their children and drowning themselves… …….this we saw over the town ditch, but had no means of preventing it. Well we killed I suppose about one hundred Chinese here. We had also some great fun with pigs as the town was full of them. There we were, officers and men, full tilt after pigs in all directions. I got sent into a ditch by one, and another ran into the big drum. We got a good many bits of loot in the town, though nothing of value ………. there was no silk or money. I got a good Chinese vase. Copper money in heaps, but not worth picking up, no means of sending it away.

I fell in with a heap of watermelons in the swell`s house, which, as you may fancy, after a long dry march and a lot of skirmishing, was very refreshing.

All events have taken place so rapidly, that I can scarcely remember from day to day, what happened yesterday; and as for Sunday, why most of our fights were fought on Sunday! To proceed we were at Tougho, and suddenly, on the 28th, got the order to move out about three miles, and camp without tents.

Away they went "sharp". I took out their provisions that day, and had to come back to the town for the next day's provisions for the men.

I got them already over night; had my Coolies and men at call near me, and about 8 a.m. pop goes a gun up where our fellows were; off I and my party start, and arrived there in no time, though under fire all the time from the Taku forts…………. and no mistake this time.

I found our fellows all except the guard which I was to bring up; and leaving my baggage escort behind, so with my men away I got to the front, shot and shell flying in all directions; very nearly knocked over twice by a round shot; crept up through ditches to the left wing, who were in the fourth ditch, saw the Colonel, who ordered me back for some rum for the men; this I had to bring up across the open plain.

I brought it up and then crept up to the right wing in the third ditch; went on fighting with them under fire from the three forts. Here we caught it awfully, and it required either brandy or nerve to stand it; I saw heaps knocked over. Then we crept on to the next ditch and no cover; balls flying like hail here; then came the cry of "Where are the scaling ladders?" None came for about 20 minutes, and then we were under a galling fire from three forts in full-blow…….. this was trying.

At length the French ladders came, and with a rush we were on the bank of the first ditch; then we dropped like sparrows, only about from 30 yards on the Fort and they firing at us like fun. Well, the ladders were placed across the ditch, so over we went……………. some in the water and some on the ladders; then the Chinese began to stone us from the parapet, but there was a breach, and we rushed into a hand-to-hand fight. I was the third officer in and then commenced the slaughter! They had to retire over a bridge and we shot them like sparrows; many cut their own throats.

I saw a heap of dead alone 5 feet high! The groans of the wounded were awful! All the other forts gave in; so we returned to Tougho, and came up yesterday by gunboats to this place from Tientsin. I am now in a jolly fort, all the natives round are peaceable. Lots of peaches, grapes, melons, sheep, eggs, poultry, except and again I say I am jolly if we are not again moved, for I am tired. I have just had a bottle of beer as a present from a naval officer…………. a luxury not tasted for weeks.

A most lovely country, quite a garden………… trees, fruits, water and climate beautiful.

Love to all.

Your affectionate son,

Charles E. Morgan

P.S. We alone, 67th Regiment, had eight officers wounded badly, one feared mortally, 10 killed, wounded, gallant fight! I am not wounded and, thank God, very well.

(The Cambrian 23rd November 1860)

Morgan (David Lloyd 1823-1892)

A Naval Officer, born at Llandeilo – Fawr the son of David Morgan. He studied medicine at the London Hospital and St. Andrew's University. Entered the Royal Navy in 1846 and became staff surgeon in 1854. During 1847 to 1849 he served on the West coast of Africa and the Crimean War 1850-1856. He was with the Chinese land forces between 1857 and 1861.

He was medical officer for HMS Euryalus between 1862 and 1865. A physician to Queen Victoria and died 3 December 1892 at Rhosmaen, Llandeilo.'

(Dictionary of Welsh Biography to 1940, page 641)

In
Memory of David Lloyd Morgan CB
Inspector General
Of Hospitals and Fleets RN
Physician in Ordinary
To the Queen
Of Rhosmaen, in this Parish
Eldest son of the Said David and Mary
Morgan
Who after a Distinguished
Career in the Service
Of His Country
Died On the 3rd of December
1892 Aged 69 Years

Inscription on the grave of David Lloyd Morgan at Llandeilo Church

Morgan (Frank Arthur 1844-1907)
'Son of Charles and Caroline Morgan of Herbert's Lodge Bishopston, Glamorgan; Commissioner of the Imperial Chinese Customs; Born 24th February 1844; Married his cousin Winifred Dorothy. '
(Burke's Landed Gentry 1952, p. 1822)

F.A. Morgan in his garden at Canton (Guangzhou) 1901

F.A. Morgan and his family at the house of the Customs Officials, Jiujiang about 1896

F.A. Morgan's house at Suzhou circa 1903

A Gower man serving the Dragon Throne: The Career of F. A. Morgan (1844 -1907)

'During the summer and autumn of 1993 an exhibition entitled 'All That Glisters' was held at the British Museum, London, by its Department of Coins and Medals, in which were displayed the various colourful and bejewelled insignia of the Order of the Double Dragon granted by the Emperor of China to one of his Mandarins, Frank Arthur Morgan. Since Morgan was a Gower man, and since this journal has over the years paid attention to local people serving overseas, such as Griffith John in China, it is surely not inappropriate here to give a glimpse of his exotic career.

Frank Arthur Morgan was born on 24th February 1844 at Cae Forgan, Llanrhidian, the third son of a barrister and a minor local landowner Charles Morgan (1796-1857) and his wife Caroline, daughter of the Rector of Penmaen, John James. He died in a London hospital on 11 February 1907 and was buried in the churchyard of Bishopston. He married in 1892 Winifred Dorothy the daughter of his cousin Stanley Morgan, and had three children, Frank Stanley born in 1893 at Seoul, Korea; Helen born at Kiukiang (now Jiujiang), in 1895, and Winifred Gordon, also born at Jiujiang in 1897. He inherited from his uncle, Henry John Morgan, the farm of Herbert's Lodge at Bishopston in 1859,

which he made his British home from 1885 onwards, rebuilding and extending it in 1886, this being in turn the home of his son, who died in his hundredth year in 1992.

F. A. Morgan's introduction to the Far East was through his elder brother, Charles Edward Morgan (1836-1911), of Oakfield Park, Berkshire and Cae Forgan, Llanrhidian, later Colonel of the 67th Regiment of Foot, who took part in 1860 in the Opium Wars, and in the sack of the Summer Palace on the outskirts of Peking. C.E. Morgan decided that the Orient was not for him, and returned to follow a military career. Frank, being a third son, found that he had to make his own way in the world. He was encouraged to sail out to China in May 1864 on the S.S. 'Far East', arriving in China in July and joining the Chinese Imperial Customs Service as a fourth class clerk.

It should be explained that as a result of the two Opium Wars, the Chinese were forced by Britain and other European countries to open up their coasts to foreign trade, and, to put a most complicated matter very simply, in exchange for great quantities of tea which was sold to Britain and some other countries, the Chinese were forced to accept great quantities of opium imported from India and elsewhere. To control the distribution of opium in China, and to prevent illicit opium imports, the Chinese Emperors were forced to accept a staff of European customs officers who lived mainly in the coastal and river ports of China.

Part of their work was bureaucratic, that is, keeping accounts of customs revenues, and part of their work was sleuthing, tracking down and punishing drug pirates. They all came under the control of an Inspector General, who for many years was Sir Robert Hart. Jiujiang, on the Yangtze River, was one of the most important ports for the passage of opium. China (with the exception of treaty ports such as Hong Kong) did not become a colony, but the Imperial Customs service closely resembled a colonial service, and it is hardly surprising that it is seen today in China as a form of 'imperialism'.

Frank Morgan appears to have spent a good deal of his time in Shanghai, learning Mandarin and other Chinese dialects, but was transferred to Zhenjiang (a river port on the Yangtze not far from Nanjing) in 1876. He appears to have returned to Swansea in 1877, possibly to attend to the affairs of his mother, who died at that time, and to help his three unmarried sisters set up home in their new house in Caswell Bay

On his return from long leave he was sent to Taiwan to look after the customs at the port of Taikuo on the south - western corner of the island, then was removed to Peking in 1880 where he was promoted to Deputy Commissioner. Here one of his tasks was to look after General Gordon, who had been invited to China by the Emperor's government, who needed him to suppress rebellions. He admired General Gordon so much that he was to name his second daughter Winifred Gordon after the General. In 1883 he was awarded a Diploma by the International Fisheries Exhibition in London, presumably, for opening up another closed part of China's coastal trade to foreigners. He was sent a long way up the River Yangtze to Yichang, returned to Peking serving as Acting Audit Secretary. In 1885 and 1886 he was at least for some time of his long leave home in Bishopston to arrange the redesigning of Herbert's Lodge by a London architect, Henry Hall. He returned to Peking and then was appointed in March 1887 to be the first Commissioner in charge of the Kowloon district in the far south of China in Hong Kong, where he worked for three years, it was said 'with distinction'.

The family tradition was that his sister Alice who came out to visit him, was the first to launch a European ship at Kowloon Harbour.

From 1890-91 he served at Zhouhai, then went on a long leave. He got married in 1892 and returned this time to Korea as Commissioner at Jenchuan and Seoul. His next five-year term of service began about 1895 at Jiujiang on the River Yangtze as Commissioner, before moving for two years to the southern coast of China at the port of Shantou. He was at home in Bishopston at least for part of the year 1900.

He was deeply interested in South Africa, because of the debatable question of importing Chinese 'coolie labour' into Africa. The family then in residence in Bishopston celebrated the relief of Mafeking by placing the large Japanese wooden fire prevention pumps (which were like mediaeval siege engines) on the lawn and the yard, and hurling huge quantities of water back and forth over the roof.

His final term from 1901-05 was at Guangzhou, Shantou and Suzhou. He left Canton in December 1902 and did not return to China until early November 1903 to be Commissioner at Suzhou, and by then his marriage had broken down, he instituted divorce proceedings, and his health, aggravated by an old wound in his leg, was also giving way.

He appears to have retired in May 1905. He held the Chinese Civil Rank of the 4th and 2nd Classes and was given the Order of the Double Dragon the third division first-class and was also given the right by Edward VII to have the equivalent knightly precedence in Britain. His wife, after the divorce, went to Canada and remarried a distant connection on her mother's side called Hanson, and died there in 1950.

Grave of Frank Arthur Morgan Morgan at Bishopston Church

F. A. Morgan, who was usually called Ma-Gen in Chinese, was a short, bearded, portly man, well educated by the famous Doctor Harper at Sherborne (later the Principal of Jesus College, Oxford), and like his father and son, had a great passion for reading and a talent for light verse. The Inspector-General (Sir Robert Hart) summed him up in a letter of 19th February 1893 regarding the need to settle the troubles in Korea:

'Morgan is getting into the saddle properly and will suit the post admirably. Merrill and Schoenicke did exceptionally well, but the times require three different kinds of man, and now it is the Morgan kind-commonsense and amiability-which will do best.'

F.A. Morgan's horse 'Silken Mead', with his Chinese servant, at Hong Kong 1890

He seems to have been humorous and amusing, and he liked travelling to and from the East on P&O ships because he found them less formal and pompous than other lines, but family tradition has it that he was also expected to be merciless in his dealings with Chinese opium smugglers, and if the story can be believed, had powers of summary punishment, trussing up the criminals along the quayside and cutting off their heads with a sword into the waters below, to set a ferocious example to others. He was a man of the world, and delighted in such luxuries as horseracing. His horse 'Silken Mead', named after the field, which had this beautiful name even in the seventeenth century, at the side of his house in Bishopston, won the Hong Kong races for 1890. Some silk racing favours have survived for these races of 1890.

He was said to have had great love for everything Chinese, and was cared for in China and at home in Bishopston by his servant Ma King Dong (or 'Ching-Tong' to the rest of the household) to whom he left a small legacy of 500 Mexican dollars in his will, and who, after returning to China in 1907, corresponded with the family through a friend, a bank clerk from Shanghai, for some years.

Morgan was also fond of sailing, had a yacht called the 'Kiddie' painted in the family livery colours of chocolate brown and blue, in which he would cruise up and down the coasts and islands of China.

Morgan was so accustomed to a life of travelling about China with his servant, that in Bishopston he built a bathroom for his guests but had King-Dong bath him always in a tub.

He always collected fossils and interesting pieces of rock as he travelled around China that he used to decorate his house in Bishopston. Until the 1950s the drawing room was hung with Chinese shop-signs, and indeed with the complete contents of a Chinese pedlar's tray.

The house was so crowded with Chinese curiosities and had so many Chinese features, such as numerous pots of chrysanthemums which was a status symbol of the mandarins, that in his day it was like an Oriental enclave in the middle of Gower.
In 1993, the opening of certain confidential files in governmental archives has cast some doubt as to the exact fate of General Gordon and even the exact date of his death. Frank Morgan enormously admired General Gordon, whom he had to look after on his last visit to serve the Chinese Emperor, and would in later years reminisce that as he was crossing the China Sea from China to Japan one day about the beginning of 1885, he was amazed when the Chinese crew, in the middle of the sea, suddenly told him that he should start to mourn for the death of his friend General Gordon.

He knew he was fighting in Sudan, but had heard nothing of Gordon's death, and asked the Chinese how they knew. The spirits had told them, they replied. He dismissed the story as nonsense.
But having arrived a few days later in Japan, he went to the nearest telegraph office to ask for the news. The clerks in the office said that the news was only arriving that minute of the death of Gordon at Khartoum. He was always a hard-headed man of the world, confessed that for once in his life he was dumbfounded.
I was invited to visit China in March 1992, among other things in order to find out a little more about the career of the man whom many in Gower called 'Mandarin Morgan' in his day, and the Mandarin's son, then in his hundredth year, insisted that I should visit his childhood home at Jiujiang on the River Yangtze, and returned to tell him all about it. I did manage, through the kindness of my hosts, to visit that beautifully sited town, on an isthmus between a lake and the great river itself, and even found the house of the Customs Officer still standing, although its garden had disappeared through road widening along the riverbank. The Mandarin's son died at the very moment of my return to Bishopston, and I was unable to tell him of my pilgrimage to his childhood haunts. I could not help thinking of the spirits of General Gordon. (Prys Morgan)
(Article and photographs by kind permission of Professor Prys Morgan and the Gower Society – XLIV 1993 pages 40-42)
(British Museum – F.A. Morgan Collection)
References
S.F. Wright 'Hart and the Chinese Customs' (Belfast 1950)
J.K. Fairbank, K.F. Bruner, E.M. Matheson (editors) The I.G. in Pekin, the letters of Sir Robert Hart, Chinese Imperial Customs 1868-1907, 2 volumes
(Cambridge Mass., 1975)
Marriages
'On the 9th instant, Frank Arthur Morgan, Commissioner of Imperial Chinese customs, of Herbert's Lodge, Bishopston, Swansea, to Winifred Dorothy, eldest daughter of the late Stanley Morgan, and stepdaughter of George A Petter, Gothic Lodge, Chiswick Mall. No cards.'
(The Cambrian 15th April 1892)
Births
'On the 10th instant, at Seoul, Corea, the wife of Frank Arthur Morgan, of Bishopston, Swansea, Commissioner Imperial Chinese Customs, a son.'
(The Cambrian 13th January 1893)

Morgan (Rev. E)
'Baptist Minister, Shanghai, China; born in Llangeitho in 1860. Worked in Qufu in 1884. He learnt Chinese and moved to Shaanxi Province before moving on to Shanxi where he had to oversee 10 schools. In 1906, he moved to Shanghai and worked on translating materials into Chinese. He was awarded an honorary Doctorate by the University of Wales in 1924. He spent forty years in China and died in Bristol in 1941.' (Who's Who in Wales 1920; Ceredigion Archives)

Morris (Alfred, A.C.P, M.R.S.I)
'Headmaster of Saiyingpun School. Born 21st June 1874 at Cwmavon. Formerly at Hong Kong Technical Institute and part-time Assistant Tutor in English at Hong Kong University. Member of the Hong Kong Volunteer Corps and Hong Kong Defence Corps.'
(Who's Who in Wales in 1920)

Morris (William John)
'Born in Llanelli in 1870. Missionary in China from 1894 and served in Guangzhou.'
(Overseas Missionary Fellowship 1991)

Moss (Gwenfron 1898-1991)
'A Pharmacist; born 1888 in Coedpoeth, near Wrexham. In 1928 sailed to China (Tianjin). She worked in Tianjin with the wife of the Rev. William Hopkyn Rees, who was also from Coedpoeth. She died in 1991 aged 93.'
(Overseas Missionary Fellowship 1991)

N

National Botanic Garden Wales (NBGW)

The Garden is situated near Llanarthne in the Towy Valley, Carmarthenshire. It is both a visitor attraction and the 'Centre for Botanical Research and Conservation', and features the world's largest single-span glasshouse measuring 110 m (360 ft) long by 60 m (200 ft) wide.

In 2012 NBGW signed a Memorandum of Understanding with Nanshan Botanic Garden in Chongqing as part of the Wales Government-China link and designed the Wales Garden for the Chongqing International Garden Expo in 2012. Three members from the Garden attended the Expo in December 2012 and the Garden is still there. It was called 'Gifted by Nature, United by Dragons'.

NBGW collaborated with Nanshan Botanic Garden in Chongqing and took an exhibition called 'Barcode beyond the Visible' there for Wales Week in Spring 2013. At that event an MOU was signed with Nanshan.

Head of Conservation and Research, Dr Natasha De Vere was in Kunming for the '5th International Barcode of Life Conference' in October 2013 that was co-hosted by the Kunming Institute of Botany. During the conference she visited the seedbank and herbarium and also had discussions on collaboration in relation to pollinators and work at the field station in the mountains near Lijiang called the Lijiang Alpine Botanic Garden and Jade Dragon Field Station.

Kunming Institute of Botany   Xishuangbanna Tropical Botanical Garden

Dr. Rosie Plummer, Director of NBGW at 5th International Barcode of Life Conference, Kunming (October 2013)

'Ni Hăo'
The Newsletter of the Wales-China Friendship Society; first published in 1987

WCFS Newsletter – March 2013

Nanjing
The Treaty of Nanjing was signed on August 29th, 1842. A Welshman was present at the signing of the Treaty on board HMS Cornwallis. Richard Woosnam, of Builth Wells, was Private Secretary to Sir Henry Pottinger who became the first Governor of Hong Kong.
(See: Woosnam)

Nantgarw (Dawnswyr)
Based in Cardiff, the Welsh dance group Dawnswyr Nantgarw was formed in 1980 with the intention of reviving the folk dancing tradition in the Taff and Rhondda valleys. They have grown to be one of the largest and most successful teams in Wales and visited China in 1999.

Nantmor
Nantmor, near Beddgelert, was the fictional city of Wang Chang, China in the film 'Inn of the Sixth Happiness' made in 1958. It starred Ingrid Bergman portraying the story of the missionary Gladys Aylward.
(See: Gladys Aylward), 'Inn of the Sixth Happiness', Beddgelert)

Nantong
The Cities of Swansea and Nantong (Jiangsu Province, China) signed a friendship partnership in 1987. A road in the Swansea Enterprise Zone is named Nantong Way. Nantong had the first museum in China and Swansea had the first museum in Wales.

Nantong Way road sign at Swansea Enterprise Park

Nantong is famous for its embroidery. The Chinese scene pictured is embroidered on fine net - a gift from the City of Nantong.

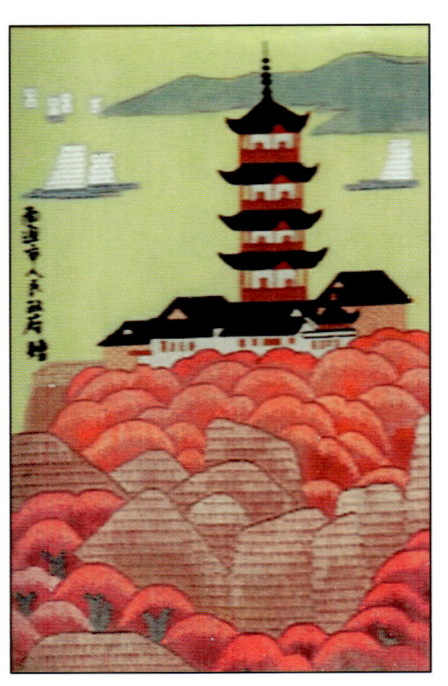

National Trust
Examples of Chinese wallpaper may be seen at Erddig Hall, Powis Castle and Penrhyn Castle. The three properties are in the possession of the National Trust.

Nantyffyllon
'Hanes Eglwys 1841-1941'
There is a section on W.T. Beynon whose family was killed by the Boxers in 1900
(See: W.T. Beynon)

Nantymoel Primary School
'The students of Nantymoel Primary School released helium filled balloons to raise money for charity in July 1993. To the students amazement they received a card written in English from Cheung Xin who worked at the Shangri-La hotel in Beijing. Cheung explained how he had found the balloon in the hotel grounds.'
(Nantymoel Primary School)

Napier (Major-General Sir Robert)
'At the taking of the Taku forts in China, Major-General Sir Robert Napier, the gallant brother of Captain Napier, of Bridgend, had his glasses broken by a gingal ball, and was also scratched in two places.'
(The Cambrian 23rd November 1860)

National Dance Company Wales (NDW)

The National Dance Company Wales made its debut visit to China in 2009. The Company visited Kunming, Chengdu and Chongqing. It was the first international company to perform at the new Grand Theatre in Chongqing.

Members of NDW rehearsing in China

National Museum of Wales (NMW) Exhibition Chongqing

An exhibition – 'Land of the Red Dragon' opened at the Three Gorges Museum in Chongqing as part of the 'Wales-Chongqing Week' in 2013 that featured Welsh culture, language, history and landscape. It was part of an on-going relationship between the NMW and the Three Gorges Museum – a Memorandum of Understanding (MOU) being signed in 2008.

Official opening ceremony at the Three Gorges Museum Chongqing (2013)

National Screen and Sound Archives (Wales)
The National Screen and Sound Archives of Wales are located at Aberystwyth. A video copy of the Wales-China Friendship Society's 'China 89' Tour to China was deposited at the Archives.
  (See: 'China 89')

Neath (Town Hall)
THE OPIUM TRADE
'A public meeting of the inhabitants of Neath was held in the Town Hall, on Monday evening last, for the purpose of adopting a petition to Parliament, praying for the total and immediate repression of the opium trade between China and India.
The Mayor, Mr James Kenway, presided, who, after briefly opening the proceedings, called upon the Rector to move the first resolution. The following is the resolution moved by the Rev J Griffiths, seconded by Mr Evans, and carried unanimously.

That, in the opinion of this meeting, the opium traffic carried on between India and China is most iniquitous and demoralising in its tendencies, demanding the exertions of the inhabitants of this town to obtain its suppression; and that the petition to both Houses of Parliament be forwarded to Mr Dillwyn in support of Mr Gilbert's motion in the House of Commons on Wednesday next'. A cordial vote of thanks was awarded the Rector for his interesting address upon this occasion, after which the petition was signed by a large number of those present, and the proceedings terminated.'
(The Cambrian 1st April 1859)

Neath (Town Hall)

THE MOST SPLENDID EXHIBITION IN WALES

```
THE MOST SPLENDID EXHIBITION EVER IN WALES
            TOWNHALL, NEATH
         FOR SIX NIGHTS ONLY, viz,
 MONDAY, TUESDAY, WEDNESDAY, THURSDAY, FRIDAY AND SATURDAY,
        NOV 9TH, 10TH, 11TH, 12TH, 13TH and 14TH, 1846.
   M. Gompertz respectfully announces SIX performances of the celebrated
         P    A    N    O    R    A    M    A,
 Painted on 4500 Square Feet of canvas, the largest ever exhibited out of
 London, illustrating in Thirteen Views, the principal events connected with

           T H E   W A R   W I T H   C H I N A!
```

(The Cambrian November 1846)

New Welsh Review
'Internal Migration in the People's Republic of China' - An article and photographs by Rhodri Jones Autumn 2008, Number 81, P. 46-56).
(See: Rhodri Jones)

Newport (Chinese Laundry)
'Friday, 6th June 1919. A Chinese laundry, refreshment houses and lodging houses were wrecked and the furniture was taken into the street and burned.'
(The Times, 10th June 1919)

Newman (Private Charles)
The 'Firing Line' Museum, at Cardiff Castle, possesses the diary of Private Newman, King's Dragoon Guard. It records the events during the Second China War of 1860.
(The QDG Heritage Trust, Cardiff Castle)

Regimental Diary of Private Charles Newman of the King's Dragoon Guards

North Wales Chinese Association (NWCA)
The North Wales Chinese Association is a non-political, non-religious organization formed to serve and represent the interests of those members of the Chinese community. The Association, based in Bangor provides a wide range of services to meet the needs of the Chinese community in North Wales and promote mutual understanding between Wales and China.

O

Odell (Rev. Collis)
MARRIAGES
'On 21 March, at Hong Kong, by the Lord Bishop of the Diocese, Miss Elizabeth Hingston, younger sister of the late Mr Hingston, of Cardiff, to the Rev Maurice Collis Odell, Military Chaplain at Hong Kong.'
(The Cambrian 9th June 1854)
BIRTHS
'On the 15th March, at Hong Kong, the wife of the Rev M.C. Odell, Military Chaplain, of a son'.
(The Cambrian 13th April 1855)

Olympics and Paralympics
Welsh athletes formed part of Team GB at the 2008 Beijing Olympics and Paralympics. On returning home to Wales, they were welcomed by rousing cheers and enthusiastic flag-waving at the Senedd in Cardiff Bay.

Onllwyn (Plate)
(See Griffith John; Wuhan)

Opium
'It looked very much like a return of 1839-40, and similar arguments were again in advance in the House of Commons." On May 7th, 1913 the Rev. Josiah Towyn Jones, the Welsh nationalist, moved that "China should be released from her treaty of obligation to admit opium, and that "she should be set free to prohibit the importation of the stocks of opium now accumulated at the treaty ports and Hong Kong". If successful, the motion would have led to enormous, perhaps crippling losses. Jones apologised for any defects in his maiden speech, as English was to him a foreign language.'
('Hong Kong' by Frank Welch, Chapter 12, P.363)

Opium Den Restaurant Swansea

In the 1990s, Tak Chan, owner of the former Opium Den Restaurant, Castle St, Swansea, commissioned a replica ceiling of the Palace Museum, Beijing. Students from the Swansea College of Art were given the commission by Mr. Chan to decorate the restaurant's ceiling with Chinese Dragons, covered in gold leaf, identical to those on the ceilings of the Palace Museum in Beijing.

Opium Trade in China
ADDRESS BY THE REV YUNG-KING YEN, M. A., AT SWANSEA
'Last (Thursday) evening the Reverend Yung-King Yen M.A., representing the native Church of China, addressed a public meeting at the Albert Hall, Swansea, to protest against the opium trade in China. There was a crowded audience, and the address was listened to most attentively. Dr Rawlins presided, and was supported by the Reverends James Owen, Eli Clarke, Dr. John Williams, O.T. Snelling, Mrs Eben Davis, Cllr. Rocke, Mr W Nicholls (secretary YMCA) etc. The Chairman read letters regretting the inability to be present from several gentlemen, including Mr R.D.Burnie, M.P., who wrote in sympathy with the crusade against opium. The Chairman introduced the Rev. Mr. Yen in a capital speech, in which he strongly denounced the use of opium, which he said was debasing physically and morally.

The Rev. Yung-King Yen was loudly applauded on rising to address the meeting. He spoke with great deliberation and clearness, and seemed to know this thoroughly. In opening, he referred to the fact that Swansea boy, the Rev. Griffith John, was championing the cause in China, and that he (the speaker) represented the opinion of the Christians and heathens in China. The Rev gentleman first dealt with a history of the opium traffic, which was encouraged by European merchants. So serious did it become that in 1839 China decided to take vigorous measures to stop the entrance of smuggled opium into the country. After repeated warnings to the English merchants Commissioner Lin surrounded their houses with troops and secured the whole quantity of opium then lying in Chinese waters, value nearly £2,000,000. This he utterly destroyed. War followed, China was defeated, and the Treaty of Nanking was signed in 1842, by which the Chinese Government was compelled to pay £2,000,000 for the destroyed opium, £4,000,000 for the expenses of the war, to open five ports for foreign trade, and to cede Hong Kong to Great Britain as a place for the refitting and careening of ships, followed by a supplementary treaty in 1843. England's part of this treaty was fulfilled by turning Hong Kong into a huge opium warehouse, by encouraging the contraband. In 1856-58 the second war arose indirectly through the smuggling of opium into China. China was again defeated, and the Treaty of Tientsin was signed, by which more ports were open to British trade, and the import of opium was legalised. The imported opium was to be subject to a tariff duty of 5 per cent 'ad velorem', amounting to 30 taels per chest of 133 pounds. Li Hung Chang, China's great statesman, declared in 1881 "China's view of the whole question from a moral standpoint; England's from a fiscal. The present duty was established, not from choice, because China is submitted to the adverse decision of arms." The speaker stated that the Chinese were not a warlike people; they were mild and peaceable, and they never had, and never would, be victorious in a war. They look down upon the military service with the results that only the riff-raff and the scum of the nation entered it. In 1869 the tariff came under revision. The leading men of the Empire were alarmed that the spread of so great an evil, and approached the British Ambassador, most pathetically begging him to use his influence with the Government to bring the traffic to an end. Eventually China's terms, fixing the 'li-kin' at 80 taels, in addition to 30 taels tariff duty, were accepted. When the agreement came up for revision in 1890 the second additional article was arranged, by which Chungking, 1000 miles up the River Yangtze Kiang, was added to the list of treaty ports, so that now it is legal to take Indian opium right into the heart of China, as well as to have it pass freely from east to west China, without further taxation in that which is paid at the port of entry. In conclusion, the Rev. Gentleman dwelt upon the evils of opium, and made an eloquent and earnest appeal for support in the cause. The meeting concluded with a vote of thanks and the singing of a hymn.'
(The Cambrian September 7th 1894)

Owen (Brigadier General Chas. S, C.M.G, D.S.O)
'Born 1879 at Ymlwch, Caernarvonshire and served in China.'
(WHO'S WHO IN WALES, 1920, P.347)

Owen (George S.)
'George Owen (1843-1914) was born in Pembroke and sailed for Shanghai with Evan Bryant. He worked in Beijing and contributed to the translation of the Bible into Mandarin. On returning home, he became Professor of Chinese at the University of London.'
(Overseas Missionary Fellowship, 1991)

Owens (Hugh)
Hugh Owens wrote home to his mother from HMS Cornwallis in Hong Kong, May 1843. The Cornwallis had returned to Hong Kong, from the River Yangtze, where the document ceding Hong Kong to Britain was signed on board the ship.

Hong Kong
HMS Cornwallis
May 4th, 1843

 '*Dear Mother,*
I embrace the excellent opportunity of writing to you a few lines hoping you are quite well as I am at present and give my kind love to my sisters as I hope they are quite well and give my kind love to Mr...... and likewise to my uncles and aunts. Dear affectionate Mother will you be so kind as to send me an answer stating me uncle William Jones' health and tell me where my uncle Richard Jones resides. Dear mother I received four letters the last one was in December 1842.
Dear mother Henry Williams was invalided home in the Apollo and there are two young men on board coming home with us James Cringely he belongs to C........ and Hugh Thomas belongs to Bungalore. Dear mother thank God I am in good health and spirits and our ship is expected to be ordered home at the latter end of August as soon as the China ransom is paid and I hope I shall find you quite well and comfortable.

Dear affectionate mother Henry Williams' cousin Henry Edwards is homeward bound in a Liverpool ship. No more at present and give my love to all especially my friends.
Hugh Owens
Seaman on
HMS Cornwallis to is affectionate mother Ellen Owen'
(Caernarfon Record Office, Gwynedd Council)

Owen (John William)
'John Owen was born, June 1881. He left for China in September 1904, aged 23 and arrived in October 1904. He studied for the Ministry and lived at Oakleigh, Brynhyfryd Road, Llandudno. He married Miss M.A. Lloyd in November, 1909.'
(Overseas Missionary Fellowship, 1991)

Owen (William)
'William Owen (1847-1925) was born at Llanharon. In 1878 he was appointed as a missionary to Sichuan. He also worked in Wuhan with Griffith John and was acknowledged as a good Chinese scholar. He died at Barry in 1925.'
(Overseas Missionary Fellowship, 1991)

Oxwich
In the graveyard of St. Illtyd's Church, Oxwich, Gower there is a grave that commemorates the death of Thomas Evans, who died at Tianjin in 1869. The grave also commemorates other family members who died abroad.
(See: Thomas Evans)

P

Palace Museum
'Clocks and watches from the Qing Dynasty. From the collection in the Palace Museum' (Foreign Languages Press 2008) compiled by Pin Liao. The collection includes clocks by William Hughes, the Angelsey-born clockmaker '(The Clocks of William Hughes)
  (See: William Hughes).

Parry (Lord Gordon)
Gordon Samuel David Parry, born Neyland, Pembrokeshire on 30th November 1925, was a Welsh Labour politician. He was created a Life Peer as Lord Parry of Neyland on 21 January 1976 by the Prime Minister Harold Wilson. He wrote about his visit to China and related the interesting story of his neighbour, Mrs Wood who had spent time in China. He died 1st September 2004.
(See: Captain Richard Wood)

Paterson (Neil)
Author of 'The China Run' – A story about a voyage between Wales and China. Christian West, on the death of her husband, became the ship's captain in the days when women were not expected to tackle such a job -let alone be a successful captain.
('The Biography of a Great Grandmother - 1829 to 1893' by Neil Paterson pub. Hodder and Stoughton Ltd 1948)
(See: China Run)

Pathfinder
SHIPPING INTELLIGENCE
'The 'Pathfinder' from Swansea to Hong Kong, September 15, 1860.'
(The Cambrian October 19th 1860)

Patterson (Sharon)
Sharon Patterson, Swansea, designed and made a Welsh Dragon stained-glass window to be displayed at the Welsh Dragon Exhibition held at the British Consulate General in Shanghai. The Exhibition was held to promote trade with China.
(See: 'Welsh Dragons for China Exhibition')

Stained-glass Dragon window by Sharon Patterson

Pearson (Gail)
International operatic soprano and singing teacher born in Neath. A former student at Cwrt Sart Comprehensive School, Briton Ferry and studied at Cardiff University and the Royal Northern College of Music in Manchester. She currently divides her time between performing and teaching singing at the Royal Welsh College of Music and Drama and Cardiff University School of Music. Soloist on the 'China 89' - Wales' first ever student's performance and cultural tour to China in 1989.
(See: China 89)

Gail Pearson with members of the 'China 89' Choir in concert at Nantong (1989)

Pearson (Robert John Charles 1907- 1983)
'Domiciled in Swansea. Chief Petty Officer on HMS Gannet (1934-1936) that formed part of the Yangtze Flotilla. During his time on the Yangtze he took many photographs of his life in China.'
(Malcolm Hansler – great nephew)
The following photographs are from a collection by Robert Pearson while serving aboard HMS Gannet of the Yangtze Flotilla.

HMS Gannet

Chinese gentlemen aboard HMS Gannet

Christmas card from Yangtze Flotilla sent home to his wife (1935)

Peking Opera

St. David's Hall, Cardiff hosted the Peking Opera in November 1986. The Chinese Theatre combined music, dance, song, acrobatics and martial arts in the performances which consisted of extracts including:-

'Stealing the Magic Herbs' 'The Jade Bracelet'   'Havoc in Heaven' 'The Red Maid' 'The Monkey King 500 Years On'

The performance and Opera School was organized by the Cardiff Laboratory Theatre (1986).

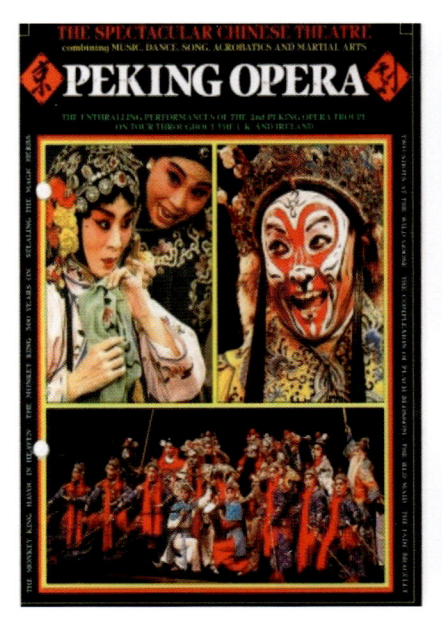

Peking Opera and School posters – Cardiff Laboratory Theatre

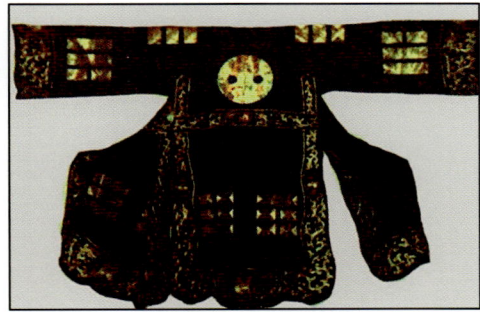

Peking Opera Robes Exhibition at the Chapter Arts Centre, Cardiff, organized by the Cardiff Laboratory Theatre (1986)

Pembroke
A CHINESE COMMISSION AT PEMBROKE
'On Tuesday a Chinese Commission paid a visit to Pembroke Dockyard, and was conducted through the various departments and over the ships under construction by Captain Morant, superintendent of the yard, and Mr JC Froyne, chief constructor. They were afterwards conveyed in the steam launch to the monster steel - clad 'Nile' lying at Hobbs point. The small august party appeared deeply interested in everything that came under their notice.'
(The Cambrian 6th July 1888)

Pembrokeshire
'The Pembrokeshire Tea Company, Nant Y Coy in the Preselli Hills, is owned by Tony Malone and Michael Ward. They are even exporting tea to China.'
(CNN 2010)

Penllergare
A drawing (c.1854) of a 'Chinese Primrose' (Primula Sinensis) by John D.Llewelyn
(See page 251 'The Photographer of Penllergare - The Life of John D. Llewellyn, 1810-1882' by Noel Chanon pub. 2013

Penpont
(See: Penry Williams)

Phillips (Arthur Noel 1841-1900)
'A soldier from Breconshire and entered the Royal Navy as Master's Assistant in 1855. He received the China Medal for the operations which ended with the taking of Canton; Died at Talgarth.
('Eminent Welshmen' by T.R Roberts, volume 1)

Phillips (Thomas 1760-1851)
He founded St. David's College Lampeter in 1822 and Llandovery College in 1848. He was 88 years of age when Llandovery College opened. He donated 7,000 books to Landovery and 20,000 books to St. David's Lampeter. Many of the books he donated related to aspects of China in which he took a particular interest especially on the subjects of Chinese religion and philosophy.

One of the many books donated by Thomas Phillips was a copy of the atlas used by the British Embassy in 1793. The atlas not only contained maps, including the route to and around China, but also illustrations of significant places the Embassy visited during its stay, including the Great Wall of China. The following illustrations are taken from the atlas.

Chinese barges of the Embassy preparing to pass under a bridge

An 18th Century engraving of the Great Wall of China

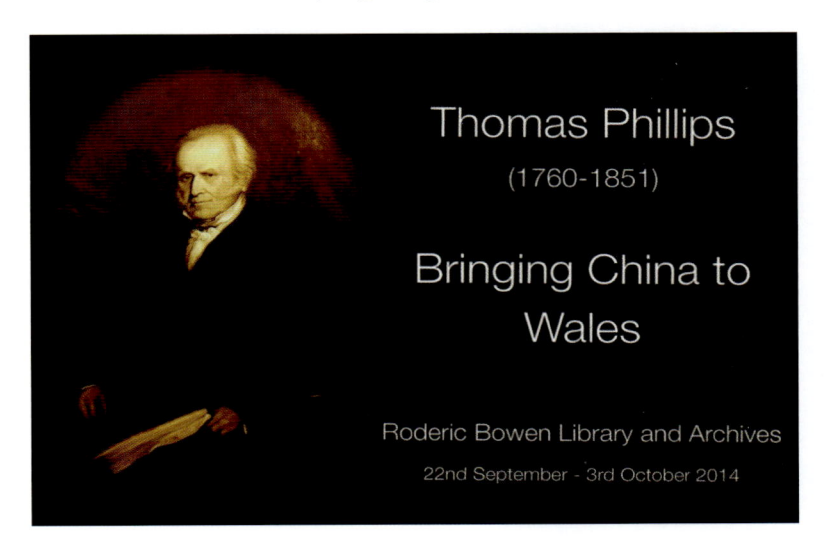

Thomas Phillips (1760-1851)
'Bringing China to Wales' (Roderic Bowen Library and Archives UWTSD Lampeter 2014)

'The Authentic Account of An Embassy from the King of Great Britain to the Emperor of China' by Sir George Staunton gave a written account of the preparations and journey of the Embassy. The frontispiece (pictured) mentions Admiral Sir Erasmus Gower as Commander of the Expedition.
(See: Admiral Sir Erasmus Gower)

AN
AUTHENTIC ACCOUNT
OF
AN EMBASSY
FROM
THE KING OF GREAT BRITAIN
TO THE EMPEROR OF CHINA;

INCLUDING
CURSORY OBSERVATIONS MADE AND INFORMATION OBTAINED IN TRAVELLING THROUGH
THAT ANCIENT EMPIRE, AND A SMALL PART OF CHINESE TARTARY

TOGETHER WITH A RELATION OF
THE VOYAGE UNDERTAKEN ON THE OCCASION
BY HIS MAJESTY'S SHIP 'THE LION', AND THE SHIP 'HINDOSTAN', IN THE EAST
INDIA COMPANY'S SERVICE, TO THE YELLOW SEA, AND GULF OF PEKIN;
AS WELL AS THEIR RETURN TO EUROPE;
WITH
NOTICES OF THE SEVERAL PLACES WHERE THEY STOPPED IN THEIR WAY OUT AND HOME;
BEING THE ISLANDS OF MADEIRA, TENERIFFE, AND ST. JAGO: THE PORT OF RIO
DE JANEIRO IN SOUTH AMERICA: THE ISLANDS OF ST. HELENA, TRISTAN
D' ACUNHA, AND AMSTERDAM; THE COAST OF JAVA, AND SUMATRA
THE NANKA ISLES, PULO CONDORI, AND COCHIN-CHINA.

TAKEN CHIEFLY FROM THE PAPERS OF
His Excellency the EARL OF MACARTNEY, Knight of the Bath, His Majesty's
Embassador Extraordinary and Plenipotentiary to the Emperor of China; Sir ERASMUS GOWER
Commander of the Expedition, and of other Gentlemen in the several departments of the Embassy

By SIR GEORGE STAUNTON. BARONET,
Honorary Doctor of Laws of the University of Oxford, Fellow of the Royal Society of London, His Majesty's
Secretary of Embassy to the Emperor of China, and Minister Plenipotentary in the absence of the Embassador.

In Two Volumes, with Engravings; beside a Folio Volume of Plates.
VOL. I.

LONDON:

PRINTED BY W. BULMER AND CO.
FOR G. NICOL, BOOKSELLER TO HIS MAJESTY, PALL-MALL.
MDCCXCVII

Phipps (John)

'Private John Phipps of the King's Dragoon Guard was awarded the China Medal with clasp. During the China war of 1860 Private Phipps was detailed to form part of the Escort to the British Envoy seeking peace with the Chinese. The Envoy and his escort were imprisoned by the Chinese and subjected to the most rigorous conditions being bound and tortured throughout their captivity. The Private showed the greatest courage and cheerfulness and continually kept up the spirits of the other captives. After weeks of continuing hardship Private Phipps eventually died just before the prisoners were released.'

The picture shows the return of bodies of the prisoners who died, and their identification by moonlight.
(See also: Thomas William Bowlby and the wreck of the 'Royal Charter' in Wales)
(QDG Heritage Trust 'The Firing Line' Cardiff Castle)

Piech (Paul Peter 1920-1996)

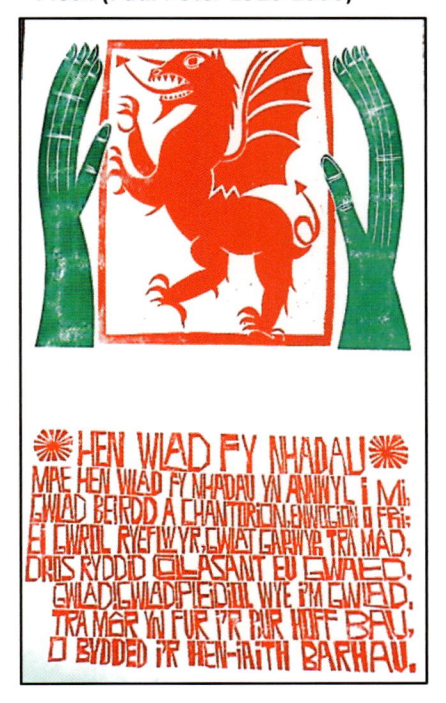

Born in 1920 in New York, USA, of Ukranian parents. He married a Welsh nurse Eileen Tomkins, in 1947. Piech was a graphic artist and printmaker; a man from Brooklyn who made his home in Porthcawl. A former member of the U.S. Army he was based in Cardiff during World War II with the U.S. 8th Army Air Force. To cheer the men up, he was asked to paint glamorous blondes on the aircraft as the planes were given female names.

Piech was to become an internationally famous graphic artist and printmaker. When he heard about the Welsh Dragon Exhibition to be held at the British Consulate General in Shanghai in 1988, he willingly and enthusiastically donated a print (Pictured) made especially for the Exhibition of a Welsh Dragon accompanied by the words of the Welsh National Anthem.

Pin Liao
(See: Palace Museum)

Polo (Marco)
'Marco Polo, Genghis Khan and his Grandson, Kublai Khan.'
'The Europa Youth Conference, hosted by Radnorshire District Council, made history at Llandrindod Wells in Wales as Conference delegates took part in one of the most historic meetings in 700 years.

Mr Mate de Polo, 22 years old a descendant of Marco Polo, from the island of Korcula, where Marco Polo was born, toasted 23-year-old Ms Dashzeveg Delegsuren, a descendant of Genghis Khan and grandson Kublai Khan from Mongolia.

'A toast to the first meeting between Marco Polo and Kublai Khan in 1271 was proposed by James A. Gilman MA President of The International Marco Polo Committee. The Europa Youth Conference, hosted by Radnorshire District Council, made history at Llandrindod Wells in Wales as Conference delegates took part in one of the most historic meetings in 700 years.
Mr. Mate de Polo, 22 years old a descendant of Marco Polo, from the island of Korcula, where Marco Polo was born, toasted 23-year-old Ms Dashzeveg Delegsuren, a descendant of Genghis Khan and grandson Kublai Khan from Mongolia. '
('Brecon and Radnor Express and Powys County Times')

Photograph shows Mayors and Council Chairmen from Welsh Councils funding the Marco Polo Project with Mr Mate de Polo and Ms Dashzeveg Delegsuren (centre) at the Lakeside Restaurant, Llandrindod Wells (1993)

'Practical Pity'
RESCUE THE PERISHING

Swansea, July 31, 1878
'To the Editor of the Cambrian,
Sir,
 Yes the perishing! I do not now mean those who perish spiritually but those who die for the want of food. I do not at present plead for those at home but for those abroad, namely the Chinese. The last tidings from there are terrible! The calamity seems like a swelling river widening and deepening in its course.
 The happy results of the relief sent to the sufferers are most encouraging. The British Council at Tientsin writing to the Committee of the Relief Fund writes, thus the effect produced on all classes of the natives in North China by the action of the missionaries who had been distributing relief:- "The officials treat the missionaries now with the most marked cordiality and assist them in every way in their power." Mr Smith (one of the distributors) triumphantly tells us that the people have at last "opened their houses", and that the distributors have, since last autumn, seen more of Chinese life than all the other missionaries put together, since China was open to them.
The advent of a foreigner in all the plans which are being resisted is now hailed with delight; and the utmost courtesy and hospitality extended to them, not only by those who taste of the generosity but by those who need it not. The distribution of funds your Committee have so kindly sent to the brave and judicious band of missionaries now engaged in the work will do more really to open China to us than a dozen wars. The outdated class the 'literati' and 'gentry' are beginning to modify their rules with regard to foreigners and are confessing that their efforts for the relief of the suffering millions not only an example for them, and have really been the incentive which has produced Chinese action.
A correspondent writes from Sweden "How is it possible that Christians should read again and again the awful reports from China and other parts, and that there should not go out a general agonised cry and shouts of "We must go and help!" I would add how little regard is the golden rule- "Do unto others as you would have others do unto you." If we denied ourselves of some of even the necessities of life it would be in one sense no wonder; but what of the feasting, drinking, and smoking, that are going on in our country, in spite of all the alarming news that reach us; thousands dying, millions suffering at the moment. There is a God that judges on earth! Will He not visit us if we are indifferent, especially if, "at ease in Zion at such a time as this." With what measure it shall be measured to you again, are ''His words''. However, much has been done for their relief, how much more may be done by use of proper means? Yours, etc., PRACTICAL PITY '
(The Cambrian 2nd August 1878)

Pope (Samuel)
LETTER FROM A DOWLAIS FUSILIER
'Private Samuel Pope (Number 4273) of the 3rd Royal Welch Fusiliers, was with the British Field Forces and took part in the capture of Tientsin, North China, writing from that city shortly after the engagement to his parents in High Street, Dowlais, says: "There are about 300 of our regiment up here. We had a bit of a fight getting into Tientsin, but we took it quite easily eventually. One of our regiment was killed and two were wounded. We were on the left flank, our sailors and marines were next, and then came the Americans. The Italians, German and Russian troops were on the right flank shelling the town with the big guns as we advanced, and they did some good work too.

I can tell you when we got within 1000 yards of the city bullets began to whizz about us, but they did very little damage, as the shots were well above our heads or else struck the ground in front. If the enemy had been any sort of marksman not one half of us would have got near. I was glad we got the order to charge for the nearer we got the safer we were. Our officers told us to take no prisoners, so that meant to kill all and spare no one.
The enemy had put their guns away when we got up as if they were innocent of firing, but we shot and bayonetted as many as we could find. We were given a fine reception by the English residents in the City. It was like a second Ladysmith, for the Chinese had been shelling the place for about a fortnight, but they did very little damage. (The Western Mail, 6th September 1900)

Porcelain (Chinese)
In 1987 the National Museum of Wales exhibited some exquisite and rare pieces of Chinese porcelain that came from the much larger collection owned by Sir Michael Butler, former Ambassador to the EEC. One hundred and thirty pieces from his collection were on display.

Powell (Amanda Elizabeth)
'Born Aberdare in 1895 and appointed as a Missionary to Guangzhou in 1901. In 1919 married Dr E.C. Peake and moved to Hangzhou and later worked at Tianjin. She died in 1939.'
(Overseas Missionary Fellowship 1991)

Presbyterian
PRESBYTERIAN MISSION TO CHINA
'On Tuesday evening, the 17th instant, a public meeting will be held in Mount Pleasant Chapel, and the Rev W.B. Swanson will deliver a narrative of mission work in China, and a collection will be made in aid of the mission.'
(The Cambrian 13th October 1876)

Price (David)
'On the 13th ult, on a voyage from China to New York Captain David Price, of the barque 'Maxima', of Swansea, died, aged 53 years, regretted by a large circle of friends.'
(The Cambrian 25th January 1878)

Price (F.S.)
In his 'History of Caio' there is a section on the Rev Timothy Richard, p.58 to 59.

Price (Frederick William)
'Originally from Darrenfelin, Llanelly Hill, Clydach, near Abergavenny, he went to China in 1911. He worked at Taizhou from 1915 to 1922, Xinzhou - 1922 to 1935 and married May Rose Nicolle, of Jersey in 1915. Senior Missionary in Taiyuan - 1935 to 1936 during the Japanese attacks and was imprisoned. On release, returned as a Minister to Abergavenny. Retired to Sussex.'
(Overseas Missionary Fellowship 1991)

Price (Pat)
Pat Price, of the Lovespoon Gallery in Mumbles, Swansea commissioned artist, John Harris, to carve a Lovespoon for the Welsh Dragon Exhibition held at the British Consulate General in Shanghai which opened on March 1st, 1988.

Prince of Wales
The Prince's Foundation for Building Community donated funds to the SHIJIA HUTONG REJUVENATION PROJECT in Beijing. A 'hutong' is the name given to the lanes in and around Beijing. Over the years many 'hutongs' have been demolished to make way for the 'new' Beijing. Courtyard 24 of Shijia Hutong has been saved from the bulldozer as it is a typical example of a Beijing 'siheyuan'-a home built around a courtyard.
It has been saved for posterity with a donation from the Prince's Foundation for Building Community.
The former home is now called Shijia Hutong Museum and will attempt to capture the sights and sounds of traditional hutong life. It was previously the home of a well-off literary family. Colin Chinnery, a Beijing artist and curator, explained that his grandparents once owned the house. He recalled that his grandmother, Ling Shuhua, the daughter of a provincial governor, had been a painter and writer and, on marrying a professor from Peking University, was given the house as a wedding gift. In 1947, Ling and her family fled to the UK to escape the Country's revolution. The house became a factory and later a kindergarten.

Shijia Hutong Museum, Beijing

The Prince of Wales and the Chinese Ambassador Liu Xiaoming opened Wales' first Confucius Classroom on St David's Day 2011 at Llandovery College in Carmarthenshire. The opening coincided with the College's 163rd anniversary.

Proctor (William)
'Sometime Assistant Under-Manager at the Britannia (Pengam) Colliery. Appointed a colliery manager in China (1919).'
(WHO'S WHO IN WALES 1920)

Prosser (Michael)
Michael Prosser held an exhibition at The Cross Community Centre, Pontardawe, in January 1983. It was called:
'AN EXHIBITION OF CHINA'S MINORITY LANGUAGES '
(South Wales Evening Post, Wednesday, February 2nd, 1983 www.southwales-eveningpost.co.uk)

Pryce (Lewis 1684-1720)
An armorial dinner plate from Canton,China bearing his coat of arms.
(See Gogerddan)
(National Museum of Wales)

Armorial plate and Coat of Arms of Lewis Pryce

Pullin (Thomas William)
'Thomas William Pullin, died aged 44 on 22nd October 1917, Welsh Regiment, Private; the son of William and Cecilia Pullin, 11 Corporation Road. Served in China. St. Woolas Cemetery, Newport, memorial Newport Cenotaph-First World War.'
(History Points)

Q

Qingdao (Former spelling Tsingtao)
The Second Battalion of the South Wales Borderers was sent to the Far East in 1912 and based in the British-controlled part of Tianjin. It landed at Lao Shan Bay for operations against the German territory of Qingdao, 4th December 1914. The Battalion provided the only British contribution to the Japanese invasion of Qingdao. The Battalion remained until the outbreak of World War I. embarking at Hong Kong and landing at Plymouth on 12th January 1915.

2nd Battalion SWB at Laoshan Bay, Qingdao, 23rd September 1914

2nd Battalion SWB landing at Laoshan Bay, Qingdao, 23rd September 1914

British Troops arrive in Tsingtao (Qingdao 1914)

'TSINGTAO' (Qingdao)
'In August, 1914, the 2nd Battalion had nearly completed two years of its tour at Tientsin, in Northern China. In early August the Japanese entered the war and sent a division to capture the German port of Tsingtao. The Twenty-Fourth and half the 36th Sikhs were sent from Tientsin in September to represent the Allies and take part in the capture. After much hard digging in heavy rain and in great discomfort Tsingtao fell on 7th November, at a cost to the battalion of 14 men killed or died of wounds or disease and 20 officers and 34 men wounded. `Tsingtao` is a battle honour held by no other British Regiment.'
(www.royalwelsh.org.uk)

BRITISH SOLDIERS` GRAVES, QINGDAO, MEMORIAL FUND
A fund referred to as the British Soldiers` Graves, Qingdao Memorial Fund was originated by the British Community of Qingdao, to care for and preserve the graves of ten men of the Second Battalion, South Wales Borderers who fell whilst serving with the British Forces co-operating with the Japanese at the siege of Qingdao, August - November 1914:

No. 10924. Private Dale	*Died 5. 11. 14*
No. 10614. Private Evans	*Died 5. 11. 14*
No. 10673. Private Pavitt	*Died 5. 11. 14*
No. 8243. Private Sewell	*Died 5. 11. 14*
No. 10019. Private Bettis	*Died 5. 11. 14*
No. 7235. Sergeant Payne	*Died 5. 11. 14*
No. 8436 Sergeant Millar	*Died 7. 11. 14*
No. 0763 Private Williams	*Died 5. 11. 14*
No. 9880 Private Sydenham	*Died 6. 11. 14*
No. 10202 Private Parkers	*Died 5. 11. 14*

These men were buried in the middle of a narrow patch of Chinese cultivated land above and on the edge of a ravine in which the British Field Hospital was situated near Sheng- Heies-Tuan-Chuang, about six miles from Qingdao. With the aid of funds raised among the British Community of Qingdao this plot of land was purchased in the November of 1915, and six months later ten marble crosses were erected.

In April 1917, F.S. Thornton, whilst on service with the Chinese Labour Corps, died at Qingdao and was buried alongside the ten men of the Borderers.
Early in 1918, a committee was formed, consisting of:
    R.E. Eckford
    A. Van Ess
    W.T. Alway
This committee, with funds augmented by a donation from Tianjin friends of F.S. Thornton, purchased an additional piece of land which provided access to the graves from the road and also permitted steps being taken to protect the graves from erosion which was, by this time, becoming a serious menace.
By the autumn of 1919, the Fund had been called upon for more repairs, additional drainage etc., and, as the ravages of erosion were again becoming evident, the Committee, then consisting of:
    Rev. F.J. Griffiths
    Allen Archer
    W.T. Alway
sent out an appeal in October for the sum of three thousand dollars - to enclose the graves with a suitable stone wall, plant pine trees and shrubs and to provide the nucleus of a fund for the general maintenance of the graves, after freeing the fund from debt.
(The debt referred to was a cash advance from Mr. Alway, which advance was later converted into a gift). With funds made available from the reception to this appeal, the committee was enabled to purchase the bank at the back of the graves and, at the cost of approximately eleven hundred and fifty dollars, to enclose the property with a stone wall.

As a result of the appeal sent out by the British Consul in April 1923, the Shanghai Race Club presented the Fund with three of the 6 % Debentures, 1923 issue, for Tls. 1000 - each (Total value Tls. 3,000).
In 1924, the sum of £30 was received from the Imperial War Graves Commission to be applied towards the upkeep of the cemetery. At the same time £750 was also received, which sum was to be utilised for the erection of a suitable monument to the men of the South Wales Borderers, through Mr. Tyrrell Adams, an American resident of long standing in Qingdao; the work was put in the hands of a local contractor and a very fine monument in Laoshan granite was raised.
It must be mentioned here that without the valuable assistance of Mr.Adams, this   cenotaph could never have been completed within the limits of the funds made available for it.
Owing to exceptionally heavy rains in July 1925, a part of the retaining wall at the back of the graves broke down, with the unfortunate result that two graves were washed away. The graves were immediately reconditioned and the retaining wall strengthened along its whole length.
During 1924 and 1925, the sum of 1,000 dollars was placed on fixed deposit with the Hong Kong and Shanghai Banking Corporation at 5% interest per annum.
Though information available is scarce, it is evident that early in 1928, a very handsome gateway to the cemetery was erected, the cost of which was defrayed by the Shanghai Race Club.
The gates are of bronze and bear, in embossed relief, the badge of the South Wales Borderers.
At this time, the care of the cemetery was somewhat lax and, upon the instigation of the British United Services Association, an unofficial committee comprising :
Mr. King H.B.M. Consul   Mr. Gray United Service Association Mr. Hearne United Service Association was informed to attend to all matters connected with the cemetery.

In 1933 a rating from H.M.S. Caradoc, Engine room Officer Harbury, died, and was buried in the cemetery. In 1934, funds amounting to 720 dollars were raised by the United Services Association from the Shanghai Branch of the Association and from other British National Societies there, to complete the wall around the cemetery. This work was put in hand under the surveillance of Mr.Hearne. At this time also, the then existing Shanghai Race Club debentures were called in and exchanged for a new issue (in dollars) and the opportunity was taken to withdraw the money in Fixed Deposit with the Hong Kong and Shanghai Bank and incorporate it in the new debentures received, and the amount of holdings in the new issue totalling 6,200 dollars.

In January 1936, A.R.T. Finch, Honorary Secretary of the United Services Association, and to whom must be given credit for most of the early part of this report, died in Qingdao and was buried in the cemetery alongside the other 12 graves. In April, the death of Major Stockwell occurred and he likewise was buried in the cemetery. In May, a sailor from H.M.S. Medway leading Signalman Moultan, died at sea and upon arrival at Qingdao, he was buried in the cemetery with full Naval honours.

Early in the current year (1936) Mr. Handley-Derry, H.M. Consul-General and administrator of the Fund, circularised the British Community proposing to purchase an additional plot of ground adjacent to the present cemetery, thereby enabling the Community to provide a suitable last resting place for any of its members who should die in Qingdao.

The proposal was adopted and, with the funds then raised by subscriptions from British firms and individuals, approximately 1240 dollars, plus a balance of 400 dollars from the Soldiers` Graves Fund, the land was purchased and enclosed with a wall. Unfortunately, the project cost more than could be afforded and, to make good the deficit, the Qingdao Times Co., donated 450 dollars to the United Services Association in memory of the late Major Stockwell.

Though, through the years many individuals, headed by Mr.Eckford, have accorded time and energy in the improvement and care of the graves, no report on this cemetery would be complete without some form of acknowledgement to Mr. Handley-Derry and Mr. Hearne. One can only wish that Mr. Handley-Derry`s zeal had been more fully exemplified by some of his predecessors. Mr. Hearne has been indefatigable and the Cemetery we have today in all its simple beauty, as compared with the arid fields of twenty years ago, is tribute in itself to the hours he has devoted to its care and attention.

South Wales Borderers Cenotaph at Qingdao

And in closing this report there is one other, of lowly rank, who is deserving of mention - the watchman. Faithfully has he served the cemetery since its inception for he was leader of the stretcher-bearers who conveyed the stricken men to the Field Hospital twenty years ago, and one item in the cash book dated May 1926, reads: Gratuity to Caretaker shot by bandits while defending Cemetery Flowers.
Hon. Secretary,
British United Services Association Qingdao, 10th December 1936.
(Regimental Museum of the Royal Welsh 23rd, 24th, 41st and 69th Foot, The Barracks, Brecon)
Note: Qingdao Museum had no knowledge of the Cemetery, Cenotaph or the Gates which must have been destroyed during the Cultural Revolution. The Author's research has been deposited at the Museum.

SWB Graves, Cenotaph and Cemetery Gates, at Qingdao

R

'Rajah of Sarawak'

GALLANT REPULSE OF PIRATES

'The ship Rajah of Sarawak, of this port, Captain Giles was attacked by pirates in June last, in the Canton River. The Rajah was aboard from Calcutta to Whampoa. The particulars of the attack are thus described in a letter from Captain Giles to his friends:- "The ship was attacked by pirates coming up the river. We, however, beat them off without losing one of our men, but killed eight of them. There were forty men in the pirate prow (vessel), thirty-two of whom made their escape, though their boat sank before reaching the shore, from the effect of our nine-pound grape." Captain Giles and his crew achieved this gallant action without injury to a single man on board the Rajah. This fine vessel, we should add, is well armed, and to this she is indebted for her preservation and that of her crew, numbering, master inclusive, twenty-five men, besides some native passengers on board.

We mention this as an indication to ship owners of the necessity of well arming such vessels as are bound for the China seas, which, we are informed, are infested by pirates of the most desperate and merciless character'.

(The Cambrian 12th September 1856)

The 'Rajah of Sarawak' was owned by William Jenkins of Swansea who commissioned the marine artist James Harris (Swansea) to paint her. William Henry Jones in his book 'History of the Port of Swansea' (1922) related that the Rajah "was so much in advance of her time that people used to come `from the hills, as far as from Merthyr district, to see her come to Port .... built and engaged in the China and Cuba trade.'

She was built in Bideford in 1850 for the East India Trade. Mr. Jones continued that 'she carried between decks for the conveyance of troops. She was brought in to Swansea two months later by Captain Brown, and her arrival with colours flying afforded a fine spectacle, which was witnessed by thousands of people.'

('History of the Port of Swansea (1922)' by William Henry Jones)

'Red Deer'

SHIPPING INTELLIGENCE

'Red Deer' from Cardiff to Shanghai with loss of some spars and four topsails, or spoken previous to May 24th at Rio de Janeiro.'

(The Cambrian 22nd June 1866)

Hopkyn Rees (Alwyn Harrison 1892-1954)

A.H Hopkyn Rees, Asiatic Petroleum Company Limited, Qingdao, China, he was the son of the Rev W Hopkyn Rees.

Hopkyn Rees (William 1859-1924))

The Rev Dr William Hopkyn Rees D.D., FRGS; Professor of Chinese at London University (1920)

Late Secretary of the Christian Literature Society of China and Principal of the School of Chinese Learning, Shanghai.

Born Cwmafon April 24, 1859; Son of Thomas Rees and Janet Hopkyn.

Married July 12, 1882 to Margaret, daughter of Alderman Harrison, Coedpoeth, Wrexham

Published in Welsh: 'Life of Griffith John, China', 'China and the

Chinese' Published in English: Jonathan Lees of Tianjin
Published in Chinese: 14 volumes
Published in English: dozens of articles as associate editor of 'Chinese Recorder'.
Religion: Congregationalist
Former President of the St David's Society, Shanghai for four years. Conducted Welsh religious services in Shanghai. Director and Principal of the Chinese School of Learning for Britons, Shanghai.
Member of The Royal Asiatic Society.
Examiner in Chinese for Hong Kong University and several Missions.
Governor of Municipal Schools for Chinese, Shanghai.
Member of British War Propaganda among the Chinese.
Writer of pamphlets and articles in Chinese for the Allies, etc.
Member of Union Lodge of Freemasons, Tianjin, China
(Who's Who in Wales-1920)

P.833 WILLIAM HOPKYN REES 1859-1924 LONDON MISSIONARY SOCIETY
'He married Margaret Charlotte Harrison of Coedpoeth and settled in Qizhou in 1888 where he founded a station. He weathered the difficulties of the 1900 Revolution and was decorated with the Blue Ribbon and given the rank of Mandarin for services of pacification. He was transferred to the Peking United Theological College and the Language School for Missionaries`, appointed to the Board of Revisers of the Old Testament Scriptures in Mandarin, and to the Shanghai staff of the Christian Literature for China Society. In 1915 he was elected Associate Secretary, with Timothy Richard (q.v.), and in 1916 General Secretary, of the Christian Literature Society for China, and member of the editorial board of the "Chinese Recorder" in 1919. He resigned in 1921 owing to ill health, and was given the chair of Chinese in the University of London. He published "China a`r Chineaid, in 1906, "Griffith John O China",1901, in Welsh, and "Jonathan Lees of Tianjin" and "How to study Chinese",1918,both in English. He died in London 4th August 1924.'
H.T. Jacob "HOPKYN REES", E. L. Evans "Cymru a`r Gymdeithas Genhadol"'
('DICTIONARY OF WELSH BIOGRAPHY DOWN TO 1940' (1959)

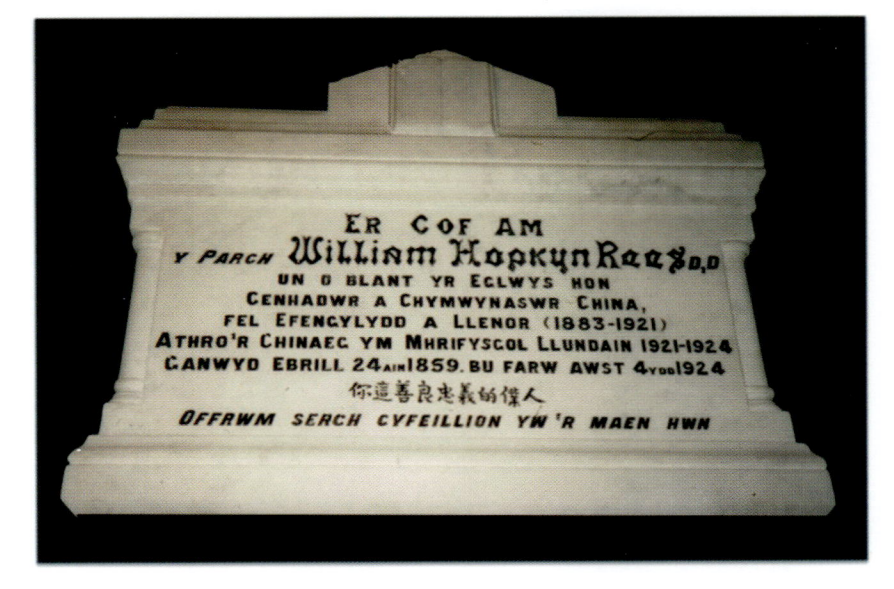

Memorial to Rev. Hopkyn Rees at Seion Chapel, Cwmafon

> 'IN MEMORY OF THE REV. WILLIAM HOPKYN REES D.D,
> ONE OF THE SONS OF THIS CHURCH,
> MISSIONARY, TO AND SERVANT OF CHINA '
> AS MISSIONARY AND SCHOLAR (1883-1921)
> PROFESSOR OF CHINESE AT LONDON UNIVERSITY 1921-1924
> BORN 24TH APRIL 1859, DIED 4TH AUGUST 1924 WE RETAIN
> FONDEST MEMORIES
> OF HE WHO LIES HERE'

Translation of the Memorial to Rev. Hopkyn Rees at Seion Chapel, Cwmafon

A brass memorial plate was sent by all the leaders of the Christian Churches in the Xiaochang County Hubei Province, China, to Seion Chapel, Cwmavon in thanks for the life and work of Dr. William Hopkyn Rees

> **TRANSLATION OF PLAQUE**
> 'FROM ALL CHURCH LEADERS IN XIAOCHANG COUNTY, CHINA IN MEMORY OF REES, THE GOOD SHEPHERD WORTHY OF BEING CALLED A FAITHFUL SERVANT OF THE LORD, AN INSPIRATION AND INNOVATOR. WE WILL REMEMBER HIM FOREVER WITH LOVE AND AFFECTION' UNVEILED 17TH JANUARY 1935

References
The Chinese Recorder, November 1924, pages 737-739'
'In Remembrance' by Frank B. Turner
William Hopkyn Rees
'Cenhadwr Crist yn China' by Idris Hopkyn
'Hopkyn Rees China' by H.T Jacob (1925)

Rhys - Davies (Sir William 1863-1939)
Born, Haverfordwest, 11th May 1863
Member of Parliament for Pembrokeshire 1892 to 1898
1907 Attorney General in Hong Kong
1908 King's Council
1912 Chief Justice of Hong Kong, Vice-President of the St. David's Society, Hong Kong
1913 Knighted
1924 Retired
1939 Died in the UK.
(WHO'S WHO IN WALES 1920 p. 400 Sir William Rhys - Davies B.A, R.C.)

Rees Brothers (George, John and Thomas)
'The three brothers - John, Thomas and George were involved in the opium trade in China. They joined the East India Company and traded with China. John Rees left a vast fortune of £34,000. Thomas was captain of various ships involved in the China trade.'
('A Legacy of Opium' by Douglas Fraser - 2010)
George Rees died in 1842 and was buried in Macau. Thomas Rees' wife was also buried in Macau.

Tomb of George Rees in Macau Protestant Cemetery

> DEATHS
> DEATH NOTICES
> DEAD
> *'Very suddenly from a stroke of the sun on the 27th September last, on board of the Brig the 'ROYAL EXCHANGE', at Hong Kong, Captain George Rees, aged 37, formerly of Tenby, and brother of John Rees Esq of that place, deeply and sincerely lamented.'*
> (The Cambrian 4th February 1843)

Tomb of Thomas Rees' wife in Macau

```
SACRED
TO THE MEMORY OF
MARIA
WIFE OF CAPT THOMAS REES
OF THE SHIP LORD AMHERST
WHO DIED AT
MACAO DEC 27 1886
BELOVED AND LAMENTED
```

Rees (Gwendoline M.)
'Daughter of W Hopkyn Rees. She was born in Xiaochang in 1889. Appointed to Tianjin in 1916. Married and lived in the Netherlands. She died in 1932.'
(Overseas Missionary Fellowship 1991)

Rees (Lyndon MBE)
Lyndon Rees, of Tonypandy, became Managing Director of Citybus Limited one of the three major bus operators in Hong Kong.
('Wales On Sunday' May 24th 1992)

Rees (Rev John Lambert)
'Ordained 1897 in Shanghai and became a Missionary in China under the American Church from 1890 to 1904. Appointed Rector of Llanddowror in 1906. Member of S.P.G deputation 1904-1906. Organizing Secretary of the S.P.G of St. David's Diocese. Honoured by the University of Wales for his missionary labours and literary work in Chinese, in which language he has written numerous theological and historical works which won the approval of eminent Chinese and have influenced the development of modern times.'
(WHO'S WHO IN WALES 1920 p.396)
'Timothy Richard called him 'the most promising young Sinologue among us'.
('Forty-Five Years in China' by Timothy Richard, Chap 9 p.228 pub. Frederick A. Stokes and Co New York 1916.

Rhosllannerchrugog (Rhos Orpheus Male Choir)

The Rhos Orpheus Male Voice Choir, from North Wales, was among the first musical groups to perform in China and Hong Kong in 1980. The 'Orpheus in the Orient' Tour took place in May-June, 1980. The Choir visited Hong Kong, Guangzhou, Shanghai and Hangzhou. The tour Programme was arranged by the Embassy of the People's Republic of China, Wales-China Friendship Society (WCFS), Society for Anglo-*Chinese* Understanding (SACU). In China, the Chinese People's Association for Friendship with Foreign Countries (CPAFFC) and the St. David's Society in Hong Kong also assisted in arranging the Tour.

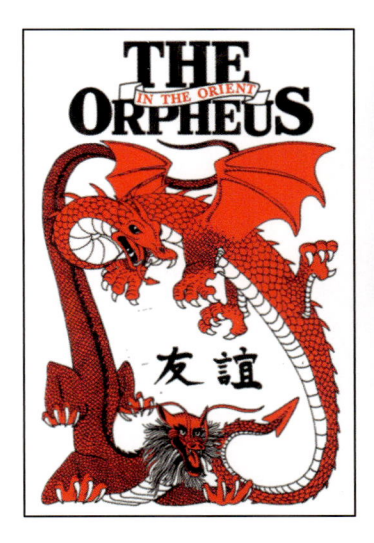

Rhos Orpheus Choir departing for China

Official Tour Programme Cover

Richard (Timothy 1845-1919)

'One of the greatest missionaries whom any branch of the Church has ever sent to China.'
(Dictionary of Welsh Biography Down To 1940)

Rev. Dr Timothy Richard (1845–1919) was a Welsh Baptist missionary to China, who influenced the modernisation of China and the rise of the Chinese Republic. Richard was born on 10th October 1845 in Ffaldybrenin, Carmarthenshire, the son of Timothy and Eleanor Richard, a devout Baptist farming family. Inspired by the Second Evangelical Awakening to become a missionary, Richard left teaching to enter Haverfordwest Theological College in 1865.

Street sign in Ffaldybrenin

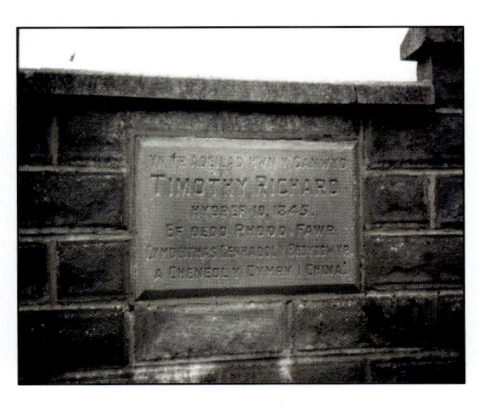

Memorial plaque to Timothy Richard in Ffaldybrenin

The wall plaque reads: "In this building Timothy Richard was born on 10th October 1845. He was a great gift of the Baptist Missionary Society and the Welsh nation to China."

Dr. Richard was appointed by the Baptist Missionary Society and sent to China in 1869. There he dedicated himself to China, where he had an active role in relief operations during the Northern Chinese Famine of 1876–1879, and was instrumental in promoting anti-foot binding and sexual equality in China. In 1878 he married Mary Martin who died in 1903. They had four daughters. In 1914 he married Doctor Ethel Tribe who survived him.

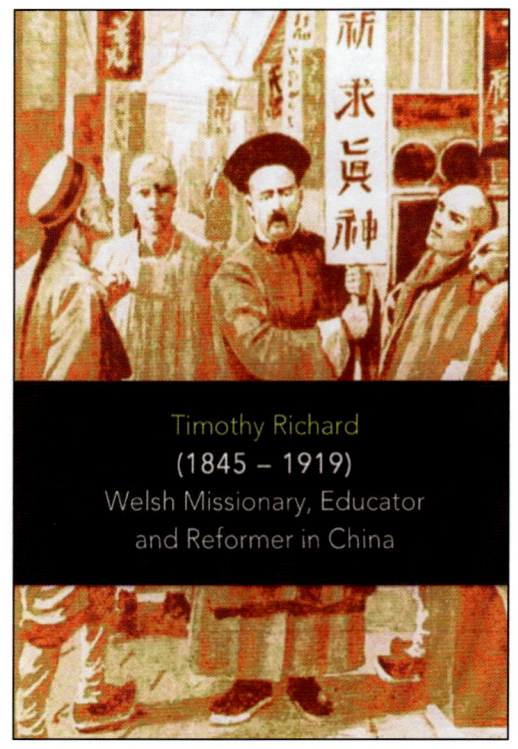

Exhibition on the life of Timothy Richard at UWTSD Lampeter Library (2014)

A booklet to accompany the Exhibition on the life of Timothy Richard by Dr. Thomas Jansen

'The Welsh Academy Encyclopaedia of Wales 2008 ' - Timothy Richard p.758
'Tim China' by David A. Chambers (2013)
'Forty-Five Years in China' by Timothy Richard pub. Frederick A. Stokes and Company, New York 1918
'Timothy Richard' – by Prof W.E. Soothill pub. Seeley, Service and Co. Limited, London 1924. 'Timothy Richard D.D., China Missionary, Statesman and Reformer' by Rev. B. Reeve pub. S.W. Partridge and Co Ltd
'Basic Themes in comparative Study of Religion (1992) by Cyril Williams (Edwin Mellen Press Ltd – March 1993) Chapter 9: 'A Baptist-Buddhist Encounter: Timothy Richard and Chinese Buddhism.'

Li Ti Mo Tai

Timothy Richard's Calling Card

Timothy Richard aged 24 years

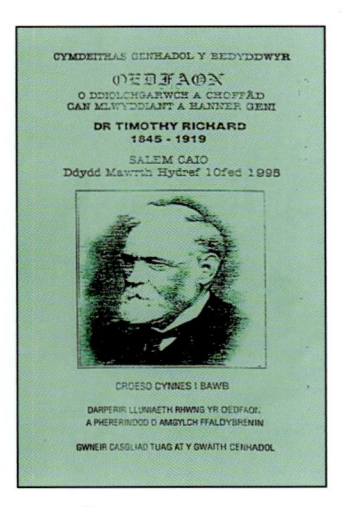

150th Anniversary Service to commemorate the birth of Timothy Richard at Salem Chapel Caio

Richards (Private Frank DCM, MM 1883-1961)
PRIVATE FRANK RICHARDS came from Blaina, Gwent and served with the 2nd Battalion Royal Welch Fusiliers
'Old Soldier Sahib' by Frank Richards D.C.M., MM 1933 Chapter 8 - North China Veterans.

Richards (Rev.)
'The Rev Richards, of Radnor, led the Welsh male choir whilst interned by the Japanese at the prisoner of war camp in Stanley, Hong Kong. He also gave Welsh lessons to the inmates.'
(St. David's Society Hong Kong)

Roath Park Cardiff
'Head gardener is to purchase for Roath Park, from the Zoological Gardens at Clifton, a pair of upland geese at £5, a pair of black swans at £4.10s, and a pair of Chinese geese at £1.'
(Cardiff City Council 1894-95)
('British History on line/ Cardiff Records Vol 5 John Hobson Matthews Editor, published 1905, p 219-230')

Roberts (Frederick Charles 1862-1894)
'Frederick Charles Roberts whose family came from Mynydd Y Gof, Bodedarn, Anglesey, studied at Aberystwyth and Edinburgh and became a medical missionary. In 1887 he left for China and assisted James Gilmore in Mongolia. Later he worked in Tientsin (Tianjin).
He was joined by his sister, Mary, who married the Rev Thomas Bryson. She took charge of the hospital named after him in Tianjin and wrote 'Frederick C Roberts of Tianjin or, for Christ in China' (London: H.R. Allenson)
(EMINENT WELSHMEN VOLUME 1)

Roberts (Mary)
'The sister of Robert Charles Roberts, she became a Congregational missionary in North China, Tianjin, 1884-1894, and Changzhou, 1916. She married the Rev Thomas Bryson. Author of 'Frederick C Roberts of Tianjin' and died in 1939.'
(WHO'S WHO IN WALES 1920)

Roberts (Mary Elizabeth)
'Born in Liverpool of Welsh parents in 1863. Appointed to Qizhou in 1893. She married GB Grant (1866-1827) a native of Scotland and associated with Bridgend. Both returned to China in 1898.'
(Overseas Missionary Fellowship 1991)

Robson (William)
Author of 'Griffith John - Founder of the Hankow Mission Central China': Pub. S.W. and Partridge (London)

Rowlands (Rev Edward)
'Congregational Missionary born in Madagascar in 1882 of Welsh missionary parents. Appointed in 1907 to central China (Wuchang 1907-1908 and 1910, Zaoshi 1908-1910) and was interned in Shanghai. Married in 1909. Returned from China in 1945.'
(Overseas Missionary Fellowship 1991)

Rowlands (Rev William Francis)
'Congregational Missionary and son of Welsh missionary parents in Madagascar. Born in 1886 and appointed in 1913 to Cangzhou, North China. He was interned with his wife and returned from China in 1950.'
(Overseas Missionary Fellowship 1991)

Royal Mint
The Royal Mint at Llantrisant struck a commemorative Silver Proof Medal to celebrate the Year of the Dragon (1988).

Year of the Dragon (1988) Silver Proof Medal

Royal Regiment of Wales

'MARCH INTO HISTORY'
'The men of B Company, 1st Battalion of the Royal Regiment of Wales are pictured marching away from a colonial outpost which has seen a British guard since 1898. History was made when the Welsh Red Dragon was finally lowered from the Hong Kong border with China and the 86 soldiers marched the 40 miles back to their base at Fort Stanley on the southernmost point of Hong Kong Island to mark the occasion.'
(Postman's Diary South Wales Evening Post Friday 10th January 1992 (www.southwales-eveningpost.co.uk)

Men of B Company Royal Regiment of Wales making history in Hong Kong

Royal Welsh Fusiliers

SWANSEA BOY IN CHINA.
Splendid work of the Welsh Fusiliers
RUSSIANS AND JAPS AS SOLDIERS.

Some Pathetic Stories
'Mr.James Evans, of No.7, Richardson Street, Swansea, has received the following letter from his son, Drummer W.J Evans, of the 23rd Royal Welsh Fusiliers, who is serving with our troops in North China. The communication is dated 1 "Field Force, Tientsin, July 29th - The sight coming down the Peiho River was something awful and ghastly. Hundreds of bodies were floating down, some with no heads or legs, and others with every limb gone, and the sun roasting them. You could see where the bayonets have been through them. Others had their faces smashed with Dum-dum bullets. I have just come in off outpost duty, capturing junks for the British transport. I am proud to be able to tell you that our regiment has upheld the credit of the flag. The Russians can't make out our plan of attack. They got in one position and won't advance or retire. The Russian General, who was in charge, paraded the Russians, and told them that he had heard of British pluck, but he did not believe it until he had seen the dash of the Fusiliers. If it had not been for our mob and the Japs it would have been all up with Seymour's lot; they were surrounded. In the same room as I am writing this letter there was a poor chap by the name of Porter, killed by a shell, which struck him whilst

he was having something to eat. We are on biscuits and bully, and it goes down all right; but the water is very dirty.

Our chaps shot a spy a couple of days ago. He was very stubborn, and would not give us any information. The Japs are good soldiers; they are all little chaps and salute us. We expect to go to the relief of Pekin to-morrow or the next day.

It seems a very curious thing that there were two chaps here named Porter, and the day that one got killed the other wrote to his mother to tell her if she saw the account in the papers not to think it was him; but he got killed the next day, shot through the head, poor chap. The both Porters are buried side by side.

We have lost nine killed and twenty-two wounded. We have one man recommended for the V.C., and another made full corporal for valour in the field. The Japs have lost about 300. They won`t have anybody with them but the British. They are too rash for soldiers; they expose themselves too much. I have been in the hospital to see Mick O` Brien, a drummer, who had his arm nearly shot off. I can tell you there have been a number of narrow escapes.'

Battle Honours of the Royal Welsh Fusiliers including Pekin 1900 on display at Royal Welsh Fusiliers Museum Caernarfon Castle.

Royal Welsh in Peking (1900)

If a man is left wounded in the field the Chinese cut his head off, and they get a nugget of silver for each foreigner's head. Poor Harry Scott, a Cardiff chap, got wounded in the advance, and he tried to roll himself to the river to drown himself out of the way of the Chinese, who would dismember him. A search party was sent out for him, and they brought him in, but he died from half drowning and loss of blood I expect a good bit of fighting before this is finished, and then we go to India, I expect, David Howell, my chum, is all right. We shall probably be on the march again to-morrow. I sent you a letter from Wei-Hai-Wei, and will write again as soon as we settle this affair."
(The South Wales Daily Post, 18th September 1900)

British Legation Peking 1900

Entrance to the former British Legation, Canal Street, Beijing (1994)

'The Battle Honour 'PEKIN 1900' awarded to the 2ⁿᵈ Battalion of the Royal Welsh fusiliers is unique to the British Army. As a result of the friendship struck between the US Marines and the Royal Welsh Fusiliers, the marines commissioned John Philip Sousa to write a special March for the RWF which was first played, with the composer conducting the band, in 1913. The plaque was placed in Wrexham Parish Church in the 1960s. There was a brass inscription which stated 'Removed from the Embassy Chapel Peking-1960.' It has now been returned to Beijing and may be found in the Garden of Remembrance in the grounds of the Ambassador's residence.'
(From Lieutenant-Colonel R.J.M Sinnett)

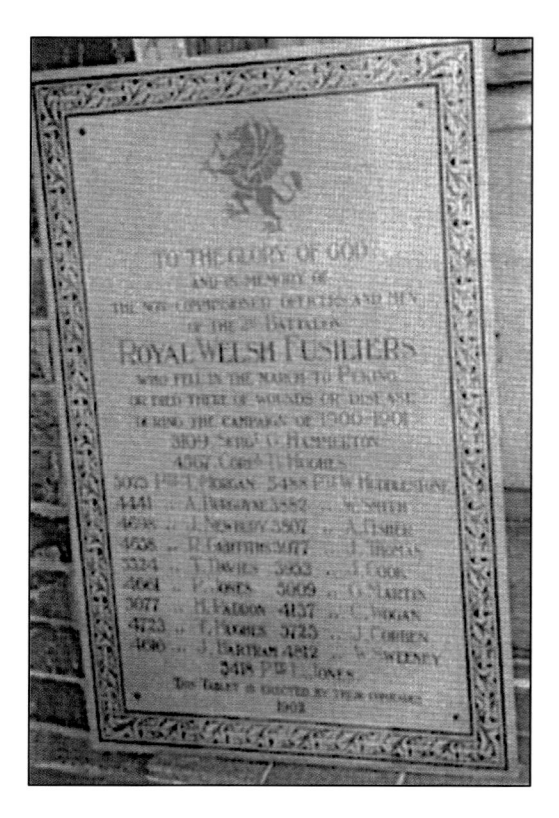

Memorial Plaque to the 2ⁿᵈ Battalion, Royal Welsh Fusiliers
In the grounds of the British Ambassador's residence, Beijing

Royal Welsh Show
In July 2010 Minister Counsellor, Zhou Xiaoming, of the Chinese Embassy, London, met First Minister Carwyn Jones at the Royal Welsh Show in Llanelwedd, Builth Wells to discuss the export of Welsh lamb to China. In 2011 a Chinese delegation led by Mr Xiang Yuzhang, Chief Inspector of Quality Supervision, Inspection and Quarantine, came from Beijing to meet representatives of Hybu Cig Cymru (HCC) - Meat Promotion Wales.

Rhydderch (Francesca)
Freelance writer and literary editor based in Aberystwyth. Author of 'The Rice Paper Diaries' the story written in memory of her great aunt Menna Willers (née Gillies 1919-1961) who was interned at Stanley POW Camp, Hong Kong Island from 1942-1945. (2014)

S

Scott (Professor Michael)
Professor Michael Scott former Vice-Chancellor and Professor of English and Theatre Studies at Glyndŵr University. His 'TEN STORIES OF KING ARTHUR' have been translated into Chinese. Published by the Foreign Language Teaching and Research Press, 2013.

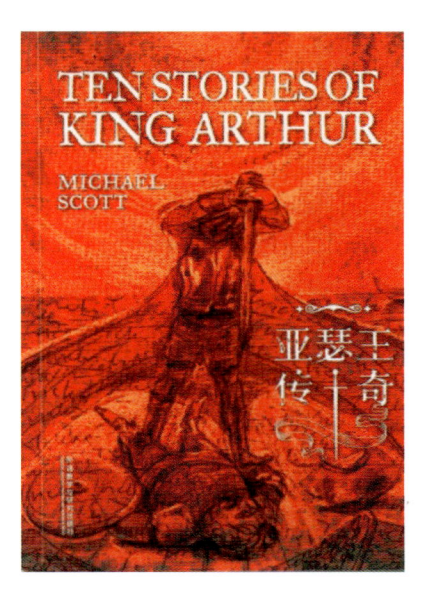

Cover reproduced by kind permission of Daphne Todd

Selby (Stephen)
Stephen Selby worked for the Hong Kong Government in various capacities. His mother lived in Llanystmdwy, North Wales. He has lived in Hong Kong for many years. His book 'Chinese Archery' (University Press HK), published in 2000 is the first detailed work on Chinese Archery since the Ming Dynasty.
(See also 'Stone house' and Percy Smith)

Shanghai Cup

The Shanghai Cup dates back to the year 1876 and the Shanghai Yacht Club. George Baillie Hill won the Club's annual regatta for three years running in his yacht 'Nimrod'. The Shanghai Cup was presented to him. It had been commissioned and made by Lee-Ching, Jeweller and Goldsmith,for $433. Mr Hill returned to Britain and when he died the Cup was passed to his son, Victor, who died in World War I.
It remained with Victor's daughter, Georgina until a chance meeting with the Commodore of Penarth Motor Boat and Sailing Club. She explained how she had been looking for a home for the trophy and a yacht club where it could be raced. The Shanghai Cup was presented to the Penarth Club and first raced for in Welsh Waters in 1998.The Penarth Yacht Club is now known as the Cardiff Bay Yacht Club.

Bill of Sale for Shanghai Cup (Penarth Motor Boat and Sailing Club)

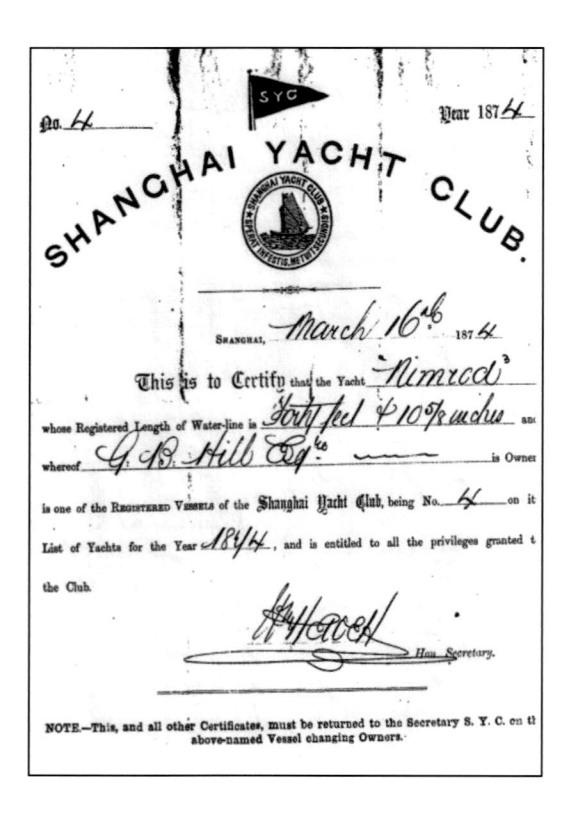

Registration for Nimrod to enter Shanghai Cup (Penarth Motor Boat and Sailing Club)

A report in the South Wales Evening Post of the penultimate leg of the Shanghai Cup race across Swansea Bay. The race from Swansea to Cardiff sponsored by Hyder is one of a series of races called 'Chasing the Dragon' (www.south-waleseveningpost.co.uk)

Shanghai Kunju Theatre
The Shanghai Kunju Theatre appeared at the Grand Theatre, Swansea in the Autumn of 1987. The performance was part of the Company's first-ever European Tour.

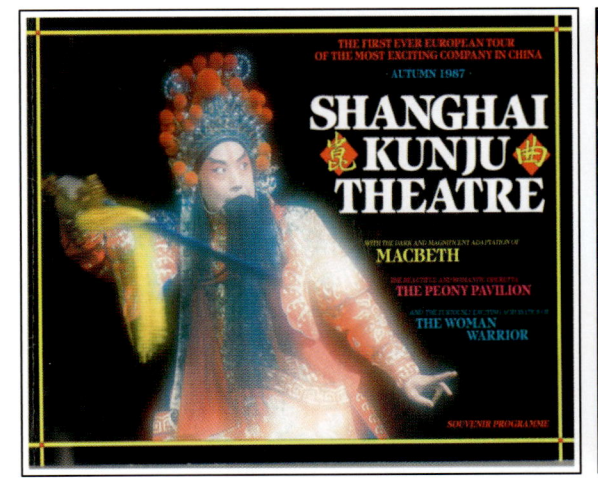

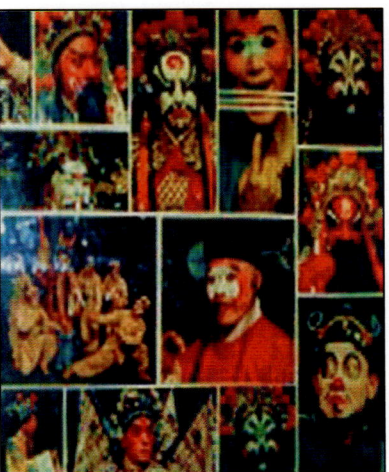

Souvenir programme of the first-ever European tour of the Shanghai Kunju Theatre Autumn 1987. Presented by Cardiff Laboratory Theatre with the assistance of Visiting Arts and the British Council.

Qiang Shen

Professor, and Director of the Institute of Mathematics, Physics and Computer Science (IMPACS) at Aberystwyth University. Fellow of the Learned Society of Wales, and a member of UK Research Excellence Framework (REF) 2014, Computer Science and Informatics. A torchbearer for the 2012 London Olympics in celebration of the centenary of the birth of Alan Turing the pioneering computer scientist, mathematician, logician and cryptoanalyst.

Shijia Hutong (Beijing)
(See: Prince of Wales)

Shoni Sguborfawr
'Shoni was christened John Jones. Although police records state that he was born in Merthyr Tydfil, the name Sguborfawr was a farm near the village of Penderyn. Before he reached 30, Shoni had made a name for himself as a hard man, and was seen as one of the toughest men in 'China', which was an undesirable area of Merthyr where the worst and most desperate of an industrial society found themselves. In 1840 the arrival of the Taff Vale Railway, which made Merthyr the industrial steel manufacturing hub of Britain, was celebrated in 'China' with a bare-knuckle boxing contest between Sguborfawr and Cyfarthfa champion, John Nash.'
(The Welsh Academy Encyclopaedia of Wales John Davies, Nigel Jenkins, Menna Baines and Peredur Lynch (2008) p.78 pub. University of Wales Press)
(See also: Merthyr Tydfil)

Silk Road East Expedition (April to July 2010)

'Beijing Trek for Riders'
'Swansea Valley man, Kevin Sanders and his wife, Julia, from Ystradgynlais, led the first-ever motorcycle team in an overland crossing to Beijing. Kevin, director of BMW rider training, led a team of 16 from Wales to London and then on to Beijing on the world's longest motorcycle journey.'
(South Wales Evening Post May 2010 www.southwales-eveningpost.co.uk)
The ten-week expedition crossed Europe, Turkey, Georgia, Azerbaijan, Turkmenistan, Uzbekistan, Tajikistan, Kyrgyzstan, and China.

At the frontier with China

At BMW in Beijing

Singleton Abbey
Singleton Abbey is a large, mainly 19th century mansion in Swansea and is the the Registry Office of Swansea University. The house is a neo-classical villa, octagonal in plan, erected in 1784 under the name of Marino by Edward King, a customs official. In 1817 it was purchased by the industrialist John Henry Vivian, who added rectangular one-bay extensions to either side. Although called Singleton Abbey it has no religious origins. The house had a 'Chinese Bedroom',

Chinese bedroom at Singleton Abbey

Slow Bikes to China
'Slow Bikes To China is the bicycle journey of a lifetime'

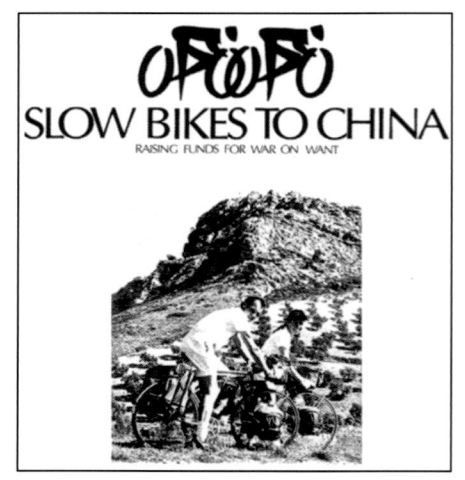

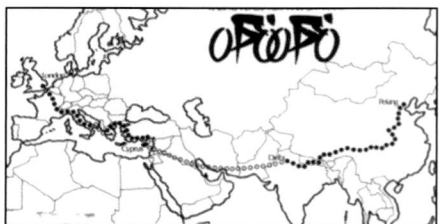

'On Monday 15th September 1986, John Wyer and Vicky Stammers will leave London, bound for China. Their journey will take them across two continents and eight countries, ending 10,000 miles from home. Their aim is to raise £10,000 for long-term aid projects in Ethiopia and Eritrea, to be carried out by WAR ON WANT.'

'John Wyer and Vicky Stammers gave up their jobs as architects to ride their bikes from London to Beijing for charity-hence the name 'Slow Bikes to China'. They were invited to speak about their experiences by the United Nations Association in Cardiff to give the Doris Hansen Memorial Lecture in November 1987. (See: United Nations)

The children of Alderman Davies' Church in Wales infant school in Neath raised £675 by having a bike ride around the school yard. The children had written letters to the couple as they travelled the globe. John and Vicky visited the children to say thank you and to collect the cheque.'
(South Wales Evening Post www.southwales-eveningpost.co.uk)

John Wyer and Vicky Stammers (Centre) with pupils and staff at Alderman Davies' Church in Wales Primary School Neath 1987
Photo: South Wales Evening Post www.southwales-eveningpost.co.uk

Smith (Percy)
Percy Smith was a chartered accountant and a collector of Chinese antiques. Whilst visiting his mother in North Wales in 1984 from his home in Hong Kong Stephen Selby called at a second-hand bookshop in Llanystmdwy and bought 21 photographs (10" x 8"). Some of the photos were pasted on cardboard mounts and others had been stripped from their backings as though removed from an album. Stephen Selby bought them as he thought that they had been taken in Hong Kong. On his return to the Island, he took the photographs to the Public Record Office and, as it turned out, sent them on a detective hunt. The Public Records Office in Hong Kong had to play detective as no one at the office knew or recognised the house. Eventually, it was discovered that the house that once was called 'Stone House' had been re-named 'Kellett Manor'. It had been the home of Percy Smith. The photos found in North Wales showed room after room in the Stone House filled floor-to-ceiling with Chinese antiques.

Percy Smith placed an advert in a Hong Kong newspaper that he was leaving Hong Kong in 1925 and retiring to 9 Marine Terrace, Barmouth. He did not seem to have any connection with Barmouth. He came with two Chinese men called Sam and Fu and all his Chinese antiques packed in large wooden crates. He died at Barmouth and it is thought that Sam and Fu returned to Hong Kong. When Percy Smith's daughter Kate died, all the effects, including the photographs, went to a dealer at Llanystmdwy so the story came full circle when Stephen Selby found the photographs and took them back to Hong Kong.
(See: Stephen Selby)

> 'Mr. H. Percy Smith regrets "that it has been impossible for him to personally say farewell to many of his friends and to thank them for all their kindness to him. He will be very glad at all times to hear from them.
> Mr. H. Percy Smith leaves the Colony on the Blue Funnel 'Rhexenor' on the 1st of June, for England, where he has taken a house known as 9 Marine Terrace BARMOUTH, North Wales.' (South China Morning Post 1925)

(Copy of original placed in South China Morning Post 1925)

Sam and Fu with John Williams, neighbour of Percy Smith, in Barmouth

Stone House, Hong Kong Island

Dinner Party at the Stone House

Percy Smith 'at home' in the Stone House

Song Qingling (1893-1981)

The second wife of Dr. Sun Yatsen, the leader of the 1911 Revolution, the first President and founder of the Republic of China. Song Qingling worked for peace in China. She established welfare institutions for women and children and believed that "if you educate a woman you educate a family". She also pioneered nursery schools and childcare facilities. In 1955, she wrote, 'children are the flowers of the country and we should take care of them'. Towards the end of her life, she was given the title Honorary President of the People's Republic of China. The Author was presented with an embroidered scarf to commemorate Song Qingling, during her visit to Shanghai in 1989 as co-leader of 'China89'
(See 'China 89')

Embroidered commemorative scarf presented to the Author, March 1989

Soothill (William Edward)
Professor William Edward Soothill (1861 – 1935) was a Methodist missionary to China who later became Professor of Chinese at Oxford University and a leading British Sinologist. Among the many works written by him was 'Timothy Richard of China' published in 1924.

South Wales Borderers
The Regimental Museum of the Royal Welsh, 23rd, 24th, 41st and 69th Foot at Brecon Barracks has many items on display pertaining to the SWB's time in Tsingtao (Qingdao). It has a vast archive of the SWB in Tianjin and Qingdao.
The following two letters are between Lieutenant-Colonel Kuhlo of the Imperial German Troops stationed at Tianjin to his counterpart Brigadier-General Barnardiston commanding the British Troops in Tianjin.
They both thank each other for their friendship during their time in Tianjin. The following week they would fight each other in Qingdao!
BATTALION ORDERS
By
Lieut. Col. H G. Casson
Commanding 2nd Battalion. The South Wales Borderers (24th Regiment.)
TIENTSIN, Wednesday, August,1914
No. 782 DEPARTURE of IMPERIAL GERMAN TROOPS.

The General Officer Commanding has received the following letter from the Officer Commanding Imperial German Troops, Tientsin
1st August 1914.

'Sir,
I have the honour to inform you that I have received telegraphic orders to move a small detachment as soon as possible to Tsingtau.

On account of the haste with which I have had to carry out this order, it has been impossible for me to say Goodbye to you personally. I therefore beg you forgive the omission which was due to the unsettled state of the Political outlook. I should also be especially grateful if you would say Goodbye for me to the Officers and Troops of your Command and to convey to them my very best thanks for the friendship and comradeship which they have extended to us, both in Tientsin and Peking. The friendly relations which have always existed between us, remain a pleasant memory. I have the honour to sign myself.'
(Signed) D, KUHLO, Lieut. - Colonel.

The General Officer Commanding has replied as follows:-
Tientsin, 4th August 1914
Sir,
I have the honour to acknowledge the receipt of your letter of the 1st instant, and thank you most sincerely for the very kind expressions in which you refer to the friendship which has always existed between the Troops of our respective Nations, here and Peking. On my own behalf and that of the Officers, NCOs and men of the British Troops under my Command. I can only say that we sincerely regret the severance of those friendly relations - a severance which, we earnestly hope, may only be a temporary one.
I have etc.
(Signed) N W BARNARDISTON
Brigadier-General,
Commanding the Troops, North China.

No. 783 BOUNDS: - War having been declared between Great Britain and Germany, the German Concession, Tientsin, is placed out of bounds for all except Officers and Sergeants living in the Concession.
GH. Birkett, Captain Adjutant, 2nd Battalion South Wales Borderers.

FALL OF TSINGTAU
VIVID NARATIVE OF WELSHMEN`S GOOD WORK
PRIVATE EVANS` HEROISM

The story of sixteen days and nights spent in the trenches before Tsingtau by the South Wales Borderers is told in extracts from the China Mail, forwarded by Private L. Craske, 9327, of the C Company, South Wales Borderers, to relatives in Camberwell.
The extracts are given by the Evening News as follows:-
Almost every man is able to recount some thrilling personal experience of the siege, and all are full of praise of the generosity and kindness of the Japanese troops and people. Gifts of cigarettes, bearing the Imperial monogram, with cakes from the Imperial bakery, reached every man were very welcome

15 OR 16 DAYS IN THE TRENCHES
For some 15 or 16 days before the fortress surrendered the men were lying in flooded trenches, and so high was the water and so bad the roads that their transport could not reach them. C Company lived for some days practically on biscuits kindly given them by their Japanese colleagues, and on sweet potatoes gathered from the fields. Tobacco was at a high premium most of the time. Many men were driven to smoking tea-leaves. In the early part of the operations, some difficulty was experienced by the Japanese, mistaking the British for Germans. Capt. Grey was captured and held for some time, and later on the Japanese infantry fired on the British advance post.
After this the Borderers were supplied with Japanese raincoats and hoods, which they always had to wear outside the trenches. This was why the German aeronauts were unable to locate the British troops till Nov. 5. This night was described as the hottest the troops experienced.

THE HEROISM OF PRIVATE EVANS
One act of bravery stands out conspicuously among the many reported. It cost Private 10614 Evans, the hero of it, his life. It was on the terrible night of the 5th, when a rain of bullets swept the British position that he ventured to bring in wounded comrades from the advanced position.

Three journeys he made to the danger zone, each time returning with a wounded man, and he had just returned and picked up a fourth when a machine gun opened fire and he fell on the comrade he sought to save. He was riddled with bullets, and his whole body acted as a shield for his comrade, who was rescued alive. The last shell fired (before the surrender of the fortress) accounted for four of the Borderers. Sergeant Millar was killed outright, Lance-Corporal Sydenham was mortally wounded, and two others received injuries. Sydenham showed rare courage on his way to the hospital. Private Gibbons, who was one of the stretcher party, recounts that one of his (Sydenham's) legs was blown off, but he sang several songs as he was borne along, two having reference to his parents and home, and one to the fact that he would need a wooden leg!

As the bearer party was taking him off, Gibbons saw the white flag was hoisted, and said, "It's all over, Sydenham." The wounded man replied, "Let's get up and have a look," and, his wish gratified, he expired.

2nd Battalion SWB Pioneers at Tianjin

A GRIM TABLEAU
Before they surrendered, the garrison blew up all their remaining guns, exploded what ammunition they were not able to fire and sank ships across the harbour mouth.

When the Borderers entered the city after its capitulation the streets in the outskirts were strewn with dead. One gruesome sight stands out. As they were marching in after the surrender, the Borderers saw on the roadside a Japanese and a German locked on each other's bayonets. Death overtook both at the same time, and they still grasped their rifles.

Captain Johnson's fearless reconnoitring work excited the admiration of the troops, and they recounted that on one occasion he chased a German sniper with only his stick. The German bolted into a hole.

Most of the men carried away souvenirs of the fight, and one proudly exhibits a part of a German flag. Some of the bayonets used by the Germans were captured from the French in 1870.

The Germans showed a great deal of ingenuity in their defence works. Much sanguinary fighting took place on the banks of the river near the entrance to the city. The bed of this stream was covered with wire, to which mines were attached, and on the banks were trip wires so arranged that anyone stumbling over them would fall upon sharpened stakes driven into the ground. Some of the wires of these entanglements were charged with high voltage electric current.

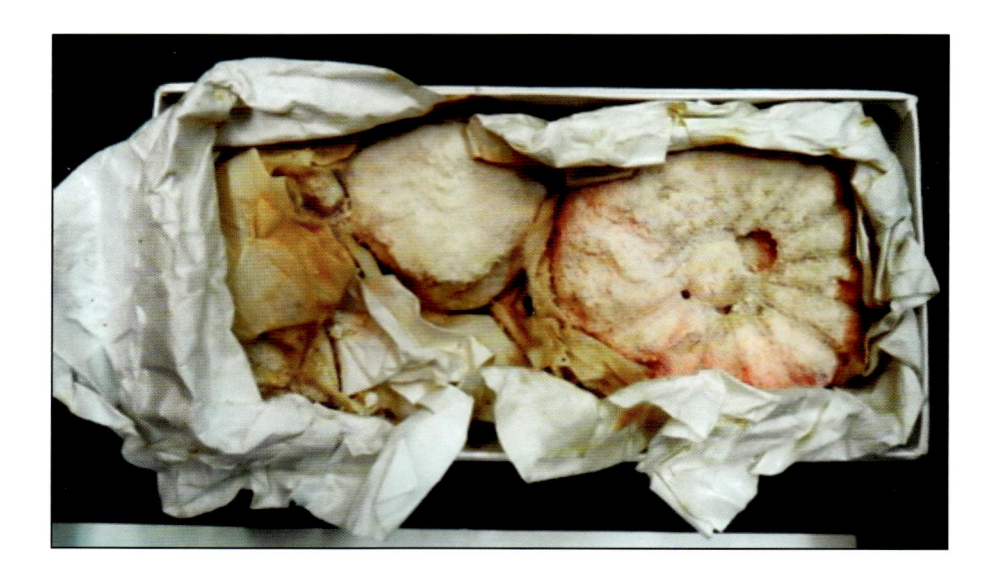

Cigarettes and cakes - presents from the Emperor of Japan to the South Wales Borderers, at Qingdao, on display at the Regimental Museum in Brecon

2nd Battalion SWB Officers at Hong Kong November 1914

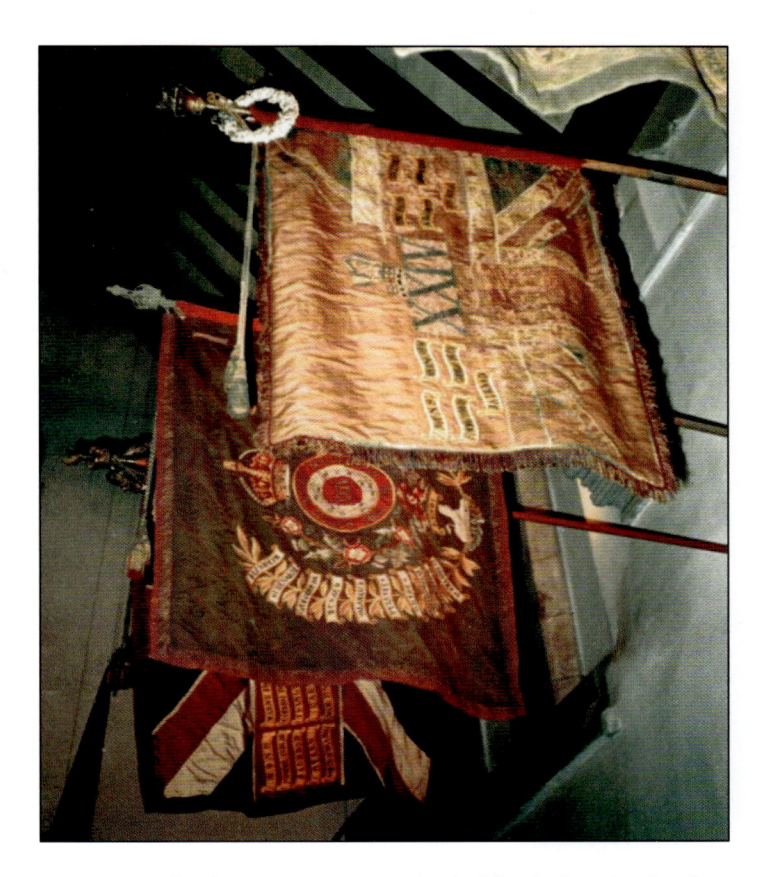

Regimental colours at Brecon Cathedral (including the Battle Honour - Qingdao 1914).

Song Renzhong
'Vice-President and Secretary-General of the Nantong City People's Association for Friendship with Foreign Countries and Foreign Affairs Office Nantong City, Jiangsu Province. Mr Song is a long-time friend of Swansea City Council and the Wales-China Friendship Society. He played a prominent part in the organization of the historic 'China 89' visit to Nantong and delegation and civic visits between Swansea and Nantong.' (1989)
(See 'China 89')

South Glamorgan Chinese Women's Association

South Glamorgan Chinese Women's Association Committee (1987)

The year 1987 was important to Chinese women in South Wales with the establishment of the South Glamorgan Women's Association in Cardiff. It was considered to be a significant step forward for the women as it established them as a 'force' within the Chinese community.
Many of the women were unable to speak English and groups such as the Cardiff Chinese Community Services Association (CCCSA) were established to provide interpretation and translation services as well as organizing cultural events in Cardiff such as celebrations for Chinese New Year.

South Wales Federation
MINUTES 1937 CHINA:
The following resolution was passed:
'This Council of the South Wales Miners Federation, representing 120,000 members, expresses its deep-felt horror at the savage and inhuman massacre of defenceless men, women and children in China by the invading armed forces of Japan. We urge the Trades Union Congress Council to make every effort through the International Federation of Trade Unions, and other working class organizations, particularly in European countries, Australia, United States and Canada, to adopt a policy of refusing to handle any goods and materials for export to or imported from Japan, and to create a world-wide movement to boycott all Japanese goods, until the Japanese have left Chinese territory. Copies to be sent to the Prime Minister, the Foreign Secretary, and the Japanese and Chinese Ambassadors in London.'

SOUTH WALES MINERS` FEDERATION
MINUTES 1938
CHINA APPEAL COMMITTEE
An appeal for financial support to the fund for the provision of medical supplies, etc., was received.
That a grant of £20 be made.
The following resolution was passed:-
'This Executive Council of the South Wales Miners` Federation expresses the strongest indignation and protest against the ruthless war of aggression which Japanese Imperialism is waging on China, accompanied, as it has been, by the systematic, barbarous and pitiless massacre of the Chinese civil population.
It hopes that the victories of the Chinese Armies over the Japanese Armies will continue, and that they will have the effect of wearing down and ultimately smashing the power of the Japanese military clique, thus opening the way of peace, freedom and democracy in Japan as well as liberating China from the danger of foreign domination.
This Executive Council therefore calls upon the members of the South Wales Miners` Federation to do whatever they can to assist the Chinese people in their struggle, particularly in regard to boycotting Japanese goods and creating a public opinion to force the British Government to adopt a more positive policy in aid of China and against the present imperialist rulers of Japan.'

NATIONAL UNION OF MINERS 1955
Minutes
P. 101 (N 0.98) The President W. Paynter submitted the resolution for discussion of the Executive committee.
"This Delegate Conference of the South Wales Area of the National Union of Mineworkers strongly condemns the policy now being pursued by the United States Government in bolstering up the regime of Chiang Kai-Shek in Formosa and other islands of the Chinese coast. Such a policy can only result in World War threatening the extermination of humanity. Conference warns the Government that it opposes such a policy and that in the event of any development of war in defence of Chiang Kai-Shek serious dislocation would result in this area of the mining industry.'

P. 143 (No. 1 18) Welsh National Peace Council visit to China .... appoint a delegate to attend delegation.
P.68l (No.378) Delegation to China
'Mr. D. D. Evans, Vice President, had been invited in a personal capacity to be a member of a good will mission to China. The delegation is comprised of Members of Parliament of all parties and other Trade Union leaders. He (General Secretary) suggested to the Executive Committee that Mr. Evans should convey the greetings of Welsh Miners to the Chinese people and also that he should attend the Delegation as official representative of the South Wales Area of the Union. '
P.891 (No.508)

'CHINA,1955.Fushen 40K from Shenyang/Lungfang/Anshan/Changchun The Vice President presented the attached report on his visit to the above country.
He further stated that the problem of pneumoconiosis was a grievous one in China and that we had a great deal to give our Chinese friends in this respect.
He had taken with him lung sections from the Welsh School of Medicine which portrayed the disease in the various stages of its development; an inhaler from the Pneumoconiosis Research Unit, Llandough; and also safety pumps from the Safety Department of the Divisional Coal Board.

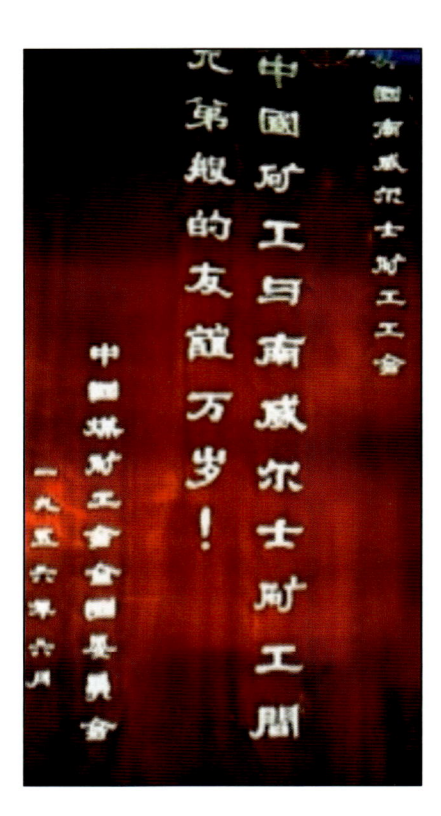

Banner presented to the South Wales Union of Miners by the National Union of Miners of China.

He had explained to the Miners` Union representatives, medical men and the administrators in the coal industry the steps which have been taken in South Wales to deal with the disease and also he acquainted them of the heavy incidence of disease in this area. He was of the view that we had a great deal of knowledge to offer the Chinese miners.

He suggested that we should invite a delegation to visit South Wales comprising of a doctor from a School of Medicine near the coalfields of China, a mining engineer and two miners` union representatives to study the problem in all its aspects, that is, medical and environmental.

Our Chinese friends were anxious to establish a close liaison between the medical schools, the industry`s administrators in both countries and with mines of South Wales.

FOREWORD

THE AREA EXECUTIVE COUNCIL was invited to appoint a representative to become one of the delegation to visit China in the summer of 1955

The delegation included many prominent Trade Union leaders, Members of Parliament and other public figures. The Vice-President, Mr. Dai Dan Evans, was appointed to the delegation. In the following pages he presents his report on what he saw, his impressions of the leaders and people of China and the many gigantic problems with which they are now grappling.

Different people see different things even when viewing the same scenes. Their impressions are determined by their understanding of the social forces producing fundamental changes in society. Their attitude to such changes is governed by the interests of the class with which they are identified.

The class approach with which "Dai Dan" reports on the 'New China', has its roots in 26 years of toil at the coal-face in the Swansea Valley; years of service in this Union as a Lodge Secretary, Miners' Agent, and more recently, as Vice-President. His understanding is that of a Socialist, whose sincerity and ability is unchallenged.

We commend this report to our members, not merely as a source of information upon New China but also as a stimulus to greater activity to ensure full recognition of the New China by the United Nations; to compel the removal of all trade barriers and to maintain peaceful co-existence between our two countries.
W. PAYNTER,
President,
South Wales Area, N.U.M.
W. H. CREWS,
General Secretary, South Wales Area, N.U.M.

NATIONAL UNION OF MINEWORKERS (SOUTH WALES AREA)
MINUTES 1956
P.487 (No.293) .... 'Delegation from China to arrive on Gala Day.
P.539 (N o.371) Chinese Miners Delegation given a great deal of information on pneumoconiosis. Visited Pathological Laboratory Cardiff Royal Infirmary
Pneumoconiosis Unit Llandough
Mass Radiography Department for Tuberculosis in Llandaff and observed the treatment at Sully Hospital, Scientific Department of National Coal Board.
Collieries Visited: Nantgarw, Britannia, Bedwas and Hafodyrynys and homes, clubs, factories and institutes.'
P.541 Mr. Chih Lien, leader of the Delegation presented a landscape scene woven on silk background.

CHINESE MINERS' GREETINGS PEKING, 19th October 1956
Thanks for the visit
'In their report they emphasised the close friendship between the miners and the peoples of China and South Wales.'
Signed Chin Chih - Fu Chairman, National Committee Coalminers` Trade Union of China.

NATIONAL UNION OF MINERS (SOUTH WALES AREA)
MINUTES Volume 1 1960
P142 CHINESE DELEGATION
'Three Chinese journalists are visiting this country.................. National Union of Miners asked to show them the life of the miners in South Wales.'

Sparham (Rev G.J. MBE 1892-1974)

Grandson of the Rev Dr Griffith John.
Griffith John Sparham was born in Hankou (Wuhan) in 1892 the son of Charles George Sparham. He was buried with Griffith John at Carnglas Cemetery Sketty, Swansea. Book of poems - 'People, Thoughts and Places'
Page 62 – 'SWANSEA AFTER 49 YEARS'

Griffith John Sparham memorial at Carnglas Cemetery, Swansea

Stamps (Postage)
The Royal Mail issued Chinese New Year stamps with 'street scenes' from cities around the UK. Including Cardiff and Swansea in 2013.

Special Chinese New Year stamps by Royal Mail

Stanley (Henry Edward John 1827-1904)
'Henry Stanley, 3rd Baron of Alderley, from Anglesey, entered the diplomatic service. He translated Morga's account of the Philippines and China at the close of the 16th Century. He also edited an English version, a CHINESE MANUAL issued in 1854. A member of the Asiatic Society and served on the Council.'
(EMINENT WELSHMEN by T.R Roberts, volume 1)

Stepney (Sir Thomas 1725-1772)
In 1762 Sir Thomas Stepney, of Llanelly House, commissioned an armorial dinner service from China. The 125 piece dinner service was discovered in Washington DC after being sold at an auction by a Portuguese ceramic dealer to a private collector in the late 1990s. It was eventually traced by the Carmarthenshire Heritage Restoration Fund. The dinner service is on display at Llanelly House.
(See: Llanelly House)

Stories ('All Our Stories Project')
The Project traced the lives of first-generation Chinese people who came to live and work in Swansea up to the present time. The Project was managed by the Swansea Chinese Co-Op Centre, Swansea University and, the West Glamorgan Archive Service. A DVD of the Project is to be found at the Archives and Swansea University Library. (2013)

'Suo Gan'
A Welsh Lullaby, performed by James Rainbird and the Ambrosian Junior Choir directed by John McCarthy, is featured prominently in the film 'Empire of the Sun' Directed and Produced by Stephen Spielberg.

Swan Gardens (Swansea)
Swan Gardens is a purpose built sheltered housing complex for retired and older members of the community, managed by the Family Housing Association (Wales), primarily for older people of Chinese origin. Regular social activities include close links with Chinese Community Cooperative Centre. (2010)

Swansea (Assembly Rooms)
'CULTURE AND THE ARTS AND SCIENCE, MUSIC, CONCERTS, RECITALS
'Concert at the Assembly Rooms by M. Richardson and Chinese Steel Band.'
(The Cambrian 2nd April 1847)

Swansea (City and County)
A sign that formerly stood at Fabian Way on the eastern approaches to Swansea showing the cities twinned with the City, including Nantong, Jiangsu Province.

Former City of Swansea boundary sign at Fabian Way

Swansea Chinese Christian Church
The Swansea Chinese Christian Church (SCCC), located in the Uplands area of the City, was set up in 1970 to reach out to the Chinese population in Swansea. The Sunday Service is conducted in Mandarin, Cantonese and English. In 2015 the Church relocated to its first permanent home at Capel Gomer, Mount Pleasant, Swansea.

Swansea Chinese Community Co-Op Centre

The Centre was established on December 1st 1996 by a group of volunteers. Since then it has set up the Chinese Woman's Group and the Chinese School, located on the Kingsway Swansea.

During 2012-2013 a project recording the oral history of the lives of older members of the Chinese community, who live in Swansea and surrounding areas, was initiated. The Swansea Chinese Community Co-op Centre, Swansea University and the West Glamorgan Archive Service managed the Project called 'All Our Stories'. DVDs of the Project may be found at the Archives and Swansea University Library (November 2013).

Launch of the Swansea Chinese Community's DVD at Sketty Hall, Swansea, 14th October 2013

15th Anniversary Celebration of the Swansea Chinese Community Co-op at the Brangwyn Hall, Swansea.

'The Centre was set up on 1st December 1996 by a group of enthusiastic volunteers who have dedicated their time and money in the Chinese community's development work for many years and, the Centre was, subsequently, registered as a charity organization.

In December 1997 we applied for funding and were granted a three-year grant by the National Lottery Charities Board for the purpose of employing a Centre Manager, paying for the rent and other running cost. The number of members increases each year covering the majority of South Wales. Currently we have over 600 members. The majority of our members are from Swansea and its nearby regions, but we also have members stretching from the West to North of Wales. The services and support we provide on daily basis targets women, young people and the elderly. We provide basic interpretation and translation of letters, organize training to build capacity and meet needs, run talks and seminars to increase knowledge, short trips to improve quality of life, and arrange workshops to promote the Chinese culture and encourage cultural diversity. Our annual Chinese New Year celebration is at the Swansea Brangwyn Hall.'
(Swansea Chinese Community Co-op Centre 2014)

Swansea Christian and Literary Association
'On Monday evening last, the Trinity Church Schoolroom, Mr Tedrake, in the absence of the appointed essayist, delivered an address on the question 'Can the British authorities be justified in entering the hostilities with China?' Mr Tedrake took the affirmative of the question, and in treating the subject he entered minutely into the facts of the case as disclosed in the dispatches of Sir John Bowring and argued the treaty of Nanking had been violated by the Chinese in boarding the lorcha 'Arrow' and seizing the crew, as the boat was under British protection. He further says that although it might be shown that the registry of the lorcha had expired, the Chinese officials were not cognisant of it and it was sufficient that the animus of the insult was there. Moreover, this was but one of many insults that had from time to time been given to British subjects, and therefore satisfaction was properly demanded to prevent their recurrence. A discussion followed, in which several gentlemen took part.
The question being put to the meeting, the numbers pro and con were equal and it was carried against the Government by the casting vote of the Chairman. The 'Gradual development of the human mind' will be the next subject that comes under the notice of the Association.'
(The Cambrian March 20th 1857) (See: Sir John Bowring)

Swansea Docks
Among the vessels visiting the port was one from China loading 3,000 tonnes of tinplate and general cargo. It was the first Chinese vessel to visit Swansea for nearly 40 years.

'D Shed ' King's Dock Swansea with cargo for a Chinese ship berthed at the Port (1987)

Swansea Market
'A Chinese tea room, designed by Swansea-based artist, Owen Griffiths and organized by Swansea City Council was set up in Swansea Market as part of a Glynn Vivian Art Galleries off-site programme of events to celebrate Swansea's Chinese links were also on display at various venues around the city featuring the work of artists Tim Davies, Paul Emmanuel, Fern Thomas, Yingmei Duan, Maleonn, and Zeng Huang.'
(City and County of Swansea Council 2013)

Swansea Parachute Club
'In May, the club chief instructor Dave Howerski and his wife Suzie were part of a nine - strong delegation of British skydivers to China as guests of the Chinese Aeronautical Society. There the team enjoyed the opportunity to make some 16 jumps using the school's Russian - built Antanov Aircraft. "The trip was a fascinating insight and experience", said Dave. "We found it a very friendly open society and were exceptionally well treated by our Chinese hosts."
(South Wales Evening Post, Wed June 22nd 1988) (www.southwaleseveningpost.co.uk)

Dave Howerski (centre facing) and three Chinese skydivers over 'An Yang', Henan Province, China

Swansea Pottery
Chinese Inspired Designs:
WILLOW – used throughout production from 1790 – 1860s
CHINESE VIEWS – produced between 1820-1830s
CANTON – produced between 1830 – 1850s
AMOY – produced between 1840 – 1850s (probably after the Port was captured by the British)
SWANSEA PORCELAIN
MANDARIN – produced between 1814–1820. It was a colourful pattern with a seated mandarin and other figures.
('The Glamorgan Pottery' (1995) by Helen Hallesy)

'THE CHINESE INFLUENCE ON SWANSEA POTTERY DURING THE LATE 18TH AND EARLY 19TH CENTURY' by Helen Hallesy
The development of the pottery industry in Britain is closely associated with the East India Company, a trading company which from the late 18th century, imported in addition to tea, silks, ivories and spices, huge quantities of blue and white porcelain at little cost.
There was a great demand for these new Chinese white tablewares but as the decline in importation steadily decreased from the Far East due to many political changes throughout Europe, a real market was created for replacements. This need was met with great success, by pottery manufacturers throughout England and also in Wales, at Swansea, who seized the opportunity in developing their own particular style and range of patterns in imitation of the Chinese.

The term 'china ware' has gradually became widely applied throughout Britain until the word 'china' is now the accepted word for any porcelain wherever it is made.

'Swansea's designs after the Chinese'

Most of the designs illustrated here are 'transfer printed' taken from a copper engraving which was then transferred on to paper and thence to pottery. The sources for the engravers ideas were therefore either direct copies or modifications from the Chinese imported wares. Imaginary scenes showing pagodas, temples, stretches of water, Chinese figures in various occupations, or any combination of these features would be incorporated in a new design.

The Willow pattern

Swansea 'Willow' pattern dinner plate

The main features of the true Willow are a bridge with 3 figures crossing it, a Willow tree, denoting the season of Spring, a boat, a tea house, two flying birds and a fence in the foreground of the garden. This was used throughout the life of the Pottery and despite being 250 years old, remains a perennial favourite in British homes today.

An early variation of this was also developed at Swansea in which there is no Willow tree, a three arched bridge with 2 figures, a temple, pavilion, a junk in the foreground and distinctive moth border. This is commonly referred to as the **Longbridge** *pattern*

Swansea 'Longbridge' pattern meat platter

Patterns introduced were often inspired by topical events in distant lands and given the name of the town associated with a memorable event. Romanticised views of oriental landscapes were common features within the compositions. In 1840, Britain became involved in the first of the 'Opium Wars' with China, and by the following year, 1841, she had captured and seized many of the Chinese seaports including those of **Amoy** *and* **Canton**, *both of which were opened up as Treaty Ports for the importation of Opium. It is recorded that the island of* **Whampoa,** *off the coast of China, is where the British ships anchored, before resuming their long voyages back to Britain. As news of these events reached Britain, it was natural that these place names would be incorporated into ideas for the engravers - thus `Amoy`, `Canton and 'Whampoa' will be found as pattern names used on pottery at Swansea.*

Swansea 'Amoy' pattern toy cup and saucer

*The **'Amoy'** pattern was used on miniature tea-sets, or toy services, and shows a lady in Chinese dress receiving tea from her servant, while a man in Chinese costume stands at her side smoking a long-stemmed pipe.*
The 'Canton' composition shows two figures on a bridge, one carrying water pails, with pagoda, temple and a stylised flowering Orange tree, denoting good luck. By the 1820's the technique of painting on top of the print was an inexpensive method of adding splashes of colour to enhance the design.

Swansea mug printed and painted in the 'Canton' pattern

*The **'Whampoa'** pattern was much used for dinner and toilet wares and shows conventional Chinese scenery of pagodas, sailing boat, a Willow tree and trellis fence.*

Swansea 'Whampoa' pattern meat platter

Swansea coffee pot printed in 'Chinese views' pattern

*A series of Oriental designs, generally printed in black called **'Chinese Views'** often show a more Europeanised representation of Chinese scenery and architecture and were used on coffee, tea and dessert wares Most of the patterns named after ports were introduced during the 1830's-40's period of production on earthenwares, although for a short period of time from 1814 until 1820 fine porcelain was manufactured at Swansea and a colourful design called the **'Mandarin'** was popular.*

Swansea 'Mandarin' pattern porcelain dessert plate

This is a hand painted design painted in the 'famille rose' style depicting a village scene with seated mandarin and group of other figures with European style houses in the background. It has a detailed border of landscapes and birds. Several other variations on these themes persisted on Swansea pottery until the middle of the 19th century when the British taste changed, moving away from chinoiserie inspired designs to the more favoured scenes depicting British rural country life.'

Footnote
There were two potteries operating in Swansea during this period, the earliest was the Cambrian 1768-1870 and for a shorter period of time, the Glamorgan Pottery, 1814-38 (Photographs and written extracts by kind permission of Helen Hallesy)

Swansea Sound
Swansea's first commercial radio station organized a live radio link between Swansea and Shanghai in March 1989 as part of the 'China 89' Project – Wales' first ever schoolchildren's performance and cultural visit to China by pupils and staff of Alderman Davies' Church in Wales Primary School, Neath and Cwrt Sart Comprehensive School, Briton Ferry, organized by the Wales-China Friendship Society. (See China 89 Project)

Swansea Theatre

PANORAMA OF CHINA

'The public are respectfully informed that the above EXHIBITION will finally CLOSE in a few nights. Therefore those PERSONS who have not already availed themselves of the opportunity of witnessing one of the finest displays of PANORAMIC and DIAORAMIC EFFECTS ever produced to their notice, should lose no time, or they will be deprived of a gratification that they may never again be presented to them.

In order to give additional effect, a splendid band is engaged, and will perform between each part a selection of music from the most popular authors.

The doors will be opened every evening at half-past 7 o'clock, the performance to commence at eight precisely.'

Boxes 2s; pits 1s; Gallery 6d. Juveniles under 12 years of age, and schools half price to the boxes and pits only.

Historical catalogues, 6d each

Places in the boxes may be taken and tickets to be had at Misses Jenkins' Library, Wind Street and also at the Cambrian office.'

(The Cambrian 11th December 1846)

Swansea Twinning

Swansea-Nantong Friendship Document – 10th April 1987
By Kind Permission of City and County of Swansea Archive Service

The City of Swansea established a formal friendship link with the City of Nantong, Jiangsu Province in 1987. However, visits between Council officials and private individuals took place in 1986 to pave the way for the formal linking between the two cities.

'HISTORIC DOUBLE CEREMONY - 6,000 mile city link'

'AN HISTORIC double ceremony was performed 6,000 miles apart today to mark the official start of social, cultural and trade links between Swansea and China. It signalled the beginning of formal twinning links with Nantong - and virtually sealed the development at the Enterprise - Zone of a multi- million pound Chinese cotton mill.

The Welsh flag was flying over Nantong, where Swansea's Lord Mayor, Councillor Lilian Hopkin, and City Council Labour Leader, Tyssul Lewis, signed a twinning agreement with their counterparts of Nantong.

Simultaneously, in Swansea's Guildhall, Deputy Lord Mayor Councillor Alan Ayres signed a copy of the document as a symbolic gesture,

A telex from the Lord Mayor in Nantong said that the outstanding welcome received from the Chinese hosts emphasised the importance that Nantong attached to the twinning arrangement. "Nothing we do matches the scale of the welcome here," she said.

300 JOBS
With Councillor Ayres, at the Guildhall ceremony today, was Councillor Trevor Burtonshaw, who made a major contribution in fostering ties with Nantong during his year as Lord Mayor in 1985/86.

The ceremony 6,000 miles away virtually clinched the long-awaited deal for a Tootal Mill at the Enterprise Zone. It will mean about 300 new jobs but, more importantly, in the long term, it could well lead to further major Chinese investment here in the same way as the Japanese are expanding operations in South Wales.

The cotton factory deal is the climax of many months of talks between the City Council and Nantong delegations. Cllr Charles Thomas, Deputy Council Leader, added his name to the agreement in the Guildhall today and helped to raise the Chinese flag above the building.

He said "History has been made in Swansea and Nantong today and we hope it will be the start of a long, happy and prosperous relationship between the two.'

(South Wales Evening Post Friday 10th April 1987 www.southwales-eveningpost.co.uk)

> **Two dragons**
>
> The Welsh Dragon flew over Nantong yesterday to mark the official start of social, cultural and trade links between the Chinese city and Swansea.

(South Wales Evening Post April 1987 www.southwales-eveningpost.co.uk)

The Author and her husband present an official gift from Nantong City to Swansea Lord Mayor Councillor Lilian Hopkyn at Swansea Guildhall, September 1986

Swansea University
Inaugural Chinese Studies course at the Department of Continuing Education (DACE) at University College Swansea in 1993/1994.
A number of participants who attended the lectures included post-graduate Chinese students at the University. They had come to learn about Chinese history as it had been forbidden study during the Cultural Revolution (1966 – 1976)

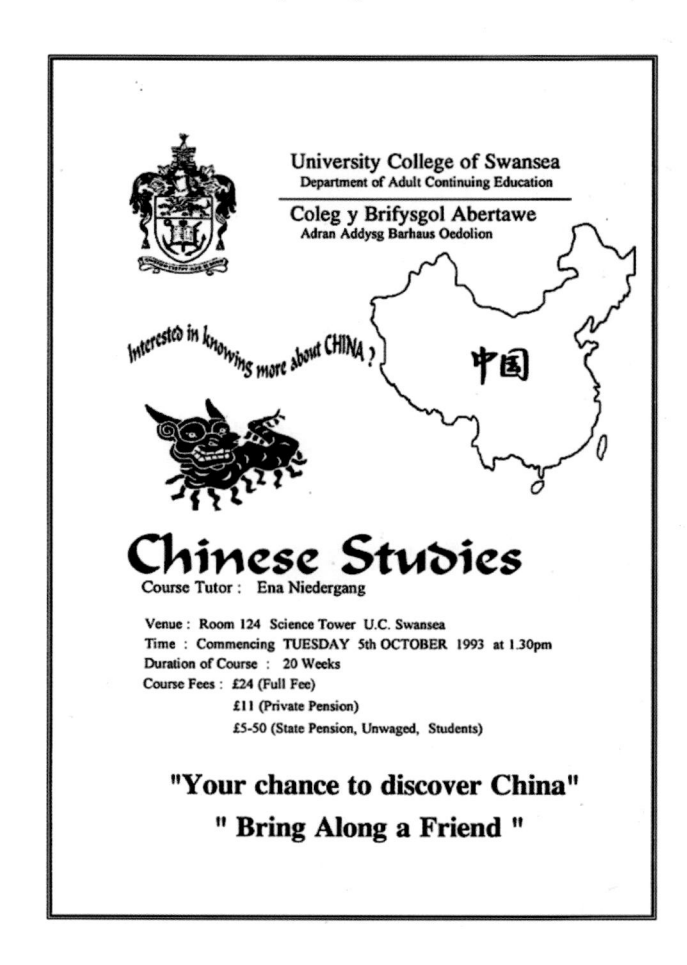

University College of Swansea
Department of Adult Continuing Education
Coleg y Brifysgol Abertawe
Adran Addysg Barhaus Oedolion

Interested in knowing more about CHINA? 中国

Chinese Studies
Course Tutor: Ena Niedergang

Venue: Room 124 Science Tower U.C. Swansea
Time: Commencing TUESDAY 5th OCTOBER 1993 at 1.30pm
Duration of Course: 20 Weeks
Course Fees: £24 (Full Fee)
 £11 (Private Pension)
 £5-50 (State Pension, Unwaged, Students)

"Your chance to discover China"
" Bring Along a Friend "

T

Talbot (Charles 1635-1737)
Armorial plate, part of a dinner service from Canton, bearing the coat of arms of the Talbot family – probably Charles Talbot from Hensol Castle in the Vale of Glamorgan.
(See: Hensol ; National Museum of Wales)

Armorial plate with the Talbot family Coat of Arms

Taliesin Arts Centre, Swansea University
The Taliesin Arts Centre at Swansea University and the Confucius Institute at the University of Wales Trinity St David hosted a performance of 'LOOK AT ME, I'M CHINESE' by the 'Mahjong Dance Shanghai Group'. (October 2010)

Tasker (Capt. John c1742 – 1800)
Captain John Tasker served in the Merchant Navy, based in Bombay, but travelled widely. A Chinese artist in Canton, China, probably painted his portrait. Captain Tasker purchased Upton Castle in Pembrokeshire and was appointed High Sherriff of the county in 1798. He died in 1800 and is buried at Upton Castle Church.

Tatford (Frederick A)
Author of: 'Born to Burn-The Story of a 20th Century Hero!' published by Upperton Press, Eastbourne (1971). The story of David and Jean Davies' time in China.
(See: David Davies)

Tea (Chinese Green)

CULTIVATION OF THE CHINESE GREEN TEA PLANT IN WALES

'Mr S Rootsey, of Bristol, in a letter to the Bristol Journal, says 'Having found the Chinese Green Tea Plant (Comellia Viridis) to be more hardy than some other shrubs which endure in the open air in this neighbourhood, I have tried it upon the Welsh mountains, and find it succeeds. I planted it in a part of Breconshire, not far from the source of the Usk, above 1000 feet, above the level of the sea, and higher than the limits of the native woods, consisting of Alder and Birch. It endured the last winter, and was not affected by the frost of 7th May. It has now made several vigorous shoots, and I have no doubt of it thriving very well in the future.'

(The Cambrian 23rd July 1831)

Tea Merchants

Swansea Street Directory 1875-76) NEW TEA SHOP CASTLE STREET

NEW TEA SHOP, CASTLE-STREET,
Opposite the Wheat Sheaf Inn, Swansea.

THE Inhabitants of Swansea and its surrounding neighbourhood are most respectfully informed, that the above premises are now open for the sale of Teas, Coffees, Spices, and Lump Sugars.

The Proprietors, in commencing business, beg to submit the system they intend pursuing, and at the same time they assure the Public, that a large capital will be employed in endeavouring to establish a Tea Business in this town, as it should be. Teas and Coffees require the greatest nicety, and it must be evident to every person, that where Bacon, Cheese, Soap, Candles, Snuff, Tobacco, and many other articles equally as nauseous and detrimental to Tea, are sold, and frequently weighed in the same scales as Tea and Coffee, it must naturally follow, that particles of the above Goods will get mixed with the Tea; and thus we account for the general complaint now being made by the Public, that Good Tea is very scarce and very dear; this we purpose remedying, as our list of prices will shew.

Our Stock is large, and comprises some of the choicest Teas and Coffees ever imported. Cash has been paid for them, combined with sound judgment and long experience in buying, and will be sold for cash, at much less prices than the Public are now paying. Our Shop is small but compact, and capable of doing a large trade, which we feel confident of doing, as we are determined to be satisfied with small profits, depending entirely upon an extensive ready-money business to make it pay. In conclusion, we ask for one trial, feeling convinced that that once will induce you to continue, and also to recommend your friends.

LIST OF PRICES:—

BLACK TEAS:	s.	d	GREEN TEAS:	s.	d.
Congou, sound and strong	3	4	Twankay, strong and good flavour	3	5
Fine strong Congou, rough full flavour	3	8	Fine Twankay, Hyson flavour	3	8
Souchong, strong, rich, and fine flavour	4	0	Hyson kind, fine flavour	4	0
Very much recommended.			Young Hyson, good	3 6 to 3	8
Fine Black-leaf Pekoe, rich Souchong flavour	4	4	Fine Ditto	4	0
Lapsang Souchong, rich Pekoe flavour, most delicious			Very fine Young Hyson, Ouchain flavour	4	6
Tea, no better required	4	8	Young Hyson, Gunpowder flavour	5	0
Pouchongs, Capers, Scented Capers, Pekoes, and every other sort of Black Tea.			Imperial Gunpowder	4	6
			Finest Imperial Gunpowder	5	0
			Fine Small-leaf Gunpowder	5	0
			Gunpowder, bright silvery leaf	5	4
			Finest quality Gunpowder, rich delicate flavour, no finer to be bought	6	0

MIXED TEAS:

A very fine Mixed Tea, consisting of Young Hysons and Souchongs .. 4 0
Howqua's Mixture, containing forty different sorts, all of the choicest quality .. 5 0

COFFEES:

	s.	d		s.	d.
Ceylon, clean and good flavour	1	0	Jamaica, rich and very full flavour (much recommended)	1	4
Java, strong and fine flavour	1	2	Finest Jamaica or Berbice	1	6
Mocha or Turkey Coffee, most delicious flavour, no better required				1	8

Shopkeepers and large Consumers, by calling upon us and examining our Stock, must return satisfied that we are in a position to supply as cheap as any Firm in London, Bristol, or Liverpool, and a great deal cheaper than many feel inclined to do.

Your obedient Servants,
An ASSISTANT WANTED   WALTON and COMPANY.
☞ Observe the Teapot over the Door.

THE MERCHANT TEA COMPANY,
ESTABLISHED FOR THE SALE OF PURE TEA AT MERCHANTS' PRICES.

The Proprietors of this Establishment have undertaken a Commercial Enterprise of no small importance to the General Public, and they would strongly urge their claim, asking for support to enable them to carry out their designs, viz.:

PURE TEA.—MERCHANTS' PRICES.

FINE BREAKFAST CONGOU - - - 2s. per pound.
CHOICE SARYUNE KAISOW - - - 2s. 6d. „
FINEST IMPERIAL SOUCHONG - - 3s. „

In ordering, please state whether Plain or Scented Teas are required.

PLAIN TEA is a mixture of India and China growths, which we recommend to those who prefer a nice, comfortable, smooth-drinking Tea.

SCENTED TEA is a more extensive mixture of the different India and China growths, and consequently has greater aroma and more pungency. Those who appreciate a real old-fashioned rough tea of this description would do well to try our Scented Teas.

The immense stock and variety of Tea which we always have on hand for customers to select from enables us to please every palate, and at such prices as cannot fail to ensure perfect satisfaction.

THE MERCHANT TEA COMPANY, 99, Oxford Street, Swansea.

(The Cambrian 1846)

CHINA TEA WAREHOUSE,
WIND-STREET, SWANSEA.

MARY WILLIAMS,
IN returning her grateful thanks for the very liberal support and preference which she has experienced in her business of Tea Dealer and Grocer, begs to announce that she has *just received a large supply* of PORTUGAL GRAPES, FRENCH PLUMS, MUSCATELLS, VALENTIA RAISINS, FIGS, and every other description of DRIED FOREIGN FRUIT, of superior quality, and in excellent preservation. Genuine Teas, direct from the East India House; fresh roasted Coffee, raw and refined Sugars, Spices, and every article in Grocery, of best quality, and on the most reasonable terms.

(The Cambrian 3rd January 1835)

THE CHINA TEA COMPANY,
NO. FIVE, CAER STREET, SWANSEA.
(LATELY OCCUPIED BY MESSRS MATTHEWS.)
WILLIAM POOLER, Manager.
WILL OPEN TO-MORROW.

(The Cambrian 16th January 1857)

CHINESE AND EAST INDIAN TEA COMPANY

HORNIMAN'S PURE TEA (Agents in Wales)

Agents in Castle Street Swansea and Orchard Street Neath
(The Cambrian 4th January 1867)

(The Cambrian 14th January 1857)

Saint Teilo

St. Teilo's skull returned to Llandaff Cathedral

'The skull of St. Teilo was given into the hands of the Matthew family over 500 years ago when Llandaff Cathedral had fallen into disrepair. The Bishop's Palace and the Archdeacon's house had been sacked by Owain Glyndwr and the tomb of St. Teilo had been vandalised.

At this time David Matthew, whose family in previous centuries had come to be regarded as keepers of the Tomb of Saint Teilo, set about its restoration. To show his gratitude the then Bishop of Llandaff gave Sir David the skull as hereditary keepers.

Over the centuries the skull followed the fortunes of the Matthew family until 1994 when it was returned to the Cathedral. The skull had travelled to the Prescelli Hills, to Southern England and to Australia, where it had been kept in a bank vault in Sydney, New South Wales and, finally returned to Llandaff Cathedral. Eventually the skull came into the possession of Captain Robert Matthew who lived in Hong Kong who deemed it right to return it to the Cathedral.'

(Extract from a sermon preached at Llandaff Cathedral by Chancellor B.M Lodwick on St. Teilo's day and the return of St. Teilo's skull)

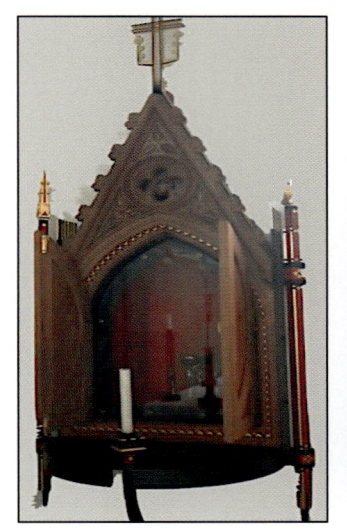

Shrine of St. Teilo at Llandaff Cathedral

Captain Robert Matthew (centre left) with his wife, members of the family and Chancellor B.M. Lodwick around St. Teilo's Skull (Western Mail)

'Terrible' (HMS)
'HMS 'Terrible' and HMS 'Spy' were put on patrol between King Road and Milford Haven, and Swansea. Skippers complained of being boarded in the channel and having their 'hands' pressed into service on the warships. Smuggled goods seized locally were sometimes auctioned locally. Bohea, Green, Congou and Hyson realised from two shillings to seven shillings per pound.'(Late 18th Century)
('The Port of Swansea………. In Retrospect' by W.C. Rogers Vol.5 p. 180)

Thomas (D.G)
'Ordinary Seaman D.G Thomas, of Swansea, was killed while serving abroad HMS Amethyst in April 1949 in what became known as the' Yangtze Incident'.
('Crippled by dash to Freedom' by Jill forward from The Way We Were Series)
(South Wales Evening Post April 23rd, 1996 www.southwales-eveningpost.co.uk)

Thomas (Dylan)
Swansea University and the City and County of Swansea are jointly funding a visit by the Chinese poet Wu Fu - Sheng, Professor at the University of Salt Lake City, who will be working on the first substantial translation of the Swansea-born poet Dylan Thomas's poetry into Mandarin Chinese. (2014)
(See Wu Fu - Sheng)

Thomas (Millicent and Margaret)
'The Years Behind the Wall', Chapter X, p.81 - How a Welshman Worked for China. The story of Timothy Richard

Thomas (Professor John David Ronald DSc, F.R.S.E)
'Born on the 2nd January 1926, at Gwynfe, and later lived at Gresford, Wrexham. Prof Thomas held many academic posts during his life. In 1991 he was Honorary Course Advisor at the Hong Kong Baptist College. From 1983 to 1985 he held the post of Foreign Expert at the Shanghai Teachers University.'
(From: Professor Thomas and The International Who's Who 1995-96, 59th Edition)

Thomas (Rev. James 1843-1933)
James Thomas was born at Stepaside in 1843. In 1868 he arrived at Shanghai, with his wife, as a newly ordained minister. He worked for the London Missionary Society (LMS) for three years and left to become Minister of the Union Chapel (Congregational). His work took him to the brothels and opium dens along the Huangpu River in Shanghai. On returning to Britain, he was appointed to the British and Foreign Bible Society becoming its Regional Secretary. The Rev Thomas retired in 1990.
('Stepaside's Man in Shanghai – Portrait of Rev James Thomas'
Pembrokeshire Mining Community
Reference: Page 109 Forty-Five Years in China by Timothy Richards, D.D, Litt.D
Timothy Richards refers to him as 'my friend'

Other Sources
The Times newspaper, 1933 ; Blackheath Local Guide newspaper, 1933
Congregational Year Book, 1934; School of Oriental & African Studies, University of London, London Missionary Society archive
Pembrokeshire Record Office, Haverfordwest Grammar School Admissions Register, 1855-1909 (cat ref. SSR/2/7/4) The History of the British & Foreign Bible Society, William Canton, Murray, 1910
The History of Haverfordwest Grammar School, G Douglas James, (no publisher's name), 1961

Thomas (Rev Robert Jermain BA 1840 – 1866)

LONDON MISSIONARY SOCIETY
'He served as a teacher at Oundle in 1856. He matriculated at University of London. Ordained 1863, he sailed for Shanghai. In 1866 he was given charge of Anglo-Chinese School in Peking. In 1931, a Robert Jermain Thomas Memorial Church was built near the spot where he died; this Memorial was erected by the natives.'
(E.L, Evans Cymru a `r Gymdeithas Genhadol)
(Dictionary of Welsh Biography Down to 1940 p.964)

Robert Jermain Thomas was a Protestant Christian missionary who served with the London Missionary Society in the late Qing Dynasty China and Korea. As a fluent Korean speaker, he agreed to accompany merchants as an interpreter aboard the American ship 'General Sherman, on condition that he could take Bibles with him.
A story is told that as the 'General Sherman' was being attacked, Robert Jermain Thomas began to throw the Bibles that he had brought with him for distribution among the people, on to the bank of the river. Everyone on the boat was killed. About twenty-five years later Korea was a more open country with more freedom for foreigners, an American stayed at an inn in the vicinity of Rev. Thomas` murder. The American found, as he looked around his room, something very strange and wonderful. He seemed to be looking at something that he knew. Then, it suddenly dawned on him that the walls of his room were covered in faded pages with Chinese writing. He was looking at pages of the Bible! The innkeeper then told the American the story of how the pages of the Bible came to be there. People, at that time, had been forbidden to read the Bible and those brought by Robert Thomas had been used as wallpaper. But one man hid his copy and read it secretly. He passed on the Bible teachings to his family and friends. The Rev. Robert Jermain Thomas had not died in vain. The Korean Protestant Church has recognised Rev. Thomas as the first Korean Christian martyr. Many Koreans make pilgrimage to Hanover, Abergavenny to visit where Robert Thomas lived. In the little three hundred year old Independent Hanover Chapel is a memorial plaque to Rev. Thomas in English, Welsh, Latin and Greek. Many books have been written about him in the Korean language.

Memorial to Jermaine Thomas at Hanover Chapel, Monmouthshire

The Author and husband (left) with the Head of the Presbyterian Church in South Korea and the Head of the Korean Presbyterian Church in the UK, their wives and Mrs Nancy Wilson, of Hanover Chapel, outside Hanover Chapel, Monmouthshire (1994)

SIR,
Thinking that numerous friends of my dear son will be glad to learn further accounts respecting his lamentable death, will you have the kindness to insert the following letter in the next impression of the 'Cambrian' which I received a few days ago from the Rev. Joseph Edkins, B.A., with whom he lived and laboured in the Missionary work at Pekin.
Yours
Robert Thomas
Hanover, near Abergavenny,
March 18th, 1867.

My Dear Sir,
Long ere this reaches you the report of what has occurred in Corea will have touched your heart with anxiety and grief. My wife and I cannot but think with the deepest pain of the sorrow that must have been caused by the tidings of what we fear has occurred not only to yourself but our lost friend`s mother and sisters. You will wonder that you have not been written to. In fact, there was nothing satisfactory in the reports that reached us, and the details conflicted each other. I waited for more definite information, and have been travelling for nearly a month in a neighbouring province. Our beloved friend left us on July 10th. I had a note from him from Chefoo, in which he informed me that he was going to Corea in a merchant ship, and expressed the hope that I would not postpone an intended journey to Mongolia on account of his absence. This journey I took in company with Mr. Muirhead and returning on the 12th October, heard for the first time the shocking news that the 'General Sherman ' had been destroyed by the Coreans, and all on board had been put to death. Then, however, as now, there were many persons who declined to believe that your son was among those who met this cruel fate. I prefer, myself, to hold by the little thread of remaining hope till the spring. The reason against hope is the belief of the French Missionaries, derived from native Corean statements, that none were spared. The reasons for hope are that our friend spoke Corean, and would be able to make the people understand that he might be useful to them, also that he had with him a young Pekinese Christian, one of my students. Why should the Coreans kill Chinese in a time like the present? However, those of us who allow ourselves to hope that your son may be still be heard of have no positive evidence

to rest on, but simply such presumptions as those I have just mentioned his having with him a Corean dress would favour his escape.

The French are in possession of an island at the mouth of the river that leads to the capital, and will commence warlike operations in the spring. They will take the capital probably with great ease, and we shall then obtain full information. The disaster to the 'General Sherman' took place in another river further to the North West, and nearer to the Chinese boundary. Up this river there is a rich Corean city, and the country in its neighbourhood constitutes the most fertile district in Corea. The city is called Pingan. The "General Sherman" went apparently to open trade there. One account said that the "General Sherman" went four tides up the river, another stated that she went aground at the mouth. The French missionary, Kidd, states that the local mandarins referred the case of all on board to the King`s father, who, as Regent, ordered the decapitation of the whole number. If he be lost, we have lost one whom we much loved who showed extraordinary linguistic talent who endeared himself much to the Chinese by his amiability, and was capable of becoming extremely useful among them as a missionary. God hath done as it hath pleased Him, and who shall say unto Him what doest thou? Anticipating that you would on hearing these gloomy tidings through the newspapers, write to Dr. Mullens for information, I sent him in October such particulars as we then had here, and thought best to postpone writing to you personally till more satisfactory communications should be obtained. Commending you to the sympathy of our compassionate High Priest on high,

I remain, faithfully yours,
Joseph Edkins.
Pekin, December 4th, 1866.
(The Cambrian 22nd March 1867)

TO THE EDITOR OF THE CAMBRIAN
Sir,
'Will you have the kindness to insert the following letter in the next impression of the 'Cambrian', which I received a few days ago from the American Ambassador at Peking.'
Hanover near Abergavenny July23rd 1867
Legation of the United States, Peking
April 23rd 1867
My Dear Sir,
I enter upon the sorrowful task of responding to your letter of enquiry touching the loss of your respected son. As the ONLY FOREIGNER IN THE EAST who could speak the Corean language, he was PERSUADED to act as interpreter for the French expedition. His reasons for embarking in the 'General Sherman' are, I think, correctly stated by you. The Sherman was chartered by Mendows and Co., of Tientsin, for a trading venture to Corea. There are various accounts as to the manner of the capture of the vessel and the destruction of the crew and passengers, 27 in all. The account is that she grounded and while in a helpless position was surrounded and burnt together with her precious freight. Another is that a fight occurred and that the natives were beaten off when the relatives of the slain, during a parley on shore, fell upon the passengers and murdered them. The former account came first through the French priests who escaped the massacre of the Christians; the latter from the Corean official who was in Peking last winter seeing information touching the future intentions of the French and the powers interested in the fate of those lost in the Sherman. The priests thought that the massacre was dictated by the King or the guardian of the King. The official denied this, and said it was an accidental collision growing out of misunderstanding. This seems to be the best authenticated statement. According to this, your son was beheaded WHILE TRYING TO APPEASE THE COREANS. An American ship of war visited the coast of Corea last winter for the purpose of inquiry, but succeeded only in ascertaining that all were lost. It was impossible to open relations with the Coreans.

Capt. Shagelat reports that a man, who from the respect paid to him, must have been a high official, came on board with much 'hauteur' ordered him to go away as speedily as possible, and said that the passengers and crew of the Sherman were not murdered by the order of the officials, and that the Coreans had beaten the French. We shall, I think make a more serious attempt to come into relations with the Coreans during the approaching summer. If we do I will see that every possible fact in relations to your lamented son shall be communicated to you. I shall be pleased to hear from you and to aid you in any way. Your son was most favourably known at the Legations and, by missionaries of the East. He was a remarkable scholar, and when he died a great light went out. Deeply sympathising with you in your great sorrow.
I am, most truly, yours,
Anson Burlingame
(The Cambrian 26th July 1867)

Thomas (Ronald Stuart 1913 – 2000)
Welsh poet and Anglican priest. Chinese academic Cheng Jia translated the 'Collected Poems 1945-1990 ' of R .S. Thomas. Two volumes, published in 2012, by Chu Chen Books (A division of Chongqing University Press Company, Ltd)

Thompson (R. Wardlow)
'Griffith John - The story of fifty years in China' by R. Wardlow Thompson London (1906)

Toke (Roundell Tristram)
Commissioned as a Second Lieutenant in the Welch Regiment (1892)
Promoted to Lieutenant (1886) and Captain (1900).
'As a Lieutenant, he was seconded to the Chinese Regiment, in Hong Kong, as Adjutant. His regiment is not recorded as being part of the relief force which relieved the legation at Pekin in 1900 but, being anxious to become involved, he, somehow or other, managed to involve himself as an observer and certainly got as far as Tientsin (Tianjin). Whether or not he got as far as Pekin is not known, but the story of the Relief is well recorded. His uniforms were donated to the Museum by his wife, sometime, during World War II.
(Bryn Owen FMA, Regimental Museum Cardiff 1997)
The uniforms are now at the Regimental Museum of the Royal Welsh (23rd, 24th 41st and 69th Foot Brecon)

Regimental uniforms of Captain Toke

Trawler (Chinese)

FIRST CHINESE TRAWLER
Leaves Swansea on Long Voyage
'The first Chinese vessel that has ever left South Wales……… One of the very few to leave any port in the British Isles……. steamed from the Swansea Fish Wharf early on Friday morning……….. the steam trawler 'HIO FUNG' that is bound for Hong Kong, a matter of 9,500 miles from Swansea.

Included in her crew is Mr Harry Richardson, a Swansea mate, who is, however, on this voyage, acting as boatswain. He has a reputation of exceptional experience in trawling matters, and he'll remain with the HIO FUNG in Chinese waters.

The HIO FUNG has been fitted out by the Castle Steam Trawling Company, who makes a speciality in this direction and has already fitted out a trawler or two for Japanese owners. This trawler is one of the finest and most up-to-date ever launched in this country, and the fact of her being fitted out at Swansea (she came all the way round from Middlesbrough for the purpose) is a tribute to the facilities offered to trawler owners at the Port.'
(The Cambrian 5th May 1911)

Treborth (Botanical Gardens)

The Treborth Botanic Garden covers an area of 18 hectares on the shores of the Menai Strait and has been owned by Bangor University since 1960. (See Bangor University)

The 'Two Dragons Garden Project' is a collaborative partnership development between:
- Bangor University
- Treborth Botanic Garden
- Xishuangbanna Tropical Botanic Garden
- Chinese Union of Botanic Gardens
- Royal Botanic Garden Edinburgh
- Botanic Garden Conservation International
- Bangor Confucius Institute

The project aims to improve capacity for teaching, research and knowledge exchange in the botanical sciences across Wales and China. Planning is currently underway to develop a Chinese herbal garden at Treborth. The team is led by Dr. Sophie Williams, Lecturer in Conservation Science at Bangor University and Xishuangbanna Tropical Botanic Garden.

Dr Sophie Williams and Yang Xi, Training Co-ordinator for the Chinese Union of Botanic Gardens at Xishuangbanna, Yunnan Province (2014).

Trevor (Thomas, 1st Baron Trevor of Peckham 1658-1730)
Thomas, 1st Lord Trevor, 1658-1730, and his wife, Ann Weldon, did not live in Wales, but his father was a descendant of the Trevor family, of Plas Teg, Mold and Trevalyn, Denbigh. Thomas' father moved to London to make his money.

Dinner plate bearing the coat of arms of Baron Trevor and his wife Ann Weldon – Canton, China c 1722 at the National Museum of Wales.

'Y Tyst'
A weekly Welsh language newspaper that was circulated in Liverpool and throughout Wales. It merged in 1871 with 'Tyst Cymreig' and 'Y dydd'. The newspaper focused mainly upon local, general and foreign news. Articles about Rev. Dr. Griffith John in China ('GRIFFITH JOHN YN CHINA') appeared in 4th May, 25th May and 15th June issues of 1883.
A review of Noel Gibbard's book 'Griffith John – Apostle to Central China' (Penybont ar Ogwr, 1998) appeared in the March 25th, 1999 edition of 'Y Tyst.

Tulloch (Major-General Sir Alexander Bruce KCB, CMG 1803-1864)
'Colonel of the Welch Regiment 1918-1920. Served as a Deputy Quartermaster General with the Gunboat Expedition to South China in 1859. He was present at the 1860 campaign at Dagu, the occupation of Tianjin, and the surrender of Pekin.'
(Bryn Owen, FMA, Curator, Regimental Museum, Cardiff Castle)
(See also: Archives Wales; Gwent Archives)

Turner (Frank B)
Writer of 'In Remembrance-Rev W Hopkyn Rees DD'. An outline of Hopkyn Rees' life and achievements in China.
(The Chinese Recorder November 1924)

Turner (John)
SURGEON, H.C. STEAM-FRIGATE 'NEMESIS' DONATES CHINESE ARTEFACTS TO ROYAL INSTITUTION
'There are some other donations which the Council wish to notice with special commendation......... there have likewise been sent home, at various times during the past year, numerous articles illustrative of the costume, civil, and domestic and military habits, arts and manufacturers of the Chinese, by Mr John Turner, also a native of Swansea, and Surgeon of the H.C. Steam-Frigate 'Nemesis', engaged in the late war.

It is particularly gratifying to know that, amidst the active pursuits in the engrossing interest of life............. the very strife of war itself and in the remotest regions of the earth, our countrymen and friends have neither forgotten their home, nor disregarded the claims of science on their patriotism.'
(The Cambrian 3rd June 1843)

MR. J.TURNER (SON OF CAPTAIN TURNER) OF SWANSEA TAKES PART IN THE CAPTURE OF CANTON
in the Gazette report for the taking of Canton, we perceive the name of Mr J Turner, surgeon of the Nemesis steam vessel, and son of Captain Turner R.N. of this town, among the gallant officers who took part in the storming of the works.
(The Cambrian 19th June 1841)
Matthew's Swansea Directory 1830
Lieut John Turner, R.N. Nelson Terrace
Piggott's Directory of England and Wales 1844
Captain John Turner, R.N. Nelson Terrace
Hunt and Companies Bristol etc. and Welsh Towns Directory 1850
Captain John Turner R.N. 9 Nelson Terrace (p.131)

DEATH OF SURGEON-GENERAL TURNER
ANOTHER OLD SWANSEA BOY GONE OVER
TO THE MAJORITY

'Our obituary column of last week contained the notice of the death, at Bath, at the age of 75, of Surgeon-General John Turner, late of the Bombay Artillery, second son of the late Captain John Turner, RN, of Swansea. Bladud, the Bath Society paper, has the following article on the event:-
The death of Surgeon-General Turner removes a familiar figure from our midst. In his earlier days he saw a good deal of active service, notably during the Chinese War. He retired from the service in 1874, since which time he has been a resident in this city. A few particulars of his career will be read with interest by his many friends. As Deputy-Inspector General he served in the steamer Nemesis, in China, in 1841-42, and was present at the attack on the Bogue Forts, the several affairs in the Canton River, attack on Canton, taking of Amoy and , second capture of Island of Chusan, occupation of the City of Wangpoo, assault and capture of the city of Chapoo, capture of the 100-gun battery at Wosengund and final operations before the city of Nankin. He was awarded a medal at the close of the campaign. Surgeon-General Turner also served with the Bhawulpur Field Force, under Lieut. -General Sir Charles Napier, in 1845-46, also with Ahmednager Field Force in 1858, under Sir Hugh Rose, when in pursuit of Tatya Tope in Kandeish and Satpura Range. For eight years he was principal medical officer at Aden, after which he was appointed Inspector of Hospitals in the Northern Division of the Bombay Presidency. He was 75 years of age. The cause of death was exhaustion, consequent upon inability to swallow, owing to cancer in the throat.
The funeral took place on Thursday last, the 28th ultimo. Surgeon-General Turner, as we have said, was the son of a Swansea man, but it is not clear that he was born in the town. His father lived in Nelson terrace; his brother, who is now living in retirement in Clifton, was for a great number of years connected with HM Customs here; and his sisters, the Misses Turner, still reside at No. 12, Mansel Street Swansea.
The deceased gentleman was a schoolmate with Jon Deffett Francis, with Mr. Edward Strick and others, at Mr. Harmsworth 's school Swansea. He went through his medical studentship at Guy 's Hospital London, at the same time as Dr. JG. Hall our veteran Swansea surgeon, and between them there existed a close life-long friendship.
Dr. Hall remembers in their student days, when Mr. Turner was about to enter London University they went to Bristol to get deceased 's baptismal certificate.

Major-General Turner was in Swansea as recently as May or June last when his trim figure, smartly dressed booted and spurred could not have failed to attract the notice of some of the more observant townsfolk. On that occasion, Dr. Hall drove his friend round the district and renewed old boyish memories of Caswell, Langland Bay and Gowerland, and on parting it was arranged that the visit should be repeated in October. But this was not to be. Cancer developed itself suddenly, and the smart and manly old soldier-doctor answered the roll-call of Death, and thus leaves another gap in the fast-thinning ranks of old Swansea Boys.'
(The Cambrian 6th December 1889)

Tyzack (Charles)
Author of 'Friends to China: the Davison Brothers and the Friends Mission to China 1886-1939', published by William Sessions Ltd, Ebor Press 1988. An account of Quaker missionary works in China. Charles Tyzack was the great grandson of Adam Davison. He was a former Secretary of the Wales China Friendship Society and lecturer in English at Cardiff University.

U

'ULearnChinese'
A Chinese language and culture teaching programme for non-Chinese speakers written and developed in Wales. A special interactive version produced in conjunction with Chinese Language Publishing Ltd has been endorsed by HANBAN (Office of Chinese Language International, Beijing)
Each set (1 to 6) contains Study Book, Revision Workbook, Teacher's Guide, and a set of interactive CDs which include a full range of back-up resources, voice recognition system and a virtual pinyin keyboard.

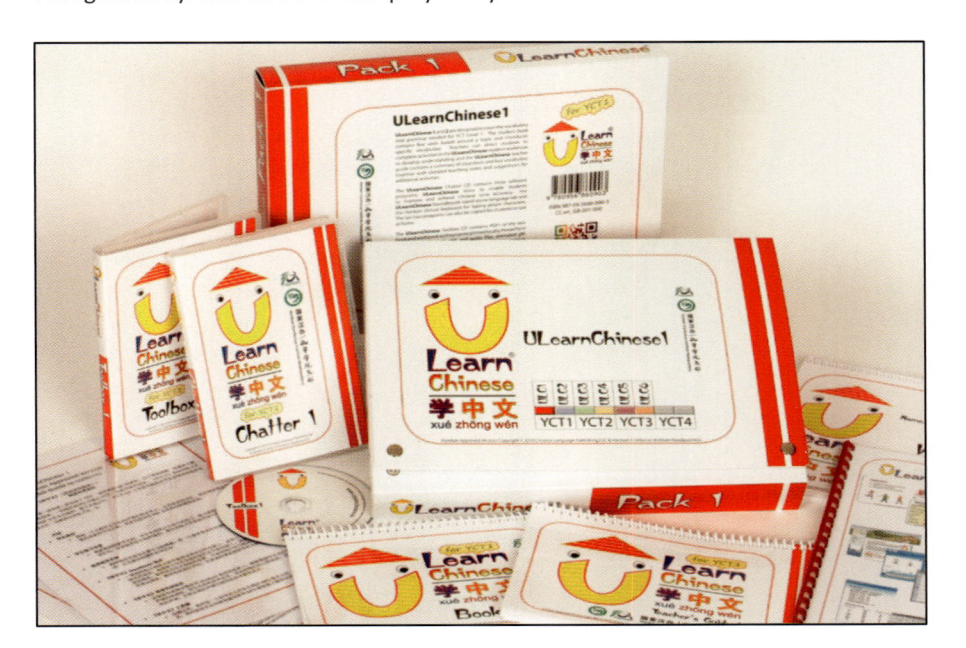

UNICEF
The Wales China Friendship Society held a fundraising event in support of a UNICEF appeal to raise money for the inoculation of children in China (Jiangsu Province) in 1987.

'Under Sail'
'An exhibition of marine painters recalling the glorious age of sail in Swansea Bay. ' The Exhibition featured Swansea cutters, tall ships and seascapes (1830-1880), and was held in July 1987 at the Glynn Vivian Art Gallery, Swansea. Included in the exhibition were works by James Harris who painted many ships on the China run.

Union Hospital (Wuhan)
The Union Hospital is located in Hankou, Wuhan. A large bust of Griffith John stands in the grounds (picture) In October 2012, a delegation from Union Hospital presented a specially commissioned bust of Griffith John to the College of Medicine at Swansea University to celebrate the linking of the two organizations. The bust is on permanent display at Swansea Museum. (See: Griffith John)

Bust of Rev. Dr. Griffith John at the Union Hospital, Wuhan.

Plaque at Swansea University College of Medicine commemorating the establishment of the Joint Medical Centre (January 2015).

Judy McKimm, Swansea University with Professor Yao at the Hospital Museum Wuhan.

Dr. Guobin Wang (centre left), President of Union Hospital, Wuhan and medical delegation at the official unveiling of a bust of Rev. Dr. Griffith John at Swansea Museum (2012).

United NationsAssociation

ANNUAL DORIS HANSEN MEMORIAL LECTURE
U.N.A - CITY OF CARDIFF BRANCH

John Wyer and Vicky Stammers (WAR ON WANT - SLOW BIKES TO CHINA APPEAL) were guest speakers at the Annual Doris Hansen Memorial Lecture, Cardiff on Wednesday 11th November 1987

```
UNITED NATIONS ASSOCIATION
CITY OF CARDIFF BRANCH
President: The Rt. Hon. The Lord Mayor of Cardiff

ANNUAL DORIS HANSEN MEMORIAL LECTURE

to be held at
Welsh Centre For International Affairs
Temple of Peace, Cathays Park, Cardiff

WEDNESDAY 11TH NOVEMBER 1987 at 7.30pm

Guest Speakers
JOHN WYER
VICKY STAMMERS
WAR ON WANT SLOW BIKES TO CHINA APPEAL
```

Universities

'All Welsh universities have signed agreements with numerous universities throughout China for collaboration in a wide range of areas. A Higher Education consortium has been established to provide a comprehensive portfolio of training and development programmes in which all Welsh universities are involved.' (2014)
(WALES CYMRU www.wales.com)

Upward (Rev. Bernard 1873-1944)

'Bernard and Kate Upward worked with the Rev. Dr.Griffith John in central China for the London Missionary Society. One of Bernard's main focuses was education and, as well as acting as a teacher at the school set up by Dr John in Hankou, he wrote in a report to the Missionary Society that "it fell to 'my lot' to take a large share of the looking after the erection of the college" – overseeing the building of what would be the first block of the Griffith John College at Han Chia Ten, some six miles outside the city of Hankou.
The main block was more or less complete by January 1908, and the following years saw steady growth in numbers of students, and of the buildings to house them. More Chinese teachers joined the staff and many aspects of school life were bilingual. A wide variety of activities and achievements was reported, from the individual attainments of leavers who went into good jobs or further education to the formation of a college choir and a fife and drum band, the holding of sports days, the building of a swimming pool and, eventually, the starting of a scout troop with its own brass band – the first scout band in China!
The College expanded, with success in University entrance exams and the training of primary school teachers, followed by the opening of a "Higher Normal School" for training high school teachers, a theology department and a medical school.

By 1919 there were 250 students at the College, and in 1920 Bernard writes of its 'coming of age' – the 21st anniversary of its founding. Record numbers of leaving certificates were gained, as well as matriculation certificates for Hong Kong University, bringing an assurance that good progress really had been made in fulfilling Griffith John's vision.'
(Jenny Childs – Great niece; 2015)

Griffith John Anglo-Chinese College Hankou

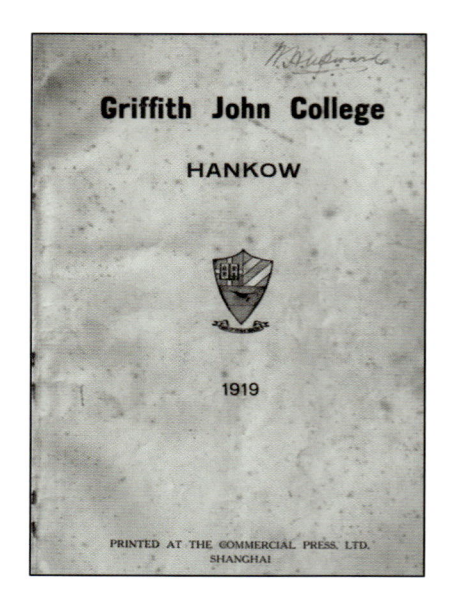

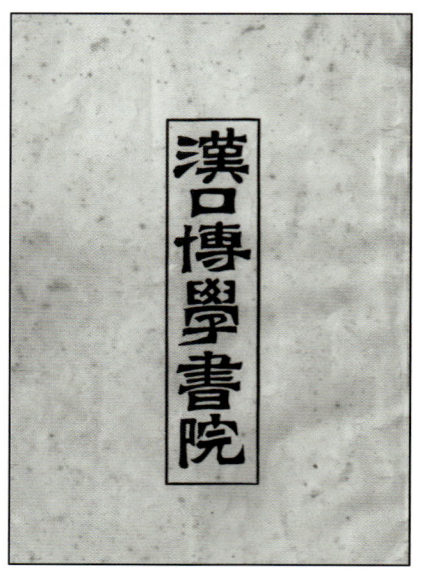

Griffith John College Handbook 1919 signed by Rev. Upward

Part of envelope with Griffith John College title and sent by Rev. Upward to his wife in UK via Siberia

V

Vaughan (Richard c 1665-1734)

Armorial dinner plate part of a dinner service from Canton bearing the Coat of Arms of Richard Vaughan of Cors-y-Gedol, Dyffryn Ardudwy at the National Museum Wales

Vicari (Andrew)
Welsh artist Andrew Vicari was invited by the Chinese Ministry of Culture to exhibit in Beijing. He was the first Western artist to be officially invited to paint China's great philosopher, Confucius. He also painted Chairman Mao Zedong and China's first emperor, Shi Huang Di. (1994)

Vivian (Admiral Algeron Walker Heneage C.B., M.V.O 1871-1952)
'Walker Heneage Algernon Vivian (1871 - 1952), admiral; b. 4 Feb. 1871, third son of Major Clement Walker Heneage, V.C., 8th Hussars, of Compton Bassett, Wilts. and Henrietta Letitia Victoria, daughter of John Henry Vivian of Singleton, Swansea. In 1886 he began a career in the Royal Navy, joining the battleship HMS Triumph as a midshipman under the command of Sir Algernon Heneage, a relative of his. He served in various parts of the world, including north China. On retirement he settled in Swansea, at first at Parc le Breos, Penmaen, an estate that he had been left by Graham Vivian. But, soon after, he inherited Clyne Castle on the death of Dulcie Vivian. Thereupon he added 'Vivian' to his surname.'
(National Library of Wales – 'WALES BIOGRAPHY ONLINE')

Vivian (Richard Glynn 1835-1910)
Richard Glynn Vivian was the youngest son and seventh child of nine children. He was the son of industrialist and politician, John Henry Vivian and his wife Sarah. On the death of his father in 1855, he inherited a quarter share in his father's copper business, Vivian and Sons, Swansea, but he preferred the arts and travel and left his brothers to run the business.

He travelled widely and, as a result, built up a large art and porcelain collection. It was during his travels to China in 1870 that he bought many pieces that form part of his collection at the Glynn Vivian Art Gallery in Swansea.

In 1885 he married Laura Halkett but they divorced six years later. He bought Sketty Hall to house his collection. By 1902, almost blind, his faith led him to use his wealth to help others. Three years later he offered his collection to Swansea Corporation, and with his endowment, the Glynn Vivian Art Gallery was built to house it. He laid the foundation stone in 1909 but did not live to see its completion as he died in 1910 at his London home.

.

GLYNN VIVIAN DIARY 1870

Glynn Vivian had the following sketches at the front of his Diary.
1. Sketch Woman Echeng 19th Feb. 70
2. Temple Echeng 15th Feb.
3. Temple Echeng 19th Feb.
4. Duck Island
5. Gate of City of Echeng 20th Feb. 70
6. Duck Island 22nd Feb. 70
7. Nankin from River 23rd Feb. 70
8. Triumphal Arch Nankin 23rd Feb. 70
9 and 10. Sketches of people

Examples of Chinese Porcelain and Cloisonné brought back by Richard Glynn Vivian from China now at the Glynn Vivian Art Gallery in Swansea

The following excerpts are taken from the diaries of Glynn Vivian.
Echeng Tuesday, 15th February 1870
Breakfast in room. Finished letters to my mother.

Wednesday, 23rd February 1870.
Later met Mr. Gordon and introduced to Capt. Hardy, Had tiffin
Began to ship at Nankin at 5, Fine American steamer. Chinese saloon.
Prints of women. Landed. Got coolies. Rode donkeys, Long ride. Desolite houses.

Thursday, 24th February 1870
Le Père Colombelle took us to the Temple of Confucius.

Saturday, 26th February 1870 - Golden Island

10th MARCH 1870 - Fine day but cold. Wrote diary & drew. Had to wait till 5 for tide outside the bar of the Peiho River. Entered forts about 6. Drew them. Yu Shan just behind us. Fine night so kept on till nearly 11. Started again at daybreak. River very narrow & great blocks of ice kept on sticking all day. Some blocks nearly a foot thick and ran aground at last turn Double Bend.

Friday, lst April 1870 - Temple of the Sleeping Buddha

Saturday, 2nd April 1870 - Dinner at restaurant with chopsticks. Bits of meat, rice, salted vegetables. Sampled Chinese white wine very strong like gin.

Sunday, 3rd April 1870 - Peitang Museum. Fine new church-………back to the Legation 6.30.

Monday 4th April – Went to Roman Catholic Cathedral. Followed two men going to execution. Saw their heads cut off in street. Their perfect immobility. Heads in basket. No motion. Brandy and water in Gardiner's room.

Tuesday 5th April 1870 – Saw funeral.

Wednesday 6th April 1870 – Temple of Agriculture. At night developed photos.

Thursday, 7th April 1870 - Bought blue and white Ming Vases. At 8 started for Yuan Ming Yuan in cart. Back to Legation. Went to church at ll. Ayrton came to look at my china. Walked with him to old Curio Shops. Bought Imperial 5 clawed dragon green and white saucer .... oval enamelled looking clip. Nankow Ming Tombs camels, elephants, griffins, horses developed photos. Not good

15th April, Good Friday - American Charge d` Affaires dined with us. Went to Curiosity Shop. Bought 2 enamel turquoise and red lacquer box with Imperial dragons.

16th April - Went to church at ll. After breakfast went with Ayrton to Chinese town, looked at silks and bought vase with pottery said to be rare (& other things)

Tuesday 10th May - Chefoo fine situation of Palace. Took photo. Saw stone boat in lake Bridge & drove to Yuan Ming Yuan. Got over lst wall. Found fragments of china. Got over 2nd wall, trees, enormous grounds, gardens, ruins.

ACCOUNTS BOOK CHINA AUSTRALIA 1871
Glynn Vivian mentions many Chinese items that he purchased.
(Diary extracts by kind permission of Cardiff Central Library)

W

Wade (Professor George Woosung 1851-1941)
Professor Wade was born in China. His father was Joseph Henry Wade, of Shanghai. During his lifetime he became a prolific author, cleric and professor. He was appointed to St. David's College, Lampeter (now the University of Wales Trinity St. David's) where he stayed for 40 years.
Reference
Welsh Biography on Line
'Wade, George Woosung' by Thomas Iorwerth Ellis MA (1899-1970) Aberystwyth
'History of St. David's University College Lampeter' by DTW Price, University of Wales Press (1990) Volume ii: 1898-1971

St. David's College Lampeter Academic Staff (1927). Professor Wade is seated in the centre of the photograph.

Wales Arts International (WAI)
2008 – 'In Search of The Red Dragon' – Eight artists from universities in Beijing, Shanghai, Guangzhou and Chongqing came to Wales in 2008 for a month-long residency at institutions and centres throughout the Country (Trinity College Carmarthen, Aberystwyth Arts Centre and UWIC School of Art and Design - Cardiff). The work was exhibited during the 'Wales in Chongqing Week' in 2009.
2009 – 'Celebrating the Dragon' – Three artists from Wales visited China in 2009 as part of 'Celebrating the Red Dragon' supported by Wales Arts International and the British Consulate. The artists were Iwan Bala, Mary Lloyd Jones and Christine Mills. Their work was initially exhibited in Chongqing and subsequently moved on to Guangzhou, Shanghai and Beijing.

Wales-China Friendship Society – Tseina a Chymru Undebol

The Wales China Friendship Society (WCFS), a registered charity, established in 1975, is among the oldest in the UK. Over 40 years, it has worked to promote and develop friendship and understanding between the people of Wales and China. The Society has worked closely with the Chinese People's Association for Friendship with Foreign Countries (CPAFFC) in Beijing and other similar organizations in the UK and Europe, and Chinese community groups including the Society for Anglo-Chinese Understanding (SACU) and the Scotland-China Association (SCA). It has also worked with the British Embassy in Beijing, the British Consulate-General in Shanghai and the Chinese Embassy. The Society also formed strong links with the Foreign Affairs Offices in the Cities of Nantong, Xiamen, Tianjin, Hangzhou and Wuhan.

It has worked on several Yangtze flood appeals, earthquake appeals in conjunction with the Chinese Embassy and with UNICEF on a vaccination programme for China's children (Jiangsu Province).

Over the years the Society has supported and organized many different cultural, educational and twinning programmes and delegation visits including:

1980 – Rhos Orpheus Choir performance tour to China.

1987 - Working with the Cardiff Chinese Community on the first Chinese New Year celebrations to be held in Wales when the Chinese brought their festival out to the community. It also designed the first course on the study of China held in Wales. The Year also marked the establishment of its first branch in China at Shanghai – the first time that a UK friendship organization had established a branch in China. The majority of the members were former post-graduate students from the West Glamorgan Institute of Higher Education (WGIHE -Now the University of Wales Trinity St. David Swansea).

Founding Members of WCFS Shanghai Branch in 1987

A WCFS logo by Xu Da a former post-graduate student at WGIHE, Swansea (1985)

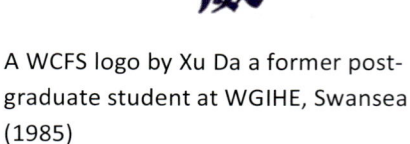

Official Seal (Chop) of the Wales-China Friendship Society

1987 - Officers of the Society received the Captain and crew of the container ship 'Ping Quan', the first Chinese vessel to dock at the Port of Swansea for nearly forty years.

1988 - Co-produced with the British Consulate General in Shanghai the first non-Chinese Dragon exhibition to be held in China.

Report in the China Daily about the 'Welsh Dragons for China Exhibition'. *'It was organized jointly by the Wales-China Friendship Society and British Consulate - General in Shanghai. The Exhibition was unique in that it was the first 'non-Chinese Dragon' exhibition to have been staged in China.'*

'Red Dragon of Wales comes to Shanghai'
SHANGHAI – Dozens of red dragons- in drawings, prints and carvings-from Wales came to Shanghai to meet their Chinese 'cousins' on Tuesday. An exhibition of 'Welsh Dragons for China', held at the British Consulate-General, included drawings of dragons by five year-old children from a school in Neath. In accompanying letters to the Consul-General Iain Orr, the young artists expressed their joy at promoting friendship between the British and Chinese peoples. Some of them even had the Chinese character 'Long' (dragon) drawn in their letters.
The exhibits had been collected from various organizations in Wales by the Wales-China Friendship Society. Some exhibits were especially commissioned for the Exhibition, including a hand-carved lovespoon, a traditional Welsh token of affection. On its handle were carved a Welsh Dragon, a Chinese Dragon, the words 'Wales ' and 'China' and two hands clasped in friendship.
The Red Dragon has been the national emblem of Wales for hundreds of years. The coat of arms of its Capital City, Cardiff bears the inscription in Welsh 'The Red Dragon Leads the Way'. March 1st, St. David's Day, is Welsh National Day and the British Consulate-General held the Exhibition of Welsh Dragons on that day to welcome the Year of the Dragon.
(China Daily 5th March 1988)

1989 – The Society organized and led Wales' first ever schoolchildren's performance, cultural and educational tour to China (CHINA 89 PROJECT). (See: 'CHINA 89')

1993 – Organized, in conjunction with the Chinese Embassy, the Ambassador's visit to Wales.

1997 - Celebration to mark the hand back of Hong Kong to China.

2008 - Inaugural Wales-China St. David's Day event with the Confucius Institute in Lampeter.

2012 - Supporting the link between Swansea University College of Medicine and Union Hospital, Wuhan.

2013 - Organizing fundraising appeals for children's hospices in Wales (Ty Hafan) and China (Butterfly Children's Hospices).

In 2015 the Society celebrated forty years of friendship and understanding between the peoples of Wales and China.

Hangzhou Peoples' Association for Friendship with Foreign Countries Delegation at Swansea Guildhall, February 1998. Lord Mayor Councillor Alan Lloyd (Centre) invited the Delegation, hosted by the Wales-China Friendship Society, to sign the visitors' book.

Wales - National Museum
The National Museum of Wales hosted the 'Ancient Chinese Bronzes' (1981) and 'Dinosaurs From China' (1987) exhibitions. The spectacular skeletons of dinosaurs from the People's Republic of China formed the centrepiece of the largest exhibition of dinosaurs ever to be staged in Britain. In 2011, the Museum, in conjunction with Chongqing Culture Bureau, exhibited ancient rock carvings from China – from the steep hillsides of the Dazu World Heritage site near Chongqing. The sculptures had never before been seen outside China. The Museum also designed the 'Land of the Red Dragon Exhibition' in Chongqing (2013)

'Wales in China'
The China-Britain Business Council (CBBC) magazine featured 'Wales in China' 2009-2010. Front cover – 'Where Two Dragons Meet'
Page 6 – Feature: 'Wales – growing links with Chongqing'
Page 7 – 'Christ College and Chinese Students'

Wales-Chongqing Week

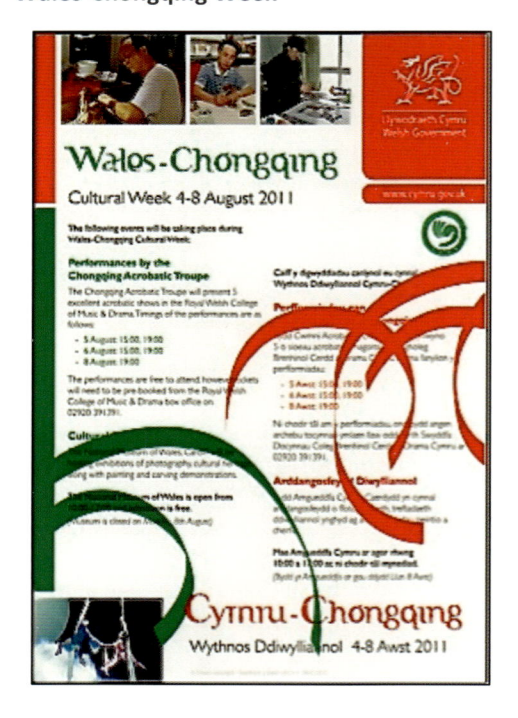

Wales Chongqing Cultural Week - 2011
'For the first time ever, the Bureau of Cultural Relationships, of the Chongqing Government is holding a Culture Week in Wales (4th – 8th August). This builds on the success of Wales Week's in Chongqing events, which have taken place around St David's Day in Chongqing for the past 5 years. You can catch performances by an acrobatic troupe and demonstrations of traditional arts from the region of Chongqing by a group of artists.'
(Wales Cymru)

Wan Xiaoqiao

Dr Wan Xiaoqiao, Professor, China University of Geosciences in Beijing worked as a Post-doctoral Research Fellow with Professor Robin Whately at Aberystwyth University (1987-1988) on samples of fossils discovered in Tibet. Professor Wan was the first academic to be awarded a Royal Society Fellowship to study at an university in Wales.

Ward – Jones (Capt. Albert Louis)
'Captain Albert Louis Ward-Jones was born at Ty'n Twll, Bryncroes and 'brought up' at Beudy Newydd and Fron Allt in the Bryncroes District, the last of eight children of Griffith and Margaret Jones.

At the age of 16 (about 1912) he went to sea until the outbreak of the First World War on sailing ships out of Liverpool. In 1914 he enlisted with the Royal Navy and became an officer in the minesweeping service. In 1918 he returned to the Merchant Navy and for the next 20 years served in the China Seas out of Hong Kong. Captain Ward-Jones joined the China Navigation Co Ltd. He received eight medals for war and civilian services.

In 1939 he piloted the 'SS Suivo' safely down the Yangtze River during the Sino-Japanese war and was awarded a solid silver dollar in the form of an ashtray by the Chinese and was one of his proudest possessions.

During the Japanese invasion of Hong Kong he was taken prisoner and interned in Stanley Camp for four years until the Japanese surrender in 1945. Captain Ward-Jones and scores of other sea captains had tried to prevent the invasion by scuttling their ships at the harbour entrance and they suffered untold privation and maltreatment at the hands of their captors. A few days before the Japanese surrender, Captain Ward-Jones and four others were ordered to dig their own graves before facing a firing squad. He survived and returned to Pwllheli in 1945 and, as his health was impaired, quit the sea. He farmed at Dynfra, Aberdaron, for four years, which was his wife's family farm, before retiring to Pwllheli where he lived at Mathan House, Penlan Street. He died on July 17th, 1975, a few days short of his 79th birthday.'
(Pwllheli - The Port and Mart of Llŷn' by Lewis Lloyd 1991 Pages 275-276)

Watkins (Martha Winifred)
'Born in Manafon, Montgomeryshire in 1881. Appointed to Guangzhou, 1907 and worked there amongst women. Later in charge of a school for girls in Hong Kong and returned home in 1931.'
(Overseas Missionary Fellowship 1991)

Welsh Government
Former First Minister Rt. Hon Rhodri Morgan AM signed a Memorandum of Understanding between the Chongqing Municipal Government and the Welsh Government in Chongqing in March 2006. A formal co-operation agreement was signed during the Former First Minister's subsequent visit to China in March 2008. The Mayor of Chongqing, Wang Honju, visited Wales in August 2008. The principal areas of co-operation include business, energy, education and health.

Eleven of Wales' Further Education Colleges formed a Wales-Chongqing Consortium under the banner of Colleges Wales (UK) International, managed by Colleges Wales. The current First Minister Rt. Hon Carwyn Jones A.M., on the 25th October 2011, while on a visit to Chongqing, officially launched the consortium. The First Minister also signed an agreement with the Mayor of Beijing, Guo Jinlong, to promote business and educational links between Wales and China.

In February 2013, Minister for Housing, Regeneration and Heritage Huw Lewis, opened an exhibition organized by the National Museum of Wales entitled 'Wales, the Land of the Red Dragon' at the Three Gorges Museum in Chongqing. Previously, the two Museums had signed an agreement to co-operate in 2008.

The Welsh Government currently has three offices in China.

The Beijing office was originally opened by the Welsh Development Agency in May 2002 with a remit to attract Foreign Direct Investment (FDI) into Wales.

The office is currently heavily involved in the developing relationship with the Beijing Municipal Government, encapsulated in the Memorandum of Understanding (MOU) signed by the First Minister Carwyn Jones during his visit in 2011.

Subsequent sub-MOUs have been signed between the Welsh Government's department of Economy Science and Transport and the Beijing Investment Promotion Bureau, and between the Welsh Government's Culture Department and Beijing Culture Bureau.

The Welsh presence in Chongqing was established following the signing of a Memorandum of Understanding with Chongqing Municipal People's Government in 2006 by First Minister Rhodri Morgan, as recommended by the Chinese Vice-Premier (later Premier) Wen Jiabao. A formal Co-operation Agreement between Wales and Chongqing was signed during First Minister Rhodri Morgan's visit to Chongqing in March 2008. A further agreement was signed during First Minister Carwyn Jones' visit to Chongqing in November 2011. In September 2006, a Welsh Affairs Officer was appointed to the British Consulate General in Chongqing to take forward the Chongqing-Wales relationship. A second post was added in September 2007. In January 2011 the two posts were relocated to a separate Wales Government office in Chongqing.

The Shanghai office was established by WDA in September 2004, again with a FDI remit. Whilst there is no MOU-type relationship with the Shanghai Government, the office has developed a good working relationship with the Shanghai Municipal Government Foreign Affairs Office and the Government Economic Development Department.

First Minister Rt. Hon. Carwyn Jones A.M. with Mr Huang Qifan, Mayor of Chongqing (October 2011)

First Minister Rt. Hon. Carwyn Jones A.M. at the signing of the Memorandum of Understanding with Beijing Municipal Government, in October 2011, in Beijing with Mr Guo Jinlong, Mayor of Beijing:

Former First Minister Rt. Hon Rhodri Morgan AM, signing the first Memorandum of Understanding with Chongqing on the 1st March 2006 with Wu Jianong, Vice Mayor, Chongqing Municipal People's Government.

Former First Minister Rt. Hon Rhodri Morgan AM meeting with Mayor Wang Hongju during a visit to Chongqing in March 2008, prior to the signing of the "Sister Region" Twinning Agreement between Wales and Chongqing.

Welsh Development Agency (WDA)
The WDA opened an office in Beijing in 2002 with the remit to recruit and attract Foreign Direct Investment (FDI) into Wales. In 2004 an office was opened in Shanghai. In 2006, the WDA was closed down and its functions transferred to the Welsh Assembly Government.

Welsh Dragon
WELSH DRAGON FOUND IN BEIJING!
'Ms Li Feng did a double take as she glanced at a shop window in Beijing on the way home from work as she saw a Welsh Dragon displayed in the shop window. She was so surprised that she bought the tea towel. Ms Li recognised the Welsh Dragon from her time spent with friends in Wales.'
(Wales-China Friendship Society Newsletter 'Ni Hao' 1994) (See: Li Feng)

Li Feng displays the Welsh flag at a reception in Beijing (1994).

Welsh Flag
A Welsh Flag shown on stage at the People's Theatre, Nantong, Jiangsu Province, China during the final concert by the 'China 89' performers from Alderman Davies' Church in Wales Primary School Neath and Cwrt Sart Comprehensive School Briton Ferry – March 1989.

Welsh National Opera
'The Welsh National Opera staged a highly acclaimed production of La Bohème at the Hong Kong Arts Festival, May 2007. Performances took place at the Grand Theatre and Hong Kong Cultural Centre.'
(Welsh National Opera)

Wen Jiabao
Former Chinese Prime Minister (2003 – 2013), Wen Jiabao, visited Wales in 2000 as Vice-Premier with responsibility for Western Provinces. He recommended the setting-up of a partnership between Chongqing Municipality and Wales.

Williams (Emeritus Professor Cyril)
Late Emeritus Professor Rev. Cyril G. Williams, Fellow of Cardiff University and former Dean of Divinity in the University of Wales served in the congregational ministry in Wales and London before entering academic life in 1958, when he joined the staff in the Department of Semitic Languages at Cardiff University. He also taught at Carleton University, Ottawa, University of Wales, Aberystwyth, and finally University of Wales, Lampeter. He was awarded a Doctorate of Divinity by the University of Wales in 1993.

Author of 'Timothy Richards (1845-1990) O Ffaldybrenin i China' (1995)
'Basic Themes in the Comparative Study of Religion' (1992) – Extract: Chapter 9 'A Baptist-Buddhist Encounter: Timothy Richards and Chinese Buddhism'

Williams (Henry Goulstone)
'Organist Trinity Church, Swansea (1852), would be glad to hear from his brother William, or any of his relations. Any old friend or pupil dropping Henry G. Williams a few lines, they will be thankfully received.
Address - Henry Goulstone Williams, Professor of Music,
St Julien Hugh Edwards, Spanish Consulate, Amoy, China
PS: As my stay will be of short duration please write by returning mail.'
(The Cambrian 17th September 1869)

Williams (Jane 1897-1994)
Jane Williams, a nurse from Llanelli, was married to a medical missionary doctor. They lived in Yunnan Province, China from 1923-26.

Mrs Jane Williams in conversation with the Author

TRANSCRIPT OF A CONVERSATION BETWEEN THE AUTHOR (E.N.) and MRS.JANE WILLIAMS (J.W.) (China 1923 – 1926)

E.N. "How long did it take for letters to arrive?"

J.W. "Six or seven weeks"

E.N. "Did you speak Chinese to them?"

J.W. "A dialect from Yunnan.........colloquial. They were so happy if they found us doing something."

E.N. "Were you called a 'foreign devil'?

J.W. "Yes, prayed to the Lord to give me patience because it wasn`t always nice.

E.N. "Did you get malaria?"

J.W. "We had to boil the water. Malaria. I had a bout of malaria. The last two years, I thank God, I haven`t."

E.N. "How long were you in Kunming?"

J.W. "Two years and a half"

E.N. "How did you get around?"

J.W. "Walking"

E.N. "There are many Minorities in Yunnan."

J.W. "I was their nurse and that gave me acceptance. They were willing to accept Western medicine. I used to tell them to be clean and not to have drugs. We had no money."

E.N. "Twenty-two Minorities."

J.W. "Embroideries from the Miao People. They were proud to take us to their homes and we were proud to go and see how they lived."

E.N. "You have some wonderful pleated skirts from the Miao People. Their skirts are very famous. They were worn for special occasions?

J.W. "They were a gift."

E.N. "What about the mandarins?"

J.W. "They were glad as we were able to do things for them and they accepted us."

E.N. "Any animosity?"

J.W. "A warlord`s son was brought to the Mission one day. The little boy was ill. Luckily, they were able to help the child. From that day on the warlord protected them. What if the story had gone the other way?"

E.N. *"What did the people call you?"*

J.W. *"Wai laoshi"(Outside teacher - meaning Foreign teacher). They used to laugh at our mistakes."*

E.N. *"Did you travel anywhere else?"*

J.W. *"Only Yunnan. The Council wasn`t willing for us to go anywhere else. I rode on a mule. The mule was cleverer than I was and tried to tip me off. You had to forget you were a lady."*

E.N. *"What about news from home?"*

J.W. *"Oh, yes, we used to go to the station to get our letters."*

E.N. *"Did they make you homesick?"*

J.W. *"Sometimes it did. Sleeping time was often a crying time. I used to say "Please Lord help me." I used to imagine what they were doing at home."*

E.N. *"What about newspapers?"*

J.W. *"Only news was by talking to missionary visitors."*

E.N. *"Kunming is known as the city of eternal spring. Was it a nice climate?"*

J.W. *"We had a garden and could go out and pick flowers."*

E.N. *"What was your job?"*

J.W. *"A nurse and teach the Gospel and live the Gospel."*

E.N. *"How hard was it to teach about Jesus?"*

J.W. *"Difficult. We had the festivals........Christmas, Easter. The Chinese would join in and make a fuss."*

E.N. *"What about supplies? Nursing supplies came from where?"*

J.W. *"The Mission Society would send them out and they were transferred to our names."*

E.N. *"When you came home was it difficult to settle down?"*

J.W. *"I was ill. I was glad to be home. I am glad I made friends in China. I`m sure if I went back they would remember "wai laoshi."*

E.N. *"Tell me about your life there."*

J.W. *"I was married in China. Twice in one day - British Consulate. We had good friends in the China Inland Mission............because I was a nurse I had open doors and they were child-like in their gratitude. I didn`t christen but accepted them into our community. Sometimes we would find baby girls thrown on the wayside and we brought them to look after them. We would rescue them. They would leave them on the roadside. Eventually, the girls would work for us.... domestic work. We used to speak English to them.*

We called the Chinese their own Chinese names. They are cleverer than us. Mr.Jiang, the evangelist, he was proud to do anything for us.

The services were at the Mission. We didn`t stop them coming and they saw how we lived."

E.N. "And these Three-inch shoes?" – "these small shoes?" (Three-inch shoes necessitated foot binding)

J.W. "They were a gift too.'

Footbinding
Footbinding was thought to have originated in the 10th Century when, according to legend, one of the emperor's concubines bound her feet to dance at court. The other concubines copied as they thought her dance was graceful. The practice spread throughout the country and down through the centuries – but only with the Han Chinese. The little shoes, about three inches long (7.5cms), that covered these dainty feet, were called 'golden lilies' or 'lotus' shoes. When a matchmaker came to discuss marriage between families, she would ask the size of the bride-to-be's feet rather than her beauty, as the smaller the feet, the bigger the marriage settlement. This custom lasted into the 20th Century, although attempts had been made to stop it, at various times, during the Qing Dynasty (1644-1911). The girls' feet were bound at a young age from 2-5 years of age. It caused great pain to both girls and women which often led to ill-health. The woman depended upon three men in her life – her father – her husband, and son – as she was unable to walk unaided. Men had to be educated, as well as the women, to stop footbinding and learn that women with 'natural' feet were beautiful.

A pair of Chinese Three-inch shoes presented, by Mrs Jane Williams to the Author.

Williams (Nicolas)
DEATH
'On 9th September, being unfortunately washed overboard from the ship'LAUGHING WATER', when on her voyage from Swansea to Hong Kong, Mr Nicolas Williams, of Swansea, leaving a wife and a large family to deplore his loss.'
(The Cambrian 9th January 1857)

Williams (Lewis)

Lewis Williams of the Rock Inn, Penrhiwfawr, was an Assistant or Deputy Viewer at Tong Colliery, Tangshan, North China. Williams arrived in China in November, 1888 and died there on June 14th, 1889. He was only 26 years of age and left a widow and young child in Wales.

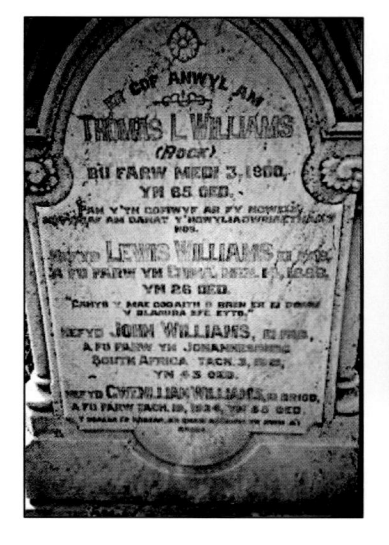

The death of Lewis Williams is recorded on the family grave at Cwmllynfell Chapel.

Site of the former European Cemetery in Tangshan where Lewis Williams was buried. The graveyard was destroyed during the 1976 earthquake.

Williams (Noah T)

'Mr. Noah T. Williams was born in Cwmllynfell 1876. His father was a colliery blacksmith. He left school and was apprenticed to the blacksmith at Brynhenllys Colliery at the age of fourteen. He took lessons from the local preacher in English, Latin and Maths (his mother mortgaged her cottage, Bryn House, Cymllynfell for £100, to pay for this). He also attended the Cymllynfell Board evening classes in the sciences. He competed for a Glamorgan County Scholarship which gave fees and maintenance to attend the University of South Wales and Monmouth, Cardiff when he was 24 in 1900. He was appointed to a Chair at the Imperial University at Shanxi, Northern China which was established by Timothy Richard. He returned to Wales in 1911.'
(Dr Peter Harries)

'It was not until September 1902 that contracts were signed for the erection of the buildings. The two departments were built on a large site inside the city near the southern wall. Those of the Western College comprised a great assembly and examination hall, library, gymnasium, museum, offices and reception room, together with lecture-rooms and laboratories. Each school had its own rooms, Chemistry, Mining and, later, Civil Engineering, each in another. The architecture was simple and in Chinese style. The whole university was lighted by electricity, the apparatus, from boiler to switches, being transported on mule-back from Tianjin, and erected by Mr. N.T. Williams the Mining Professor.'
Chapter XXIII 'The Shansi University: A Dream Fulfilled' (p.260)
Timothy Richard of China (1924) by Professor W.E. Soothill

Williams (Penry)

Penry Williams II succeeded his father Penry Williams of Penpont near Brecon, in 1743. He commissioned a tea and coffee service, bearing his coat of arms, from China, examples of which can be seen at the National Museum of Wales.

Part of a tea and coffee service dating from about 1770, from Jingdezhen, China with the coat of arms of Anne (1713-1778) and Penry Williams (1714-1781) of Penpont.

Williams (Rowan Douglas, Baron Williams of Oystermouth, Swansea)

The former Archbishop of Canterbury, Dr Rowan Williams, who was born in Ystadgynlais, and brought up in Swansea, and his wife, Jane, visited China in the autumn of 2006. They visited Shanghai, Nanjing, Wuhan (Visited the 'Glory Church' built to commemorate the birth of the Rev Dr Griffith John), Xi'An and Beijing. Dr Williams was the most senior Church of England prelate to have visited China in more than a decade.
(See: Wuhan)

Winch (F.R (Fully Rigged) Ship 'Henry Winch')

'The 'Henry Winch' a fully rigged ship of 474 Tons was built in 1845 at Pwllheli by W. Jones and owned by James Baines', "Black Ball Line" and launched on January 14th 1846.
She was the largest vessel ever built in any of the Welsh ports. The Henry Winch sailed for Hong Kong and was employed chiefly in the China trade under the command of Captain Evans Williams.'
(Pwllheli - The Port and Mart of Llŷn' (p. 111 /112) by Lewis Lloyd 1991)

Wood (Captain Richard MC, DCM, MM)

Captain Wood and his wife, a military nurse, spent time in China. Lord Parry wrote about his former next-door neighbours as having an exciting life in China. Mrs Wood had related how she and her husband had been guests of Dr Sun Yat Sen and Mme Song Qing Ling and also General Chiang Kai-shek.

Sun Yat Sen had presented Richard Wood with the sleeve from his embroidered robe as a mark of respect. The Woods had treasured the sleeve and had it framed to hang at their home in Neyland.

(Source: Lord Parry of Neyland)

Wood (Myfanwy)

'Miss Wood, a missionary under the London Missionary Society has been in China since 1908, engaged in educational work. She is at present a General Secretary of the Committee on Preparation for the National Christian Conference.
(The Chinese Recorder, Volume L111, March 1922 Number 3, Notes on Contributors)

Miss Wood was present at Griffith John's funeral in Swansea in 1912.

'A member of the Welsh Congregational Church at Y Boro London. In 1908 appointed as a teacher to Xiao - Chang, North China she later served as Headmistress at a girls school in Beijing. In 1926 she was appointed to the Yenching University in Beijing. She returned home in 1951 and died in 1967.'
(Overseas Missionary Fellowship 1991)

A report by Myfanwy Wood

WOMEN AT THE NATIONAL CHRISTIAN CONFERENCE

'The reports from the various Commissions appointed to prepare material for the coming National Conference, are almost ready for the press, and as one has read rapidly through them, one rejoices at the clear, sane vision of the work and position of women in the Chinese Church that is revealed through all these reports. But when one comes to consider the personnel of the Conference, one`s rejoicing is checked. It is to the delegates to the Conference that the full printed reports of the Commissions will go. It is they who will share the experiences of the days of the Conference, share the fresh baptism of the Holy Spirit that we believe God will give to this gathering of His servants in China. They will share the corporate fellowship of those days, together will they see visions and dream dreams, and with the strength of Pentecostal inspiration will they go out to prophesy and meet the challenge of our times.

In the article by Mr. T. Z. Koo in last month`s RECORDER, attention was drawn to the need of helping every individual Christian to understand the purpose and hopes of the Conference, and this will be no less true after the Conference. It has always been a truism of work in China that women are most effectively reached by women. What, then, shall we say of the following figures?

I have analysed the Conference delegates according to the divisions used in the Directory of Protestant Missions in China, and I give the figures for the first seven divisions.

	Chinese		*Foreign*	
	Women	*Men*	*Women*	*Men*
Anglican	1	20	11	21
Baptist	2	14	9	22
Congregational	1	15	4	18
Lutheran	0	27	5	22
Methodist	10	71	18	44
Presbyterian	5*	33	21	53
China Inland Mission	0	30	10	27

*These five women have been appointed by the churches of the Irish Presbyterian Mission and the United Free Church of Scotland Mission in Manchuria. Some churches and some missions have still to appoint their delegates.

Would it not be regrettable if after the generous recognition given by the Commissions to the place of women in the new Chinese Church, there were not enough Women delegates present at the Conference adequately to receive and report back to the 129,000 women church members whom they should represent, the attitude and findings of the Conference on the new responsibilities opened to them?'

(The Chinese Recorder Pages 195 - 196) March 1922 by Myfanwy Wood

Woosnam (Richard 1815 - 1881)

'Third son of Bowen Woosnam, solicitor of Llanidloes, Montgomeryshire. Richard Woosnam was present at the signing of the Treaty of Nanjing on board HMS Cornwallis on the 29th August 1842. Final ratification of the Treaty took place in Hong Kong on the 26th June 1843.

In 1841, he was appointed Surgeon and subsequently Private Secretary to Sir Henry Pottinger during the Chinese War of 1842, and was present at most of the combined naval and military actions which led to the conclusion of the treaty of peace. He received a medal for his services, and was appointed assistant Secretary of Legation to Her Majesty`s Mission. He afterwards filled successfully the appointment of Deputy Colonial Secretary of Hong Kong. Returned to this country to Cheltenham 1861. Settled down at Glandwr, Llanidloes.' – 'Active in public life and political affairs. (Mont. Worthies).'
(EMINENT WELSHNIEN by T.R.ROberts VOL.1 p.604)

'The Signing of the Treaty of Nanjing' by John Platt (artist) and John Burnet (engraver).

'Richard Woosnam of Glandwr, Montgomeryshire, and Tyn-Y-Graig, Breconshire, J.P. for both cos. MRC.S. London, Surg. in Bombay Army, accompanied Sir Henry Pottinger on his Special Mission as Plenipotentiary to China 1841, as Surg. to the Mission, and he subsequently acted as Sec. of Legation, and was Deputy Colonial Secretary at Hong Kong; present at most of the operations of the United Naval and Military Forces, which resulted in the conclusion of the first Treaty with China, which was dictated by Sir Henry Pottinger at Nanjing in 1842, and he bore the medal granted for the occasion.'
(BURKE`S LANDED GENTRY 1952 ps.2790-2791)

Richard Woosnam died at Builth on 27th November 1881 and is commemorated on the Woosnam family memorial at St. Idloes' Church, Llanidloes

Woosnam family memorial and grave at St. Idloes' Church, Llanidloes

Wu Fu-Sheng

Professor of Chinese Literature, Comparative Literary and Cultural Studies at the University of Utah. He is the author of many books including 'The Selected Poems of Cao Zhi' which he co-wrote with Graham Harthill. Professor Wu is a student of the Swansea-born poet, Dylan Thomas and has translated a number of Thomas' poems into Chinese. He visited Swansea University and gave a presentation in the City as part of the Dylan Thomas Centenary Celebrations. (2014)

Wu Hu

'Deputy-Director of the Chinese People's Association for Friendship with Foreign Countries (CPAFFC) arrived in Pontardawe today as part of a friendship visit arranged by the Wales-China Friendship Society'
(WCFS June 2nd 1992)

Wu Jianzhong

Director of the Shanghai Library-one of the 10 largest libraries in the world- returned to Aberystwyth University where he had gained a Ph.D. in library services in 1992. He was made a fellow of Aberystwyth University in July 2012.

Wu Xinyu

Dr. Wu is Director of International Development at the International Education Centre, Bangor University. As Director she represents the University at national and international levels.
(See: Bangor University)

Wuhan
The following buildings in the City of Wuhan are associated with the Rev Dr. Griffith John, the Swansea-born missionary, that continue to live on after him.

Wuchang Church built by Griffith John in 1864. The Church celebrated its 150th Anniversary in 2014. It is now known as Chongzhen Tang – 'Worship Truth Church'

Congregation at the special service to celebrate the 150th Anniversary of Chongzhen Tang, Wuchang (19th October 2014) established by Rev. Dr. Griffith John.

Ladies choir and choristors at the special service to celebrate the 150th Anniversary of Chongzhen Tang, Wuchang (19th October 2014) established by Rev. Dr. Griffith John.

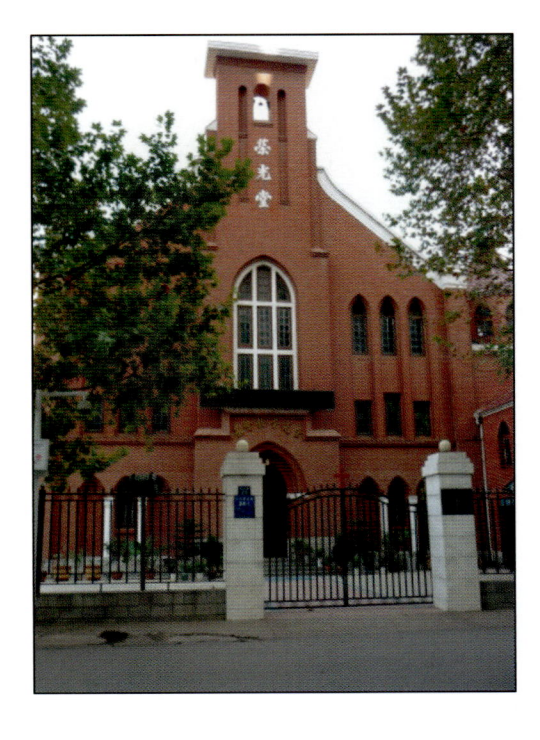

The Glory Church was built in 1931 to celebrate the Centenary of Griffith John's birth.

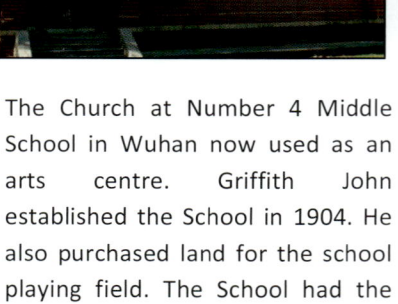

The Church at Number 4 Middle School in Wuhan now used as an arts centre. Griffith John established the School in 1904. He also purchased land for the school playing field. The School had the first football team in Wuhan.

The 'Griffith John School' Wuhan now re-named the Number 4 Middle School.

Wuchang Hospital – now The Hospital for Traditional Chinese Medicine

Wuhan (Museum)
The Museum has a display of people who have influenced the City and encouraged its move into the 20th Century; among those featured is Griffith John.

英国杨格非牧师是近代最早到汉口的基督教传教士
British priest Griffith Young is the earliest Christian preacher to Hankou

Tribute to Rev. Dr. Griffith John displayed at Wuhan Museum

X

Xia (Zhidao)

Dr Xia (D.Phil Oxon) is a Senior Lecturer in Regenerative Medicine at the College of Medicine at Swansea University, and a former Senior Research Fellow at Oxford University. His home City of Wuhan, is where the Rev. Dr. Griffith John, the Swansea – born Missionary lived and worked for over 50 years. Dr Xia worked as an Associate Professor in Orthopaedic Surgery at the Union Hospital, Hankou, Wuhan, established by Griffith John. Dr Xia played an important part in setting up the link between Union Hospital and the College of Medicine at Swansea University.

Xiamen

The City of Xiamen (formerly Amoy) in Fujian Province is twinned with Cardiff. The establishment of the link in 1983 was the first between a UK city and a city in China. The City was a treaty port in the 19th century and, in the 1980s, one of the four original Special Economic Zones opened to foreign investment and trade when China began economic reforms. Xiamen University has a long established link with Cardiff University in a number of different fields including the China Studies Centre in the 1980s.

In 2011 Aberystwyth University hosted a delegation from Xiamen University. Both institutions have been active in co-operating in the fields of International Relations and Computer Science. The photograph shows the boundary sign originally placed at the northern approach to Cardiff on the A470, listing the twinning cities including Xiamen.

Embroidery from the City of Xiamen – A gift to the City of Cardiff now on display at the Mansion House.

Xiaogan City

About 40 miles from Wuhan is the city that the Rev Dr Griffith John would have known as 'Hiau-Kan'. It was where he built a home for lepers that opened on 7th April 1895. Once the Belgian - built railway was finished, he took his grandson, Griffith John Sparham, on a visit to Xiaogan. The Mission at Xiaogan consisted of two residences, a chapel, school and a small hospital. The home for lepers was built outside the city walls. Xiaogan Central Hospital – Non Medical Technology was established by Griffith John.

(See: Griffith John)

Bust of Griffith John at the Xiaogan Central Hospital (Note: Griffith John's name in Chinese characters – Yang Ge Fei)

Xu Da

A member of the first group of students from Fudan University in Shanghai to study for a Master's Degree in Education at the West Glamorgan Institute for Higher Education now the University of Wales Trinity St. David, in the mid-1980s. During his time in Swansea, he and fellow members of the group became active within the Wales-China Friendship Society, including designing a proposed new Society logo (See: Wales-China Friendship Society). On his return to China he became a founder member of the Society's Shanghai Branch (which no longer exists).

Y

Yale (Elihu)
Elihu Yale (1649 – 1721) of 'Plas Grono', the family mansion near Wrexham, was a British merchant and philanthropist, Governor of the East India Company settlement in Bengal, at Calcutta and Chennai and a benefactor of the Collegiate School of Connecticut, which in 1718 was renamed Yale University in his honour. After his retirement in 1699, he spent time at Plas Grono until his death in 1721. Yale is buried at St. Giles Church, Wrexham. Plas Grono reverted to the Erddig estate and was pulled down in 1876. The 'Yale' name continues through the 'Yale-China Association', founded in 1901 to promote education in China.
(Yale-China Association)

Tomb of Elihu Yale at St. Giles Church Wrexham

Yang Xin
Director of the Palace Museum, Beijing. The Author, during a visit to Beijing in the early 1990s, was invited to the Palace Museum to meet Mr Yang Xin and Mr Yun Li Mei of the Imperial Court History Department to see one of the clocks by William Hughes, the 18th Century Angelsea - born clockmaker, which had recently returned to the Museum from an exhibition of clocks in Japan. In conversation with the Director, she mentioned a William Hughes Automata Clock that had been stolen from the Summer Palace in 1860, during the Second China War. The Director stated that they had no knowledge of this particular clock and requested information for the Imperial Archives. The Author presented her research on this 'unknown' timepiece to the Palace Museum Archives. (1994)
(See: William Hughes)

Yangtze Incident
Lady Susan McLaren, wife of Former British Ambassador to China, Sir Robin McLaren, unveiled a memorial plaque to the ship's crew. The crew included members from Wales. A plaque commemorating a local sailor, who served on the 'Amethyst', is displayed at the Council Offices in Port Talbot. The event became known as the 'Yangtze Incident, and was the basis for the film of that name.
(See: HMS Amethyst, Owen Baker, Geoffrey Locke, Len Ley, Sir Edward Youde)

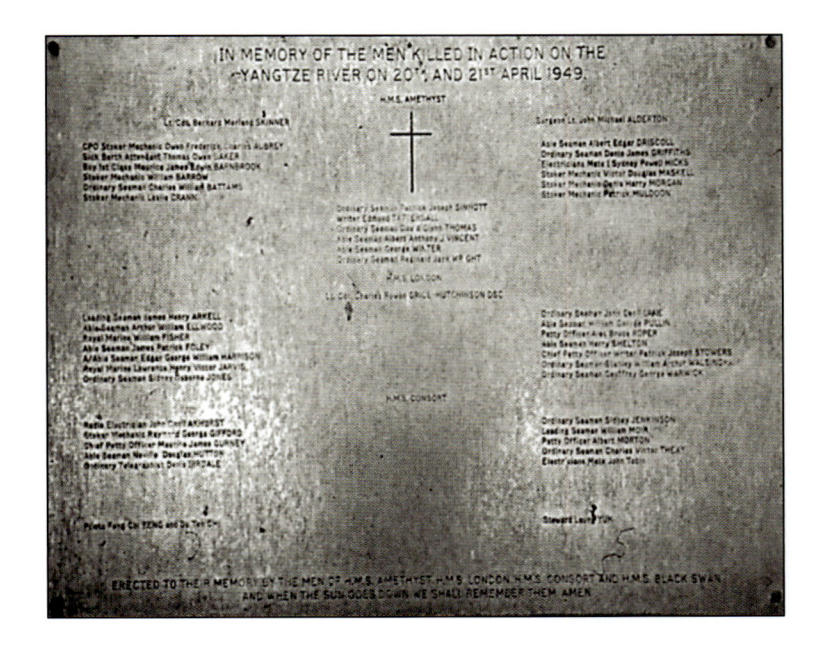

Plaque to the crew of HMS Amethyst in the Memorial Garden of the British Embassy in Beijing

Yao Xinzhong

Yao Xinzhong Professor of Chinese Religion in the Department of Theology & Religious Studies at King's College, University of London read philosophy and ethics at Renmin University of China (BA, MA, PhD) and Religious Studies at the University of Wales (PhD). He started teaching religion at the University of Wales (Cardiff and Lampeter) in 1991 and became a Professor of Religion and Ethics in 2002. He was the holder of a four-year grant awarded by the Templeton Foundation for the project 'A Comparative Study of Religious Experience in Britain and China' for which he was appointed Senior Research Fellow at the Ian Ramsey Centre, the University of Oxford (2004-07). He is a visiting professor in a number of Chinese universities and an honorary President of the Confucian Academy of Hong Kong. In 2007 Professor Yao was instrumental in establishing Wales' first Confucius Institute at Lampeter now part of the University of Wales Trinity St. David.

Yen (Rev. Yung-King)

'Mr Yen, who, as representing the native Christian Churches of China, will address a public meeting at Swansea on Thursday next to protest against the Opium trade in China. Mr. Yen has come to England in response to an invitation from the Anti-Opium Organizations, in order to give his personal testimony as to the curse that has fallen on China and their people through the vicious opium habit. Rev. Yung-King Yen is a Presbyter of the American Protestant Episcopal Church Mission in China, was educated in the United States being a distinguished graduate of Kenyon College. He refused lucrative appointments to become a preacher of the Gospel to his countrymen.

He has laboured in connection with his own Mission as teacher in Wu Chang, the Capital City of Hupeh; and latterly has had charge of the native Church of "Our Saviour " in Hong Kew, a suburb of Shanghai, and has been a Professor in the Divinity School of St. John`s.
He is regarded by the Foreign Community as the fair-minded and cultured exponent of the views and feelings of his own countrymen in any matters affecting the relations between Chinese and Europeans. He speaks English with great deliberation and clearness.'
(The Cambrian, Friday September 7th 1894 (See: 'Opium Trade in China P.144)

Yiling Group – Cardiff University

Cardiff University has been collaborating with the Yiling Group Medical Research Institute since 2012, initially investigating the potential mechanisms of some anti-cancer medicines. Cardiff, in conjunction with Pekin University and the Yiling Group have been testing the benefits of the Chinese herbal medicine 'Yangzheng'. The collaboration with Yiling has resulted in the creation of scholarships and new opportunities for bi-lateral exchanges between the UK and China to undertake study and training. The venture between Cardiff University and the Yiling Group is supported by the Wales Government.

Launch of the Cardiff University-Yiling Group Joint Medical Research Centre by Professor Yiling Wu and Cardiff University President and Vice-Chancellor Professor Colin Riordan

Yan Ying

Lecturer in Translation Studies at the School of Modern Languages, Bangor University. Dr Ying was the Editor of a special issue of 'Foreign Language and Art' – contemporary Welsh literature and art. As a literary translator, she promotes literature exchanges between Wales and China. Dr Ying is Co-Director of the Centre for Asian Studies at the University. She co-organized the 'Symposium: Reading China,Translating Wales' (May 2014)

Youde (Sir Edward KCMG, GCVO, MBE 1924-1986)

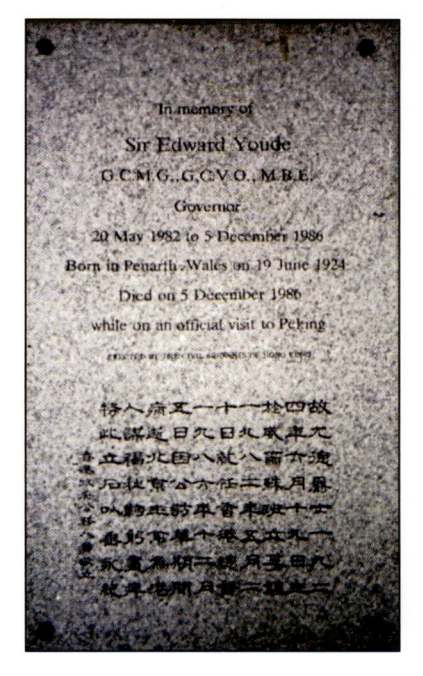

Sir Edward Youde was a British administrator, diplomat and Sinologist. He served as Governor of Hong Kong between 20 May 1982 and 5 December 1986. Born in Penarth, he attended the University of London's School of Oriental and African Studies.

In 1949, Youde was serving on the frigate HMS Amethyst during the Chinese Civil War when it came under attack from the People's Liberation Army forces. The frigate was heavily damaged by artillery fire and became stranded in the Yangtze River. Using his skills in Mandarin, Youde negotiated with the PLA commander to secure the release of the Amethyst. Following the Amethyst's escape from enemy territory, Youde was awarded the Member of the Order of the British Empire (MBE). He is mainly remembered as the Governor during whose time in office the Joint Declaration on the future of Hong Kong was signed in Beijing in 1984. This, amongst other things, made it clear that the British would leave Hong Kong in 1997 after 156 years of colonial rule.

A plaque in honour of Sir Edward Youde is at Saint John's Cathedral, Hong Kong. His legacy continues in Hong Kong through the Sir Edward Youde Memorial Fund Scholarship Schemes for Hong Kong students – Sir E.Y. Scholars Association (S.E.Y.S.A.).

Sir Edward Youde, Hong Kong's only Welsh Governor was said to be widely respected by the Chinese population of Hong Kong.

The idea of setting up a secondary school to develop students' potential in sport and the visual arts together with a normal academic syllabus was first mooted by Sir Edward Youde. Based upon this idea, the Jockey Club Ti-I College was founded in 1989. During a visit to Beijing, Sir Edward suffered a fatal heart attack in the early morning of the 5th December 1986 at the British Embassy, while he was sleeping. A small Memorial Garden is located in the grounds of the Ambassador's residence. (See also: Owen Baker; Geoffrey Locke and Len Ley – 'Yangtze Incident')

Sir Edward Youde's memorial garden at the British Ambassador's residence in Beijing

Yu Shao
'Miss Yu, from China, visited the Llangollen International Music Eisteddfod as a guest of the United Nations Association (Wales) as part of its Volunteering Programme. This was the first time that a Chinese volunteer had participated in such a project. She was featured on a special Llangollen Eisteddfod HTV Wales programme televised on 13th July 1986.'
('Ni Hao' Newsletter WCFS - Summer 1986)

Yuan Ming Yuan (Old Summer Palace)
The Old Summer Palace, known in Chinese as Yuan Ming Yuan (the Gardens of Perfect Brightness), and originally called the Imperial Gardens, was a complex of palaces and gardens in Beijing located 8 kilometres (5 miles) northwest of the walls of the Imperial City. It was built in the 18th and early 19th century as the place where the emperors of the Qing Dynasty resided and handled government affairs as the Forbidden City was used for formal ceremonies. It was often referred to as the 'Versailles of the East'.
In 1860, during the second Opium War, two British envoys, a journalist for 'The Times' newspaper and a small escort of British and Indian troops were imprisoned and tortured, resulting in twenty deaths. The British High Commissioner to China, Lord Elgin, retaliated by ordering the destruction of the Palace, which was then carried out by British and French troops including the 67th Regiment of Foot which included C.E. Morgan of 'Cae Forgan', Gower (He eventually became Colonel of the regiment). Ten years later (1870) Glynn Vivian visited the remains at Yuan Ming Yuan and recorded it in his diary.
In 1994, the Author and her husband visited Yuan Ming Yuan, the remains of the Palace and gardens were still in a ruinous state. In 2012, they re-visited Yuan Ming Yuan. The stone-built Palace was still a ruin but the surrounding gardens had been restored to their former splendour.
(See: Charles Morgan; Glynn Vivian)

Ruined buildings at the Old Summer Palace Yuan Ming Yuan

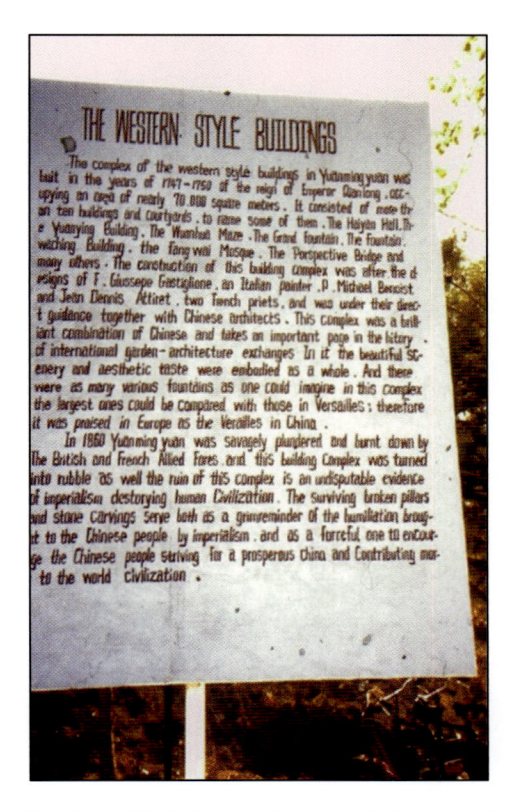

*Notice at Yuan Ming Yuan (1994) describing the brilliance of Yuan Ming Yuan and its destruction by the British and French Allied forces in 1860 as an 'indisputable evidence of imperialism'.

*Yuan Ming Yuan Notice (Original transcription by the Chinese.)

THE WESTERN STYLE BUILDINGS
'The complex of the Western-style buildings in Yuan Ming Yuan was built in the years of 1747-1750 of the reign of Emperor Qianlong, occupying an area of nearly 70,000 m². It consisted of more than 10 buildings and courtyards, to name some of them, the Haiyan Hall, the Yuanying Building, the Wuanhua Maze, the Grand Fountain, the Fountain Watching Building, the Fangwai Mosque, the Prospective Bridge and others. The construction of this building complex was after the designs of F. Giuseppe Castiglione, an Italian painter. P. Michael Benoist, Jean Denis Attiret, two French priests, and was under their direction and guidance together with Chinese architects. This complex was a brilliant combination of Chinese scenery and western architecture and takes an important page in the history of international garden architecture exchanges. In it the beautiful scenery and the aesthetic taste were embodied as a whole. And there were as many various contents as one could imagine in this complex the largest brands could be compared with those in Versailles; therefore it was praised in Europe as the Versailles in China.
In 1860 Yuan Ming Yuan was savagely plundered and burnt down by the British and French allied forces and this building complex was turned into rubble as well the ruin of this complex is an indisputable evidence of imperialism destroying human civilisation. The surviving broken pillars and stone carvings serve both as grim reminder of the humiliation brought to the Chinese people by imperialism and to encourage the Chinese people striving for a prosperous China and contributing to the world civilisation.'

Yun Li Mei
Member of the Imperial Court History Department at the Palace Museum, Beijing. He showed the Author around the Clock Museum within the Palace Museum (Forbidden City) in 1994. The Author donated her research on William Hughes, Clockmaker, to the Museum Archives.
(See: Yang Xin, Director of the Palace Museum Beijing; William Hughes.)

Z

Zhao Yanxia

Dr Zhao was appointed Director of the Centre for Daoist Studies at the University of Wales Trinity St. David in 2013. She is a member of the Department of Humanities and a lecturer in Chinese, teaching Chinese Religion and Philosophy.

Zienkiewicz (Olgierd Cecil, CBE, FRS, 1921 – 2009)
Former Professor and Head of the Civil Engineering Department at Swansea University, who made the Department a leading centre for the research and development of FEM (The "finite element method" of computer-aided engineering). During his time at Swansea Professor Zienkiewicz's research and reputation attracted some of the first ever-Chinese students to study engineering at the University. A number of his Chinese students were to become distinguished academics and holding Professsorships in China, Australia and the UK.

Zhu Limin

In 1982 Dr Zhu graduated in Traditional Chinese Medicine (TCM) from the University of Liaoning, China, where she studied both Chinese and Western Medicine. Worked for nine years as Physician in Charge at Liaoning Hospital for TCM. In 1991 she came to Swansea to join her husband, Shiying Zhao, who was studying for his Ph.D at Swansea University. Before arriving in Swansea, Limin did not know any English as she had studied Japanese in China. She spent the next two years learning English before going to work at The Swansea Natural Medicine Clinic. In 2000 she opened The Clinic of Chinese Medicine in Swansea. Over the years, Dr Zhu has worked for friendship and understanding between Wales and China.

ZOAR
'Chinese shoes and other curiosities from China, presented by Mrs Griffith John, to be sold at the first Bazaar held at any of the Welsh churches in Swansea.'
ZOAR CONGREGATIONAL CHURCH BAZAAR
'We desire to call the attention of the public to the above Bazaar, which will be held on Monday next, April 24th, in the large and commodious school-room underneath the church, to commence at 2 o'clock in the afternoon. A host of ladies and gentlemen in Swansea and the neighbourhood have taken a deep interest in it, and have, most generously, sent in hundreds of every variety of fancy, but chiefly, useful articles, which will be disposed of at very reasonable prices.
Mrs John, the wife of the Rev. G John, Missionary from China, who has lately returned with her husband, has very kindly presented to the Bazaar a pair of Chinese lady's shoes and other curiosities from China, which will be sold.

We understand this is the first Bazaar held by any of the Welsh churches in Swansea and it promises well; for the friends at Zoar have deviated a little in some things from their usual custom. A great number of tickets are already sold, and daily called for.'
(The Cambrian 21st April 1871

WALES-CHINA 250 YEARS OF HISTORY

PART TWO
STORIES BEHIND MY RESEARCH

Of the many entries in the book there are just two that 'got away'! The first was that of a Samuel Lloyd, who was one of the 'Council of Five' chosen to assist the President of the East India Company to China in 1699 and is thought to have been the first Briton to learn Chinese. Was he Welsh?

The second may be described as, a fascinating 'got away' entry - the result of a story related to me at the National Trust's Tudor Merchant's House in Tenby. It was about black woollen cloth in the 1200s known as the 'Black Cloth of Carmarthen', which was traded along the Silk Road to China. A member of staff at the National Woollen Mill in Drefach, Carmarthenshire, explained that, at that time, black was the hardest colour to dye, and, consequently, black cloth would have been very expensive. The story continued that during excavations in the Gobi Desert, skeletons were found with DNA leading back to West Wales. If only a smidgen of the story was true - then it would be remarkable.

The following are extracts from just some of the stories behind the entries in the book. In fact, each and every entry could form the basis of a story in itself.

Gladys Aylward

The Jago Family were Swansea friends of the Missionary Gladys Aylward who worked with John and Evie Jago during her time in Swansea before leaving for China in 1930. In 1963, she returned from China and stayed with them. On departing for China, she left a Chinese jacket and dress with John and Evie for the 'next time' she would visit them in Swansea. Unfortunately, there was not to be a next time as Gladys died in Taiwan in 1970. Evie kept the clothes as she realised their historic value.

After her death, her son and daughter-in-law, Jack and Val, looked after them. About twenty years ago, they very kindly allowed me to photograph the clothes for my research.

In 2014, I phoned Jack to ask if I could photograph the garments again. Jack said that he was just about to phone me and said he wished to see me. Jack and Val, 94 and 91 years old respectively, had been wondering what to do with Gladys Aylward's clothes after their day. Jack prayed to God and sought his help. God told Jack to leave them to me. So, I have become the 'guardian' of Gladys Aylward's Chinese clothes. The film 'Inn of the Sixth Happiness' (1958) led me to North Wales where I met Jane Pedley. During the weeks leading up to our meeting I had sent and received numerous e-mails from Jane that started with an enquiry to the Nantmor Mountain Centre asking if there was anyone who could tell me about the making of the film 'Inn of The Sixth Happiness'.

I received a reply from Jane who said that my request had sparked off her imagination and could she help me. Jane went around Nantmor and Beddgelert talking to people and, almost everyday, I would receive e-mails from her full of interesting information. She discovered that people in the area still had memories of the making of the film and where certain scenes had been filmed. She had a story of the Director who had to re-take a scene as one of the little boy extras had forgotten to take off his white ankle socks before crossing a stream. Jane had arranged an interview in Beddgelert with Mrs Jean Owen, the understudy to Ingrid Bergman who starred in the film - taking the part of Gladys Aylward.

Jean had vivid memories of being Ingrid Bergman's understudy. She commented that Ingrid was a gracious, gentle lady who was full of consideration for her in the roll of understudy. I am indebted to Jane who did so much to make my visit to Beddgelert and Nantmor such a memorable experience.

On returning home to Swansea I visited Jack and Val Jago and told them about my trip to Beddgelert and Nantmor. They were delighted that two remarkable women had played the missionary who, herself, had been a remarkable woman.

Rev. William Thomas Beynon

A number of years ago I gave a talk at Cowbridge Historical Society about my research. I asked for help on the whereabouts of the William Thomas Beynon plaque that used to be at Nantyffyilon Chapel before it closed. No one at the meeting knew anything about the plaque.

A few days later I had a letter from John Lyons, who had been at the meeting, but had to leave early. John spent time searching for the plaque's whereabouts. He failed to discover the plaque but sent me a photograph of it. I am very grateful to John.

In 2014 I was at Saron Chapel, Crynant, in the Dulais Valley where I met the Rev. Gareth Thomas, formerly the minister at Nantyffyllon Chapel. He told me a remarkable story of meeting three Chinese men at Nantyffyllon, who were members of the church that had been established by the Rev. Beynon, in China. They wanted to buy the plaque and take it back to their church in China.

Cenhadwr Americanaidd (1842)

Several copies of Cenhadwr Americanaidd were saved from ending up in a rubbish bin by Mrs Jeremiah of Rhiwfawr (Swansea Valley). She said that the owner of a junk shop was throwing them away!

Captain Henry Davidson

The plaque to Captain Davidson at Llansteffan Church was a surprise discovery. He had helped to save the Frigate 'Alceste' with Ambassador Amherst aboard who was returning from the Second Embassy to China in 1816.

A short while before the discovery of the plaque, a Mrs Williams wrote to me from Morriston. She asked me to come and collect an old book on China that she had rescued from a bonfire that her husband had lit to burn some old books. The 'old book' she referred to was 'China and Its Inhabitants (Parts I and II)' by John Francis Davies, Governor of Hong Kong (1851), and referred to Lord Amherst's Embassy to China. I wondered what other 'old books' had hit the flames? In 2014, on a visit to Anglesey, my husband Barry, and I visited 'Chateau Rhianfa' at Menai Bridge (formerly Plas Rhianfa) which was the former home of Sir John Hay Williams, who married Sarah, the daughter of Lord Amherst - Three connections with the Second Embassy to China and Lord Amherst.

Hannah Davies

On a visit to London, my husband and I happened to pass an hotel that advertised an antique book sale. We went to have a look. One particular book caught my eye as its cover stated it was by a 'Hannah Davies'. As it was the same name as my grandmother, I took it off the shelf. On doing so, a cutting from a newspaper fell to the floor, I picked it up to read 'Pontardawe Lady Missionary in China'. I had to buy the book as the coincidence was too great- as I also come from Pontardawe!

Rev. Robert Kenneth Evans

Several years ago I was invited by radio presenter Ray Gravelle to talk about my work on China on his BBC Radio Wales programme. It turned out to be a catalyst for several letters from listeners. One came from a Rev. Paul Flavell, of Llanaber, near Barmouth. He wrote about a grave with three Chinese characters in the cemetery of St Mary's Church Llanaber.

He had even gone to the trouble of taking a greaseproof paper rubbing of the characters on the grave and sent it to me. The three characters were 'Yi Wen Si' which were the three Chinese characters nearest in sound to 'Evans'.

It was the grave of the missionary, Rev. Robert Kenneth Evans, who had drowned at Barmouth.
He was the husband of Janet Evans, who was the daughter of the Rev. Hopkyn Rees, missionary to China.
My husband and I decided to visit the cemetery and as we were searching for the grave, a man called out, "Can I help you?" I explained what we were looking for and he replied that we were in the wrong cemetery. By this time, I was almost opposite him and I said, "I don't know how to tell you this but you're standing next to it"
He was amazed as he frequently came to tend his family grave and had made an inventory of all the graves in the cemetery.

John Reginald Harding
After long hours of researching in archives, I came across John Reginald Harding of 'The Hendre' near Monmouth. My letter was delivered to his grandson, Christopher Harding- Rolls, who invited me to visit his home. Christopher showed me mandarin robes and honours bestowed on his grandfather by the Emperors of Korea and China respectively. He also showed me a photograph of the Royal Palace in Seoul designed by his grandfather. Christopher went on to explain that his grandfather had, originally, designed and made a model of an Oriental-style palace. The Emperor of Korea exclaimed that he wanted one 'like your Queen's'. This was Queen Victoria and Buckingham Palace. Harding then designed a 'Buckingham Palace' for the Emperor that is now used as a museum in Seoul. John Reginald Harding had kept a diary of his time in China .... a China long gone! On examining the diary Christopher, very generously, said "Take it home and read it." I replied, "You do not know me". "I know you'll bring it back!" Christopher said.
Sadly, Christopher died a few years ago but I shall always remember his warm welcome and generous nature. His wife Jenny continues to update me with family information for which I am most grateful.

Thomas Harries
When I met Edwin Harries, Thomas Harries' brother, he had not long come out of hospital and was very frail. Before his hospital visit, I had asked to see him, but on hearing how weak he was, I did not wish to impose. However, Edwin insisted that he wished to see me and talk about his brother Thomas - he said that he wanted his brother's work and time in China to 'live on' through my research for the book. He proudly showed photographs of Thomas and his house in China. Edwin's sheer determination, despite his frail condition, to make sure his brother's achievements in China were to live on was very humbling. I was so sad to hear that a few weeks after my visit Edwin had died. Edwin's contribution, in many ways, sums up the principal reason for my research and subsequent book - recording historical events about China before becoming lost in time.

William Hughes
I read about William Hughes' automata clocks and watches that had been bought by the Chinese Emperor Qianlong. I wondered if they were still in China and began to make enquiries. This was not an easy task in the early 1990s as at the time China had a lot of red tape but, with the help of my Chinese friend, Li Feng, I got an interview with Mr Yang Xin, Director of the Palace Museum in Beijing and Mr. Yun Li Mei, from the Imperial Court History Department of the Palace Museum.
One of the clocks by William Hughes was permanently on display at the 'Clocks and Watch Museum' located within the Palace Museum.
Another had just returned from a major exhibition in Japan and had been returned to the Archives. Director Yang, kindly, asked for it to be brought from the Archives.

It arrived in a small wheelbarrow, covered in sacking, which, when removed, revealed the magnificent piece made by William Hughes in the 18th Century. It shone in the sunlight as we stood outside in the courtyard.

It was a wonderful occasion! I asked Mr Yang and Mr Yun about a William Hughes' clock that had been stolen from the Summer Palace outside Beijing during the Second China War of 1860. They replied that they had no knowledge of this clock. I had a photocopy of the clock with me. I showed it to them and they replied they had never seen it before and asked if my research could be given to China.

I was delighted to give my research on the William Hughes automata clock to the Archives of the Palace Museum, Beijing.

Gareth Jones

During one of many visits to Hay-on-Wye I bought a book called 'Gareth Jones - A Manchukuo Incident' by Margaret Siriol Colley, Gareth Jones' niece. Inside the book was a letter from the author, mentioning some background information about her research for the book about her uncle who had been murdered in Inner Mongolia on the eve of his 30th birthday in 1935.

Siriol wrote to me saying it would be good to meet up. Unfortunately, she passed away before we had a chance to meet. So, when I saw her letter in the book, it was meaningful. I wrote to her nephew, Nigel Colley, and asked if he wanted his aunt's letter. He wrote back, "So, in case you did not know about the programme, then perhaps the letter falling out of the book and you contacting me was meant to be! – Spooky?" The programme Nigel referred to was BBC 4's - 'Hitler, Stalin and Mr Jones'. I did not know about the programme; so, perhaps it was 'Spooky'.

Kenrick Brothers

A puzzle that took us across North Wales!

In September, 2014, Dr Wu Xinyu, Director of the International Department at Bangor University, invited Barry and I to see 'things Chinese' at the University. Alaw Wyn Jones, her P.A., had designed a two - day Chinese-themed programme. Part of the programme took us to the University Archives, where we met Elen Wyn Simpson, the Archivist, who, very kindly, had items with a China link waiting for us. Among the items were two albums containing photographs taken of, or by J.P. Kenrick who worked for the Pekin Syndicate Ltd in China at the beginning of the 20th century. It seemed that he came from Wynn Hall in Ruabon.

Wynn Hall is a beautiful mansion on the outskirts of Ruabon. A woman came out of the house and, from her response to my question, was French. She said "Go inside, it's an hotel - Just walk in." I entered the building to realise, immediately, that it was not an hotel. The large room I entered had several settees placed, informally, around what would have been the entrance hall. A man was sprawled out on a settee on the left of the door and a woman sat, curled up, reading a book on a settee on the right. "Can I help you?" asked the man. I apologised to him for walking in. He said that they were part of a film company and had rented the Hall to make a horror film.

From the Hall we went to Ruabon Library where we met Alison Anderson, who brought out several books and newspaper cuttings about the Kenrick's of Wynn Hall. She told us about a woman, who came to the Library about 20 years ago with a batch of letters she had found whilst walking her dog in the woods near the Hall. Alison realised that they must have some value as they were addressed to a 'Mrs A. Kenrick, Wynn Hall'. She had passed them on to the Wrexham Archives. The story had led us from Bangor to Ruabon and, now, to Wrexham - the story was becoming more intriguing and had to be seen through to the end.

The letters were a mystery themselves - how had they got into the woods? How long had they been left undiscovered?

They were not in a very good condition and were over 100 years old and, being discarded in the woods, had not enhanced their condition.

The letters were addressed to Alice Wynn Kenrick and her son, Hubert and were written by Hubert Wynn Kenrick, her husband, at the beginning of the 20th century. I felt intrusive as I opened the letters but intrigued by what I should find.

It seemed that Hubert had been a Captain with the P&O Line and wrote frequently to his wife and son from the Far East.

Some of the letters had been sent from Shanghai. The Archivist at Wrexham showed me a Kenrick family tree, written in white ink on dark blue paper, tracing the family line back a few centuries.

The dark blue paper was torn in several places and the white ink was quite difficult to read but, on one line, the names J.P. Kenrick and Hubert Kenrick could be made out - they were brothers! The puzzle that had taken us across North Wales and the centuries was solved!

Private Z. Lewis

An amazing experience surrounded a Royal Welsh Fusilier's medal that my husband and I purchased in the late 1990s. The medal had been awarded to a Private Z. Lewis who had served with the Fusiliers (China 1900). I phoned John Griffiths (Pontardawe) whom I knew possessed a vast knowledge on the history of Welsh soldiers. I did not tell him about the citation on the medal. A few days later, John came to our house with a large file of papers relating to Welsh soldiers who had served in China. I could hardly believe what happened next - John opened the file and on the first page was an account about Private Z. Lewis!

Rees Brothers

An article in the Cambrian Newspaper, February 4th, 1843 was about the death 'from a stroke of the sun' in Hong Kong, of Captain George Rees, aged 37, from Tenby. My husband and I visited Hong Kong and searched the cemeteries but with no avail.

We then decided to try the Protestant cemetery in Macau. It was almost a lump in the throat moment to have matched the entry in The Cambrian with the inscription on George Rees' grave in Macau.

Years later, Douglas Fraser, from Tenby, wrote to me saying that he had found a letter that I had written to Tenby Museum about ten years ago asking for information on the Rees brothers. Douglas and his wife, Elizabeth, had bought the house built by George Rees and was intending researching the history of the property. We met and exchanged information we both had compiled about the brothers.

Timothy Richard

It was a beautiful Sunday afternoon so Barry and I decided to visit the village of Ffaldybrenin, in Carmarthenshire, as I had been told that there was a plaque to Timothy Richard set into a wall near the chapel. As Barry was photographing the plaque, a man walked by. "Can I ask you what you doing?" he enquired, politely.

On hearing about my research, he introduced himself as Professor Cyril Williams. He said that our meeting was a coincidence. He went on to say that he shouldn't have been preaching at the chapel that Sunday but had changed days as a favour to a friend. Professor Williams insisted we went home with him to meet his wife, Irene. She, over the years, has been a great support to me on the project, even after the death of her husband. Professor Williams wrote to me, following our chance encounter, that he was writing a book about Timothy Richard, and unbeknown to me, I had been the catalyst for him to finish it.

Percy Smith

Bill Williams, from Barmouth, wrote after he had heard me being interviewed on the BBC Radio Wales programme about my research. In his letter he mentioned that his neighbour Percy Smith, an accountant, had retired to Barmouth from Hong Kong along with two Chinese servants and a collection of Chinese antiques. On visiting Bill he told me stories about Mr Smith and gave me photographs and an intriguing newspaper article from the South China Morning Post.

Bill mentioned that the Chinese servants became friends with his brother John. On a visit to Hong Kong, my husband and I chased up the story and contacted the Hong Kong Record Office and the South China Morning Post.

Rev. Robert Jermain Thomas

On a visit to the chapel where Robert Jermain Thomas would have attended in the village of Hannover near Abergavenny, Barry and I happened, by chance, to be there on the day that the Head of the Presbyterian Church in South Korea and the Head of the Korean Presbyterian Church in the UK were visiting with their wives- a chance encounter!

Union Hospital

During our visit to Wuhan in October 2012 my husband Barry and I visited Union Hospital to photograph the bust of the Rev. Dr. Griffith John, located in front of the main hospital building. As we photographed the bust, a gentleman came towards us, stopped and looked at the bust. He then turned towards us and said in perfect English "That man (Dr. John) did great good for the Chinese people." He smiled and then walked away.

Jane Williams

The meeting with Mrs Jane Williams came about after the BBC Radio Wales programme when I was interviewed about China. Her daughter and son-in-law, Betty and Peter Frazer, invited me to their home to meet her. We must have talked for over an hour and, as she was frail and elderly, I was very aware that she might be becoming tired. "No!" she exclaimed and insisted on carrying on talking about the China she remembered so many years ago. Several weeks later Betty and Peter came to our house and presented me with a little parcel. On opening it, I discovered the little pair of pink three-inch shoes (Lotus or Lily shoes) that Mrs Williams had shown me during our talk. She had insisted that I have them as I had been the only one, for several years, whom she had been able to talk to about 'her China'. By presenting the Chinese shoes to me, she started my collection of the 'Lily' shoes.

Richard Woosnam

I came across the name Richard Woosnam while researching an archive. I discovered that he had a descendant called Charles Woosnam living near Builth Wells and wrote to him asking for information. He invited Barry and me to visit his home. His ancestor, Richard Woosnam, was Private Secretary to Sir Henry Pottinger and was with him at the signing of the 'Treaty of Nanking' aboard HMS Cornwallis that ceded Hong Kong to Britain. Charles Woosnam showed us the print of the signing. I had only ever seen it in a book before and here was one of the original prints. He told me that if I hadn't got in touch he was considering sending the print to the then Governor of Hong Kong, Chris Patten.

I advised that he should re-consider owing to the historical importance and rarity of the print. A few days later he phoned me saying that the print was staying in the family.

Wuhan
In the early 1990s I worked in Wuhan, the capital city of Hubei Province, central China. It was the city and province where the Swansea-born missionary, Rev. Dr. Griffith John, had spent over fifty years of his life. During this time he established schools, colleges, hospitals and churches. In 2012, the centenary of his death, Barry and I revisited Wuhan to find out what, if anything, remainerd of his legacy.
The Curator of Wuhan Museum and two of her colleagues arranged a programme for us to visit the places associated with Griffith John.
We were taken to the Glory Church, Hospital of Traditional Chinese Medicine, Number 4 Middle School and Chongzhen Tang – all established by by the missionary. It was a most memorable visit to the city where I had worked and called 'my home in China' and to find that Griffith John's legacy alive in the 21st century.

GLOSSARY – PLACE NAMES
China modernized its language in the 20th Century. Chinese characters and Romanization of the language were simplified.

Former Name	Present Name	Pinyin /Characters
Amoy	Xiamen	Xiàmén 厦门市
Peking	Beijing	Běijīng 北京
Canton	Guangzhou	Guǎngzhōu 广州
Chapoo	Zhapu	Zhàpǔ 乍浦
Chefu	Qufu	Qūfù 曲阜
Chengtu	Chengdu	Chéngdū 成都
Chichou	Qizhou	Qízhōu 祁州
Chingtechen	Jingdezhen	Jǐngdézhèn 景德镇
Chinkiang	Zhenjiang	Zhènjiāng 镇江
Chongking	Chongqing	Chóngqìng 重庆
Chowtsun	Zhoucun	Zhōucūn 重庆
Chusan	Zhoushan	Zhōushān 舟山
Foochow	Fuzhou	Fúzhōu 福州
Hankow	Hankou	Hànkǒu 汉口
Hsingchow	Xinzhou	Xīnzhōu 忻州
Ichang	Yichang	Yíchāng 宜昌
Kiujiang	Jiujiang	Jiǔjiāng 九江
Mukden/Monkden	Shenyang	Shěnyáng 沈阳
Ningpo	Ningbo	Níngbō 宁波
Nanking	Nanjing	Nánjīng 南京
Newchang	Zhuhai	Zhūhǎi 珠海
Pehtang/Peitang	Beitang	Běitáng 北塘
Peiho	Baihe	Báihé 白河
Siaochang	Xiaochang	Xiàochāng 孝昌
Suchow	Suzhou	Sūzhōu 苏州
Swatow	Shantou	Shàntóu 汕头
T'ai Yuen Fu	Taiyuan	Tàiyuán 太原
Taichow	Taizhou	Tàizhōu 台州
Tchao-Tchou	Chaozhou	Cháozhōu 潮州
Taku	Dagu	Dàgū 大沽
Tientsin	Tianjin	Tiānjīn 天津
Tsingtao	Qingdao	Qīngdǎo 青岛
Tsangchow	Cangzhou	Cāngzhōu 沧州
Tsowping	Zouping	Zōupíng 邹平
Tungchow	Tongzhou	Tōngzhōu 通县

Wei-hai-wai	Weihai	Wēihǎi 威海
Whampoa	Huangpu	Huángpǔ 黄埔
Woosong	Baoshan	Bǎoshān 宝山
Yungcheng	Yungcheng	Yùnchéng 运城

ILLUSTRATION AND PHOTOGRAPH CREDITS

The photographs and illustrations contained in this book were obtained from a variety of sources, including private collections, libraries, old books, newspaper archives, individuals, local and national governments.
A special debt is owed to the following for their kind permission to reproduce the photographs and illustrations set out in the book:

Every reasonable effort has been made to trace and acknowledge the copyright holders. I apologise for any errors or omissions in the following list and would be grateful to be notified of any corrections that should be incorporated in any future editions.

2 Ah Chow Marriage Certificate, (West Glamorgan Archives Service); **3** HMS Andromeda, (Pembroke Dock Heritage Centre); **5** 'China Project', Ye Yang (UWC Atlantic College-2014); **6** Austin Family Grave, (Niedergang Collection); **6** 'Extraordinary Novelty', (southwales-eveningpost.co.uk); **7** Gladys Aylward, (Jago Family); **7** Gladys Aylward's Clothes, (Niedergang Collection); **8** Owen Baker, (Neath-Port Talbot CC); **8** Owen Baker Plaque, (Niedergang Collection); **8** Bangor College (China), (Bangor University); **9** Launching Bangor University in China, (Bangor University); **9** 'Reading China-Translating Wales', (Bangor University); **10** Dr Owen Pritchard Collection, (Bangor University); **11** 'Inn of Sixth Happiness' Plaque, (Niedergang Collection); **12** Thomas Beynon Memorabilia, (Pontypridd Museum); **13** Beynon Grave (Aberkenfig), (Niedergang Collection); **13** Memorial Plaque Siloh Chapel, (John Lyons); **17** Bowrington Arcade, (Niedergang Collection); **19** Ancient Chinese Bronzes, (National Museum of Wales) (NMW); **21** Buddha at Portmeirion, (Robin Llewellyn) (Portmeirion Ltd); **21** Bute Park (History Points); **26** 'SS Carmarthenshire', (National Museum of Wales) (NMW); **29** Kam Yau Chen (Niedergang Collection); **29** Cheng Jia,(Cheng Jia); **30** 'China 89' Cover, (Niedergang Collection); **30** 'China 89' Party,(Neath Borough Council); **31** 'Friendship Lasts Forever', (Niedergang Collection); **33** 'China Ginger', (South Wales Evening Post); **34** Chinese Armorial Porcelain (Private Collection); **37** Chinese memorial in Cardiff, (Niedergang Collection); **40/41** CHINESE JUNK, (South Wales Evening Post); **41** CPAFFC Delegation, (Niedergang Collection); **42/43** Chinese - style staircases (Pembrokeshire), (Niedergang Collection); **43** Chinese – style staircase (Bishopsgate House Hotel), (Hazel Johnson-Ollier); **46** Chinese Temple Tea Warehouse, (West Glamorgan Archives); **47** Wales Week in Chongqing, (Wales Government/NMW); **49** Confucius Statue (Swansea University), Niedergang Collection; **49** Confucius Conference (1994), (Niedergang Collection); **50** Presentation Watch and Case, (Niedergang Collection); **51** Confucius Institute, (University of Wales Trinity Saint David Lampeter); **52** Cwrt Sart Comprehensive School, (Niedergang Collection); **53** Chinese Porcelain Bowl, (Cyfartha Castle Museum, Merthyr Tydfil); **53** Chinese Celadon glaze ceramic dish, (Cyfartha Castle Museum, Merthyr Tydfil); **54** Decorative roof tiles, (Cyfartha Castle Museum, Merthyr Tydfil); **55** Chinese fortress at Dagu (Taku), (Tianjin Museum China); **56** Capt. Henry Davidson, (Niedergang Collection); **57** David and Jean Davies' Grave, (Niedergang Collection); **58** Hannah Davies, ('Among Hills and Valleys of Western China') (1901); **60** Day Family Honours, (Tenby Museum); **60** 'From Steep Hillsides' (Dazu), (National Museum of Wales) (NMW); **61** Deer (Père David), (Neath-Port Talbot CC); **62** 'Dinosaurs from China' Exhibition, (National Museum of Wales) (NMW); **62** Dixon Memorial, (Tabernacle Chapel St. David's) (Niedergang Collection); **62** Herbert Dixon and Family (Cambrian News and County Echo); **63** Thomas William's grave (St. David's), (Niedergang Collection); **64** Dixon Memorial Service, (Cambrian News and County Echo);

65 Welsh Dragon Boat Championship, (Ken Morgan Narbeth & Whitland Rotary Club); **65/66** Dragons (Shanghai and Swansea), (Niedergang Collection); **66** ADS Primary Neath,(southwales-eveningpost.co.uk); **67** Bronzes at Dyffryn Gardens, (Niedergang Collection); **68** St. David's Day poster, (Niedergang Collection); **69** Thomas Edwardes memorial (Llanllwch Church), (Niedergang Collection);

70 Wrexham Eisteddfod Chair, (National Museum of Wales) (NMW); **72** Janet Evans at a school in China, ('Hopkyn Rees China' H.T. Jacob 1923); **73** Rev. Robert Evans grave at Llanaber, (Niedergang Collection); **74** Thomas Evans grave at Oxwich, Gower, (Niedergang Collection); **75** 'Riversdale' by Lai Fong, (Ceredigion Museum, Aberystwyth); **76** Chinese Imperial Robe, (Fonmon Castle); **76** Chinese High Official's Robe, (Fonmon Castle); **77** Chinese ornamental vase and plate, (Fonmon Castle); **77** Armorial plate with Jones Family Crest, (Fonmon Castle); **78** Simon Francis, (Simon Francis); **78** 'Legacy of Opium', (Douglas Fraser); **81** Glory Church, Wuhan, (Niedergang Collection); **81** General Gordon 'The Story of Chinese Gordon' (A. Egmont Hake 1884); **82** 'China – A Study' (Niedergang Collection); **82** A student at Gorseinon College, (southwales-eveningpost.co.uk); **83** Sir Erasmus Gower, (National Museum of Wales) (NMW); **86** Griffith Griffith's House, Gwynfe, (Mrs M.H. Jones Gwynfe); **87** Keith Griffiths, (Keith Griffiths); **88** Presentation to Captain of 'Ping Chuan', (Niedergang Collection); **89** Guo Brothers, (Niedergang Collection); **84** Major Gwynne's memorial at St.Tetti's, (Niedergang Collection); **90** J.R. Harding, (Jenny Harding-Rolls); **90** J.R. Harding's lighthouse, (Jenny Harding-Rolls); **90** J.R. Harding's Decorations and Orders, (Jean Harding-Rolls); **90** Royal Palace, Seoul, (Jenny Harding-Rolls); 90 Book Plate, (Thomas Lloyd); **91** Thomas Harries' House and Garden, (Edwin Harries); **92** James Harris grave at Reynoldston, Gower, (Niedergang Collection); **95** Huang Xiuqi, (Niedergang Collection); **95** 'Rhament Plat y Pren Helyg', (Y Casglwr); **96** William Hughes, (National Museum of Wales) (NMW); **97** Automata Watch , (Anitquarian Horologist Dec 1955); **97** William Hughes Mirror Clock, (Palace Museum Beijing); **98** India and China Tea Company, (Mrs. Elsie Jones Brynamman); **98** Ingrid Bergman, (Jean Owen Beddgelert); **99** Location scenes at Nantmor, (Jean Owen Beddgelert); **100** Jack and Val Jago, (Niedergang Collection); **100** Heather James, (Heather James Pontardawe); **101** Eli James grave, St. Mary's Swansea, (Niedergang Collection); **102** William Jenkins grave, St. Mary's Swansea, (Niedergang Collection); **103** Rev. Dr Griffith John, (West Glamorgan Archives Service); **104** 'Onllwyn Plate, (Niedergang Collection); **104** Griffith John Blue Plaque, (Niedergang Collection); **104** Griffith John Bust, (Niedergang Collection); **104** Griffith john Memorial Garden, (Niedergang Collection); **105** Griffith John Memorial Plaque at Brynmelin, (Niedergang Collection); **107** Griffith John Fundraising Tour,(Unknown); **107** Griffith John event, (Norman Burns and Dr. Tom Davies Cwm Dulais Historical Society); **107** Centenary of the birth of Griffith John,(Llynfa Thomas); **108** Griffith John grave at Carnglas, Sketty, (Niedergang Collection); **108** Margaret John, (West Glamorgan Archives Service); **109** Captain John Jones, (National Museum of Wales) (NMW); **110** St. Helen's House, Swansea, (National Museum of Wales) (NMW); **111** Porcelain cup with monogram of Ann Jones, (National Museum of Wales); **112** John. T. Jones Grocer, (West Glamorgan Archives Service); **113** Admiral Oliver Jones, (Fonmon Castle); **115** 'Migrant Worker', Rhodri Jones; **115** 'China Caves Project', (Steve Jones); **116** Tom Jones 'Hong Kong', Clydach, (West Glamorgan Archives Service); **117** Pekin Race Course, (Bangor University Archives); **117** Pekin Syndicate, (Bangor University Archives); **118** Thomas Kymer, (National Trust, Parc Dynefwr); **118** Angela Kwok, (Angela Kwok); **119** John. M. Leeder, (www.southwales-eveningpost.co.uk); **120** China War Medal-1860, (Niedergang Collection); **121** Wei Fong Lee, (Wei Fong Lee); **122** Dragon Moon Flask, (Bonhams London); **123** Li Feng, (Niedergang Collection); **123** Underground Orchestra, (Wuhan Provincial Museum); **123** Li Hong Zhang, (Wikepedia Public Domain); **123** Lin Jixi, (Niedergang Collection); **124** Llangollen Int. Eisteddfod, (The Shropshire Star); **124** Llanelly House, (Niedergang Collection);

124 Stepney Armorial Dinner Plates, (Stepney House); **127** Lovespoon, (Niedergang Collection); **129** Margaret Memorial Hospital, (West Glamorgan Archives Service); **132** Missionary Doll, (Niedergang Collection); **132** Ludwig Mond, (Niedergang Collection); **136** David Lloyd memorial, Llandeilo Church, (Niedergang Collection); **136** F.A. Morgan at Canton, (Prys Morgan); **136** F.A. Morgan and family, (Prys Morgan); **137** F.A. Morgan's house at Suzhou, (Prys Morgan); **138** F.A. Morgan grave at Bishopston Church, (Niedergang Collection); **139** F.A. Morgan's horse 'Silken Mead', (Prys Morgan); **142** Kunming Institute of Botany, (National Botanic Garden of Wales); **142** Xishuangbanna Botanic Garden, (National Botanic Garden of Wales); **142** Dr. Rosie Plummer, (National Botanic Garden of Wales); **143** 'Ni Hao' newsletter, (Wales-China Friendship Society); **144** Nantong Way, Swansea, (Niedergang Collection); **144** Chinese scene embroidery, (Niedergang Collection); **145** National Dance Wales at Chongqing, (National Dance Company Wales) (NDW); **145** 'Land of the Red Dragon Exhibition', (Welsh Government); **146** THE WAR WITH CHINA', (southwales-eveningpost.co.uk); **147** Diary of Private John Newman, (Niedergang Collection); **148** Ceiling at the Opium Den Restaurant, Swansea, (Niedergang Collection); **152** Stained glass window by Sharon Patterson), (Niedergang Collection); **153** Gail Pearson with 'China 89' Choir, (Niedergang Collection); **153** HMS Gannet, (Malcolm Hasler); **154** Chinese Gentlemen, (Malcolm Hasler); **154** Christmas Card, (Malcolm Hasler); **155** Peking Opera, (Cardiff Laboratory Theatre); **155** Peking Opera Robes, (Niedergang Collection); **157** 'Chinese barges of the Embassy', (Roderic Bowen Library UWTSD Archives Lampeter); **157** 'Great Wall of China', (Roderic Bowen Library UWTSD Archives Lampeter); **157** Thomas Phillips Exhibition, (Roderic Bowen Library UWTSD Archives Lampeter); **159** 'Return of bodies', (Niedergang Collection); **159** 'Hen Wlad Fy Nadhau' (Paul Peter Piech); **160** Marco Polo International Conference, (James A. Gilman); **160** Marco Polo Project Conference, (Brecon and Radnor Express and Powys County Times); **163** Shijia Hutong Project, (Ying Chinnery Beijing); **164** Armorial dinner plate of Lewis Pryce, (National Museum of Wales) (NMW); **165** South Wales Borderers at Laoshan Bay, (Regimental Museum Brecon); **166** British troops arrive in Qingdao 1914 (Regimental Museum, Brecon); **168** Cenotaph at Qingdao (Regimental Museum, Brecon); **169** South Wales Borderers Gate, Cemetery and Cenotaph, (Regimental Museum, Brecon); **170** Hopkyn Rees, 'Hopkyn Rees China' (H.T. Jacob C.C. Llundain); **171** Hopkyn Rees Memorial, Seion Chapel, (Niedergang Collection); **172** Brass memorial plaque, (Niedergang Collection); **173** Tomb of George Rees in Macau, (Niedergang Collection); **174** Tomb of Maria Rees in Macau, (Niedergang Collection); **175** Orpheus Choir Tour to China, (Rhos Orpheus Choir, Brin Jones); **175** Timothy Richard, 'Forty-five Years in China' (Timothy Richard-1916); **175** Heol Timothy and Memorial plaque (Ffaldybrenin), (Niedergang Collection); **176** Timothy Richard Exhibition, (U.W.T.S.D Lampeter); **177** Facsimile **of** Timothy Richard's Calling Card (1924), '**177** Timothy Richard 150th Anniversary service programme, (Niedergang Collection); **178** Year of Dragon (1988) commemorative medal,(Niedergang Collection); **179** 'B Company' Royal Regiment of Wales, (southwales-eveningpost.co.uk); **180** Battle Honours of the Royal Welsh Fusiliers, (Niedergang Collection); **180** Royal Welsh in Peking (1900), (Royal Welsh Fusiliers Archives Caernarfon); **181** British Legation Peking (1900), (Royal Welsh Fusiliers Archives Caernarfon);; **181** Entrance to former British Legation, Beijing (1994), (Niedergang Collection); **182** Memorial plaque to the 2nd Battalion Royal Welsh Fusiliers, (Niedergang Collection); **183** 'Ten Stories of King Arthur'- Michael Scott, (Daphne Todd); **183** Shanghai Cup, (Niedergang Collection); **184** Bill of Sale and Registration for 'Nimrod', (Penarth Motor Boat and Sailing Club); **185** 'Chasing the wind into port',(www.southwales-eveningpost.co.uk); **185** Shanghai Kunju Theatre Programme, (Cardiff Laboratory Theatre/CPR); **186** Qiang Shen, (Qiang Shen); **186/187** 'Swansea to Beijing', (Kevin and Julia Sanders); **187** The Chinese bedroom at Singleton Abbey',(Richard Burton Archives, Swansea University); **188**'SLOW BIKES TO CHINA', (John Wyer and Vicky Stammers); **188** John Wyer and Vicky Stammers at Alderman Davies' Church-in-Wales Primary School Neath,(www.southwales-eveningpost.co.uk); **189** Sam and Fu with John Williams, (Bill Williams); **189/190** Stone House, Dinner Party and Percy Smith 'at home', (Hong Kong Archives); **190** Song Qingling, (source unknown);

191 Embroidered commemorative scarf to Song Qingling, (Niedergang Collection); **193** 2nd Battalion South Wales Borderers Pioneers at Tianjin, (The Regimental Museum of The Royal Welsh 23rd, 24th, 41st and 69th Foot, Brecon); **194** Presents from Emperor of Japan, (The Regimental Museum of The Royal Welsh 23rd, 24th, 41st and 69th Foot, Brecon **195** Officers of the 2nd Battalion South Wales Borderers at Hong Kong, (The Regimental Museum of The Royal Welsh 23rd, 24th, 41st and 69th Foot, Brecon); **195** Regimental Colours of the South Wales Borderers at Brecon Cathedral, (The Regimental Museum of The Royal Welsh 23rd, 24th, 41st and 69th Foot, Brecon); **196** South Glamorgan Chinese Women's Association, (Niedergang Collection); **198** Banner presented to South Wales Union of Miners, (South Wales Miners Library Hendrefoilan); **199** Rev. G. J. Sparham, 'People Thoughts And Places' (G.J. Sparham); **199** Rev. G. J. Sparham memorial at Carnglas Cemetery (Sketty), (Niedergang Collection); **200** Chinese New Year commemorative stamps, (Royal Mail); **200** Sir Thomas Stepney, (Carmarthenshire Heritage Regeneration Trust); **201** City and County of Swansea boundary sign, (Niedergang Collection); **202** Launch of Swansea Chinese Community DVD, (Swansea Chinese Community Co-op Centre); **202** 15th Anniversary Celebration of Swansea Chinese Community Co-op Centre at the Brangwyn Hall, Swansea, (Swansea Chinese Community Co-op Centre); **203** The 'D Shed' at Swansea Docks, (southwales-eveningpost.co.uk); **204** Dave Howerski and three Chinese skydivers, (Dave Howerski and John Hitchen); **205** Swansea 'Willow' pattern dinner plate, (Helen Hallesy); **205** Swansea 'Longbridge' pattern meat platter, (Helen Hallesy); **206** Swansea 'Amoy' pattern toy cup and saucer, (Helen Hallesy); **206** Swansea mug with 'Canton' pattern, (Helen Hallesy); **207** Swansea 'Whampoa' pattern meat platter, (Helen Hallesy); **207** Swansea coffee pot with 'Chinese views', (Helen Hallesy); **208** Swansea 'Mandarin' porcelain dessert plate, (Helen Hallesy); **209** Swansea-Nantong Friendship Document at Swansea Guildhall, (Kim Collis, City and County of Swansea Archives); **210** Two Dragons', (southwales-eveningpost.co.uk); **210** Presentation of Nantong City gift to Lord Mayor of Swansea, (Niedergang Collection); **211** 'Chinese Studies' course brochure, Swansea University/Niedergang Collection; **212** Armorial plate with Talbot family coat of arms, (National Museum of Wales) (NMW); **212** Captain John Tasker, (Tasker Family); **213** Merchant Tea Company, (West glamorgan Archives Service); **213** The Tea Shop, Castle Street, Swansea; **214** The Tea Company; **214** China Tea Warehouse; **214** Chinese and East Indian Company; **214** Horniman's Pure Tea, (213 to 214 south-eveningpost.co.uk); **215** Shrine of St. Teilo, Llandaff Cathedral, (Niedergang Collection); **215** Capt. Robert Matthew and family, (Western Mail); **217** Rev. James (Thomas, Pembrokeshire Mining Community); **217** Rev. Jermaine Thomas, (Hanover United Reform Church, Llanover); **217** Rev. Jermaine Thomas memorial, (Niedergang Collection); **218** Leaders of the South Korean Church and South Korean Church in UK group at Hanover Chapel, (Niedergang Collection); **220** Capt. Roundell Toke dress uniforms, (Niedergang Collection); **221** 'Two Dragons Garden', Treborth, (Bangor University); **221** Dr. Sophie Williams and Yang Xi, (Dr. Sophie Williams); **222** Armorial dinner plate with coat of arms of Baron Trevor, (National Museum of Wales) (NMW); **225** 'ULearnChinese' teaching pack, (Niedergang Collection); **226** Bust of Rev. Dr Griffith John at Wuhan Union Hospital, (Niedergang Collection); **226** Judy McKimm and Professor Yao at Wuhan Union Hospital, (Dr. Zhidao Xia); **226** Professor Wang Guobin and medical delegation at Swansea Museum (Niedergang Collection); **226** Commemorative plaque at Swansea University School of Medicine, (Niedergang Collection); **227** 'Doris Hansen Memorial Leacture', (United Nations Association City of Cardiff Branch); **227** Rev. Bernard Upward, (Jenny Childs); **228** Griffith John College, Hankow, (Jenny Childs); **228** Griffith John College Handbook, (Jenny Childs); **228** Griffith John College envelope, (Jenny Childs); **229** Armorial dinner plate with Vaughan family coat of arms, (National Museum of Wales) (NMW); **230** Chinese Porcelain and Cloisonné, (Glynn Vivian Art Gallery and Museum Swansea); **232** St. David's College Academic Staff (1927), (Roderic Bowen Library and Archives UWTSD Lampeter); **233** WCFS Logo, (Wales-China Friendship Society); **233** Founding Members of the Shanghai Branch of the Wales-China Friendship Society (1985), (Xu Da); **234** The Wales-China Friendship

Society Official Seal (Chop), (Wales-China Friendship Society); **235** Hangzhou Delegation Chinese Peoples Association for Friendship with Foreign Countries (CPAFFC) Delegation at Guildhall, Swansea (1988), (City and County of Swansea); **236** 'Wales in China', (Welsh Government); **236** 'Wales-Chongqing Cultural Week (2011), (Welsh Government); **238** First Minister Carwyn Jones and Huang Qifan, (Welsh Government); **238** First Minister Carwyn Jones and Guo Jinlong, (Welsh Government); **239** Former First Minister Rhodri Morgan(Chongqing 2008), (Welsh Government); **239** Former First Minister Rhodri Morgan (Chongqing 2006), (Welsh Government); **240** Li Feng with Welsh flag (Beijing 1994), (Niedergang Collection); **240** Welsh flag at the People's Theatre, Nantong (1989), (Niedergang Collection); **241** Professor Cyril Williams, (Irene and Eirian Williams); **241** Mrs Jane Williams (Five Roads, Llanelli) with the Author, (Niedergang Collection); **244** Chinese Three-inch Lotus Shoes, (Niedergang Collection); **245** Lewis Williams, (Hywel Gwyn Evans); **245** Williams family grave at Cwmllynfell, (Niedergang Collection); **245** Site of the former European Cemetery at Tangshan, (Niedergang Collection); **246** Armorial china with coat of arms of Penry Williams II, (National Museum of Wales) (NMW); **246** Dr. Rowan Williams, (Dr. Rowan Williams); **248** 'Signing of the Treaty of Nanking', (Charles Woosnam); 249 Woosnam memorial at St. Idloes Church Llanidloes, (Niedergang Collection); **249** Wu Fu-Sheng, (Wu Fu-Sheng); **249** Wu Xinyu, (Wu Xinyu); **250** Chongzhen Tang, Wuchang, (Niedergang Collection); **250** 150th Celebration of Chongzhen Tang, (Chongzhen Tang); **251** Ladies choir and choristers at Chongzhen Tang, (Chongzhen Tang); **251** The Glory Church, Wuhan, (Niedergang Collection); **252** Wuchang Hospital for Traditional Chinese Medicine, (Niedergang Collection); **252** Number 4 Middle School,Wuhan, (Niedergang Collection); **252** The Church at Number 4 Middle School, Wuhan, (Niedergang Collection); **253** Tribute to the Rev. Dr. Griffith John, (Wuhan Museum); **254** Dr Zhidao Xia, (Dr Zhidao Xia); **254** Embroidered panel from Xiamen, (City and County of Cardiff); **254** City of Cardiff Boundary Sign, (Niedergang Collection); **255** Bust of Rev. Dr. Griffith John at Xiaogan, (Wuhan Museum); **255** Xu Da, (Niedergang Collection); **256** Tomb of Elihu Yale at St. Giles Church, Wrexham, (Niedergang Collection); **257** Memorial plaque to HMS Amethyst, (Niedergang Collection); **257** Yao Xinzhong, (Yao Xinzhong); **257** Rev. Yung-King Yen,(soutwales-eveningpost.co.uk); **258** Launch of Cardiff University - Yiling Group Centre at Cardiff University, (Cardiff University); **258** Yan Ying, (Yan Ying); **259** Sir Edward Youde Memorial Garden Beijing, (Niedergang Collection); **259** Sir Edward Youde memorial at St. John's Cathedral, Hong Kong, (Niedergang Collection); **260** Yuan Ming Yuan, Beijing, (Niedergang Collection); **261** Notice at Yuan Ming Yuan, Beijing, (Niedergang Collection); **263** Zhao Yanxia, (Zhao Yanxia); **263** Zhu Limin, (Zhu Limin).

WALES-CHINA 250 YEARS OF HISTORY

INDEX

A

'A Legacy of Opium' (Douglas Fraser), 78
Aberaeron, 75
Aberavon, 1, 19
Aberconwy (Henry Duncan McLaren, 2nd Lord Aberconwy), 1
Abergavenny, 1
Aberkenfig Church, 13
Abernant House, 1, 22
Africa, 1
Ah Chow, 2
Ai Wei De (The Virtuous One), 7
'Alacrity' (HMS), 120
'Alceste', 56
Alderman Davies' Church in Wales Primary School, 2, 30, 31, 32, 52, 66, 240
Allen (C.F. Romilly J.P.), 2
Allen (E.L.B.), 3
Allen (Herbert James – 'Early Chinese History or are the Chinese Classics Forged?'), 3
'Amelia', 3
'Amethyst' (HMS), 3, 8, 94, 121, 127, 259
Amoy Pattern, 206
'Andromeda' (HMS), 3
'Ann Lucy', 4
'Anna Maria', 4
Arber-Cooke (Alfred Theodore), 4
Armorial Dinner Services, 34, 35, 77, 124, 164, 200, 212, 222, 246
Arthur (William C.), 4
Arthur (William Hawken), 4
Atlantic College, 5
Austin (Dr. Clifford), 5
Austin (Griffith Rosser), 5, 6
Aylward (Gladys), 6, 7, 21, 57, 98, 99, 143

B

Baker (Owen), 8
Bala (Iwan), 8
Bangor University, 8, 9, 10, 221
Baoyueping (Moon Flask), 121, 122
Barnard (Sir Charles Louden), 10
Barnwell (Rachael), 44, 45, 46
BBC ('Cardiff Singer of the World' Competition), 10
Beddgelert, 7, 11, 98, 99, 143
Bei Dao, 11
Beijing Acrobatic Troupe, 11
Beijing Art Museum, 123
Beijing Haidian Foreign Language Middle School, 11
Bell (Prudence), 11, ('Lives from a Black Tin Box'), 59, 62
'Bella Donna', 11

Benton (Gregor), 12
Bergman (Ingrid), 7, 98
Betts (George Edgar), 12
Beynon (Owen Gwynne Richard), 12
Beynon (Rev. William Thomas), 12, 13
Bianhu (Moon Flask), 122, 123
Bishopsgate House (Beuamaris, Anglesey), 42, 43, 44
Bitten (Nelson – 'The Story of Griffith John – Apostle of Central China'), 14
'Black Swan' (HMS), 94
Bodnant, 1, 42
Bonhams, 121, 122
Bonello (Gareth), 14
Bowen (Professor Huw), 109, 110, 111
Boxers (China), 11, 12, 13, 55, 62, 63, 64
Bowen (William), 14
Bowlby (Thomas William), 14, 158, 159
Bowring (Charles Algernon), 14
Bowring (Sir John), 15, 16, 17, 18
Brecon (Theatr Brycheiniog), 18
Brecon Cathedral, 195
Bridge (Albert Henry), 18
British Council, 8, 14
British Consulate – General (Shanghai), 60, 61, 127, 152
British Embassy (Beijing), 3, 156, 157, 256, 257
British Library, 30, 61
'British v Chinese', 18, 19
Britten (F.J. – 'Old Clocks & Watches and their Makers'), 19
'Brodland', 19
Bronzes (Ancient Chinese), 19
Brownell (Charles), 20
Bryant (Evan), 20
Bryant (Myfanwy), 20
Brynamman, 98
Bryson (Mary), 20
Buddha, 21, 60
Bute Park (Cardiff), 21

C

Caccia (Harold Anthony), 1, 22
Cadwaladyr (Betsy), 22, 23, 24
Cambria Magazine, 24
'Campbell', 25
Campion (Mary Anne J), 25
Cardiff (Anti Chinese Sentiment), 25
Cardiff and Xiamen, 25
Cardiff Chinese Community Association, 118
Cardiff Chinese Christian Church, 25
Cardiff Laboratory Theatre, 155, 185
Cardiff University (China Studies Centre), 25

'Carey' ('William Carey'), 26
'Carmarthenshire' (S.S.), 26
Cathays Cemetery (Cardiff), 37
'Celebrated Chinese Steel Band Concert', 48
'Celebrating the Red Dragon' (Exhibition), 8, 232
Cenhadwr Americanaidd, 26, 27, 28, 29
Chan (Tak), 148
Chang Jung, 29
Changsha, 8
'Charlotte' (HMS), 29, 113, 114
'Charlie and the Chocolate Factory' (Roald Dahl), 55
H'E. Chen Zhaoyuan, 25
Chen Cam Yau, 29
Cheng Jia, 29, 220
Chin (Fong Sui), 30
China ('Treasures from China', July 1842), 51
'China 89', 2, 30, 31, 32, 146, 153, 234
China Caves Project, 115
China Challenge Cup, 32, 33, 80
China Contract, 32, 33
China Cup, 32, 33, 80
China Ginger, 33
China Ocean Shipping Company, 88
China Project (Atlantic College), 5
'China Run' (Neil Patterson), 33
'Chinaman John', 33
Chinese and the Language Test, 35
Chinese Armorial Porcelain, 34, 35
Chinese Attack, 35, 36, 37
Chinese Bedroom, 187
Chinese cemeteries, 37
Chinese craftsmen, 70
Chinese Crew Mutiny, 38
Chinese Crews from British Ships, 38, 39
Chinese Dragon, 31, 65
Chinese Dragon Bowl (Dyffryn Gardens), 67
Chinese geese, 177
Chinese Imperial Robe, 76
Chinese Official's Robe, 76
Chinese Junk (Tea), 40, 41
Chinese laundry, 25, 30
Chinese roof decoration, 54
Chinese poems, 42, 128
Chinese Porcelain, 10, 53, 54, 77, 162, 230
Chinese shoes, 241, 244, 263
Chinese State Circus, 42
Chinese Staircases, 42, 43, 44, 45, 46
Chinese Studies (Swansea University), 211
Chinese Temple Tea Warehouse (Swansea), 46
'Chinese Views' (Pattern), 207
Chinese Wallpaper, 1, 144
Chongqing, 8, 46, 47, 60, 232, 235, 236
Chongqing Int. Garden Expo, 142
Christ College (Brecon), 47, 235

Church in China, 5
Cilgerran, 83
City of Cardiff Mansion House, 254
Clapton (Mr.) 'Exhibition', 1
Clements (Ronald), 'Lives from a Black Tin Box', 11
Clydach (Swansea), 47
Clyn Castle (Swansea), 219
Coal in China, 32, 33, 47, 49, 131
''Y Cocatw Coch' (Cedric Maby), 42, 128
Confucius statue, 49
Confucius Classroom (C.C.), 50
Confucius Conference, 49, 50
Confucius Institutes (C.I), 8, 50, 51, 68, 75, 83, 156, 157, 158, 176
'Consort' (HMS), 128
Contract for China (Coal), 32, 33
' Conway' (HMS), 51
Cordell (Alexander), 51
'Cornwallis' (HMS), 143, 150, 248
Cors – Y- Gedol, 52
Cory (Reginald), 52
CPAFFC (Chinese People's Association for Friendship with Foreign Countries), 41, 80, 233
Craft Council for Wales, 52, 66
Crawshay Family, 53
Cresselly House, 43
Cultural Revolution, 49
Cwmdulais Ichaf ('Links with China'), 52
Cwmllynfell, 91, 245
Cwrt Cadno, 119, 120
Cwrt Sart Comprehensive School, 2, 30, 52, 234
Cyfartha Castle Museum and Gallery, 53, 54

D

Dagu (Taku) Forts, 55, 144
Dahl (Roald), 55
Dale (Arthur Leonard), 56
Dalian, 4
Davey (William James), 56
Davidson (Henry, Capt. Hon. East India Co.), 56
Davidson (Robert), 57
Davies (Arnold), 57
Davies (D.), 57
Davies (David), 57
Davies (Evan), 57
Davies (Florence M. E.), 58
Davies (Hannah), 58
Davies (Jean), 57
Davies (H. Tudor), 59
Davies (Murray), 59
Davies (Nia), 9

Davies (Peter B. S.), 59
Davies (Tanya), 59
Davies (William), 59
Day (Lieut. Colonel H.J.), 59, 60
Dazu Stone Carvings (Chongqing, China), 60
Deer (Père David), 61
Dey (Emily Maude), 61
Diamond Sutra, 61
'Dinosaurs from China' Exhibition, 61, 62
Dixon (Herbert and Elizabeth, nee Williams), 11, 62, 63, 64
Doré (William), 64
Dragon Boat Race, 65
Dragon Moon Flask, 121, 122
Dragon music, 65
Dragons, 65, 66
Dragons ('Welsh Dragons for China' Exib.), 66
Dyffryn Gardens (National Trust), 52, 67
Dymond (Emslie Chambers), 67
Dymond (Ruby), 67
St. David's Day, 68
St. David's Society (Beijing), 68
St. David's Society (Hong Kong), 68
St. Donat's, 5

E

East Hook Farm (Pembs.), 42
East India Company, 1, 22, 56, 69, 109, 110
Ebbw Vale, 69, 131
Edwardes (Thomas), 69
Edwards (Jack), 70
Eisteddfod (National Eisteddfod of Wales), 70
Elba Tinplate Company (Swansea), 70
Emperor of China, 1, 23, 24, 90
'Emperor of China' (S.S.), 71
Emperor of Korea, 90
'Empire of the Sun', 201
Evans (Professor David), 71
Evans (Pte.), 192, 193
Evans (W. J. RWF), 179
Evans (Elizabeth Gwendoline), 71
Evans (F. W. Price), 72
Evans (Hywel Gwyn), 72
Evans (Janet nee Rees), 72
Evans (Rev. Alfred and Bessie), 72
Evans (Rev. Robert Kenneth), 73
Evans (Thomas), 74
Exhibition ('War with China'), 74

F

Film Festival (Chinese), 75

Fitzwilliams (Edward Crawford Lloyd), 75
Fong (Lai), 75
Fonmon Castle, 76, 77
Footbinding, 244
'Footsteps of Our Fathers' (Peter B. S. Davies), 59
Fordyce (Emilie), 77
'Forerunner', 78
'Fort Regent', 78
Fossils, 78
Francis (Simon), 78
Fraser (Douglas), 78
Freestone Hall, 43
'Friendship', 31
'Friends to China' (Charles Tyzack), 57
Fund (China Relief), 79
Funeral (Chinese), 79

G

Garden Festival (Ebbw Vale), 80
Garnier (Albert J.), 'Maker of Modern China', 80
Genghis Khan, 80, 160
Gibbard (Noel), 'Griffith John – Apostle to Central China', 80
Gingko trees, 21
Gladstone (William), 80, 123
Glamorgan University, 80
Glamorganshire Rifle Association, 80
Glory Church (Wuhan), 80, 81, 251
Gogerddan, 81
Gordon (Gen. Charles George), 81, 82
Gorseinon College, 82
Gower (Sir Erasmus William), 83, 93, 158
Gower (Jon), 9
Graham (Angus Charles), 84
Great Hall of the People, 49
Great Wall of China, 157
Griffiths (Griffith), 84, 85, 86
Griffiths (Capt. John), 87
Griffiths (Keith), 87
Griffiths (Capt. William), 87, 88
Grove (William), 88
Guangzhou (COSCO), 88
Guang Yang, 10
Guo Brothers, 89
Gwynne (Maj. J.H.), 89

H

Hamilton (George), 118
Hallesy (Helen), 204, 205, 206, 207, 208

Hangzhou People's Association for Friendship with Foreign Countries, 235
Hanover Chapel, 217, 218
Harding (John Reginald), 90
Harries (Thomas), 91
Harris (David), 92
Harris (James), 92
Harris (John), 92
Hay-Williams (Lady Sarah), 93
Hearst (William Randolph), 5
'Hendrina', 93
Hensol, 93
Hickey (Frederick, Capt. RN), 93
Hill (David), 94
Hillier (Raymond), 94
Hinton (Wilfred John), 94
Holtam (Sidney Harry), 94
Hornby (Sir Edmund), 94
Huang Xiuqi, 95
Hubei Provincial Museum, 123
Hughes (Hugh Brythan), 95
Hughes (Michael), 96
Hughes (William), 96, 97
Hu Dong, 9
Hunter (Jerry), 9
Huws (Lucy), 97

I

India and China Tea Company, 98
Inglis (Iain), 98
'Inn of the Sixth Happiness', 11, 21, 98, 143
Inwood (Heather), 9
'Inspired by Wales' (Feng Jianxin and Liu Jianchun), 99
'International Migration in P.R. China' (Rhodri Jones), 114, 115
'Isabel', 99

J

Jacob (Henry Thomas), 100
Jago, 7, 100
James (Heather), 100
James (Ivor), 101
James (William), 101
Jansen (Dr. Thomas), 176
Jasper (Vincent John and Ceridwen nee Lloyd), 101
Jeffreys (George B.), 101
Jenkins (Frank), 102
Jenkins (Karl), 102
Jenkins (Richard Ceredig), 102
Jenkins (Robert), 102
Jenkins (William), 102
H.E. Ji Chaozhu (former Ambassador to UK), 103
Jiang Zemin (former President PRC), 49
John (Dr. Griffith), 24, 80, 103, 104, 105, 106, 107, 108, 128, 246, 247, 253
John (Margaret Jane), 103, 108
Johnson (Dudley Graham), 108
Jones (Benjamin), 108
Jones (Rt. Hon. Carwyn AM), 238
Jones (Edward), 108
Jones (Eleanor), 109
Jones (F. Elwyn), ' Justice in Modern China', 109
Jones (Gareth Richard Vaughan), 109
Jones (Hannah), 109
Jones (Capt. John and Ann), 109, 110, 111
Jones (J. Frank), 111
Jones (John), 111
Jones (John Robert), 111, 112
Jones (John T.), 112
Jones (Lewis), 112
Jones (Mark), 112
Jones (Admiral Oliver John RN), 76, 113, 114
Jones (Owen), 114
Jones (Rachel), 114
Jones (Rhodri), 114, 115
Jones (Steve), 115
Jones (Tom), 116
Jones (Sir William), 116
Jones (William), 116
Jones (William and Son), 116
St. John's Cathedral Hong Kong, 116

K

Kenrick (John P. and Hubert Wynn), 117
Kymer (Thomas), 118
'Kingfisher', 118
Kitto (Mark), 'China Cuckoo', 118
Kublai Khan, 118, 160
Kunming Institute of Botany, 142
Kuo (Jimmy), 118
Kwok (Angela), 118
Kwouk (Bert), 11

L

Laozi, 67
'Laughing Water', 119
Laundry (Chinese), 119, 147
Learned Society of Wales, 186
Lee Kuan Yew, 49
Lee Wai Fong, 121

Leeder (John M.), 119
Lewis (Benjamin Thomas), 119
Lewis (Sir David), 119
Lewis (David William), 120
Lewis (Dr. John), 120
Lewis (Megan), 120
Lewis (Pte. Z.), 120
Ley (Lennard), 121
Liddell (Sir Charles Oswald), 121, 122
Lighthouses in China, 90
'Lion' (HMS), 83, 93, 158
Li Bai, 14
Li Feng, 123, 240
Li Hong Zhang, 55, 80, 123
Li Ti Mo Tai, 177
Li Yuyan, 9
Lin Jixi, 123
Llandaff Cathedral, 215
Llandovery, 4
Llandovery College, 156
Llanelly House, 124
Llangollen Int. Musical Eisteddfod, 11, 124, 260
Llansteffan Church, 56
Llanthetty Church, 89
Llanuwchllyn, 111
Llewellyn (William Dillwyn), 125, 126
Lloyd (Ceridwen), 126
Lloyd (Elizabeth), 126
Lloyd (Professor Sir Geoffrey), 126
Lloyd (Miss), 126
Lloyd (Thomas), 34, 35
Lloyd George (Hon. Robert John Daniel), 126
Local Intelligence, 127
Locke (Geoffrey), 127
'London' (HMS), 127
'Longbridge' Pattern, 205
Loveridge (Miss), 127
Lovespoon, 127
Lovespoon Gallery (Mumbles), 66
Lushun, 4

Margam Country Park, 61
Margaret Memorial Hospital (Wuhan), 108, 128, 129
Marier (Frances Edith), 129
Marquis Yi, 123
Marriage (St. John's Cathedral Hong Kong), 130
Matthews and Company, 130
Matthews (Capt. Robert), 215
McFarlane (Rev. A.J.), 130
McGuiness (Patrick), 9
McClaren (Henry Duncan Second Lord Aberconwy), 1
Medhurst (C.S.), 130
Merthyr Tydfil, 53, 130, 186
Migrant Children Foundation, 71
Milledge (James Sibree), 130
Milledge (Miriam nee Thomas), 131
'Mimosa', 131
Min (Anchee), 'The Last Empress', 131
Minhinnick (Robert), 131
Miners (Coal), 131
Missionaries Remembered, 132
Missionary Dolls, 132
'Mitchell' (The Hamilia), 132
'Moldairen', 132
Mon (Ludwig), 71, 132
Monmouth, 90
Moon Flask, 121, 122
Moore (Sir John), 133
Morgan (Charles Edward), 133, 134, 135
Morgan (David Lloyd), 135, 136
Morgan (Frank Arthur), 136, 137, 138, 139, 140
Morgan (Rev. E.), 140
Morgan (Professor Prys), 140
Morgan (Rt. Hon. Rhodri), 46, 99, 27, 239
Morris (Alfred), 141
Morris (William John), 141
Moss (Gwenfron), 141
Mount Pleasant Chapel (Swansea), 7

M

H.E. Ma Zhenyang (former Ambassador to the U.K), 124
Maby (Cedric), 128
Macartney (Earl George), 83, 93, 158
Macao Cemetery, 173, 174
Madden (Richard), 128
'Magic Lantern on China', 128
'Magicienne' (HMS), 35, 36, 37
'Magna Bona', 128
'Mandarin' Pattern, 208

N

National Botanic Garden Wales (NBGW), 142
National Union of Miners (China), 196, 197, 198, 199
Nanjing, 143, 248
Nantgarw (Dawnswyr), 143
Nantmor, 7, 98, 99, 143
Nantong, 30, 143, 144, 201, 240
National Trust, 118, 144
Nantyffyllon, 144
Nantymoel Primary School, 144

Napier (Maj-Gen. Sir Robert), 144
National Dance Company Wales (NDCW), 145
National Museum of Wales (NMW), 19, 26, 60, 61, 62, 83, 96, 109, 110, 111, 145, 237
National Screen and Sound Archive (Wales), 30, 146
Neath (Town Hall), 146
Neath-Port Talbot Council, 8, 61
New Welsh Review, 146
Newport (Chinese laundry), 147
Newman (Pte. Charles), 147
'Ni Hao' magazine, 5, 143, 239, 260
'Ni Hao' song, 31, 32
North Wales Chinese Association (NWCA), 147
Number 4 Middle School (Wuhan), 252

O

Odell (Rev. Collis), 148
Old King's Arms Hotel (Pembroke), 42, 43
Olympics and Paralympics, 59, 120, 148
Onllwyn Plate, 103, 104, 148
Opium, 148
Opium Den Restaurant (Swansea), 148
Opium Trade in China, 15, 78, 146, 257
Opium War (Second), 4, 55, 96, 260
Owen (Brigadier-General Charles), 150
Owen (George S.), 150
Owen (Hugh), 150
Owen (John William), 150
Owen (William), 151
Oxwich, 74, 151

P

Palace Museum (Beijing), 19, 97, 148
Parry (Lord Gordon), 152
Paterson (Neil), 152
'Pathfinder', 152
Patterson (Sharon), 66, 152
Pearson (Gail), 153
Pearson (Robert John Charles), 153, 154
Peking Mining Syndicate, 91, 117
Peking Opera, 51, 155
Peking Opera Robes, 155
Pekinese dog, 89
Pembroke Dock, 3, 81, 82, 156
Pembrokeshire Tea Company, 156
Penarth, 259
Pennard (Gower), 4
Penllergare, 156
Penpont, 156, 246

Phillips (Arthur Noel), 156
Phillips (Thomas), 156, 157, 158
Phipps (John), 158, 159
Piech (Paul Peter), 159
Pilgrim's Flask (Moon Flask), 121, 122
Pin Liao, 159
'Ping Chuan', 88
Pitt (Jeffrey William), 56, 93
Plas Chateau Rhianfa (Anglesey), 93
Plummer (Dr. Rosie), 142
Polo (Marco), 160
Pontardawe, 58, 89, 164, 249
Pontypridd Museum, 12
Pope (Samuuel), 161, 162
Porcelain (Chinese), 162
Port Arthur, 4
Port Meirion, 21
Powell (Amanda Elizabeth), 162
'Practical Pity', 161
Presbyterian Mission to China, 162
President of China, 49
Price (Angharad), 9
Price (David), 162
Price (F.S.), 'History of Caio', 162
Price (Frederick William), 162
Price (Pat), 66, 127, 163
Prime Minister (Peoples Republic of China), 72
Prince of Wales, 163, 164
Prince's Foundation for Building Community, 163
'Princess Charlotte' (HMS), 113, 114
Pritchard (Dr. Owen), 10
Proctor (William), 164
Prosser (Michael), 164
Pryce (Lewis), 164
Pullin (Thomas Williams), 164

Q

Qingdao (former spelling Tsingtao), 165, 166, 167, 168, 169
Qinlong Emperor, 96, 121, 122
Qu Yuan, 65

R

Red Deer, 170
Rees (A.Hopkyn), 170
Rees (William Hopkyn), 72, 100, 170, 171, 172
Resolven (Vale of Neath), 109
Rhys - Davies (Sir William), 173
Rees Brothers (George, John and Thomas), 78, 173, 174

Rees (Gwendoline M), 174
Rees (Lyndon), 174
Rees (Rev. John Lambert), 174
Rees (Peter), 66
Reynoldston (Gower), 92
'Rhament Plat y Pren Helyg' (Hugh Brythan Hughes), 95
Rhosllannerchrugog (Rhos Orpheus Male Choir), 175,233
Rhydderch (Francesca), 9,182
Rice (George Talbot), 118
Richard (Timothy), 29, 162, 174, 175, 176, 177
Richards (Frank) (RWF), 177
Riordan, (Professor Colin), 258
Richards (Rev.), 177
'Riversdale', 75
Roath Park (Cardiff), 177
Roberts (Brian), 65
Roberts (Frederick Charles), 177
Roberts (Mary), 178
Roberts (Mary Elizabeth), 178
Robson (William), 178
Rowlands (Rev. Edward), 178
Rowlands (Dr. Sioned Puw), 9
Rowlands (Rev. William Francis), 178
'Royal Charter', 14
Royal Commission on Ancient and Historiacal Monuments (R.C.A.H.M.S), 44,45,46
Royal George Hotel (Pembroke), 42
Royal Mint, 178
Royal Palace (Seoul - former), 90
Royal Regiment of Wales, 179
Royal Welsh Fusiliers, 13, 89, 108, 120, 161, 162, 177, 179, 180, 181, 182
Royal Welsh Show, 182

S

St. David's (Pembs.), 59, 62, 63, 64
St. David's College (Lampeter), 87, 156, 176, 241
St. David's Day, 68
St. David's Society (Beijing), 68
St. David's Society (Hong Kong), 68
St. Helen's House (Swansea), 110
St. Teilo, 215
Saunders (Kevin and Julia), 186, 187
Scott (Professor Michael), 'Ten Stories of King Arthur', 183
Selby (Stephen), 'Chinese Archery', 183
Shanghai Cup, 183, 184,185
Shanghai Kunju Theatre, 185

Shen Qiang, 186
Shen Yang, 10
Shijia Hutong Regeneration Project (Beijing), 163
Shoni Sguborfawr, 130, 186
Silk Road (East Expedition 2010), 186
Singleton Abbey, 187
'Slow Bikes to China', 188
Smith (Percy), 189, 190
Song Qing Ling, 190, 191
'Sons of the Rock' (Hywel Gwyn Evans), 72, 245
Soothill (William Edward), 'Timothy Richard of China', 191
South Glamorgan Chinese Women's Association, 196
South Wales Borderers, 56, 108, 120, 165, 166, 167, 168, 169, 191, 192, 193, 194, 195
South Wales Borderers Cemetery (Qingdao), 165, 166, 167, 168, 169
South Wales Federation (Miners), 196, 197, 198, 199
Song Ren Zhong, 196
Sparham (Rev. Griffith John), 199
Stamps (Royal Mail), 200
Stanley (Henry Edward John), 200
Stepney (Sir Thomas), 124, 200
Stone House (Hong Kong), 189, 190
Stories ('All Our Stories Project'), 200
Strick (James), 4
Summer Palace (Beijing), 54, 61, 96, 133, 260, 261
'Suo Gan' (Welsh Lullaby), 201
Swan Gardens (Swansea), 201
Swansea (Assembly Rooms), 201
Swansea (City and County sign), 201
Swansea Chinese Christian Church, 201
Swansea Chinese Community Co-op Centre, 121, 202, 203
Swansea Christian and Literary Association, 203
Swansea Docks, 203
Swansea Grand Theatre, 11, 42, 84, 185
Swansea Market, 204
Swansea Parachute Club, 204
Swansea Pottery-Porcelain, 204, 205, 206, 207, 208
Swansea Sound, 208
Swansea Theatre, 209
Swansea Twinning, 209, 210
Swansea University, 49, 211, 226, 254, 263

Symposium ('Reading China – Translating Wales'), 9

T

Talbot (Charles), 92, 212
Taliesin Arts Centre (Swansea University), 212
Tan yr Allt House (Bangor), 42, 44, 45
Tangshan, 245
Tasker (Capt. John), 212
Tatford (Frederick A.), 212
Tea (Chinese Green), 213
Tea Merchants, 40 46, 213, 214, 216
Tenby, 59, 60, 78, 173
'Terrible' (HMS), 216
Thomas (D.G.), 216
Thomas (Dylan), 11,216
Thomas (Ian), 66
Thomas (John David Ronald), 216
Thomas (Millicent and Margaret), 216
Thomas (Rev. James), 216, 217
Thomas (Rev. Robert Jermaine), 217, 218, 219, 220
Thomas (Ronald Stuart), 29, 220
Thompson (R. Wardlow), 'Griffith John', 220
Three Gorges Museum (Chongqing), 145
Toke (Roundell Tristram), 220
Tomb of the Underground Orchestra (Wuhan), 123
Tong Shuo Ti, 72
Trawler (Chinese), 221
Treboth Botanical Gardens (Bangor), 221
Trefeilir House (Anglesy), 42, 44, 45, 46
Treleddyn (Pemb.), 42, 43
Trevor (Thomas 1st Baron Trevor of Peckham), 222
Tulloch (Major-General Sir Alexander Bruce), 222
Turner (Frank B.), 222
Turner (John), 222, 223, 224
Tyzack (Charles), 57, 224

U

'ULEARN CHINESE', 225
UNICEF, 225, 233
'Under Sail', 225
Union Hospital (Wuhan), 225, 226
United Nations Association, 188, 227
Universities, 227

Upward (Rev. Bernard), 227 228

V

Vaughan (Richard), 229
Vicari (Andrew), 229
Vivian (Admiral Algeron Walker Heneage), 229
Vivian (Richard Glynn), 229, 230, 231

W

Wade (Professor George Woosung), 232
Wales ('Land of the Red Dragon' Exhibition), 46
Wales Arts International (WAI), 8, 232
Wales-China Friendship Society, 30, 41, 49, 65, 66, 68, 80, 82, 123, 143, 225, 233, 234, 235, 255
Wales Film Archives, 30, 146
Wales Literature Exchange, 9
'Wales in China' (Magazine), 236
Wales Week Chongqing, 46, 47, 236
Wang Guobin (President Union Hospital Wuhan), 226
Wang Honju (Mayor of Chongqing), 46
Wan Xiaoqiao (Dr.), 237
Wang Cheng, 7, 98, 99
Ward-Jones (Capt. Albert Lewis), 237
Watkins (Martha Winifred), 237
Welsh Government, 46, 99, 237, 238, 239
Welsh Development Agency (WDA), 239
Welsh Dragons, 31, 66, 239, 240
Welsh Dragon Exhibition (1988), 66, 127,152, 159
Welsh Flag, 210, 240
Welsh National Opera, 240
Wen Jiabao (former Prime Minister PRC), 46, 241
Westwood (Mary Jane), 2
'Whampoa' Pattern, 207
Williams (Professor Cyril G.), 241
Williams (Henry Goulstone), 241
Williams (Jane), 241, 242, 243, 244
Williams (Jane), 22
Williams (Nicolas), 244

Williams (Lewis), 245
Williams (Noah T.), 245
Williams (Penry), 246
Williams (Dr. Rowan Baron Williams of Oystermouth, Swansea), 246
Williams (Dr. Sophie), 221
'Willow' Pattern, 95, 205
Wilson (Nancy), 218
'Winch' (Fully Rigged Ship 'Henry Winch'), 246
Wood (Capt. Richard), 247
Wood (Myfanwy), 247, 248
Woosnam (Richard), 248, 249
'Woosong', 87, 88
Wordsworth (John), 1
Wordsworth (William), 1
Wrexham (St. Giles' Church), 182, 256
Wu Fu-Sheng, 249
Wu Hong, 9
Wu Hu, 249
Wu Jianzhong, 249
Wu Xinyu, 9, 249
Wu Yiling, 258
Wuhan, 24, 246, 250, 251, 252, 253, 254
Wuhan Chime Bells, 123
Wuhan Museum, 253

X

Xia Zhidao, 254
Xiamen, 25, 95, 254
'Xiao Pengyou' ('Little Friend'), 32
Xiaogan Central Hospital, 255
'Xie Xie' ('Thankyou'), 32
Xinzhou, 62, 63
Xishuangbanna Tropic Botanic Garden (Yunnan, China), 142
Xu Da, 255

Y

'Y Tyst' (Magazine), 222
Yale (Elihu), 256
Yang (Professor Zhuqing), 9
Yang Ge Fei, 103
Yang Xi, 221
Yang Xin (former Director of the Palace Museum, Beijing), 256
Yangtze Incident, 3, 8, 94, 121, 128, 256, 259
Yao (Professor Xinzhong), 257
Yen (Rev. Yung-King), 257, 258
Yiling Group, 258
Ying (Dr. Yan), 9, 258
'Yi Wen Si' (Evans), 73

Youde (Sir Edward), 116, 259
Yu Shao, 260
Yuan Ming Yuan (Old Summer Palace Beijing), 260, 261
Yuan Shih K'ai, 72
Yun Li Mei, 262

Z

Zhao Yanxia, 263
Zienkiewicz (Prof. Olgierd Cecil), 263
Zhongguo ('China'), 32
Zhou Xianyan, 9
Zhu Limin, 263
Zoar Chapel (Swansea), 263, 264